& Other Fun Destinations

The Essential Guide to Surviving Startup
— & cashing out!

David Smith

2006 Edition

■■CambridgeManhattan■■■■

Published by:
Cambridge Manhattan Group, LLC
www.cambridgemanhattan.com

Preface

The book was written following the bursting of the dot-com bubble, the collapse of the technology sector and the slump of the Silicon Valley economy. Hopefully, in some small way, it can help entrepreneurs in Silicon Valley and beyond to reboot the technology sector—one startup at a time.

Zero-to-IPO plots out the life of a high-tech startup in the context of a journey. The journey starts at *Zero* with the formation of a private company to commercialize a new technology or invention. This journey terminates when the company reaches its destination, and ceases to exist as a private, independent corporation—at *IPO*, *Acquisition* or *Shutdown*.

> *IPO = 'Initial Public Offering' = 'Going Public' = 'Floatation' = Sale of shares to the public.*

The roadmaps and principles laid out in this book are specific to product-oriented technology startups that require up-front investment in research and development before they have a product to sell. It is not intended for Mom and Pop stores, service companies, product distributors or retailers. However, some of the principles and ideas may apply to other industries and situations—especially where investors in a company are looking for an exit route.

As the title suggests, the book plots out the route from Zero-to-IPO and identifies the milestones and stepping stones along the way. However, it points out that this route may be inappropriate for many startups today and identifies an alternative direct route from Zero-to-Acquisition. This route stimulates the reader to question some of the fundamental principles of business.

Among other things, the book provides simple step-by-step instructions to help:

- ✓ Guide your startup along the route from Zero-to-IPO.
- ✓ Structure your company into an appealing M&A target and drive it toward acquisition.
- ✓ Inject momentum into a company that has slowed or ground to halt.
- ✓ Navigate a distressed company through a cash crisis.

Written in an easy- and fun-to-read style, *Zero-to-IPO* includes detailed roadmaps, travel guides and directories of investors, lawyers, banks, publications, agencies and other resources you're likely to need on your journey.

About the Author—David Smith

Since the birth of the personal computer, over 20 years ago, David Smith has been a high-technology entrepreneur founding several startups in Europe, Asia and the U.S. He has secured tens of millions of dollars in funding and led his technology-oriented teams through all stages of growth.

In the mid-1980's David created one of the fastest growing PC clone manufacturers in the UK. As Apple World Marketing Manager for Apple Computer in the late 1980's, he led the corporations branding and distribution efforts in Europe, Africa and the Middle East. As a technologist and software inventor in the 1990's, he created the worlds' first virtual tradeshow on CD-ROM, the first CD-ROM to be filled with paid advertising and the leading web browser and safety service for kids. His products have won critical acclaim all over the world.

An accomplished speaker, David has been invited to speak at international conferences in Europe, Asia and the U.S. He has addressed U.S. government congressional hearings and appeared on numerous radio and TV shows.

David has a BS Honors Degree in Computer Science & Economics from the University of Leeds and a Postgraduate Diploma in marketing from the University of Westminster, London. An avid landscape photographer, he moved to Silicon Valley, California from Europe in the mid-'90's where he now lives with his wife Michaela and two sons.

Acknowledgement

Writers can be very boring people. Just ask my kids. Instead of going out to play soccer or driving to Toys-R-Us, for some unfathomable reason, they sit in front of a computer screen for hours, days, weeks, months and years on end. I would like to thank my children for putting up with me. I'd also like to thank my wife for understanding, or pretending to understand, that I had to invest so many hours into this project— with no obvious return on investment. Instead of freaking out, she actually helped me to research and produce the book.

Special thanks go out to Arnold, Craig, David, Dene, Enoch, Ephraim, Fabrice, George, John, Jon, Mark, Michaela, Mike, Morten, Nina, Oliver, Peter, Phil, Rebecca, Ruth, Sebastian, Steve, Veronica and Wendy for their encouragement, support, donations and advice.

I am indebted to virtually every coffee shop in Silicon Valley and Santa Cruz for providing me with desk space, electricity for my laptop and regular injections of caffeine to maintain my momentum. Having spent a large proportion of my recent life in coffee shops, I am now planning a career consulting for Starbucks.

Notices, Warnings & Disclaimers

Warning

This book may change the way you think about business. By reading these pages, you may well become a social outcast—don't be surprised when your ideas and proposals encounter wide eyes and gaping mouths in the boardroom.

Trademarks

All brand names and product names used in this book are trademarks, registered trademarks or trade names of their respective holders.

Disclaimer

Read on at your own risk!

Contents at a Glance

Table of Contents

10

14

Chapter 1—Introduction

You have a new technology, invention or idea that's going to change the world. You're going to start a company, hire a team, bring in investors, dominate your market and everyone involved will become rich beyond their wildest dreams. Realists may accuse you of being a deluded fool, however, the Nasdaq and other stock markets list plenty of companies that started out with no more than a couple of hippies, a garage, a dream and a credit card. Unfortunately, for every company that succeeds in reaching the Nasdaq there are many more that fail somewhere en-route.

When describing the story of Apple Computer, Steve Jobs used to use the immortal words 'the journey is the reward'. I'm sure the journey was rewarding enough for Mr. Jobs but he and his merry band of pirates also became gazillionaires when their stock options hit pay dirt and Apple became the first technology *IPO* of the modern era. The journey that started out with a couple of barefooted hippies working from a garage, and went on to form a profitable corporation that put PC's on desktops all over the world, has inspired a whole new generation of hippies to set out on journeys of their own.

Taking your company from *Zero-to-IPO* is one of the most challenging, exciting and rewarding journeys you're ever likely to undertake. After a few minutes flicking through the pages of this book, a shrewd reader will realize that *IPO* is not the holy grail it's made out to be, avoid getting involved in any form of technology startup, take a sensible job—and live happily ever after. If you're one of the poor souls stricken with the entrepreneurial disease, you relish working long hours and you're attracted to almost unimaginable levels of stress and risk, this book could help you avoid taking your company off in the wrong direction. When you finish this book, you should be able to plot your own route from *Zero-to-IPO* with a comprehensive travel plan detailing precisely how to get from here to there. You'll be armed and prepared to deal with most of the obstacles that you're likely to encounter on the way and you'll have a list of many of the resources you're going to need.

The route for the journey from *Zero-to-IPO* for high-tech entrepreneurs is surprisingly uncharted today, however, there is a well trodden path that an elite group of venture investors have been guiding their companies along for years. It took me twenty years as a high technology entrepreneur to discover this route. I've spent the last few years plotting it out—so that you and other travelers don't have to spend twenty years figuring this out for yourselves.

Entrepreneurs have traditionally looked to venture investors to guide them through the early part of the journey and then introduce them to investment banks to guide the company through the later *IPO*-preparation stage. This model works well when the lead venture investor knows the route and has the time to provide continuous guidance to management. However, venture investors don't always make good guides—and they've allowed many a good company to veer off track.

The title of this book refers to the journey from *Zero-to-IPO*, however, we also look at the best way of reaching other destinations such as selling the company and how to survive some of the difficult terrain that we're likely to encounter en-route.

Dreams of the land of milk and honey attract many adventurers. If you can make it through the *IPO* and the subsequent restrictions on selling your stock, there's a good chance that you can cash out and live the rest of your life in luxurious ignorance of the financial worries of the rest of the world. This is one of the reasons it's unusual to find people making the whole *Zero-to-IPO* journey for a second or third time around. Some successful travelers move on to drive their public corporations and endeavor to take over the world—but many prefer to spend time on their yachts, the golf course or hanging out in one of their beachfront homes. The point is that once someone has successfully completed the journey, they rarely come back to *Zero* to start all over again, unless it's as an outside investor. So, many entrepreneurs that start the journey are doing so for the first time—they're heading out across new terrain. Typically, they need as much help and guidance as they can get.

Of course, you'll find all the resources you need to complete the journey in Silicon Valley, however, other high-technology hubs have sprung up in recent years with their own venture capital and professional service organizations. If you're living with the hillbillies you're going to have a real struggle attracting investors and bringing together the resources that you're going to need—it could be time to relocate. If you're near one of the top technology schools in the country and your office (or garage) is within walking distance of a good sushi bar, Indian restaurant and Starbucks coffee shop, then you're probably in a high-tech hub and it may not be necessary to take a one way ticket to San Jose, California.

Alternative Routes and Destinations

In the context of this map, 'Zero' means that you have an earth-shattering invention or idea but no company, team, business or business plan. Starting out from Zero, the journey you embark upon with your startup will conclude in one of only five realistic destinations:

1. *IPO*—shares become publicly traded on stock market.
2. *Cash-flow sale*—acquirer buys the company as a profitable going-concern with positive cash flow.
3. *Asset Sale*—the sale of a company that has not reached profitability or positive cash flow. Rather than buying cash flow, the acquirer is buying the product, the intellectual property and the supporting team.
4. *Orderly Shutdown*—a carefully planned *Shutdown* with sufficient cash to pay all outstanding bills and avoid problems with disgruntled creditors.
5. *Bankruptcy*—Chapter 7 or Chapter 11 *Shutdown*.

Destination	Result
IPO	
Cash-flow sale	You win! Shareholders get to exchange their private
Asset Sale	company shares for cash or something with at least a hope of one day being converted to cash. Company does not continue as a private independent entity.
Orderly Shutdown	Company is liquidated and dissolved, the shares become worthless, investors receive nothing in return for their investment but the founding team gets to walk away and start again.
Bankruptcy	The shares become worthless, bills go unpaid and angry creditors may seek revenge.

* ranked in order of joy, pain and suffering

What about Just Building a Profitable Independent Business?

Isn't there something missing from this list? What happened to the notion that you could start a small business that goes on to generate positive cash flow and sustain itself forever as a profitable private business?

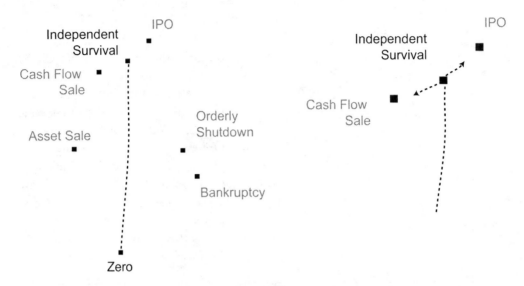

Well, for high technology startups today, *Independent Survival* is not really a sustainable situation because it provides little or no return to the outside investors. Huge cash investments are typically required today to develop the technology and accelerate the company along the route quickly enough to take a market leadership position and make it to *IPO*. Of course, a private business can distribute profits by paying dividends to shareholders, but it would likely take years, even decades for investors to recover the cash they injected to fund the up-front research and development costs of a technology company—and even longer for them to see a positive return on investment. Without an exit route, these companies are like the 'living dead'—the company is living but the stock is dead. Not surprisingly, you're unlikely to find any investors today that are prepared to sit around for years patiently waiting for their annual dividend checks—sooner or later they're going to push the board to seek a *Cash Flow Sale* or *IPO*. Although it may be appealing to service companies, low-tech sector companies and small mom and pop operations that are free of outside investors, independent survival is not a viable destination for technology startups. It is, however, a great place to hang out for a little while before you push ahead with a sale of the company or *IPO*.

A Setting for your Journey—Startup Island

OK, I have a twisted mind, but when I think of the journey from *Zero-to-IPO*, I imagine an island surrounded by shark-infested seas—see the maps on the book cover. The challenge is to take your startup from *Zero* to one of the distant peaks— *IPO*, *Cash Flow Sale* or *Asset Sale*.

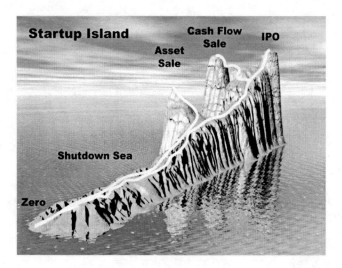

The fastest and safest way of reaching your destination is to stick to the route. However, the path is very narrow and it's easy to wander off course. Climbing back up the slippery slope to get back on track takes time, energy and, at best, slows your progress along the route. If you can't make it back up the slope, you're destined for the shark-infested seas. After making an elegant and staged descent, you get to safely sail away to your next adventure. If you splash into the sea itself, you become the main course for a feeding frenzy of hungry sharks.

Chapter 2—Preparing for your Journey

This chapter contains vitally important information to prepare you for your journey including a travel plan template, a series of questions that help you select the best route, a simple technique for taking bearings and fixing your position, tips and advice on picking your team, harnessing momentum and raising funds from investors.

Poor Preparation Leads to Poor Performance—and can affect your Diet!

Many people flooded into Silicon Valley in recent years, especially in the dot-com gold rush years, but technology entrepreneurs are not the first people to head West in search of a better life. People have been migrating West for as long as anyone can remember—and there are things that we can learn from their experiences. Today's companies are drawn by the nurturing business environment and the skilled workforce of Silicon Valley. In the last century, good weather and farming land was enough to entice people to embark on a dangerous westward journey. Back then, the challenge was to find a good road map, select a route and travel plans that would enable you to get your family through the mountains before the winter storms arrived. Some people made it through without a scratch, others were not so lucky.

© 1996 Travis Kelly

Many years ago the California Star newspaper in San Francisco published a delicious account of the rescue of the Donner Party, a group of several families of migrants trying to cross the Sierras from Independence, Missouri to the Pacific in 1846 that ground to a halt mid-winter in the Sierra Mountains near Lake Tahoe. It told of how the lucky travelers had survived by eating the flesh of the other, less fortunate, members of the party and that when they were discovered they were actually broiling and preparing the body parts of close family members for a juicy meal.

When we look back at the story of the Donner Party today it's difficult to understand how they could have been so foolish as to find themselves trapped in such an inhospitable place mid-winter without appropriate supplies. They embarked on the journey thinking that if they could just get over the mountains they'd find a land of milk and honey in California. Of course actual cannibalism is quite rare (or well covered up) in corporate America today but many of the journeys taken by technology startups end in similarly ugly conditions and there's a great deal to be learned from the journeys of our adventurous forefathers.

Seven Point Travel Plan

Surely with a little planning, each member of the Donner Party should have been able to make it through without having to snack out on the body parts of family and friends—indeed many other parties had successfully completed the journey before. Wouldn't you like to have the opportunity of advising the leaders of the Donner Party before they set out on their fateful journey? As a modern traveler your advice could likely be summarized as follows:

- ✓ *Target your destination*—make sure you know precisely where you're going. If you don't, what chance do you have of ever getting there?

- ✓ *Pick your team*—choose team members that are headed to the same destination and are prepared to pull their weight on the journey. Oh yes—try to avoid cannibals, especially if there's a possibility that your food provisions may run low. You want a team that's prepared to back itself and is more interested in stock options than salary.

- ✓ *Plot your course*—get hold of the best map you can and select a course that doesn't go through snowy mountains in mid-winter. Identify all the steps and milestones that you're going to need to hit along the way.

- ✓ *Gather your provisions*—prepare a comprehensive list of everything that you're going to need to complete each stage of the journey. Make sure you can make it to the next staging post with food to spare!

- ✓ *Maintain your momentum*—keep the wagons rolling.

- ✓ *Take your bearings*—regularly check and cross-check where you are against the map to avoid straying off course.

✓ *Prepare for contingencies*—carry extra food, clothing and shelter, just in case you get trapped by a snow storm. Should the snows come in, plan to send a party out on foot in search of help the moment the wagons grind to a halt.

This advice seems to be just common sense, however, I'm confident that the Donner Party would have made it through in one piece if they'd put together a detailed travel plan based on these seven points. In fact these principles can be applied to any type of journey. Many of the most successful corporations in business today, including Compaq Computer and Southwest Airlines, started out with a simple plan drawn up on the back of a napkin.

All the essential elements of a successful business plan can be condensed onto a single page to whet the appetite of a potential investor. If it can't be summarized onto a single page, the plan is probably too complicated to realistically put into action. In fact, I'd question any plan that was so complex that it failed the 'napkin test'.

Of course, the napkin would have to be backed up with more detailed information—but bigger is certainly not better when it comes to creating plans that normal people are likely to use as working tools. Technology markets move so quickly these days that detailed plans are invalidated in the blink of an eye—after weeks or months of painstaking preparation they inevitably wind up gathering dust on some investors bookshelf.

Preparing for a journey, let's take the seven tips we prepared for the Donner Party and draw up a short, working travel plan that can be pinned on the wall and easily communicated to the rest of the team.

Back-of-a-Napkin 7 Point Travel Plan Template for Any Journey

Team
Team Members & Responsibilities

Identify the optimal size of the team for this journey. List team members with roles and responsibilities.

Provisions
Budget & Resources Required

List all the resources that you're going to need for each step of the journey and identify where you plan to acquire them.

Taking Bearings
How to Fix your Position

Fix your position on the course as you start the journey. Identify accurate ways of pinpointing your position as the journey progresses. Remember to take your bearings regularly.

Plotting your Route

Enter the target date for reaching each milestone and stepping stone.

Starting Point
Identify Starting Position

It's important to fix your starting position.

Target Destination
Where do you Want to Be?

Here you state clearly and concisely where you want to go. Keep it simple.

List all the major milestones and minor stepping stones

Maintaining Momentum
How to Keep the Wagons Rolling

Identify the pace at which you want to progress along the course. Plan how you're going to encourage the team to keep the wagons rolling.

Contingencies

What Can Go Wrong?

List all the potential obstacles that you could encounter on the journey.

How Will you Fix It?

Identify all the ways that you will overcome each of the obstacles.

Targeting your Destination

In the good old days, you could set out with a simple mission to design a great product and build a profitable private business—you didn't have to think about whether this would lead to a subsequent sale of the company or *IPO*. Today, facing fierce competition, huge startup costs and fast moving markets, this is no longer possible—if you don't target your destination and drive directly toward it at full speed, you have little or no hope of getting there before the competition. Your investors are going to want to see a clear exit route where their shares convert back to cash and they get to receive a return on investment—designing a great product and building a good business no longer sufficient reward.

Targeting your destination is a core component of your travel plan—if you don't know where you're going what chance do you have of ever getting there? It's not a guarantee of success though—even the Donner Party had a destination in mind when they set out, and their journey didn't exactly end in idyllic conditions. Once you've targeted your destination you can plot your route, pick your team and start to generate some momentum.

Picking your Team

Do you remember those long arduous road trips with friends and family members that seemed to get more irritating the longer the journey went on? We've all had them. Tempers fray when previously friendly traveling companions grow tired and irritable—especially when the trip doesn't go smoothly and the party fails to reach its chosen destination on schedule. I recently read that scientists have figured out that putting several astronauts into a space ship for a mission that could take several years would create the perfect conditions for murder. Bear this in mind when you pick your founding partners, investors, executives, directors, advisors, managers, bankers, lawyers, accountants, consultants, suppliers, contractors and employees for this long and arduous road trip:

- ✓ *Pick traveling companions that all target the same destination*—if there's any disagreement about where the party is headed, you're definitely in for trouble sooner or later.

- ✓ *Avoid cannibals*—pick personality types that support the team and don't cannibalize their own team members when the going gets tough.

- ✓ *Pick good navigators*—people that can read maps, take bearings to fix your position and help plot out the best route forward can be worth their weight in gold.

✓ *Avoid traveling companions that want a chauffeur-driven limo service*—pick the candidates that are prepared to walk, run, climb, jump or do whatever it takes to make progress on the journey.

✓ *Pick team members that can help identify the provisions the team is going to need and helps gather them together*—avoid the person that would steal the last cookie, deny stealing it and wait for someone else to buy more.

✓ *Keep your team as small as possible*—large teams are very difficult to control and keep headed in the same direction.

✓ *Pick people that know the route*—the practical experience of seasoned travelers can be invaluable.

Founding Partners

When you start a new business, you have to decide whether you want to go it alone or bring in partners. It's natural to feel more exposed and vulnerable when you go it alone, but bringing in partners needs to be carefully thought through and can easily destroy the business.

It can be very tempting to invite your buddies to join your startup. Inviting them in before the company has any momentum, however, can be very costly. Don't be surprised if they ask for equal partnerships. Equal partnerships are never exactly equal. Two partners may have the same stock options and remuneration package, but it's impossible for two people to make precisely the same level of contribution—one partner is sure to take more responsibility and pull more weight than the other. How would you feel if you were working 80-hour weeks while your 'equal' partner was sipping gin and tonics on the beach? It can happen, believe me.

Sometimes collaboration sparks ideas and releases untapped talents. John Lennon's collaboration with Paul McCartney in the 1960's resulted in some of the most popular music in history. I don't think they would have achieved any success without this collaboration, however, The Beatles was essentially Lennon's baby. He needed other musicians and he offered McCartney an equal founding position in the band. If he'd written a few songs and generated some momentum beforehand, I'm sure he would have been able to bring in McCartney on better terms, and the relationship might have actually gone on for a few more years. After the band split up, Paul Simon says he had dinner with Lennon in New York and John explained that the reason for the split was that McCartney was challenging him for leadership of the band. Perhaps this wouldn't have happened if Lennon had set things up differently at the start. I would have loved to have been a fly on the wall at that dinner. Paul Simon was clearly the driving force in Simon and Garfunkel—he wrote almost all the songs and Garfunkel seemed to get half the credit. Lennon and Simon must have been bitching about how they'd do it differently in future. They obviously learned from the experience and did do it differently next time around. Simon hired musicians instead of partnering with them. They didn't expect to be full partners or challenge for control as they realized that it was Simon's baby and clearly accepted that he'd generated the momentum before they appeared on the scene. Lennon did the same, after he reappeared from hibernation. And so did McCartney. If you were a musician invited to an audition for Paul McCartney and Wings, you had no hopes of getting an equal share of the pie or of becoming the leader of the band. Paul did bring in his wife Linda, and this partnership seemed to go as smoothly as possible. Husband-wife teams have been quite successful in high-tech as well as music.

So, the message from the stars seems to be 'go it alone'. If you really can't make it a success without bringing in a collaborator, generate some momentum on your own first, then you can bring them in without giving away the farm. If it's your baby and they know it, you'll be able to negotiate reasonable terms:

- ✓ *Go it alone as long as you possibly can before you bring in a partner*—at least write the business plan, hire the lawyers and form the company. It's a good idea to have the lawyers help you negotiate the terms with your partners.

- ✓ *Make it clear who's in charge, and agree on the business plan up-front*—you need everyone pulling together in the same direction from the very start.

- ✓ *Don't give them a share of the business up-front*—reward them with stock options that vest over 3 or 4 years. If it doesn't work out you'll be in a position to part company without losing half the business.

- ✓ *Protect the intellectual property*—with an employment contract assigning ownership to the company (see *Write an Employee Handbook*, page 116).

Maintaining Momentum

My friend once took me on a ride in his new sports car through the French countryside. I knew he was a former racing driver but I thought he would drive like I do, only a little faster. I was wrong. So wrong that after about 5 seconds I was foaming at the mouth and hanging onto my seat. This friend is also an avid skier and I was surprised to discover that he didn't have a 4-wheel drive sports utility vehicle but took his sports car on ski trips. He drives his 2 wheel drive sports car up icy mountain roads during blizzards. I asked how he could get through the snow and ice without 4-wheel drive. It's impossible isn't it? How can you move forward if you can't get any traction on the tires? His answer was a short, simple and important word that you're going to hear a great deal in this book—'momentum is a wonderful thing'. OK it's more than one word, but the sentiment is true—if you gather momentum and you don't come to a dead stop at the bottom of an icy hill, then you can drive quite a long way in apparently impossible conditions.

The Magic of Positive Momentum

In business it's momentum that attracts customers, investors, employees and other members of the team. People like to be associated with the Company when they hear the buzz and feel the enthusiasm—everyone wants to be part of a success story.

Positive Momentum

In the context of your startup, positive momentum is the invisible force that thrusts the company forward toward it's chosen destination. Momentum is evidenced by the company's progress—its repeated achievement of milestones and stepping stones.

Positive momentum is generated by, and somewhat synonymous with, a collective sense of approval, enthusiasm, excitement and passion in favor of the company and its products, an upbeat buzz or hype emanating from the company's insiders, customers, press and other respected independent outsiders. Enthusiasm is contagious and positive momentum creates more positive momentum.

Upbeat Team   Marked Progress

Progress Cycle

Positive momentum comes from an upbeat team making marked progress along its chosen route. Evidence of the progress makes the team more enthusiastic and energetic, helping the company to achieve more milestones and stepping stones at an accelerated rate in a cycle of progress.

The Menace of Negative Momentum

In the same way that positive momentum is a magical force that drives the company toward it's chosen destination, negative momentum is a menace that paralyses progress and ultimately destroys the company.

Negative Momentum

Negative momentum is the force that prevents the company from generating traction or making progress towards its target destination. Evidenced by a lack of achievement, or a backwards step, negative momentum features a pessimistic opinion of the company, it's products and/or its prospects in the market. Unchecked, negative momentum accelerates into a freefall as word gets out that the company is in trouble and team members bail out.

The company has no momentum when it fails to achieve its milestones and stepping stones. The team gets despondent when it fails to see any evidence of progress. If they feel that the company has no plan and no future, the employees spend their time polishing their resumes instead of building products or closing sales—paralysis sets in and the whole operation grinds to a halt.

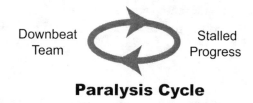

Downbeat Team   Stalled Progress

Paralysis Cycle

The despondency deepens as key team members bail out. Soon, word spreads to customers, competitors, journalists and the company's troubles become public knowledge. Instead of people being attracted towards the company, they suddenly want to distance themselves as far away from it as they can. Like any stampede, people get knocked down and trampled on the way out.

Loss of momentum is the most dangerous threat to survival for many distressed companies. In conjunction with a developing cash crisis, negative momentum often develops into freefall momentum that can be very difficult to escape.

Gentle Momentum Maneuvers

The company can start out with positive momentum, however, for a variety of reasons, it can stall somewhere en-route:

- ✓ *Fundamental problem*—the product doesn't match market demands or there's some other form of deep-seated problem with the business plan.
- ✓ *Excess baggage*—the company could be saddled with debt, lots of bickering investors or pending lawsuits.
- ✓ *'We're lost'*—the team has no vision of where the company is going, or how it's going to get there.

✓ *Unattainable destination*—some immovable barrier is blocking the company from reaching its goal.

✓ *Cash crisis*—even the prospect of a distant cash crisis can paralyze the team and halt progress. Well before the cash burns out entirely, the company can go into a state of freefall.

Fortunately, there are a number of maneuvers at your disposal designed to boost lagging momentum, kick start stalled momentum and reverse negative momentum.

Inertia Warning!

Some of the momentum maneuvers will be simple and relatively painless to implement, however, the more radical maneuvers are going to cause tremendous upheaval. In a times of crisis, upheaval is often a necessary part of saving the company. Be prepared—people seem to be resistant to change, all forms of change, and some energy will be required to break the status-quo and overcome this state of inertia.

Spread the Good Vibes

Companies at all stages of growth can boost momentum by spreading the good vibes. Steve Jobs used to regularly send out propaganda e-mails to friends, colleagues and virtually every e-mail address he could lay his hands on. It has since become a management feature for virtually all successful startups. En-route to a spectacularly successful dot-com *IPO*, my friend became a master of momentum—sending out good vibe press releases on a daily basis and whipping his team into a frenzy of excitement.

Five tips for Spreading the Good Vibes:

1. *Maintain your own level of enthusiasm*— team leaders need to stay upbeat regardless of whether they're having a bad hair day.
2. *Maintain a general level of excitement in the team (at all cost)*—feel-good beer busts, gatherings and social events can help boost morale. Any employee that persistently keeps spreading bad vibes by shouting (or whispering) 'we're all doomed, we're all going to die' or 'our competitors are going to kill us', needs to be taken out as quickly as possible.
3. *Look for good news and spread it*—evidence of marked progress is ideal, but even small wins are worth getting excited about.
4. *Don't hide from bad news, but don't dwell on it*—if there's bad news, show that you acknowledge it and move on.
5. *Expose the passionate people to as many as you can*—momentum is contagious.

Question:	When is a good time to *Spread the Good Vibes?*
Answer:	Always.

Plot the Route Ahead

People always like to know where they're going and how they're going to get there. At the very least, they need to feel that the team leaders have a map and a well-considered route. This is particularly important in times of crisis. On a long arduous journey, it's not exactly uplifting to hear your team leader say that she doesn't know where you're going and has no idea of how you're going to get there.

Question:	When is a good time to Plot out the Route Ahead?
Answer:	Always, especially when you're lost.

When they're lost, we teach our kids to stay where they are—if they continue to wander into the unknown they'll be more difficult to find. Without a clear destination or route, the natural instinct for most employees is to sit tight and wait for a roadmap and new instructions. If the team can only see a few steps ahead, that's as far as it will plan. This short horizon prevents product designers from designing new products (as they don't know if these products will ever be built), prevents engineers from engineering (they don't know if the product they're building will ever ship) and prevents sales people from selling (as they don't know if the orders will ever be fulfilled). The team becomes downbeat and progress stalls. The lack of progress brings the morale of the team down even further and the company is in a cycle of paralysis.

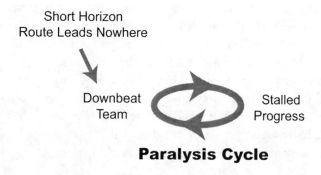

To convert negative momentum to positive momentum, you need to break the cycle. This starts by restating your target destination, taking your bearings, fixing your position and plotting out a clear route from here to there. Identify small stepping stones as well as large milestones along the way—make sure the route is realistic and each step is achievable.

With a clear route ahead, the team will realize that the company has a real future and see that work done today is not in vain. This long horizon will lift the team, marked progress will be made and a new cycle of progress established.

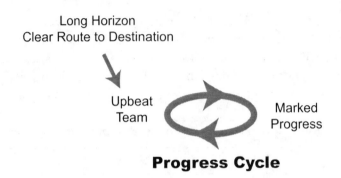

Long Horizon
Clear Route to Destination

Upbeat
Team

Marked
Progress

Progress Cycle

Taking your Bearings

<u>Why it's Important to Regularly Pinpoint your Position</u>

I recently took my young son on a weekend camping trip to Yosemite. We traveled with my friend in his car. Apart from encountering several bears, the weekend went well until the journey home. I took the wheel for the first couple of hours while my friend read the map and gave directions. When he took over the driving seat, he told me that he knew the route so I decided to catch up on some of the sleep I'd missed the previous evening—for some reason, I don't tend to sleep well when deadly, 400lb carnivorous animals are scavenging for food outside my flimsy tent. Anyway, instead of waking up to see the car pulling into my drive, I awoke two hours later on some unfamiliar highway with my friend frantically shaking my arm telling me to take out the map. Looking at the map we discovered, to our horror, that instead of being in San Francisco, we were on the outskirts of Los Angeles! By taking the wrong exit, we'd been heading South instead of North for two hours! Of course, my wife thought it was hilarious when I called to tell her why we hadn't yet arrived home—now she had perfect proof of her theory that men never look at maps or ask directions. A journey that should have taken four hours ended up taking eight!

So what did we learn from our extended weekend? Other than learning that my friend can't be trusted alone at the wheel of a car, the main lesson is this—the sooner you discover you're off track, the easier it is to correct. If we'd regularly taken our bearings and checked them against the map we'd probably have discovered and corrected our error within a few minutes and saved ourselves four hours of driving.

We all make mistakes but good navigators don't deviate too far from the track because they regularly ask themselves 'where are we now and is this where we planned to be at this point in the journey?' Unfortunately, we're often so wrapped up driving or building a business that we forget to check where we are and by the time we discover that we've deviated from the track it's too late.

As my wife frequently reminds me, car drivers don't have much of an excuse for veering off track—there are plenty of road signs and maps, even GPS navigation systems, to tell you exactly where you are and provide precise directions. Without the luxury of business roadmaps or GPS systems, many technology startups have blindly headed off in the wrong direction for years. The roadmaps in this book should help you target your destination and plot out a route to get there, however, they're of little use if you can't fix your position and figure out, with any accuracy, where you are.

So regularly taking your bearings enables you to identify when you're off course and take remedial action before it's too late, but it also helps track the company's progress—and this can boost team morale and accelerate the momentum.

Company Navigator

Thousands of years ago, successful explorers figured out that they had a much better chance of reaching their destination with a specialist navigator to read the maps, take bearings and plot out the route ahead. Often ships that set out without maps or navigators were lost at sea—so the position of navigator was created to prevent ships from sailing off the edge of the world. Fortunately, the accuracy of maps has improved over the years, and navigators are used to safely guide ships, airplanes, even spacecraft to and from exotic distant destinations.

The Art & Science of Marine Navigation
(Source: Bowditch's Navigator)

Marine navigation blends both science and art. A good navigator gathers information from every available source, evaluates this information, determines a fix, and compares that fix with his pre-determined 'dead reckoning' position. A navigator constantly evaluates a ship's position, anticipates dangerous situations well before they arise, and always keeps 'ahead of the vessel'.

You have to pass a navigation test to sail even the smallest boat. There are no such restrictions to prevent you from setting out on a costly and potentially treacherous journey with your technology startup. The position of 'Company Navigator' doesn't really exist for technology startups today. Perhaps this explains why so many companies end up sailing off the edge of the world. Successful large corporations, however, often keep teams of navigators in their strategic planning departments.

The captain of a ship has many pressures and responsibilities, especially in times of crisis. Ancient mariners quickly discovered that they were more likely to safely reach their destination if they freed the captain of the day-to-day duties of navigation and allocated this function to a specialist navigator able to dedicate more time and attention. Of course, the navigator reported to the captain. Would you feel comfortable getting on a flight in the knowledge that the captain had to single-handedly take care of navigation, monitor all those dials and controls, communicate with air traffic control and resolve any potential mid-flight crisis? For important modern-day journeys and missions, on sea, air and even in space, the captain is rarely the navigator and the navigator is rarely the captain of the craft—for exactly the same reasons, in your tech startup it may be unwise for the CEO to attempt to take sole responsibility for navigation. The company navigator should report to the CEO and the board of directors—the individuals with legal responsibility for company navigation. For a startup, Company Navigator is probably not a full time position but a function to assign to one of the board members, the management team or a specialist outside consultant.

To supplement the input from company insiders, the Company Navigator might want to seek the perspective of independent outside observers like investment bankers and merger & acquisition agents. In addition to providing a much-needed reality check, this could help identify potential obstacles and provide valuable information on the state of the route ahead.

Role of the Company Navigator

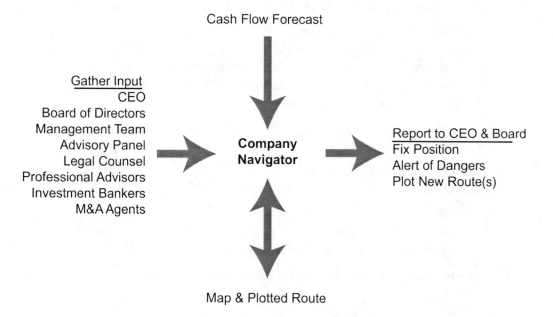

Cash Flow Forecast

Gather Input
CEO
Board of Directors
Management Team
Advisory Panel
Legal Counsel
Professional Advisors
Investment Bankers
M&A Agents

Company Navigator

Report to CEO & Board
Fix Position
Alert of Dangers
Plot New Route(s)

Map & Plotted Route

1. Prepare a map with milestones and stepping stones.
2. Take bearings and accurately fix position on the map.
3. Plot out a viable route, or a number of alternatives for the CEO & Board of Directors.
4. Alert the CEO and Board of upcoming dangers.
5. Go back to 2. above. Repeat regularly until the journey is complete.

What you're Looking For

In taking your bearings, you're really checking to see if there's sufficient reason to change your current course:

✓ *Are any obstacles blocking your route?*—is anything blocking the company from hitting one of its upcoming stepping stones or milestones? Is the obstacle insurmountable or can it be overcome?

✓ *Is the route still open?*—poor weather conditions on Wall Street often lead to the closure of the route to *IPO*.

✓ *Have any of your contingencies been triggered?*—in preparing your travel plan you identified certain events and situations that would require changes to your route.

✓ *Do you have sufficient momentum?*—are you hitting the milestones and making marked progress along your chosen course?

✓ *Are you heading for a cash flow crisis?*—averting a cash crisis is a priority activity!

Taking your Bearings in 2 Simple Steps

With an accurate map, a cash flow forecast and details of the company's progress and achievements, the process of pinpointing your position takes just two simple steps:

1. **Mark your progress**—check off the milestones and stepping stones achieved. Identify obstacles that could block your progress.
2. **Identify whether you're on track or on the slippery slope heading for a cash crisis**—compare your cash flow forecast with the status of your fundraising efforts. Be realistic here—it can be dangerous to rely only on a best case scenario.

Step 1) Mark your Progress

Example Map

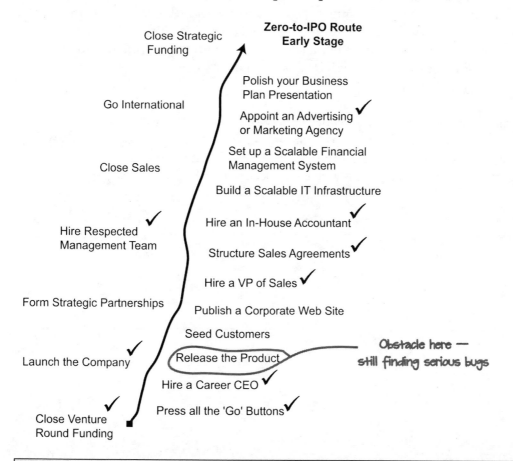

Zero-to-IPO Route
Early Stage

Close Strategic Funding

Polish your Business Plan Presentation

Go International

Appoint an Advertising or Marketing Agency ✔

Set up a Scalable Financial Management System

Close Sales

Build a Scalable IT Infrastructure

Hire an In-House Accountant ✔

Hire Respected Management Team ✔

Structure Sales Agreements ✔

Hire a VP of Sales ✔

Form Strategic Partnerships

Publish a Corporate Web Site

Seed Customers

Launch the Company ✔

Release the Product   *Obstacle here — still finding serious bugs*

Hire a Career CEO ✔

Close Venture Round Funding ✔

Press all the 'Go' Buttons ✔

Momentum Gauge

Comparing the company's current position with previous snapshots, you're in a position to show progress. Here are three indicators of positive momentum:

a) **Marked progress**—are you consistently checking off new milestones and stepping stones?

b) **Upbeat team**—are the staff enthusiastic & excited? Momentum is damaged if any of the key individuals quit and head for the hills.

c) **Market buzz**—is the company generating positive press coverage, expert product endorsements, etc?

Step 2) Are you On Track or the Slippery Slope to Cash Crisis?

If you fail to detect, or ignore, a distant or looming cash crisis you're putting the whole company in danger. Don't be lulled into a false sense of security if you have good momentum and you're hitting your milestones—a cash crisis can kill the company at any stage along the route. Actively raising funds or cutting costs can certainly slow your momentum but it has to be given priority attention—good progress and momentum are meaningless when the company runs out of cash and is forced to shut down.

As the company descends down the slippery slope toward a cash crisis, it becomes progressively more difficult to raise funds—as time ticks by and cash burns away, the slope becomes ever-more steep and increasingly difficult to ascend. So detecting a distant or looming cash crisis is a vital component of taking your bearings.

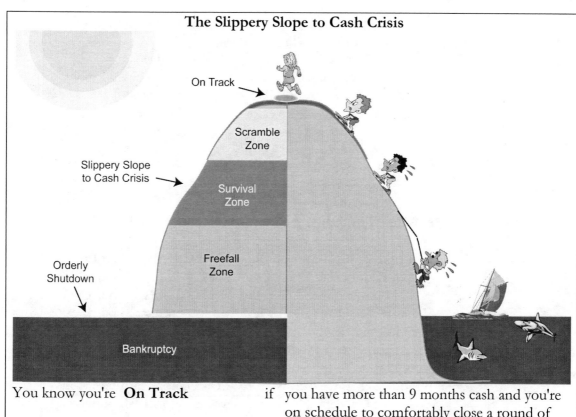

The Slippery Slope to Cash Crisis

You know you're **On Track**	if	you have more than 9 months cash and you're on schedule to comfortably close a round of funding or sell the company before the cash burns out.
You know you're in the **Scramble Zone**	if	acceleration of your efforts could compress the process and you could realistically close a round of funding or sell the company before the cash burns out.
You know you're in the **Survival Zone**	if	accelerated fundraising and M&A efforts are unlikely to avert the looming crisis. You have to lighten the load and cut the burn rate to buy more time.
You know you're in the **Freefall Zone**	if	you have less than 4 months cash and it would take something close to a miracle to close funding or sell the company before the cash burns out.

Fundraising Process	Takes in the Region of	
Appoint Fundraising Team	2	weeks
Formulate the Pitch	4	weeks
Identify Target Investors	2	weeks
Create Investor Info. Packs	4	weeks
Prepare to Approach Investors	2	weeks
Approach & Present to Investors	12	weeks
Negotiate & Agree Terms	3	weeks
Sign Term Sheet	1	week
Complete Due Diligence	4	weeks
Close Round of Funding	1	week
The Whole Fundraising Process	**35**	**weeks**

Fundraising Process	Should be Completed At Least	
Appoint Fundraising Team	*33*	weeks before cash burns out.
Formulate the Pitch	*29*	weeks before cash burns out.
Identify Target Investors	*27*	weeks before cash burns out.
Create Investor Info. Packs	*23*	weeks before cash burns out.
Prepare to Approach Investors	*21*	weeks before cash burns out.
Approach & Present to Investors	*9*	weeks before cash burns out.
Negotiate & Agree Terms	*6*	weeks before cash burns out.
Sign Term Sheet	*5*	weeks before cash burns out.
Complete Due Diligence	*1*	week before cash burns out.

The Process of Selling the Company	Takes in the Region of	
Take Decision to Sell	1	week
Pick M&A Team	5	weeks
Prepare your Paperwork	5	weeks
Dress the Company up for Sale	1	weeks
Identify, Approach & Present to Buyers	16	weeks
Negotiate Terms	4	weeks
Agree Terms	4	weeks
Board & Other Approvals	1	week
Prepare Agreements	2	weeks
Complete Due Diligence	4	weeks
Close Sale	1	week
The process of selling the company	**44**	**weeks**

Selling the Company		Should be Completed At Least
Take Decision to Sell	43	weeks before cash burns out.
Pick M&A Team	38	weeks before cash burns out.
Prepare your Paperwork	33	weeks before cash burns out.
Dress the Company up for Sale	32	weeks before cash burns out.
Identify, Approach & Present to Buyers	16	weeks before cash burns out.
Negotiate Terms	12	weeks before cash burns out.
Agree Terms	8	weeks before cash burns out.
Board & Other Approvals	7	weeks before cash burns out.
Prepare Agreements	5	weeks before cash burns out.
Complete Due Diligence	1	week before cash burns out.

When to Take your Bearings

At a minimum, you need to take your bearings and provide a status report for inclusion in the board package that's mailed out to the directors a few days ahead of each board meeting. A quarterly navigation check may be sufficient if you're on track—hitting your milestones with plenty of cash in the bank. However, as a cash crisis develops it becomes increasingly important to pinpoint your position on a regular basis—monthly or even weekly if you reach the survival and freefall zones.

What's the Best Route for You and your Product?

The starting point of the seven point travel plan is to target your destination—if you don't know where you're going you have little chance of actually getting there. Of course it is possible to embark on a journey without targeting a specific destination—people do it all the time. They're the people that never really get anywhere—you see them every day aimlessly wandering around with no sense of purpose or direction. Mercifully, the laws of natural selection and survival of the fittest come into force. A company without a target destination or clear sense of direction will soon lose momentum, find itself in a cash flow crisis that quickly advances from *survivable* to *terminal*.

Once you've decided to target a destination, which one do you choose? There are only five to choose from so your options are somewhat limited. You're not likely to target *Bankruptcy* or *Shutdown* as destinations for your startup so we can cross them off the list. The only other destinations to target are *IPO*, *Cash Flow Sale* and *Asset Sale*. *Independent survival* is of no interest to the investors, so there are only three possible routes you could realistically select for your company—*Zero-to-Asset Sale*, *Zero-to-Cash Flow Sale* and *Zero-to-IPO*.

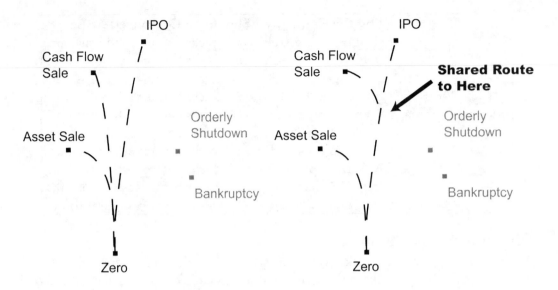

A candidate for *Cash Flow Sale* is also a candidate for *IPO* and vice versa. Companies heading for each of these destinations follow very similar routes, so we can merge these two routes into one, at least for the first part of the journey.

So, by a process of elimination, we're left with only two alternative travel plans for you to select for your startup—the long haul from *Zero-to-IPO* and the short sprint from *Zero-to-Asset Sale*.

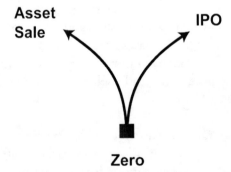

So do you choose to take the long haul to *IPO* or the short sprint to *Asset Sale*? To find out which is the best option for you I suggest you start by asking yourself some searching questions.

Make a note of your answer to each of the following questions:

1. *Are you prepared to endure the hardships of a long and harrowing journey?* After reading this book from cover to cover you should come away with a good understanding of the challenges you're going to face in a technology startup. It's not all plain sailing—as a general rule everything that can go wrong will go wrong. Virtually everyone that's been on this journey from the beginning will attest that they've been through a grueling time. Cash flow crises can be particularly painful—trying to run a business and a home on fumes can take years off your life. Don't be afraid to admit that it's not for you.

2. *Do you have a personal support network?* Do you have a shoulder to cry on? Someone to buck you up when you need a boost? However, confident you are, you're going to need a personal support network to help you make it through the ups and downs of this journey. If your partner is not behind the idea, then you could run into problems. One of the most stable and recession-proof occupations in Silicon Valley is that of divorce lawyer. When entrepreneurs strike it rich, families and relationships go through turmoil and it's boom time for divorce lawyers. When entrepreneurs strike out, it puts tremendous stress on relationships and the divorce lawyers win again. A list of good divorce lawyers may come in handy whether you succeed or not. If your spouse is behind the idea at the start, I suggest you make sure he/she reads this book after you and has a full understanding of the challenges and milestones that lie ahead. Your friends and former colleagues could come in useful as well. You're going to need personal introductions to investors, board members, management hires and your personal network will become invaluable. Lead investors are likely to carry out detailed background checks and ask for a list of professional references before they hand over their cash. So the strength of your personal and professional network could be a key factor determining your chances of success.

3. *Is the market immature enough?* Don't enter the market if it's too late. Mature markets with entrenched competitors are very difficult to penetrate. Is this market young enough for a new entrant to carve out a market-leadership position? Investors like to see independent market metrics and forecasts, but if they're readily available, it means the major analysts are tracking the market

and other companies are paying for the information, presumably to support their plans to develop products that are competitive to your own. So, if you can get good market metrics focused on your specific market niche, then it may be already too late. Is the window of opportunity still big enough for you to squeeze through? Remember, if it's going to take 18 months to release your product, the competitive landscape will have moved on. You need to predict what your competitors are going to look like in 18 months time rather than what they look like today.

4. *Is the market mature enough?* There are real dangers in being too early into a market. If you're a lone visionary predicting the emergence of a new market, then you could find yourself on the 'bleeding edge' for some considerable time. Bleeding edge companies often bleed to death before the market takes off. If you can't realistically see any customers prepared to stump up cash to buy the product within 18 months or 2 years, then you're going to need very patient and long-term investors.

5. *Is your invention sufficiently unique?* It's normally very difficult to enter an established market with a 'me-too' product and win any significant market share. In some cases it can happen, when the established players are in death spirals or they're following an inferior business model, but it's not the sort of scenario that most investors are looking for.

6. *Do you have a long enough lead?* What's stopping competitors from stealing your idea? Most venture capitalists refuse to sign non-disclosure agreements (NDA's) and your idea will soon become public knowledge when you start looking for funding. If it's a good idea and it's easy to reproduce, it will be copied and there's not a lot you can do about it. Patents can help but they will never provide full protection. However, as a patent application often takes years to process and is accompanied by legal fees that would buy a nice car, very few startups have the luxury of patent protection. Nevertheless, people are often deterred by the prospect of hard work—if you can show that you're ahead and that it's going to take time, money and hard work to catch up, then your competition may be deterred. The ideal scenario is that you've done your research at college or in your day job and, working in your garage in your spare time, you're already 6 months into your product development. In this case you have some protection as you already have a significant jump on the market and it's going to take a lot of time and energy for a competitor to catch up. If you're paranoid that someone reading the executive summary of your business plan might be able to steal the idea and beat you to market then you're probably justified in keeping things under

wraps for a while. You really need to be in the position that you feel you could give the business plan and product specifications to all your competitors and sleep soundly in the confidence that they'll take at least 6 months to catch you up.

7. *Do you have the financial wherewithal to survive a startup situation?* Can you keep the wolves from the door if you're forced to skip a few pay checks? If you went without salary, could you survive 3 months, 6 months, a year? Believe it or not, with a wife, baby and 2 mortgages to cover, I went 3 years without salary in one startup situation. Of course, by the end, I owed money to every member of my family, all my friends, distant relatives and numerous strangers I'd met in the street. This type of situation doesn't exactly ease the stress of running a startup. So, before you leave your day job, I suggest you have a plan for how you're going to survive if your pay checks dry up for a while.

8. *Are you prepared to commit 3-5 years, or more, to this journey?* You're gambling with a big chunk of your working life and your chances aren't exactly great—after all the adversity, hard work and stress you could easily come out of this journey empty handed. If you do, don't be surprised if your friends that take relatively easy corporate jobs and spend their weekends with their families, while you're slaving away at work, end up striking it rich on their stock options. Of course, building a cool product and completing the short sprint to Asset Sale can take as little as 1-2 years—much quicker than building a world-beating profitable company and taking the long haul to IPO.

9. *Are you hell-bent on world domination?* One characteristic of virtually all the people I've seen lead their companies to IPO is that they're determined to WIN at all costs and they have enough ego to carry it off. Although you probably wouldn't want one as your neighbor, egomaniacs seem to be very good at targeting a destination, leading a team and maintaining momentum— so they're well suited to this journey. As a result, savvy investors appreciate this and don't shy away from backing them. If they were born in the second half of the 20th century, Hitler, Mussolini and Stalin would probably be heading up technology startups today. No, come to think of it they'd be heading up huge technology leaders like Oracle, HP and Microsoft.

10. *Are you prepared to share the pie with everyone, and his brother?* By the time you reach IPO, you're sure to have seen your shareholding diluted by all the stock issued to seed investors, venture investors, strategic investors, mezzanine investors, investment bankers, lawyers, accountants and umpteen employee

stock option pools—not to mention huge chunks issued to the career CEO and other 'Johnny come lately' executives. Virtually everyone that gets involved with a hot IPO candidate company will want to get a piece of the action. It's like you make a pizza and head out with your buddies to find a safe place for a picnic but you find that you have to give a slice of the pizza to everyone you meet on the journey. On a long journey, your slice could be reduced to a paper-thin sliver. As Zero-to-Asset Sale is a shorter 'sprint', you'll end up with a larger share than you would after a long haul to IPO.

11. *Is your idea big enough?* Just how big is the problem that your invention solves? With hand on heart, can you realistically see a multi-billion dollar market developing for this product?

12. *Is the revenue model realistic?* Since the dot-com crash, investors are no longer prepared to invest in imaginative revenue models. There was a time when dot-coms would develop products, pay AOL millions of dollars for the privilege of giving them away for free and convince venture capitalists that stupid Wall Street investors would line up to buy stock in the excited belief that irritating, dull web page banner ads would generate zillions of dollars downstream. It worked well for a while. The stocks soared after IPO, investors cashed out and funded new dot-com startups that bought traffic from older dot-coms in a brilliant pyramid scheme, possibly engineered in the secret VC labyrinth beneath Sand Hill Road. Alas, those days are over. Wall Street investors finally figured it out and the whole pyramid scheme collapsed. Today you're going to need to show that your targeted buyers have budgets and a track record of spending cash. You're also going to have to identify and quickly establish distribution channels or other routes to market.

13. *Do you enjoy working in large teams?* Keeping a large team moving forward on a long haul can be like herding cats. In fact, it would be easier to herd cats as there'd probably be less whining, complaining and cannibalization. Small teams can be much easier and more fun to motivate and lead toward the Promised Land. On the other hand, some people relish the challenge of managing large teams—the sense of power can certainly fuel the ego of individuals hell-bent on world domination.

14. *Can you give up control without freaking out?* You may be the product inventor, company founder and see the company as your own baby, but at some point on the long haul to IPO you're likely to have to give up control to investors and career executives that are sure to make decisions that you don't agree

with. It's a frustrating feeling when you know the company is heading in the wrong direction but you can't convince anyone to turn around. Some personalities patiently stick around to gently guide the team back onto the track, others scream, stamp their feet and quit.

15. *Are you prepared to sell out for a modest price?* Imagine that a competitor turned up at your office and put a valuation on your product that you thought was lower than you deserved. Would you feel insulted and throw them out of the office or take them out to dinner? This happened to a friend of mine—his competitor turned up and offered him $70m for his company. Although he personally owned over 95% of the shares and the company was only 18 months old, he actually threw the bedazzled visitors out of the building! Nothing less than IPO was enough for this guy—he readily admitted that he was hell-bent on world domination. Of course many people would be happy to pocket the $70m and live happily ever after.

16. *Are you prepared to travel on a budget?* It's very difficult to put a value on a company that's being acquired for its products, technology or some other asset and the sale price can be relatively low. After outside investors have taken their share, there can be very little left over for the founders and employees from an Asset Sale. So you want to maintain as large a share of the pie as possible and keep your outside funding to a minimum if you're going for the short sprint to Asset Sale. This means flying in the back of the plane, making your own coffee and keeping your costs to an absolute minimum.

I can't tell you what's the best course for you—it's a very personal decision influenced by many different factors. However:

→ *If you answered 'No' to any of questions 1-7* You're probably best advised to stay where you are—forming a high tech startup could be damaging to your bank balance, your health or both.

→ *If you answered 'No' to any of the questions 8-14* The long haul from *Zero-to-IPO* is probably not for you.

→ *If you answered 'No' to any of questions 15-16* The short sprint from *Zero-to-Asset Sale* is probably not for you.

Completing the long haul to *IPO* will likely provide you with the highest possible valuation for your company and it's the only route for you if you're hell-bent on world domination. There's a feeling of safety in numbers—working as part of a relatively large team you may not feel so personally exposed as you would in a small, cash-constrained startup. The down-side of this route is that your shareholding will become increasingly diluted with each of the successive rounds of funding and you'll probably be locked out from selling your shares for some time after the *IPO* itself. If you don't make it all the way to *IPO*, you may have the opportunity to switch to *Cash Flow Sale* or *Asset Sale* as alternative destinations. The Zero-to-IPO journey can take a long time and constantly looking for new funding can be very tiresome.

On the short sprint to *Asset Sale* you're not building a viable stand-alone company and you can focus a small team on building a killer product without a lot of business distractions. There's little need to bring in a career CEO and you should be able to maintain more control. The proceeds of the sale could be tiny in comparison to a *Cash Flow Sale* or *IPO* and you're going to want to maintain a large share of the company by keeping outside investment to a minimum. This means keeping a tight control on costs, living without luxuries and, when times are tough, you may be forced to supplement your income with service work.

Chapter 3—The Long Haul to Destination *IPO* (or *Cash Flow Sale*)

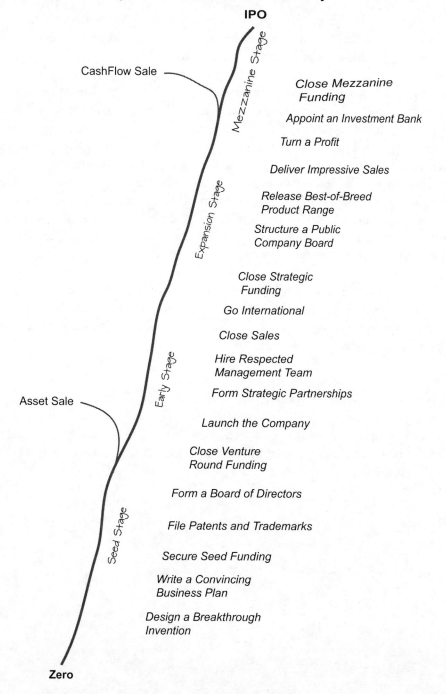

IPO

Mezzanine Stage

CashFlow Sale

Close Mezzanine Funding

Appoint an Investment Bank

Turn a Profit

Deliver Impressive Sales

Release Best-of-Breed Product Range

Structure a Public Company Board

Expansion Stage

Close Strategic Funding

Go International

Close Sales

Hire Respected Management Team

Form Strategic Partnerships

Early Stage

Launch the Company

Asset Sale

Close Venture Round Funding

Form a Board of Directors

File Patents and Trademarks

Secure Seed Funding

Write a Convincing Business Plan

Design a Breakthrough Invention

Seed Stage

Zero

Destination IPO

A Nasdaq *IPO* is the destination that most entrepreneurs are aiming for when they lose all sense of responsibility and launch a high-tech startup.   From the Wall Street investors' perspective, the *IPO* is a vehicle for previously-private companies to raise funds to fuel growth. From the private company investors' perspective, the *IPO* is an exit route—or an important step in the process of unlocking the value in its shares and generating a tangible return on investment.

If you were ready for *IPO* today (after the dot-com bubble has burst and most investors have come to their senses), you'll have sales revenues of at least $10m a quarter, profitability and solid confidence that you're going to achieve good growth in the coming 3 or 4 quarters. You're also going to need to show that you have a market-leadership position in a high growth sector with a strong management team, top-tier investors, top-tier customers and unique technology that's sufficiently solid to provide a defensible barrier to competition. If you're already at this point, put this book down right now, call Morgan Stanley and Goldman Sachs and start the push toward *IPO*. If you're not quite in this position, read on—there may be some tips contained in these pages to help you get from here to there.

The technology sector moves at lightning speed. The first few companies in each market that target *IPO* and drive toward it at full pace will likely be the first to get there and shut everyone else out.   If you're not one of them, you'll get there too late and miss your chance.

Unfortunately, many of the startups today are working with a travel plan somewhat similar to that of the Donner Party: *"..we'll head off in this direction and push through over the mountains—and through hard work and perseverance we'll make it to the promised land..".* If you're going to have any chance of completing this journey today, you'll need a well-prepared travel plan that's somewhat more detailed than this. Like all good plans, it starts out on the back of a napkin.

<u>Back-of-a-Napkin Travel Plan for the Long Haul from Zero-to-IPO</u>

Team
Team Members & Responsibilities

You'll need to find investors and founders that all want to target IPO. You'll need a substantial sized team with a wide range of skills to deal with all the different obstacles and terrains that you're likely to encounter. Plan to pick up new players with special skills as you make your way along the route.

Provisions
Budget & Resources Required

You're going to need several rounds of funding to make it all the way to IPO - plan on funding from angel, venture capital and corporate investors.

Taking Bearings
How to Fix your Position

Track your progress with regular cash flow forecasts, board and management meetings. Seek independent reality checks from outside experts as well as insiders.

Plotting your Route

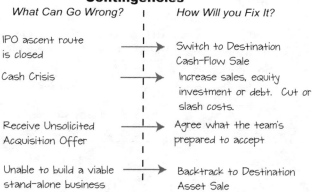

Break the Journey into 4 Stages

IPO

Mezzannine

Expansion

Early

Zero **Seed**

Starting Point
Identify Starting Position

Earth-shattering invention or technology ("Zero").

Target Destination
Where do you Want to Be?

IPO on Nasdaq or another major stock market.

Maintaining Momentum
How to Keep the Wagons Rolling

Be prepared to create a positive buzz and constantly whip the whole team up into a frenzy of enthusiasm and excitement.

Contingencies

What Can Go Wrong?	How Will you Fix It?
IPO ascent route is closed	Switch to Destination Cash-Flow Sale
Cash Crisis	Increase sales, equity investment or debt. Cut or slash costs.
Receive Unsolicited Acquisition Offer	Agree what the team's prepared to accept
Unable to build a viable stand-alone business	Backtrack to Destination Asset Sale

A Team for the Long Haul

This is a long route requiring a relatively large team with a multitude of skills. The team consists of founders, directors, advisors, executives and various assortments of investors—seed, venture capital, strategic and mezzanine. You'll likely pick up a career CEO and other key team members en-route.

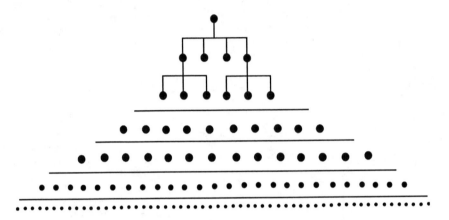

Board of Directors

Seed Stage

Don't stack your board of directors with founders and friends when you form the company. A successful CEO once told me that a board should always have an odd number of directors—and that 3 was too many! Seriously, with a Delaware corporation one person can act as the sole director and officer of the company. '1' is a nice manageable number in the seed stage—decisions are quick and simple to make and you won't have to throw someone off the board to make room for VC's and other directors later on. Instead of giving them board seats, you can appoint angel investors, founders and friends to your advisory panel—you can still invite them to attend board meetings and participate in strategic decision making without asking them to take on the associated responsibilities and liabilities.

> *A camel is a horse designed by committee..*
> *.. keep the board as small as you can!*

Early Stage

The VC leading the first round of funding is almost certain to demand a seat on the board. At this point, you can increase the size of the board to three people, and leave one of the seats vacant until you appoint the CEO. In addition to the lead VC, other investors may request board seats at this stage. To avoid moving to a 5 person board, you may want to offer them 'observation rights' to sit in on board meetings or positions on the advisory panel.

	Seed Stage	Early Stage	Expansion Stage	Mezzanine Stage
Founder	✓	✓	✓	✓
Lead VC		✓	✓	✓
CEO		✓	✓	✓
Strategic Investor			✓	✓
Outside Director			✓	✓
Marquee Name				✓
Marquee Name				✓

Expansion Stage

Strategic investors may demand a board seat and you'll likely be forced to grow the board to five people for the expansion stage. Investors and management have their own agendas and sometimes this can cloud their judgment—they're sometimes tempted to look out for themselves instead of looking out for the company. When you add a strategic investor to the board, it's a good opportunity to bring in an outside director—someone with experience and an independent perspective. In the expansion stage, two of the board seats are held by management and two are held by investors—so the choice of outside director can be quite important as it affects the balance of power.

Mezzanine Stage

Wall Street investors look for marquee names on the board of directors when it comes time to *IPO*. They're more likely to invest if they see that the company is backed by known and trusted individuals. A board made up of 7 people with 4 insiders and 3 outsiders is what most Wall Street investors expect and feel comfortable with at *IPO*. Don't just choose anyone that looks good to Wall Street— make sure he/she has good synergy with the rest of the team and that he/she's prepared to attend board meetings and make a sustained long term contribution to the company.

Who Controls the Board?

At the seed stage, there's little dispute over who controls the board. In the *early stage*, control depends upon where the CEO's alliances lie—if the CEO was brought in by the founder, together they could vote as a block and override the lead VC—but not for long. It's important to remember that preference shareholders normally have the power to change the whole board if they so wish. When it comes to the expansion stage, the choice of the outside director can be pivotal in deciding whether the board power rests with management (CEO and founder) or the outside investors (lead VC and strategic investor). At the mezzanine stage, with seven people on the board, it's anyone's guess where the control could rest. As the founder, if you want some control or influence over the board, it's important to play an active part in attracting, selecting and schmoozing the CEO and the outside directors.

Advisory Panel

The advisory panel is like an extension of the board of directors—providing advice, introductions and credibility without responsibility of being an official member of the board. It can be very valuable, especially in the seed and early stages when the board is not exactly huge. You can appoint as many advisors as you think you can manage—however, in my experience, one is way too few and ten is too many.

Executives & Management Team

Wall Street investors like to back individuals with a track-record of running public companies and providing shareholders with a good return on investment. If you're serious about making at all the way to *IPO*, you'll satisfy the investors, spread the workload and bring in a career CEO, CFO and other high-priced executives.

Investors

You're going to need several investors to fund each stage of the *Zero-to-IPO* route— seed investors, lead investors, strategic investors and later-stage or mezzanine investors. Ideally, you'll find seed investors that introduce you to lead investors, and lead investors that introduce you to strategic investors, mezzanine investors and investment banks—and they all collaborate with management and the board of directors in one big happy family. Good luck.

Although you're not always lucky enough to pick and choose your investors, it is important to find a group of shareholders that agrees on your *Zero-to-IPO* travel plan. Asking investors to target *IPO* should not be difficult at all. Agreement on the selection of the team could be a little more contentious but should be possible with some work if there's flexibility on all sides—so could the selection of the milestones and the route itself.

Of course, everyone will be happy when things are going well and you're making good progress along the route, but all hell can break loose when you stray off course or lose momentum. Some investors may have difficulty agreeing to switch the target destination from *IPO* to *Cash Flow Sale*. An investor with aggressive return-on-investment guidelines may find it impossible to support the radical decision of backtracking to an *Asset Sale*, even when this may look like the best option for everyone involved. Ideally, you'll have your contingency plans agreed with investors ahead of time so that you're ready to implement them the moment you come across an obstacle blocking your path.

For the *Zero-to-IPO* route you likely need lots of investors, you need them to work closely together to help propel the company along its journey—and you need them to be prepared to quickly switch routes if things go wrong.

Zero-to-IPO—a Multi-Stage Route

→ *Seed Stage*—this startup phase is very busy—there's a lot to do in a very short space of time! You're going to have to secure seed funding and put all the basic foundations of the business in place before your seed funding provisions run dry.

→ *Early Stage*—when you've secured your lead venture capital investor and first round funding, you're now in the Early Stage—a whole new phase of the journey. With additional management hires and a completely new scale of operation, the company will take on a whole new personality. There's still foundation building to do, but by now, you're going to have to start to show some results so that you can attract new investors and move into the next stage.

→ *Expansion Stage*—although you're still building on the company foundations, your main focus will be to *sell, sell, sell* your way to a market leadership position. When the numbers start to look good, you could be ready to start talking to the underwriters and start the preparations for *IPO*.

→ *Mezzanine Stage*—the Mezzanine Stage is when you make the final ascent to *IPO*. This is when you're 'discovered' by an investment bank, the microscopes come out and every aspect of the business is analyzed in minute detail. The company will have to continue its tremendous growth on its own as the CEO and most of the senior management team will be tied up in the *IPO* preparations. You'll then need to brace yourself for the drama and excitement of the *IPO* itself. You've reached your target destination but from the perspective of Wall Street and the investment banks, the journey is only just beginning.

Zero-to-IPO Milestones

1. *Design a Breakthrough Invention*—the journey starts with a breakthrough idea, technology or invention.

2. *Write a Convincing Business Plan*—describe as clearly and concisely as possible how the invention can be commercialized to dominate a huge, emerging market.

3. *Secure Seed Funding*—ideally from professional angels or corporate investors that can guide the company through the seed phase and provide introductions to venture investors and other key players.

4. *Form a Board of Directors*—that ideally consists of one director in the seed phase, three in the early stage, five in the expansion stage and seven in the mezzanine stage.

5. *File Patents and Trademarks*—to protect and defend the company's major asset: its intellectual property.

6. *Launch the Company*—establish your presence in the market, make sure industry insiders know who you are and what you do.

7. *Form Strategic Partnerships*—with powerful, respected corporations that appreciate and endorse your business and technology.

8. *Close Venture Round Funding*—with respected venture investor like a top-tier Sand Hill Road firm.

9. *Hire Respected Management Team*—you'll need a professional CEO with an impressive track record supported by a trusted CFO, legal counsel and other respected executives.

10. *Close Sales*—long-term contracts with top-tier corporations are ideal.

11. *Go International*—establish the channels, partners and operations to enable you to dominate a global market.

12. *Close Strategic Funding*—with respected high-tech corporations offering marketing and distribution muscle.

13. *Structure a Public Company Board*—strengthen your board with outside directors that are known and respected on Wall Street.

14. *Build Best-of-Breed Products*—ideally win industry awards and endorsements from respected experts like journalists, analysts and strategic partners.

15. *Deliver Impressive Sales*—report strong sales revenues (of perhaps $10m/quarter). It's important that you have a solid pipeline to deliver growing sales revenues through the *IPO* and several quarters beyond.

16. *Turn a Profit*—profitable results are now important—again! What better way to validate that the company has a viable business, that management can effectively deliver sales and control costs?

17. *Appoint an Investment Bank*—that's prepared to lead the underwriting and guide the company to *IPO* and beyond. Bear in mind that Wall Street investors are easily impressed by the underwriters name and reputation.

18. *Close Mezzanine Funding*—in the run-up to *IPO*, show Wall Street investors that you have the financial backing of respected corporations and top-tier investors. Continue the pattern showing a steady growth in valuation at each round of funding.
19. *Go Public—IPO.*

Although hardware, software, Internet, biotech and most forms of technology company follow a similar route from *Zero-to-IPO*, you'll likely want to use this as a guide to help you plot out a specific route with milestones that reflect your specific company, product and market conditions. Deadlines are a great motivator and you will want to attach dates to some of your milestones, however, some of the steps in the journey can take much longer than you expect—so don't be surprised to find that you have to adjust the dates from time to time.

Long Haul Contingency Plans

Even if you don't digest this whole book, make sure you read the chapter on the *Slippery Slope to Destination Shutdown*, page 251, before you form your startup. Encountering obstacles blocking the route, you really want to be able to quickly switch to a pre-prepared contingency plan. Valuable days, weeks or months can be lost if you haven't agreed on your contingency plans and identified alternative routes in advance.

With a good travel plan and momentum, you should be able to overcome most of the challenges on the *Zero-to-IPO* route, however, at some point you may find yourselves facing an obstacle that's totally blocking the path. For reasons out of your control, like unpredictable gyrations on Wall Street, *IPO* may realistically become an unattainable target. The sensible thing to do at this point is switch destinations and target selling the company instead. If you have a viable stand-alone business, now is the time to switch destinations and target a *Cash Flow Sale*. If you've been unable to build a viable stand-alone business then you need to backtrack and target *Asset Sale*. Almost every major problem you encounter will result in a cash flow crisis sooner or later. When it does, you have to either bring in more cash— from sales, equity investment and debt, or cut your costs.

Not all your surprises will be unwelcome. Heading out on the long haul to *IPO*, you may be pleasantly surprised to receive an unsolicited offer of acquisition. In the early stage, a larger company may take an interest in your technology and provide you with the opportunity to go directly to destination *Asset Sale*. In the expansion or mezzanine stages, after sales have started to flow in, a potential competitor may come in with an offer to buy the company in a *Cash Flow Sale*. In these, as well as the other contingency scenarios, you need to react quickly. It's sure to help if you've thought through the issues and formulated your plans ahead of time.

Long Haul Contingency Plans -- If IPO Becomes Unattainable

After a hard struggle through the expansion stage, you may find that you have a viable ongoing business with positive cash flow however, for some reason or another, the route to *IPO* is closed. After a valiant attempt, you may fail to attract an investment bank to underwrite the public offering. Perhaps Wall Street has an aversion to all *IPO* listings, all technology listings or just listings in your specific market sector.

The closure of the ascent route from expansion to *IPO* could be either temporary or permanent. If it's a temporary closure and you have patient investors, you could wait for the route to reopen as Wall Street comes to its senses. Otherwise, this is the time to switch destinations and target *Cash Flow Sale*.

Switch to Cash Flow Sale

Switching target destinations from *IPO* to *Cash Flow Sale* does not mean putting a 'For Sale' sign outside your office. Initially, the switch could be very subtle, almost undetectable to employees and the outside world, however, eventually it's very likely to have a profound effect on shareholders and everyone else involved with the company.

Switch to Cash Flow Sale

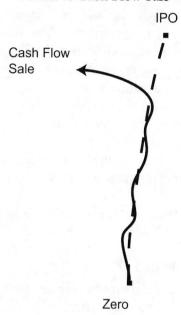

Of course you could aimlessly wander around and survive as an independent business for several years. Perhaps you could hang around looking attractive and playing hard-to-get in the hope that a well-heeled suitor is going to beat a path to your door and make you an offer that's too good to refuse. Unfortunately, buyers don't like to have to do all the hard work in tracking down potential acquisitions, so consciously targeting *Cash Flow Sale* and driving toward it at full speed will dramatically increase your chances of selling the company for a good price and converting your near-worthless private company shares into hard cash.

Here's how you make the switch:

1. Read the *Selling the Company* map and destination guide (page *351*).
2. Make sure investors and the rest of the team are aware that the *IPO* route is closed—misconceptions or misunderstandings could hinder your progress.
3. Prepare a new plan to reach *Cash Flow Sale* as your destination.
4. Win board support for a switch in destination.
5. Plot out the milestones on the route to selling your company.
6. Pick your M&A team and start the process (you may want to keep this information under wraps).
7. Offload all the components of the business that a buyer is not going to want to buy. This could include cutting out the staff that an acquirer is not going to need.
8. Recast your financials and dress the company up for a sale.
9. Continue to maximize your sales and profits.

Receive Unsolicited Acquisition Offer

Once the company starts to generate momentum in the market, it becomes a target for possible acquisition. Don't be surprised when you receive an invitation to lunch from an M&A firm or one of the executives of a potential acquirer—perhaps one of your competitors, strategic partners or someone already selling in to your target customer base. Before you turn down the date, remember this—there are plenty of entrepreneurs out there that kick themselves for turning down an offer of acquisition, then stumble en-route to *IPO*. To them, the old saying that a '*bird in the hand is worth two in the bush*' could never be more true. An *IPO* is likely to provide the highest valuation for your company, but there are many reasons why an acquisition could be very much more appealing—see *Selling the Company*, page 351. A serial entrepreneur told me a familiar story of how he created an early competitor to DOS and received the invitation to visit Bill Gates and Steve Ballmer in Seattle. Apparently, Bill was very charming, commended them on their product, and offered the entrepreneur a position heading up an exciting division of the company. Mr. Ballmer was a little more direct when he made an offer to buy them out—if you don't accept we'll put you out of business in 6 months. The entrepreneur was interested in taking the deal but the venture capitalist on his board convinced him that they would make more money by rejecting the offer, continuing as an independent and heading toward *IPO*. They turned the deal down. True to his word, Steve Ballmer stepped on the gas, put a crack development team in place, built a competitive product and the entrepreneur was out of business in 6 months. Fortunately, the entrepreneur has learned from this mistake, sold several of his subsequent startups, taken some through *IPO*, now he's started to sleep at night and no longer gets teary-eyed when he laments about his visit to Seattle.

As soon as the company completes a round of funding with an outside investor, the founders and employees lose all control over important decisions—like accepting or declining an offer to acquire the company. It's at this point that the common shareholders in private companies realize that their share certificates are worth little more than the paper they're written on—in most cases only preference shareholders get to vote on such important decisions. People tend to become emotional in M&A (merger & acquisition) situations, and the company is in danger of being damaged, or even destroyed, by a disagreement over whether to accept or refuse an offer of acquisition. Where the founders and employees want to accept the offer but the investors refuse to sell, the contention could cause an irreparable split. So, before closing your first round of funding and handing these decisions over to the investors, it would be useful to discuss how the team would handle an offer of acquisition.

If they were solely motivated by return on investment, investors would accept most offers of acquisition. However, when flushed with success, the prospect of success, or just the satisfaction of gathering momentum, shareholders often lose their ability to make sensible decisions, become hell-bent on world domination and decide to continue on and build an empire instead.

These decisions normally come down to investor expectations—some investors are only interested in *IPO* and refuse to entertain any talk of acquisition. It's useful to know this before you embark on this journey together—at the very least, agree up-front how a potential acquisition offer would be evaluated and avoid painful misunderstandings later on. When evaluating an offer, don't forget to take into consideration the issues of time and dilution—it could take several years before you reach *IPO* as an alternative destination, and as you continue on the journey, you invariably dilute your shares with issues to new investors. Your choice is between a larger share of the pie today versus a smaller share of the pie tomorrow, or at some time in the future.

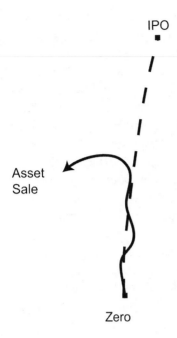

In the technology sector, it's very common for companies with established routes to market to buy new products and technologies from companies that are not yet profitable, or viable as stand-alone businesses. They usually buy the whole company and dispose of the unnecessary components. Of course, an unprofitable company won't receive the same valuation as a profitable one, but in the early stages there are usually fewer investors to share the proceeds—and the return on investment can be appealing to everyone involved.

In normal market conditions, a technology company that's profitable with positive cash-flow, is a good candidate for *IPO*. It's also a good candidate for acquisition. A *Cash Flow Sale* valuation of the company could reach 75% or more of the *IPO* valuation, however, the process can be less risky, less painful and cash has many advantages over the restricted stock shareholders receive from *IPO*.

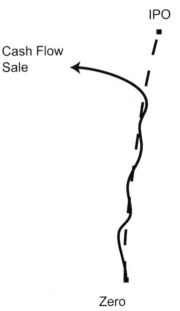

Long Haul Contingency Plans—Cash Crisis on the Zero-to-IPO Route

On the long haul to *IPO*, you're in a constant race to hit milestones before your cash burns out. Stumble and you're sure find yourself in a cash crisis. When this happens, you need to make good decisions and act very quickly to prevent the company from entering a death spiral and heading for *Bankruptcy*. For this reason, I've devoted a whole chapter of the book to *'The Slippery Slope to Shutdown'* page 251—make sure you read it, understand it and know exactly how you're going to react when you find yourself in this position. This will help to prepare a survival plan and plot out your route.

Cash Crisis on the *Zero*-to-*IPO* Route—Some Alternative Maneuvers

✓ *Increase sales*—not always a reliable source of funding in the early stage.

✓ *Raise a new 'Up' round of funding*—(see *Raising an 'Up' Round*, page 260).

✓ *Cut costs*—and lighten the load (see *Cutting Costs*, page 264).

✓ *Slash costs*—by reinventing the company (see *Reinventing the Company*, page 276).

✓ *Raise a new 'Down round' of funding*—(see *Raising a 'Down-Round'* page 260).

✓ *Bridge loan*—or other form of debt (see *Raising a Bridge Loan*, page 262).

✓ *Shutdown*—(see *Making an Elegant Descent—Orderly Shutdown*, page 291).

It's not just the sick companies that find themselves in a cash crisis. 'Healthy' companies with insanely great products and strong market momentum often leave it too late to raise their next rounds of funding—and find themselves in this precarious position. On the *Zero-to-IPO* route, you're constantly raising money. If you get the chance, raise more money than you need—this will buy you more time to hit milestones, add value to the company and raise your next round.

In the ideal situation, you fix your cash crisis by simply increasing sales. In a technology startup with a huge investment in research and development, this is seldom possible. Cutting costs is the next place to look—the elimination of unnecessary headcount and general cost cutting may help, but if you're hell-bent on reaching *IPO* as quickly as possible, you're also sure to need to raise more outside funding—so there's little time to waste. What you really want to do is raise an 'Up' round—at a company valuation and share price that's somewhat higher than the previous one. People always like to see charts with trends that start in the bottom left and head upwards to the right, especially when it comes to share prices—a series of Up-Rounds will produce a pretty chart and make everyone happy. Unfortunately, a cash crisis often leads to a 'Down' round as it puts the company in a weak negotiating position with investors. You guessed it, a 'Down' round is agreed at a valuation and share price lower than the last—producing an ugly shaped chart that no one seems to like. If you can't close a round of funding, you may have to take a bridge loan—often forcing you to give up your first-born child and accept similarly aggressive terms.

When the going gets tough, it's more important than ever to maintain positive momentum. Negative momentum can throw the company into a death spiral—transforming a survivable cash crisis into a terminal one. When the cash crisis is terminal, your target destination switches to *Orderly Shutdown* and your mission is to avoid *Bankruptcy*. See 'Orderly Shutdown & Bankruptcy', page 291.

Companies on the route to *Asset Sale*, with just a small product development team, typically have a great deal of technical expertise and a relatively low burn rate, giving them the option of generating revenues by selling consulting and other services—basically prostituting their staff. This is unlikely to be a viable option for companies on the route to *IPO*—with large sales and marketing teams to support and proportionally large burn rates. Even if it would make a difference, it would not be very easy to rent out a salesperson, administrator or CEO!

If cutting costs and raising new funds doesn't provide sufficient relief, and the company continues to burn up cash, it's time to slash costs. This may involve going back to basics, revisiting the company's mission, its sense of identity and reinventing the company itself. If you realize at this point that you have little chance of making it all the way to *IPO*, it's time to consider switching destinations and backtracking to *Asset Sale*.

Long Haul Contingency Plans—Unable to Build a Viable Stand-Alone Business

Taking your bearings you might find that you have a tremendous product, team, technology and good market momentum, but you don't have the muscle to capitalize on these assets, build your own route to market and create a viable stand-alone business. This is the time to stop what you're doing, take a deep breath and go through the exercise of reinventing the company.

Reinventing the Company

See *Reinventing the Company, Page 276.*

With infinite time and infinite budget you could build a wonderful route to market—but, alas, these days infinite quantities of anything are few and far between. You have to cross *IPO* and *Cash Flow Sale* off your list of potential destinations when you figure that you're not in a position to establish a sales, marketing and distribution infrastructure that's capable of delivering sufficient revenues to support the company and start to show a profit.

On your current route, you can't realistically reverse the flow of cash from an outward direction to an inward one. In other words, you can't see when or how you're going to stop burning up cash. This situation can't continue forever—sooner or later you're sure to exhaust every possible source of funding, every bank account, credit card, credit line and piggy bank at the company's disposal will be depleted and the wolves will be howling at the door. Unless you take immediate action, your company is destined to become yet another case of corporate road-kill on the route from *Zero-to-IPO.*

The only alternative destinations are *Asset Sale*, *Orderly Shutdown* or *Bankruptcy*. This might be a good time to check out the direct route from *Zero-to-Asset Sale* to get some understanding of what this is all about. Now let me see, which is the best one to choose? Hmm, we have to rule out *IPO* and *Cash Flow Sale*. *Shutdown* and *Bankruptcy* don't sound like fun—so I guess the only real option is *Asset Sale*. The logic is unquestionably sound and this is clearly the only choice, however, unless all your investors and board members have read this book, prepare yourself for serious resistance.

Your logic goes like this:

> *'Realistically we're not in a position to build a viable stand-alone business, so let's forget that idea and build a valuable asset that someone is likely to buy instead. Otherwise we're sure to eventually find ourselves dealing with a Shutdown or Bankruptcy'*

When your colleagues realize that this route involves a radical change in the status quo, don't be surprised to encounter logic that's somewhat different:

> *'I'd prefer not to talk about selling the company'.*
> *'My job is to build a profitable business. I know that the chances are slim at best, but let's just work on the assumption that we're going to be able to raise more money, buy ourselves more time and generate miraculous hockey-stick sales growth.'*
> *'Backtrack route? What backtrack route? I only know how to head in this direction'.*
> *'It took a lot of time, energy and money to get to where we are today—I don't like the idea of taking a backward step.'*
> *'This change may put me out of a job so I'll resist it'.*

'Asset Sale is never going to give me the return I'd like on my investment. OK, OK, it's a better return than Shutdown and Bankruptcy but I don't like to think about that.'
'My MBA course taught me that every company should drive towards sales revenue and profits'.
'I'm not prepared to make any radical change unless it's forced on me'.

When you come up against logic like this, it's natural to feel that your colleagues are hell-bent on a suicide mission to force the company into *Shutdown* or *Bankruptcy*. It might not be easy to help these people see sense, but you have to win a consensus and encourage everyone on the team to target *Asset Sale*—otherwise disagreement in the ranks is sure to thwart your progress.

Backtrack to Asset Sale

Switching from *IPO* to *Asset Sale* is a pretty radical 'U'-turn that often involves backtracking over previously covered ground—cutting the team, reducing the cash burn and offloading all the pieces of the business that an asset buyer is unlikely to want. The core asset is typically the product and its supporting team—primarily the product designers and developers. So, this backtrack route involves offloading your executive management, sales, marketing and administrative teams and stripping the company down to its core asset.

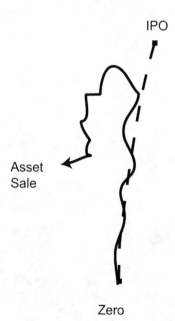

Of course, you couldn't operate a company with engineers alone—who would order the pizza and tell the engineers when to eat, wash and sleep? You need a skeleton crew to run the basic business operations, prove the existence of a market and manage the process of selling the company.

Here we have something of a conundrum. Heading out on the route to *IPO*, you probably acquired a CEO and executive team that's accustomed to growing a company from a mere handful of employees to an empire of hundreds. These executives are not accustomed to making a U-turn, heading in the opposite direction and shrinking the company down. They're probably not comfortable reciting the Asset Sale Mantra (page 238) and they're certainly not accustomed to firing themselves. On the backtrack route, however, they are undoubtedly surplus to requirement and can prove to be something of a hindrance.

On the backtrack route, the CEO is going to have to slash costs, lay off whole departments of staff, help build a killer product, sell it to an acquirer and then prepare himself for termination when the acquisition is complete. These are not skills that you often find in career CEO's—especially those that are hired for their skills in growing companies through to *IPO*. Indeed many career CEO's have no concept of how you could run a company with a tiny product-oriented team and minimal budget—they have a natural desire to keep spending and continue pressing on toward *IPO*. Chances are that the switch to the backtrack route requires a new CEO. The old one is unlikely to fire himself so the board and shareholders have to be prepared to take this step.

Implementing an effective 'U'-turn and backtracking to *Asset Sale* is probably one of the most difficult maneuvers for any company to undertake. Unfortunately, this maneuver may take a whole new generation of CEO's, board members and investors to perfect.

Destination IPO Seed Stage

Close Venture
Round Funding

Complete Due Diligence
Agree Terms with your VC
Agree Valuation with your VC

Form a Board of Directors
Find a Lead VC
Establish a Preference Share Agreement
Test the Market
Launch the Company

File Patents and Trademarks
Appoint a PR Agency
Hire a Head of Marketing
Write an Employee Handbook
Establish a Benefits Package
Define your Corporate Values

Seed Stage

Secure Seed Funding
Outsource Everything
Prepare for a Recruitment Ramp-up
Hire a Head of HR
Set Up an Accounting System
Structure a Management Team

Write a Convincing Business Plan
Build a Product Prototype
Publish a Technical White Paper
Create and Launch your Web Site
Create a Stock Option Plan

Design a Breakthrough Invention
Set Up your Capitalization Table
Select a Good Company Name
Form a Corporation
Formulate your Core Messaging & Corporate Identity
Lease an Office
Negotiate and Secure Seed Funding
Listen and Adapt to Investor Reaction
Present to Investors
Prepare to Approach VC Investors
Identify Seed Investors
Recruit an Advisory Panel
Hire a Good Firm of Accountants
Find a Good Bank
Form the Founding Team
Hire a Good Startup Law Firm
Take the Leap

Zero Write a Business Plan

Write a Business Plan

Before you leave your day job and spend your life savings committing to an office lease, I suggest you write a business plan. After it's finished, put it under the bed for a day or two and forget all about it. Then read it with a clear mind and cross out all the things you don't like with a red pen. At this point you get to write it all over again. Repeat this process ad-infinitum, until you're out of red ink or until you've shortened it to around 5 pages and wrestled every strategic issue into submission. If you're struggling to keep it to 5 pages, you could write an additional longer operating plan that you keep up your sleeve and produce when requested by an investor.

Some investors take great pleasure in selecting one word or number from your plan, apparently at random, ignoring all the important issues and quizzing you about this piece of minutia for hours on end. You need to be confident that you can defend every square inch of paper before you're ready to start taking the plan out of the house.

You could hire professional business plan writers, graphic artists, page layout designers and produce a glossy, colorful plan with detailed projections for the next 20 years and hope that it sings and dances itself to the top of the business plan pile on the investors desk. But it may be a wasted effort as many investors have no sense of humor whatsoever and are actually turned off by glitz.

A good plan should clearly and concisely show that you have a unique invention with the potential to dominate a huge emerging market. It also shows that the founder knows, at the very least, how to write a business plan. A well thought-out and well-presented plan should attract investors. If you take it seriously, the business plan can actually help you, and your future team, make day-to-day business decisions for years to come. It can also help keep board members and investors off your back. Once they've agreed to the plan, the management team has a mandate to execute it without having to defend all your actions. When you get the investors call questioning a decision, you can perfect the response: 'we're following the plan that you and the rest of the board signed off at the beginning of the year', politely put the phone down and get on with your work. So, it's worth putting some time and energy into your business plan and getting as much buy-in as you can.

How is your Technology Deployed?

Technology can be packaged up and delivered to the customer in various ways:

- ✓ *Complete end-user product*—the company packages up the technology into a product that is sold to the end use through various channels of distribution.
- ✓ *Product component*—the company sells the technology to another company that packages it with other technologies forming a complete end-user product.
- ✓ *Platform component*—the technology provides part of a platform that other developers use to create products of their own.

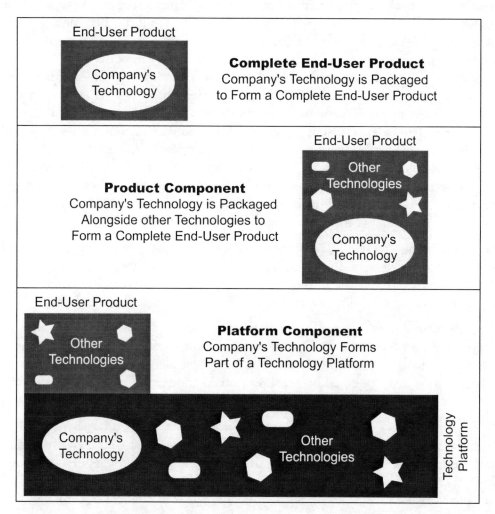

Each model has a profound effect on your strategy, so it's important to figure out how the technology will be deployed before you write your business plan.

Although I don't remember ever buying anything or responding in any way to junk mail, somehow, my name and correct address seem to have found themselves on several direct marketing mailing lists. As a result I receive between three and six inches of letters, leaflets and details of numerous once-in-a-lifetime opportunities each day. After years of practice, each pile can be 'filed' with expert precision in the circular filing cabinet beneath my desk within a matter of 3 or 4 seconds. As the papers hit the bottom of the garbage can, I get a real sense of achievement that I've managed to overcome this little challenge in world record time. This is followed by a a pang of guilt that it's a waste of good paper—at least junk e-mail doesn't require us to chop down perfectly good trees. Anyway, business plans sent to investors follow a similar route. I'm sure that I'd be facing experienced VC's if this became an Olympic event. VC's have the additional challenge of one intermediate step—the short, sharp letter of rejection. Secretaries have taken years to perfect this letter—I suspect that they go on retreats and hold conferences to brainstorm ways that they can pack as much venom as possible in 2 or 3 paragraphs. They generally read as follows: 'you're a loser and you have no chance of success, please don't bother us with your pathetic idea'. Well, that's not exactly what they say but it is the way you'll read the letters when they land on your desk. At a recent conference, one of the delegates came up with the idea of actually returning your business plan together with the letter. The inference, that your plan isn't even worthy of being thrown in the garbage, was brilliant and the concept went on to win several industry awards and standing ovations at VC conferences and retreats worldwide.

Here's the point—to avoid having your business plan hit the rejection pile within the first few seconds, you need a compelling introductory letter and executive summary. Then, to keep them moving through the plan, you need to make all the other information easily accessible with a good table of contents and logical layout.

There are plenty of books detailing how you can write the perfect business plan. There are even web sites and CD-ROMs that claim to write the plan for you. As someone once said: 'you can't please all of the people all of the time'—a plan that appeals to one investor could be a real turn off to another. There's no cookie-cutter business plan formula that appeals to everyone. If one investor doesn't like it, don't get too upset—move on to the next.

To make sure you're hitting their hot buttons, you could stalk your investor targets for months and try to figure out what turns them on. If everything goes well, you don't get arrested, and you get to meet and present to them, you'll probably be recognized as a stalker. This does not bode well for your chances of getting a commitment to invest. So, don't get too ambitious in trying to figure out what will turn on a specific investor. Your plan should simply cover all the bases in a neutral, uncontroversial and professional way.

Here are some of the bases you're going to have to cover in the document:

- ✓ Executive Summary
- ✓ Vision & Mission
- ✓ Objectives
- ✓ Technology
- ✓ Market
- ✓ Competition
- ✓ Product Strategy
- ✓ Sales Strategy
- ✓ Partnership Strategy
- ✓ Distribution Strategy
- ✓ Marketing Strategy
- ✓ Management Team
- ✓ Financials

You may be asking yourself whether you should hire a professional business plan writer. My advice is to write the plan yourself first. Give it your best shot, then have it reviewed by a bunch of experts—a friendly investor, lawyer accustomed to dealing with VC's, accountant, that 'successful' writer you know who works part-time in the local bar. With their feedback you should be able to decide whether you need to bring in a professional writer. If you do, by drafting the first version yourself, you've been forced to think through all the issues and pull together all the information he's going to need.

Here are 5 tips to bear in mind when writing your plan:

1. *Keep it short and simple*—don't elaborate when it's not necessary. You may notice that I just elaborated unnecessarily. I could have just said 'keep it short and simple' and left it at that. It would have been better if I had.
2. *Highlight any momentum you've managed to generate so far*—if you haven't managed to get the personal endorsement of Bill Gates or win a Nobel prize, you may, at the very least, be able to refer to articles highlighting the need for the product in the market.
3. *Run a speelling and grandmar checks*—sloppy English is a sure-fire way to get your plan rejected.
4. *Tell a story*—if you can weave a story into the plan, it might help keep the reader flowing through it. A story might include how the idea was hatched,

how it was developed, how the company was formed, etc. Alternatively the story could be from the customers perspective—how they currently have a painful problem, how the product solves the problem and what effect this has on the customer and the market as a whole.

5. *Have it checked by a lawyer*—when you've run out of funding, the creditors are knocking on the door and you're having a bad hair day, you really don't need to receive a letter from an investors' lawyer informing you of impending legal action to recover funds from your personal 'estate' on the basis that your business plan contained the words 'guaranteed success' or something that could be construed as a guarantee or warranty. On the other hand, as always, you need to restrain the lawyer from running up legal fees by turning the document into an unreadable piece of legal gobbledegook.

Take the Leap

Many entrepreneurs live in hope that they can come up with an idea, write a plan, get it funded and running at full speed without leaving the cozy security of their regular day jobs. Alas, this is rarely possible. Investors generally back existing entities that have some momentum generated by a fully committed founding team. Some investors, particularly overseas, need to know that you're on the line to lose your family home if the venture fails. They want to see you totally committed before they even consider getting involved. Fortunately, most Silicon Valley VC's are a little more flexible. But your own personal commitment is an important factor in building momentum and, at some point, you're going to have to take the plunge. This means leaving your day job and committing to the venture full-time.

As always, it's important that you don't burn any bridges in the transition process. Investors are going to ask for references from your previous employers, so you'll want to leave on good terms. You also don't want your previous employers to sue you for stealing their ideas, information or the 'secret recipe'—so I recommend you hire a lawyer to guide you through the process of terminating your employment agreements. Your lawyer may advise you to keep your new venture under wraps and hold off from forming a new company until you've officially parted company with the old employer. Normally, you'll have 30 days to exercise your vested stock options—don't forget and miss the deadline.

Telling your spouse and your mother that you've taken this radical step before anyone else can save you some grief.

If you have the chance, before embarking on this challenging adventure, take a relaxing vacation—it's probably the last one you're going to get for several years and a good chance to clear your mind and prepare for the journey ahead.

Hire a Good Startup Law Firm

It's somewhat unfortunate that one of the first things you need to do in your startup is hire a bloodsucking lawyer.   There are many different types of lawyers and at this stage it's important to find a law firm specializing in structuring high-tech startups. A litigation lawyer or divorce lawyer is not going to be much use to you—although you're likely to need their services, and those of other specialist lawyers, later on. There are a number of marquee-name law firms preying on startups in Silicon Valley and the other tech centers across the U.S. (see *Resource Guide*, page 400 for a more comprehensive list). They're mostly very expensive and very good. They have most of the resources in house to take you all the way from *Zero-to-IPO*.

In dealing with these larger firms, it's important to make sure you get some mind-share from the senior lawyers as well as the junior interns.   If you want a more personal and responsive service you may choose to go with a boutique firm like White and Lee—they have about 30 lawyers. Although they don't do *IPO*'s and some other specialist matters in house you'll probably get the personal attention of the senior partners. I like working with lawyers that have some experience of being entrepreneurs themselves, otherwise they can have a very unbalanced view of the world.

You'll certainly get mind-share from a small one-man-band lawyer. However, at IPO stage, you're going to need to move up to a larger firm—as they're in a position to open more doors for you in the process of early stage fundraising, it may be better to go with a larger firm from day one.

It's good practice to meet with several law firms and check them out. If they like your business plan, they may offer to reduce their fees in exchange for a small percentage of the company's equity. I've negotiated a 25% discount for the first 12 months of bills in exchange for 1% of the company. This seems to be the norm.

> *Contract lawyers are one of the most ancient forms of software engineer. Their contracts are laid out in the same way as software programs—definitions and reusable modules at the top, the actual logic below. Unfortunately the code is never actually compiled and executed, until something goes wrong. Then the contract (program) is linked and run through an ancient form of processor—a Judge.*

Assuming they're excellent practitioners of corporate law, you need to determine if they're going to actively help you in the process of structuring the company and attracting investors, board members and management team hires. As the law firm is going to represent your company in negotiations and has the ability to personally make or break important deals, you need to make sure that the personal style of the lawyer you're working with is consistent with that of your company. It's not a good sign if you cringe when the lawyer opens his/her mouth in your negotiations. This may be a little too much to ask of a lawyer, but you're going to have to spend a lot of time working together in the coming years, so it's important to find a personality that fits with yours and the type of company you want to build.

Find a Good Bank

It was always fun talking to my bank manager in the 1980's about my latest high-tech startup business. The banks were still in the industrial age—looking for strong balance sheets with real, solid bricks and mortar or industrial equipment as assets. He just couldn't get his head around the idea that the assets could be purely ideas or software code. I was something of an oddity when I visited his office—he'd been talking to butchers and bakers all day and just didn't know what to do with me. There's no way that an industrial age bank would ever be a source of funds or proactive help for an information age technology startup—beyond providing a checking account and ATM machine, they were totally useless.

The good news is that things are different today. Boutique institutions like Silicon Valley Bank have achieved great success by taking an interest in technology startups and providing a range of value-added services.

In addition to letters of credit, equipment financing and corporate credit cards, here are some of the services available from some of the more progressive banks today:

- ✓ *VC and other investor introductions (some banks even have their own funds).*
- ✓ *Business plan feedback and advice.*
- ✓ *Credit facilities to supplement equity investments.*
- ✓ *Introductions to service providers such as attorneys, accountants, HR and PR firms.*
- ✓ *Regular networking events and opportunities to meet and schmooze with other clients and service providers.*
- ✓ *Referrals for office space.*
- ✓ *Newsletters with relevant news and market updates.*
- ✓ *Bridge financing.*
- ✓ *Merchant banking services to help you raise later rounds of funding.*

You're likely to be able to supplement your equity investment funds with debt financing in the form of equipment leasing and receivables financing. The debt will normally be secured against some asset—like equipment, your house or first-born child.

So, don't just open a checking account at your local bank, if you shop around you may be surprised by the range of services that you could get from a bank that specializes in technology startups.

Hire a Good Firm of Accountants

As a startup with a limited budget, you may think that the big accounting firms will be out of your price range. But they're not. They make a fortune from audits for later stage *IPO*'s and other financing events and they try to win the accounts of hot technology startups as early as possible—so if they like your story, they'll likely offer cut-price services.

My advice is to go with a specialist high-tech startup unit of one of the big four firms (of course we used to refer to the big five firms, but Enron collapsed, Arthur Anderson took some of the blame—and then there were four):

- ✓ *KPMG*
- ✓ *PricewaterhouseCoopers*
- ✓ *Deloitte & Touche*
- ✓ *Ernst & Young*

These firms obviously have the expert resources you're going to need at all stages of the journey from *Zero-to-IPO*, but I've also been surprised at the added-value services they provide, often without charge. In the early stage they'll review your business plan and provide you with some good insightful comments and pointers. They'll also open some doors with investors—and I've found that investors often sit up and listen when one of these firms recommends they meet with you. Choosing a big 4 firm can help smooth fundraising or acquisition deals later on the journey—investors feel comfortable working with a known entity.

Which one should you choose? It's probably worth meeting with several, or all, of them (see *Appoint a PR Agency*, page 120 for a discussion on the agency selection process). Choose the one that takes the most interest in your business, gives you some mind-share with senior partners and other senior staff and has a good relationship with your lawyer and other professional advisors. The best time to put a good tax and financial structure in place is at the beginning—so bring them in early when the company is being formed.

Recruit an Advisory Panel

There's no legal obligation to form an advisory panel and it's not an official decision-making body like the board of directors, but it can be an invaluable source of help and support for you and your startup. As it doesn't carry the official responsibilities or liabilities of the board of directors, you'll likely find it much easier to recruit marquee names onto the advisory panel.

The panel could be made up of angel and other investors, outside experts in technology, finance, law, industry specialists and marquee names. Although marquee names are very busy, they're often flattered at being invited to share their hard-earned wisdom and get involved in a hot startup that's headed up by a bright and trustworthy team. Some may have time to attend regular board meetings and others may offer their advice over the telephone and attend the odd meeting when they get the chance. By offering a modest number of stock options and asking for nothing more than one returned phone call each month, I managed to pull together an impressive advisory panel quite quickly. Surprisingly, all the members, even the marquee names, were quite prepared to go above and beyond the call of duty—they attended meetings, helped structure compensation packages, provided introductions, even helped structure and close sales deals. Since stock options are no longer viewed with the same respect as they were in the days of the dot-com bubble, and the advisory role is becoming much more professional, you're likely to be asked to pay a monthly retainer and consulting fees if you want to attract an active and effective advisor to the team.

It's sometimes worthwhile thinking out of the box when drawing up lists of potential advisory panel members—one company hit the headlines when it appointed a child onto the advisory panel. I brought in some VIP's from the world of finance, law and technology, however, after coming painfully close, I was disappointed not to bring Michael Jordan onto the panel—an obvious coup for any company.

Your lawyer can provide you with a short agreement for the advisory panel members to sign—basically addressing issues of confidentiality, expectations and remuneration.

Some companies establish a number of advisory panels—each focused on a specialist topic like technology, finance, business planning, etc. Obviously it takes a good deal of management to coordinate a set of panels like this and many companies keep the advisory panel down to a manageable size—like 5-10 individuals.

Secure Seed Funding

Gone are the days when you could walk into a meeting with a top-tier VC holding nothing more than a business plan and walk out with a multi-million dollar funding commitment. In reality, those days never really existed at all—even in the dot-com dreamtime. Investors, even specialists in seed stage deals, rarely become interested in a business plan until it has a company with momentum behind it (see *Take the Leap*, page 76 and *The Fundraising Process*, page 325). This means you need to have an upbeat team and show marked progress along your chosen route *before* you approach investors.

You can't get serious funding without a team—but how can you hire a team without funding? This little chicken and egg conundrum offers a challenge to virtually every a startup entrepreneur—and successfully weeds out the creative and resourceful individuals from the rest.

Like Steve Jobs, many entrepreneurs kick-start their companies during the evenings and weekends from a parent's garage—or another low cost location like the closet under the stairs or the office cubicle (when no one's looking). They build an early product prototype (out of duct tape and string), put up a simple web site, print business cards, write a business plan and pull together a 'virtual' team. If you took a random sample of seed-stage business plans mailed to a VC, I'm sure you'd find that the vast majority of the team members listed are virtual—the individuals have indicated that they'll consider joining the team if the company gets funding but they're not yet employed by the company.

However, you manage it, let's assume you figure out how to kick-start the business, gather a virtual team and start to generate momentum. Now you're in a position to go hunting seed investors. The seed funding is essentially a bridge to your first real round of funding. This may be your first exposure to the *Fundraising Process*—good luck!

Seed funding is very risky. On average, less than one in ten startups survives. One in ten! Nine out of ten ends in closure—and all the investors typically lose every penny invested. A statistician could argue that seed investors would be better off gambling their money in Las Vegas, at least the casinos would give them the royal treatment as they watch their fortunes disappear.

If you're in a position to generate sufficient momentum without seed funding, the ideal scenario is that you go directly for VC funding and skip the angel rounds altogether. You may think this is wishful thinking, but it's sometimes possible to fund the startup phase through consulting and service revenues—I've done it myself on more than one occasion. With service revenues paying the bills, you may be able to build a product prototype and start the transition from a service company to a product company. Of course, carrying out contract service work can be a distraction when you really want to focus all your efforts on your own project, but it may be no more distracting than fundraising—seeking seed funding can take up a huge percentage of your time.

Identify Seed Investors

If you have no alternative but to go out and raise outside funding for the seed phase, you need to pull together a list of potential seed investors from the following pool:

- ✓ *Seed-Stage VC's*
- ✓ *Individual Angels*
- ✓ *Angel Groups*
- ✓ *Corporate Investors*
- ✓ *Family & Friends*

In addition to the investors lists provided in the resource guide, a good lawyer or accountant will be able to provide a list of potential seed investors and provide valuable introductions.

Seed-Stage VCs

Since the Wall Street crash, many VC investors have opted to focus on later-stage instead of early-stage deals—as lower-risk later-stage investment opportunities are now available at valuations that were previously only available for early-stage companies. You may need to look a little harder, but there are still a number of seed stage VCs out there. The company's chances of survival are significantly improved with a VC as a seed investor—as they're in a better position to lead follow-on rounds and make introductions to other investors.

Individual Angels

It's estimated that angels invest three to five times more money than venture capitalists and fund thirty to forty times more ventures, making them the primary source of outside capital for entrepreneurs. The phrase "Angel Investor" originally referred to investors in Broadway plays—they invested in Broadway plays for the excitement and opportunity to associate with the theatre personalities they admired, as much as the expectation of a return on their investment. Most angels have a net worth in excess of $1 million or an annual salary in excess of $200,000. With this, they qualify, under SEC guidelines, as 'accredited investors'—thus making them eligible to lose all their money by investing in risky startup ventures. Typically, angels have hit it big by taking a previous company from *Zero*-to-*IPO*, they have a rolodex of contacts and a stack of spare dollars to invest.

A number of measures, including 'Regulation D' have been taken by the SEC to protect small, unaccredited, investors from investing in ventures without full disclosure of the risks involved. To exploit loopholes in these regulations, and help private companies raise funds from a number of small investors, several weird and wonderful schemes are on offer to entrepreneurs. They typically involve the entrepreneur paying the fundraiser for a variety of services. These fundraising activities are sometimes frowned upon by serious investors—and many entrepreneurs have found them costly, time-consuming and ineffective.

Angel Groups

In recent years, angels have reduced their individual risks by pooling together and forming funds that invest in a number of startups. Angel groups like Garage.com and Band of Angels tap into huge networks of contacts and resources. Don't expect a free ride with angel funds these days—they've become aggressive investors negotiating valuation downwards, putting a representative on the board—and charging for the privilege. Angel groups are increasingly charging professional service fees for their involvement. Nevertheless, a good angel fund can provide valuable introductions to VCs and other investors.

Corporate Investors

Large corporations sometimes spin out new companies with seed money, back former employees or provide funding to develop new products that are complementary to their own.

The upside of corporate investment is that it provides a credible endorsement for the product, the team and the company. The downside is that seed-stage corporate investments often come with strings attached—very expensive strings.

Your objective, and that of most other investors, is to build a killer product and take your company to *IPO* or acquisition (*Asset Sale* or *Cash Flow Sale*). At some point, you want to sell your shares in the company for the maximum price possible. The objective of the corporate investor may be to help you build a killer product—to add to its own product line. If it's a hit, the corporate investor will likely want to buy the product from you for the minimum price possible. So, after the product is released, you may find that your objectives and those of your corporate investor start to diverge. This is when it's important to understand the difference between common stock and preference shares. Preference shareholders, like outside investors, normally get to vote on whether to accept an acquisition offer for the company— common shareholders like founders and employees, do not (see *Preference Share Agreements,* page 342). So, although you want to sell the company to another corporate buyer, your investor may block the deal—the investor gets to vote, you don't, so there's nothing you can do about it. Be warned—a seed-stage corporate investor could have the power to turn down alternative acquisition and investment offers and steal the company at some point in future when it runs out of cash.

As well as getting significant control of the company through preference shares, the corporate investor may attach other strings to the deal—like distribution rights for the product or an option to buy the company. If you are forced to sign a distribution agreement giving a corporation access to your product, make sure that it's for a limited length of time. By signing away rights to your product or technology for an infinite (or infinitely renewable) period of time, you could render your company worthless—a technology company without full ownership of its technology is of little or no value (see *Distribution Trap*, page 245).

When setting out on your startup journey, it's important that your investors are targeting the same destination—*IPO* or acquisition. This may be something of a challenge for corporate investors at the seed stage—unless they're acting exclusively as financial investors.

Family & Friends

You may be tempted to tap rich uncle Orville when you look for seed funding. Be warned—after investing his hard-earned cash, your relationship with uncle Orville will never be the same again. There's very little upside to taking money from close family and friends, even if they're sophisticated investors with very deep pockets, and they claim to be fully aware of the risks.

Obviously, uncle Orville loses his money if your startup is not lucky enough to be the one in ten to survive. When the company has disappeared and the professional investors have written off the losses and ridden off into the sunset, you, your family and friends stick around. You may be forced to deal with the after-shocks for years to come.

> **Family & Close Friends as Investors**
>
> When a friend becomes an investor, you gain an investor..
>
> .. and strain a friendship (Plato).

Relationships can become quite complex if your company goes bust. Let's say you pick yourself up, dust yourself off and move on to your next opportunity, which happens to be a great success. You're driving your Ferrari when you bump into uncle Orville, who lost his shirt in your previous venture, driving a beaten up VW. Although it was not part of the original investment agreement, you'd likely feel some sense of obligation to return his money out of your own pocket. He may well feel you have such an obligation himself. I've actually heard a couple, that lost their investment in their daughters' startup, complaining that the daughter and her husband had bought themselves leather jackets and booked a vacation several months after the startup closed down—they were upset that the daughter was not saving every penny she earned to pay them back the money they'd lost.

Even if the company is a success, making it all the way from *Zero-to-IPO* and beyond, uncle Orville can still get upset. Let's say the share price rises to $60 a share and you sell a bunch of stock. For some unforeseen reason, the stock then crashes to $20. Even if uncle Orville himself isn't upset that you didn't tell them to sell when the stock was at the top, Aunt Maude, his wife, may be. From her perspective, they lost money and you could have helped them avoid it.

Whatever scenario you project, there's very little upside in tapping family and friends for seed funding. It places personal pressure on you when you least need it.

If you are going to take money from close family and friends, consider structuring it as a personal loan rather than an equity investment in the company. If you suspect that you'll be pressured, or guilted, into personally compensating any losses, you may as well take the upside potential—borrow the money and invest it yourself.

Structuring the Seed Round

Ideally, your seed investors will agree to wire you cash in exchange for notes that convert to equity on the terms of your first round of funding. Essentially these investments are accounted for as loans that convert to shares at a later date. You're offering seed investors an opportunity to take a slice of the company before the door is closed by the lead VC—VC's are unlikely to see much value in letting angels or other seed investors into a subsequent round. This can appear a little unfair to a seed investor that's getting in earlier and taking significantly more risk than an investor in the subsequent round. So, you normally have to sweeten the deal for the seed investor by offering a discount on the share price of the subsequent round. In this way, the seed investors get more shares than they would if they invested the same amount in the first round. The advantage of this structure is that it doesn't present any constraints or obstacles to scare off lead VC investors, unless they feel that the discount offered to the seed investors is too steep. The other advantage is that a convertible note funding can be quick and easy to document and close.

What discount should a seed investor receive on the first round? That depends on how much they're investing and how long that enables the company to operate before the next round of funding needs to be closed. If the company has been operating on seed funding for a year, generated momentum and made significant progress before the VC's come in, they can't really object to the seed investors getting a significant discount on the round. In this scenario 50% shouldn't be at all unreasonable—but the lead VC may have a different perspective. If the seed funding only gives the company a few months of life and very little progress is made before the subsequent round, the VC leading the next round may object to a discount any higher than 15 or 20%.

Personally, if I were an angel investing, say $100,000, in a startup as a short-term bridge to the first round of funding, I wouldn't object to getting a convertible note with a discount, of say 15%, on the first round, if the round was led by a strong lead VC. If I were injecting $1.5m to fund the company through it's first year, I'd want to structure the investment as a Series A round of funding at a pre-money valuation somewhere between *Zero* and $3m—a valuation higher than $3m on a seed round would be very unusual.

Depending on how much you're able to raise in the seed round, you could structure the deal as a convertible note or a series A round. The ideal scenario is that your business plan is so strong that you can raise seed funding with a convertible note—without offering huge discounts. Then you can let the lead VC negotiate the first round without worrying about conflicts with seed investors.

Lease an Office

As the company grows, the challenge is to grow the office space and facilities in line with staffing and to minimize the trauma of moving from one office to another. The ideal office arrangement for a high-tech startup is as follows:

✓ *Large office complex with plenty of smaller units*—so that you can expand in modules as and when you need more space.

✓ *Short lease that doesn't tie you into any long term commitments*—although you want a short minimum commitment, you need the option to stay as long as you like. Also bear in mind that a long lease commitment can be a turn-off for potential acquirers in future.

✓ *Attractive work environment*—you'll have problems attracting good staff if you put them in a cubicle farm or a windowless dungeon that's miles from any restaurants or shops.

✓ *Central location with easy access to airports & major freeways*—many VC's only consider companies located within a short drive from their own office. I was surprised when, prepared and ready to talk about the details of the business plan, I called investors and found that the first questions they asked was where the company was located. If you're targeting Sand Hill Road VC's, you'll better your chances if you're located in Silicon Valley or San Francisco.

Before the Internet boom, landlords were desperate for tenants and I negotiated some great deals on office space. Since the market crash, supply is again outstripping demand in most technology centers and landlords are offering flexible deals to increase occupancy levels. Although they're going to ask for huge deposits and rent advances, you'll be in a good position to negotiate if the market's a little depressed.

By and large, investors aren't impressed by plush offices—so don't go paying a premium for the cachet value. In many cases, expensive offices can be a turn-off for investors—they like to see that your feet are firmly planted on the ground. Some investors get a kick out of finding you in a garage or some ramshackle room above a liquor store and seeing you grow into ever larger and more impressive offices—as a result of their investment and expert guidance.

I've also found it very useful to establish a good relationship with the landlord. When I was out fundraising and the company was running on fumes, I managed to persuade the landlord to allow us skip a few rent checks—hey every dollar counts! One of my other landlords was a huge property tycoon—after a little schmoozing, he invested in the company, joined the advisory panel and made some very useful introductions. He then proceeded to sell our office to another company—unfortunately we never got the chance to leverage the relationship to put the fear of God into the property managers.

Finally, choose a real-estate agent that has good personal hygiene and a good driving record—as you'll probably end up spending many hours together hopping from one office to another in his car.

Formulate your Core Messaging and Corporate Identity

I was a marketing executive for Apple Computer in the late 1980's and early 1990's (unfortunately stricken with the entrepreneurial disease however, I spent my weekends and evenings setting up a property business). In the 1980's, Apple had a commanding technology lead over Microsoft and everyone else in the PC market—with a graphical user interface, the Macintosh operating system was way ahead of MS-DOS. I've heard Steve Jobs say that he left Apple with a ten year lead over the competition when he stormed out in 1985. That's probably true—but by 1990 Microsoft was catching up with early versions of Windows.

At this time I was working in Apple European's head office in Paris, liaising with marketing managers in each of the European countries as well as the head office in the U.S. With strict branding guidelines and teams of internal brand police, Apple's logo was consistent and well recognized all over the world. However, in each European country Apple had a totally different brand image—'Apple' meant 'desktop publishing' in the UK, 'productivity' in Sweden, 'engineering' in Germany and 'something cool' in France. With the release of Windows, Apple was now facing a different form of competition. As marketers we could no longer simply ridicule DOS to position Macintosh as the clear technology leader—Macintosh and Windows actually looked quite similar on the surface. I thought it was vital for Apple to differentiate itself and redefine its brand positioning in Europe, U.S. and the rest of the world. This became a very interesting project for me.

How do you change a brand? A brand image is an awareness and perception in the minds of customers. How do you get into the minds and change perceptions for millions of people all over the world? You do it by defining a core marketing message and then make sure this message is delivered consistently over a number of years through all forms of communication with customers, press and anyone else that might influence a customer's perception. For a large company like Apple Computer, this takes lots of international flights, meetings, videoconferences, dinners, lunches and conference calls to rally consensus around a single core message. It then means brainwashing everyone involved in the company with the message and making sure they deliver it consistently through all forms of customer communications. A product brochure in Finland should deliver the same core message as an infomercial in Canada.

Looking back, this task was virtually impossible. It was already far too late—changing the behavior of employees and agency staff is like trying to teach thousands of old dogs new tricks. With Windows and a strong coordinated worldwide marketing campaign, Microsoft simply swept Apple aside. The good news is that it's not too late for you—startup time is the perfect time to define your core marketing message and start to build a strong brand image. It's important that you get this right now—as I found at Apple, fixing it later is very difficult and costly.

The other good news is that there's expert help available—a good PR agency can guide you through the process. Alternatively, you may find a good branding expert working freelance or through an advertising agency.

The first thing you need is a one pager that positively positions the company and the products and clearly differentiates them from the competition. Agencies use various formats, but this is the layout I personally like best:

- ✓ *Company*—sometimes known as the 'elevator pitch' or 'value proposition', this describes, in as few words as possible, what the company does, how it does it and why it's important.
- ✓ *Market*—this defines the market in which the company operates, identifying the current and projected demand for the company's product.

- ✓ *Product*—here you describe the product strategy, the product range and identify the key features and benefits.

- ✓ *Competition*—this is where you identify and position the competition and describe the company's key competitive advantages.

- ✓ *Direction*—outline here where the company is headed in future.

It may be easy to write a first draft, but it can take some time to brainstorm different approaches and select the very best way to articulate each point. Identifying the company's strengths, weaknesses, opportunities and threats will help clarify your thinking here, but you don't want to include all this analysis in the one-pager—keep it short and sweet. After you've spent many agonizing hours holed up with your branding advisors, you should emerge with a one-page document that everyone feels comfortable with. Here are some of the things you should do with this document:

- ✓ *Stick a copy above your desk*—so that you can refer to it when you get phone calls from journalists, investors, customers or anyone wanting to know about the company. Always make sure you get these key points over.

- ✓ *Brainwash your staff with it*—make sure everyone has a copy, understands it and can recite it almost verbatim. Every time they talk about the company in meetings, on the phone, in e-mail or printed documents, they should present the same messages.

- ✓ *Use it to create derivatives*—you'll want to use this as the basis of a more elaborate briefing document for all PR agency staff. At some point you're also going to need briefing documents for sales staff, advertising agencies, web site producers and anyone else likely to articulate the company's message.

The brand is heavily influenced by how the company looks as well as what it says. Your core messaging document will be vital in helping brief the team you hire to define your visual corporate identity. In addition to designing your logo, letterheads and business cards, make sure you ask the designers to produce templates for letters, web pages, presentations and a document laying out the branding guidelines with rules and regulations that you're going to need to police in future.

Investors, customers and anyone else coming into contact with the company will be impressed if you have a professionally designed set of logos, color schemes, and a consistent look and feel across all your communications materials. Don't be tempted to cut corners here—you're investing in a valuable asset, so pay whatever it takes to hire experienced professionals.

Form a Corporation

If you're targeting *Asset Sale,* as opposed to *IPO,* you may be able to create a tax-efficient structure using offshore corporations, limited partnerships and other weird and wonderful forms of corporate entity. But when it comes to *IPO,* investment bankers and Wall Street investors prefer to work with familiar Delaware corporations. They're also accustomed to working with Californian and some other corporations, however, as more than half the Fortune 500 companies are incorporated in Delaware, this is the corporate entity they know best.

Why Delaware? Where is Delaware anyway? I just sat down with a piece of paper and wrote down everything I know about Delaware. The list was so small that it could have been written on a toothpick. If you're from Delaware, I apologize—I'm sure there's a tremendous amount going on in Delaware that I'm not aware of. I do have an excuse in that I'm not actually American and, although I've traveled to many weird and wonderful corners of the world, I've never had any good reason to go to Delaware. I'm sure I'm missing out on something.

Well, for some reason, that I haven't yet been able to figure out, Delaware has become the company incorporation capital of the U.S.A. There are some very good reasons why you should incorporate your company in Delaware:

- ✓ *The corporate, limited liability and limited partnership law is well known and trusted.*
- ✓ *You can form a Delaware corporation, limited liability company, or business entity without actually going to Delaware (phew!).*
- ✓ *One person can act as the only officer, director and shareholder of a corporation.*
- ✓ *The owners and operators of a Delaware corporation are not required to be identified in the public records of the State.*
- ✓ *Delaware has a minimal corporate franchise tax (as low as $50 per year) that is not based upon income.*
- ✓ *There is no Delaware income tax for Delaware corporations or limited liability companies that do not do business in Delaware.*
- ✓ *Delaware has no sales or personal property tax.*
- ✓ *Different kinds of business can be transacted under one corporate roof.*
- ✓ *Shareholders can act in writing instead of holding meetings.*
- ✓ *You can add people to the board that are not shareholders.*
- ✓ *Corporate records need not be kept in Delaware.*

✓ *You're likely to end up a Delaware corporation if you IPO or you are acquired, so you may as well start out that way.*

Wherever you choose to incorporate, it's a good idea to use your lawyer to form the corporation. It may cost a little more, but you want to make sure that the corporate entity is suitable for your business activities and the structure doesn't ring any alarm bells for future investors.

Your corporation is a business entity that's separate and distinct from yourself. It can conduct business, sue and be sued in its own name. As an officer of the company, this limits your personal liability from creditors and legal claims. But don't get too complacent—if you're really naughty, the IRS and courts can bypass the company and go for you and your personal assets directly (see *Bankruptcy,* page 295).

As you form the corporation, you're going to have to authorize a number of shares to issue to founders, employees and investors at various times as the company grows. You can authorize more shares later on—but it shows investors that you're planning ahead if you do it up-front. Take a look at the capitalization table for AcmeTech Startup, Inc. (page 93) you'll see that 9.05 million common shares and 19.55 million preference shares are projected to be issued to founders, employees and investors up to the point of *IPO.* So, to cover these projected share issues, AcmeTech Startup, Inc. could authorize at least 10m common shares and 20m preference shares when the company is formed. These shares are not issued, they don't have any voting rights and they hardly exist at all, but they are available to be issued at some time in the future.

My advice is to let your lawyer take care of all the corporate papers, binders and documents—just check in from time to time to make sure they're properly updated and maintained as the company grows.

Congratulations—you now have a company, even if it's just an empty shell. You can now join the ranks of people that carry business cards with jumped up titles like: *'CEO, President, Chairman of the Board, Shareholder and Board Member'.* Of course, you need to bear in mind that if you put this title on your card, the recipient will read it as *'Mom and pop operation run by an egomaniac'.*

Select a Good Company Name

A good name for your company is easy to remember and creates a positive image. You could spend a fortune selecting a name if you get marketing agencies and lawyers involved. Here's the quick, low cost way of choosing a good company name:

1. Draw up a list of potential names—bring in creative colleagues, friends, neighbors and brainstorm to make the list as long as possible.
2. Choose your favorites and rank them.
3. Check if the domain name is available for your top ranked name:
    *   http://www.godaddy.com (or one of the other domain search and registration sites)
4. Check if the trademark has already been registered for your type of business:
    *   http://tess.uspto.gov/
5. Check how the name is being used online today:
    *   www.google.com.
    *   www.altavista.com
    *   www.yahoo.com
6. Check current registered company names with your Secretary of State:
    *   www.ss.ca.gov (for California only—other States have their own sites)
7. Loop back to 1. above until you go crazy or find a name that works.
8. Conduct a more comprehensive trademark search using a professional search service to make sure that the trademark is available.
9. Register the domain online with GoDaddy or one of the similar services.
10. Register the trademark—through your lawyer or the www.uspto.gov web site.

As it costs several hundred dollars to register the trademark online and only a few bucks to buy a web domain, you're likely to find that almost every domain of any value is registered already. If a short, memorable URL is critical to your business, and you'd like the URL to contain your company name, it's important to complete a thorough web domain search before you waste time searching through trademarks.

If you find a trademark that isn't registered to someone else, you can't assume the mark is available for you to use. If another company has been using the (unregistered) trademark for some time, a court may decide that your use of the mark constitutes infringement, dilution or blurring of the other company's brand image— and this could be costly to your startup. Now you know why large organizations fabricate completely new words like 'Kodak' and 'Xerox' to trademark and associate with their products.

Set Up your Capitalization Table

The capitalization table is essentially a shareholder list showing who owns what percentage of the company. It's important that your capitalization table is accurate, up-to-date and looks familiar to investors—some of them, especially lead venture capitalists, have been known to study the capitalization table for days! The following AcmeTech Startup, Inc. table follows the cookie cutter style that most high-tech investors would be familiar with:

AcmeTech Startup Inc.	Valuation[1] (m)	Round Size (m)	Valuation/Post(m)	Price per share	Early[2]	Expansion[2]	Mezzanine[2]	Post IPO[2]
Common Stock								
Founder Stock					2.50	2.50	2.50	2.50
Employee Stock Options					5.00	5.00	5.00	5.00
Career CEO						1.55	1.55	1.55
Total Issued Common					7.50	9.05	9.05	9.05
Authorized Common					10.00			
Preference Shares								
Angel[3] (Converted in Series A)								
Series A	$10	$8	$18	$ 1.33	6.00	6.00	6.00	6.00
Series B	$30	$15	$45	$ 1.99		7.53	7.53	7.53
Series C	$75	$20	$95	$ 3.32			6.02	6.02
Total Preference					6.00	13.53	19.55	Converted*
Authorized Preference					20.00			
Total Shares Issued					13.50	22.58	28.60	34.31
Total Shares Authorized					30.00			
IPO[4]	$400	$80	$480	$ 13.99				5.72

Notes
1 -- Pre-money valuation
2 -- Millions of shares
3 -- Angel funds raised as loan that's converted to stock in series A
4 -- Price not adjusting for pre-IPO split
5 -- Preference shares convert over to regular shares at IPO.

Like all capitalization tables, the sample AcmeTech Startup, Inc. table tells a story:

a)   After the company was formed, 10m common shares and 20m preference shares were authorized—to be issued at a later date.

b)   Some seed funding was raised from angel investors as a loan that was converted to shares when the series A round was closed.

c)   2.5m common shares were issued to founders (probably on a vesting schedule of 3 or 4 years).

d) $8m was raised in a series A round of funding by selling 6m shares at $1.33 each—a pre-money valuation of $10m.

e)   An employee stock option pool of 5 million shares was authorized and carved out for current and future employees.

f)   A $15m series B round was raised to fund the company through the expansion stage by issuing 7.53m shares at a price of $1.99 each—a pre-money valuation of $30m.

g) $1.55m common shares options were issued to the new CEO.

h)   A $20m series C round was raised to fund the company through the mezzanine stage by issuing 6.02m shares at a price of $3.32 each—by this stage the pre-money valuation had increased to $75m.

i) $80m was raised at an *IPO* by selling 5.72m shares at $13.99 each—a pre-money valuation of $400m.

j)   All the preference shares converted over to common at the *IPO*.

An unusual capitalization table can raise questions and slow your progress. Too many small shareholders on the table can deter some investors—obtaining shareholder approval for new rounds of funding and other strategic issues can become a logistical nightmare. Alarm bells can also ring if the founders' shareholdings are too high or the employee stock option pool exceeds 20% of the total.

There are no corporate rules that dictate how many shares should be authorized or issued—but an experienced lawyer will know what investors expect and make sure that the company follows a cookie cutter formula. In fact, until you have a lawyer on staff, it's a good idea to let your outside counsel maintain the capitalization table. To avoid any confusion, you may want to appoint one in-house designee to work with the lawyer on capitalization issues and try to have an up to date table available for each board meeting.

It's important to structure the capitalization table properly before you start the fundraising process—as it shows investors that you know what you're doing and avoids the time, cost and embarrassment of having to restructure it later on.

Create a Stock-Option Plan

I sold my PC company to a competitor in the mid-1980's and stayed on board with the acquiring company for about 18 months. When I told the CEO that I was leaving to join Apple Computer, he wanted details of the package they'd offered so that he could try to match or beat it. When I told him that the package included stock options, he burst into laughter—he couldn't believe that I was stupid enough to think stock options were worth anything. This was not unusual in the 1980's—a friend was offered the position of CFO at Intel and turned it down because a large portion of the package was made up of stock options. Like most people at the time, he thought stock options were 'funny money' and he was looking for hard cash in the form of salary and bonus checks. Of course when he looks at the value of those options today, he kicks himself.

Initially reserved for key managers and executives at high tech companies, stock option plans have become the norm for virtually all high-tech employees and now they're a common part of the incentive package for companies of all types. Companies in all industries now give stock options to most, or all, of their employees.

Stock option plans can be a flexible way for companies to share ownership with employees, reward them for performance, and attract and retain a motivated staff. For growth-oriented startups, options are a great way to preserve cash while giving employees a piece of future growth.

A stock option gives an employee the right to buy a certain number of shares in the company at a fixed price for a certain number of years. The price at which the option is provided is called the "grant" price and is usually the market price at the time the options are granted. Employees that have been granted stock options hope that the share price will go up and that they will be able to "cash in" by exercising (purchasing) the stock at the lower grant price and then selling the stock at the current market price. There are two principal kinds of stock option programs, each with unique rules and tax consequences: non-qualified stock options (NSOs) and incentive stock options (ISOs). ISOs are the standard practice for pre-*IPO* companies because there are no tax consequences for the company. As a result, Wall Street investors are used to seeing ISOs and calculating the consequence of these options on dilution—they're easily confused and an NSO plan is sure to raise questions when it comes time to *IPO*.

Investors in Silicon Valley startups are normally comfortable authorizing employee stock option plans that account for 15-20% of the total number of outstanding shares. In the example of AcmeTech Startup (see *Setup your Capitalization Table*, page

93), you'll see that the employee stock option pool is 5m shares, or 17% of the company prior to *IPO*. This is in addition to the founders stock and the CEO share allocations. It's unlikely that all 5m shares would be allocated to a single employee stock option pool—as the investors in the series A round would find it difficult to allocate 5m shares to employees when they're getting only 6m shares themselves! You're more likely to be forced to ask investors to approve new stock option allocations as part of each new round of funding to keep the total within the 15-20% guidelines.

Be careful—don't allocate too many options too early. You're going to need a spreadsheet forecasting the number of employees you're likely to need between startup and *IPO*, with the associated allocation of options for each position. Save a pool for the mezzanine stage, the run up to *IPO*, when you're likely to need large chunks of options to attract expensive talent like CFO's and General Counsel. Here's the forecast for AcmeTech Startup, Inc:

	Stock Allocation Per Position	No. of Staff	Total Options Issued
Exec VP/CFO	300,000	2	600,000
VP	200,000	4	800,000
Director	100,000	5	500,000
Senior Manager	75,000	8	600,000
Manager	50,000	8	400,000
Senior engineer/ other employee	40,000	15	600,000
Engineer/ other employee	30,000	25	750,000
Junior engineer/ other employee	20,000	35	700,000
		102	4,950,000

In normal Silicon Valley market conditions, each individuals options would vest over a period of 4 years—assuming the share price increases, this provides a good incentive for employees to stay with the company throughout the startup phase. Typical vesting would be as follows:

4 Year Vesting Schedule	First 12 months	First Anniversary	Months 13-48
Stock vested	0%	25%	2.08% per month

A quarter of the stock vests in one block after the employee has successfully stayed with the company for 12 months—this is known as the 'cliff'. After that, the remaining stock vests evenly on a monthly or biweekly basis. To hire good staff in the middle of the dot-com bubble, I was forced to offer 3 year vesting with a 6 month cliff. This enabled me to make the package more attractive without having to offer more shares—which would have forced me to go back to the investors to approve a new stock option pool. Since things have gone back to normal, the regular 4 year plan with 12 month cliff should be enough to hire anyone, but there are no hard and fast rules so you can get creative when you have to.

How are stock options priced? For public companies this is normally quite straightforward. When I joined Apple Computer, the share price on the Nasdaq was $30, so my options were priced at this level. As an employee, the stock option plan incented me to stay with the company and help increase the stock price for myself as well as the other shareholders. After 4 years, when all my options had vested, the share price on the Nasdaq was $65—so I could buy my shares at $30 and sell them on the Nasdaq at $65 (which I did, thank goodness because the price plummeted from there).

For a private company, pricing the shares is a little more complicated as there's no real market price, from the Nasdaq or anywhere else, and there's the added distinction between preference shares and common stock to take into consideration. The price of preference shares is set by negotiated agreement between investors and management. However, the price of common stock, which is used for stock options, is set by the board of directors. To make employment packages more appealing and attract good talent into the company, you're going to want to set the price of common stock as low a possible. However, this can come back to bite you when you *IPO*, as the SEC frowns on 'cheap stock'.

Although common stock in a private company is often worthless prior to *IPO* (because of the liquidity preferences and other issues), it does become valuable when the company goes public. If the common stock price was set too low, employees enjoying a stock-option bonanza at *IPO* will face tax liabilities. The profits made by the employees could be categorized as benefits and the company could be forced to account for huge charges against earnings. How low is too low? Well, guidelines by the North American Securities Administrators Association ("NASAA") define cheap stock as being less than 85% of the *IPO* price. But this is only an issue when you're in the mezzanine stage preparing for *IPO*. In the early stages, it's common for startups to set the common stock at 30% of the preference price, or even lower. So, after closing the series A round of funding at $1.33/share, the board of directors at AcmeTech Startup, Inc., may set the share price at, say $0.40 or even lower. As they get closer to *IPO*, unless they're prepared to take a huge earnings hit, they'll be forced to bring the price in line with the preference shares.

Your lawyer and accountants should guide you through the process of setting up an employee stock option plan. Another reason for selecting a specialist firm of high-tech startup lawyers is that they have experience of structuring and managing stock option plans. I once used a small independent lawyer to structure a stock option plan and he unfortunately forgot to file an important tax exemption called '83b'. Filing this election within 30 days of the purchase of vesting stock, the employee elects to be taxed now on the difference between the purchase price and the fair market value of the stock. As incentive stock is typically priced at its fair market value, there is no difference between price and value, and hence, no tax. By forgetting to file the 83b elections, employees with stock options would be liable for tax as each block of stock vests—they could still find themselves owing Uncle Sam a small fortune for tax on shares they were never able to sell and revenue they never actually received. Fortunately for us, the mistake was identified early enough to avoid such catastrophic effects, but make sure your lawyer and accountants are fully conversant with stock option plans and they're well organized enough to file the appropriate papers on time.

File Patents and Trademarks

It's important that you start the process of protecting your intellectual property as early as possible. This includes filing patents to provide some protection for your inventions and registering trademarks to protect your identity as expressed in brands names, logos and marketing slogans.

Patent

A patent can become a valuable asset—providing you with 'exclusive rights to make, use, import, sell and offer for sale the invention for up to 20 years'. The only problem is that it can take 20 years to get the patent approved—not ideal when you're on an *IPO* fast-track.

You can search through existing patents online:
http://164.195.100.11/netahtml/search-bool.html.

After looking through this database you'll understand why Charles H. Duell, Commissioner of the U.S. Patent Office is reported to have urged President McKinley to abolish the office in 1899 saying 'everything that can be invented has been invented'. Although there is no evidence, whatsoever, of this, or any other commissioner ever making this statement, or anything similar, the quote is often reported and the myth has taken on a life of its own. Nevertheless, there are a lot of patents out there! Some companies, like IBM, seem to spend all their time filing patents. Whenever I come up with a new idea and check the patent database, it seems to have been registered by someone working for IBM several years earlier.

Many technology companies offer bonuses to staff that come up with new patent ideas—even if the invention has no practical value whatsoever, they're happy to pay out the employee bonus and file another patent.

Even if your invention is new and unique, chances are that it overlaps with some existing patent. Although you can pay as little as $355 to file your patent directly on the U.S. Patent and Trademark Office site (www.uspto.gov), you'll pay them at least $4,000 over the life of the patent. You're going to need to pay $6-9,000 for the services of a specialist intellectual property lawyer if you want some security that it's being filed properly. Investors love patents, but as they take at least 3 or 4 years to get them granted, all you're likely to be able to say to an early stage investor is that the patent application has been filed, that it's being handled by a reputable set of lawyers and that you're hopeful that it will be granted. So, you're going to need another bloodsucking lawyer—this time specializing in patents. You can't seem to avoid having to pay lawyers at every step of the journey from *Zero-to-IPO.*

The ideal scenario is that your invention is found to be unique, you're issued with a patent before it's completely obsolete, and you can then go out and charge royalties to any future infringers. More likely, a patent will provide you with some protection against other patent holders forcing you to pay royalties to them. It's unlikely to become a profit center in it's own right.

It's important that you keep the essence of the invention under wraps before you file the patent. Distributing detailed descriptions of the invention worldwide can destroy the novelty, so in your white paper and other promotional and presentation materials, it's normally OK to talk about it in general terms—but don't get too specific. Although it conducts huge marketing campaigns, Coke keeps it's recipe a trade secret.

After you've filed your patent in the U.S., you have a one-year grace period to file in most foreign countries. You can buy more time by filing under the Patent Cooperation Treaty which has 57 varieties of country members. This gives you a window of 20 months before you have to go ahead and cough up the cash to file patents all over the world.

Trademarks

To restrict others from using your logo, product name or company name, you can register a trademark with the U.S. Patent and Trademark Office staking a claim to words, names, symbols, sounds, or even colors that distinguish your goods and services. Trademarks, unlike patents, can be renewed forever as long as they are being used in business. The roar of the MGM lion, the pink of the Pink Panther and the shape of a Coca-Cola bottle are familiar trademarks. You can even trademark slogans like 'Where do you want to go today". I always wanted to trademark the word 'the' so that I could force everyone around the world to add a little ® sign whenever they used it, but you can't register common words like 'the' or 'shoe' or 'car' unless you combine them together in some way.

You don't have to register a trademark, copyright or patent to own your intellectual property—if it was created by the company, it normally belongs to the company under common law. Registration does give you a better defense against infringers. Nowadays you can make an official U.S. Patent and Trademark Office filing your trademark directly online. Go to http://www.uspto.gov/teas/ fill out the forms, enter your credit card and you're done. As you probably guessed, it's not usually that simple—the forms can be confusing and it's normally advisable to get a registered patent attorney to handle the whole process. This can cost about $2,000 for each trademark and take around 18 months.

During the process, holders of other trademarks may be alerted about your application, and you can expect calls from unusually aggressive people claiming that your mark infringes on theirs. This is one reason why it's advisable to have a lawyer handling the process for you.   Your trademark will be restricted to a specific class— this defines the type of products and services for which it can be used. If someone holds a trademark that's similar to yours within the same class, and you can't buy it from them, you'll likely be forced to drop your trademark application and come up with another name. That's why I recommend you run trademark searches *before* you choose a name! To determine whether there is a conflict between two marks, the Patent and Trademark Office determines whether consumers would be likely to confuse your goods or services with those of the other party. But this can take months or years so it's normally better to negotiate and reach a settlement with the holder of the other mark whereby you both agree to restrict the use of your trademarks to your specific classes and take steps to avoid market confusion. As you need to start using your mark immediately, you may have to come up with a payment or some form of incentive for the other party to quickly reach agreement.

If you suspect you're going to want to trademark anything at some point in future, you need to start adding the 'TM" notice whenever you use the mark. This indicates that you're claiming rights in use of the trademark, even before you've filed a federal registration. If you're selling a service rather than a product, you use 'SM' (service mark) instead of 'TM'. The '®' designation may be used once the trademark is actually registered in the U.S. Patent and Trademark Office.

Your filing with the U.S.PTO covers all 50 U.S. states. It's important to file the trademark in your primary overseas markets as many of them are 'first to file' jurisdictions. Although you may have been using the mark for years, if someone else files before you do in many overseas countries, chances are that they'll get to use it and you won't—unless you buy it from them, which can be expensive. As in the U.S., it can cost you around $1,500 and take around 18 months to file in each country if you go through local agents. These costs obviously add up when you go for protection in several countries to cover the major international markets.

Copyright

To help protect your work from infringers, you should register your intellectual property with the Copyright Office within three months of first publication or release. This involves providing them with copies of the work—they're accustomed to receiving things like manuscripts, books, sheet music, videotapes, microfilms, cassette tapes, CD's and LP records. For software, you can send them a source code file together with print-outs of the first and last 25 pages. This gives you protection for up to 100 years—that should be long enough for anyone! This is not an expensive process and the single filing covers most major countries in addition to the U.S. The Library of Congress registers copyrights which last for the life of the author plus 70 years.

Create and Launch your Web Site

You're not a legitimate company these days until you have a professional looking web site. With your corporate identity guidelines, core messaging, company name and trademark, you now have everything you need to publish an impressive site.

At this stage, you need the site to appeal primarily to an audience of potential investors, customers, and employee candidates looking for a quick snapshot of the company. Keep it simple with as few pages as possible—updating lots of pages can become unmanageable. At the very least, you're going to need the following sections:

- ✓ *Company Overview*
- ✓ *Products*
- ✓ *Management*
- ✓ *Contact Details*
- ✓ *We're Hiring*

All the information you need for these pages could be copied and pasted from your business plan and core messaging documents. Your corporate identity guidelines should provide the web designers with everything they need to create impressive-looking pages consistent with your corporate look and feel. Create a layout and menu structure with room for growth as you're going to be adding new sections, like corporate values, technology white paper and press releases, in the coming weeks.

If you're not an Internet guru, you're going to need the following services:

- ✓ *Hosting service*—to host the web site, provide e-mail accounts and regular reports.
- ✓ *Domain registration service*—to register the domain and park it until you're ready to publish your site.
- ✓ *Web site design service*—to design the site, upload it to the servers, update and manage it moving forward.

You'll find a list of some of these service providers later in the resource guide. See *Web Hosting Services*, page 405, *Internet Domain, Search & Registration*, page 405, *Web Designers*, page 407, see *Web Site Promotional Services*, page 407.

I have a vivid childhood memory of leaving on a family vacation to London. Our guidebook must have been somewhat out of date because when we arrived at the hotel, the whole street was a pile of rubble—the hotel had been demolished and the only thing left standing was the front door (with the frame). Of course, before we went off in search of a new guidebook, we decided to snap a picture of the family eagerly knocking on the lone door with suitcases in hand—strangely enough there was no reply. This image comes to mind when I direct my browser to a web site only to receive the 'Cannot Find Server' message. Not everyone would think of a pile of rubble, but investors, customers and other important visitors are not going to be impressed to find that your site is down when they try to visit you. So, whatever hosting service you decide to use, make sure your site is up and running 24/7.

There are some people out there that still use Netscape—some of them even access the Internet with weird and wonderful devices like Mac's, Unix boxes, PDA's, TV's and high-technology toothpicks. My philosophy is this—later versions of IE and Netscape running on Windows are de-facto standards and you should design your pages to work in these two browsers. If someone wants to design a browser for a Mac, PDA or toaster-oven then it's *their* responsibility to make their browser compatible with *your* pages.

When you have your site up and running, you want to have it listed with all the major search engines. I may have mentioned earlier that investors can do very unpredictable things—after listening to my presentation, one VC investor took me to his desktop PC and ran a search on Yahoo for my company name. It failed to find our site. He then went on to other engines and proceeded to run various searches to see if he could find our site. He was disappointed not to find us—in his mind, a company is only legitimate if its site is listed on the search engines. Even if you don't come across this particular investor, it's a good idea to subscribe to one of the many services that list your site on numerous search engines—it may only cost a few dollars but it can take up to an hour of your time to select the appropriate categories you want to be listed in.

Publish a Technical White Paper

You want your audience of potential investors, customers, new hires, press and other key influencers to appreciate the strength of your technology and understand how it enables you to deliver superior products. The best way to do this is through a technical white paper—normally a 10 to 15 page document that's detailed but easily understood by business people as well as propeller-head techies.

According to February 2001 statistics compiled by eMarketer.com, white papers are the second most consulted source of information by corporate end users (strangely, employee phone directories are first—just imagine thousands of corporate employees spending their days flicking through employee phone directories). There's even a white paper portal and annual white paper awards: http://yahoo.bitpipe.com. Although they're mostly related to corporate IT technology, it's interesting to check out how the papers are written and presented.

To keep the reader interested, you might want to thread a storyline through the document that identifies the problem, then shows how it's solved by your technology. As well as learning about the technology, the reader should come away with a full understanding of the bottom line business benefits. On the bitpipe site you'll see that the award winning papers are written in plain English with clear explanations of terminology. They follow an ordered, logical structure with summaries, graphics and case studies. Readers could be turned off if you write the paper with a glossy sales spin—you'll get more respect if it's dry, accurate and to the point.

This is an important document that will be studied in detail by potential investors and customers. If you're not an accomplished author, you may want to hire a technical writer with experience of writing white papers to make sure that you're putting your best foot forward. It could take weeks and cost thousands of dollars to educate a writer on your technology—so I recommend you write the first drafts of the paper in-house, then hire a technical writer to apply the finishing touches. Here's an example of a company that specializes in writing technical white papers: http://www.whitepapercompany.com.

Although you can talk about your technology and approach in general terms, it's important that you don't give away details of precisely what's going on under the hood—as this could invalidate your patent application.

As most readers print the white papers out onto good old-fashioned paper, they are usually distributed over the web as Adobe Acrobat files. As well as publishing the paper on your site (depending on your industry) there may be other sites that are interested in publishing and syndicating it to a wider audience.

Build a Product Prototype

The key to building a good promotional prototype is that it has to look good, even if the beauty is only skin deep. A glossy front-end with fancy graphics and presentation make a huge difference. The underlying engine of the technology you're demonstrating can be simulated—behind the scenes use smoke, mirrors, trick photography, duct tape, string, whatever it takes to make it look like it's working.

Bill Gates dies and meets St. Peter at the Pearly Gates. St. Peter asks him whether he'd like to go to Heaven or Hell. Naturally, Bill says 'well I was thinking of Heaven'. St. Peter says 'I ask because some people do prefer Hell. You don't have to decide now—would you like to take a tour first and then give me your decision?' Bill figures he has nothing to lose and heads off on his tour of Heaven. When he gets there he finds it extremely dull—just a few monks and nuns reading bibles and not much else going on. Next stop is the tour of Hell. On arrival, he's amazed to find that it's a fun, friendly place with lots of bright young people singing, dancing and generally having fun. He checks it out as best he can and it seems like a pretty cool place—certainly more interesting than Heaven. So, when he has his audience with St. Peter he tells him what he found there and chooses Hell instead of Heaven.

Immediately he's transported to Hell. But when he arrives there he finds that it's not at all the same. He gingerly opens a huge door and he's astonished at what he finds—fire, brimstone, blood curdling screams, everything you'd expect from Hell. Standing at the door, mouth aghast, he sees the Devil wandering towards him. Bill stops him and says 'I don't understand—I was here a few minutes ago and it was fun and friendly, now it's totally different'. With a sinister smile, the Devil says 'Oh you mean you saw our demo—this is the shipping product!'

Bill Gates knows, as well as anyone, that customers, investors and normal people can be fooled by a cool demo. Behind the scenes the whole demo can be simulated with smoke and mirrors, but if you pull it off, even the smartest people can be fooled into thinking that you have a hot product.

Unfortunately, most people have no vision whatsoever and they can't visualize your product until they see it. A prototype can be a valuable tool to sell your dream to investors, customers, journalists and new hires.

Form a Board of Directors

A board of directors is a group of people legally charged with the responsibility to govern a corporation. The CEO is selected-by and responsible-to the board of directors. The board of directors is elected-by and responsible-to the shareholders. As the company grows, you need to be very careful about how you grow and structure the board.

One of the board members will be appointed Chairman of the Board and will have additional duties including:

- ✓ *Ensuring that all board members, when taking up office, are fully briefed.*
- ✓ *Setting dates for the board meetings.*
- ✓ *Ensuring that decisions are taken and minutes are accurately recorded.*
- ✓ *Setting the board meeting agenda.*
- ✓ *Representing the views of the board.*
- ✓ *Working with the CEO to formulate the boards' business strategy.*

The board is responsible for the governance of the company. If the company does something naughty, it's the board of directors that's often held accountable. Even if the company does nothing untoward, it could still find itself on the receiving end of lawsuits from disgruntled customers, former employees, suppliers and those little old ladies that fall down the stairs. For this reason, anyone with any sense would avoid sitting on the board of directors and opt for the advisory panel—a much safer place. To provide some liability protection for the unfortunate ones that find themselves as official directors, the company needs to take out Directors and Officers Insurance. In fact, it's unlikely that you'll be able to attract any outside directors or marquee names unless you have this insurance in place. To qualify for the insurance, you're going to have to jump through a few hoops—for one, you're likely to have to customize an employee handbook and make sure that all employees sign it.

Where do you find these outside director types? A good place to start would be your lawyer, accountant and other entrepreneurs. Look around industry associations—there's even a National Association of Corporate Directors. Check out annual reports of high profile public companies in your space to find their directors or perhaps their senior management. As with any hire, do your homework and check the references and reputations of your potential directors—with a few checks I discovered that one person I was planning to invite on my board had a criminal record and was quite a notorious personality on Wall Street.

Most directors value the experience of working with energetic management and other quality people. "The opportunity to contribute and be part of a force for change" was cited by 74% of Fortune 1000 directors as the single most important reason for being a director, followed by "respect for the CEO" at 61% (source: Deloitte & Touche). Still, you're going to have to put together a remuneration package for outside directors—comprising stock options, expenses and possibly consulting fees. Investors have traditionally not requested any compensation for their board participation—this situation is changing and many VC's are now requesting stock.

In recruiting a director, you should have worked out his level of activity and attention both in terms of the number of board meetings expected and, if the "job description" includes it, interactions outside of the board room. These outside interactions with individual directors are your opportunity to obtain one-on-one advice and assistance. Establish a format that works for both of you—a monthly breakfast, weekly telephone call, tennis match followed by a half hour discussion by the juice bar—whatever works.

Board Meetings

Because your directors are very busy people, you're going to have to schedule meetings months in advance. Many early stage growth companies have board meeting once a month—but in my experience these regular meetings are very difficult to coordinate and lose their impact. Bimonthly or quarterly meetings are often more effective. Meeting dates often coincide with financial reporting periods (like 15 to 20 days after the end of a quarter) or major industry events (such as a major trade show). Special meetings will be needed to approve financings. The time of day for the meeting will depend on whether your directors are all locally based or have to travel and whether you and they are "morning" or "afternoon" people. I find morning meetings, like morning doctor visits, work best because people tend to get behind schedule as the day progresses. Most meetings are held at the company's office so make sure the place looks presentable and that your people are aware that the "suits" are coming in.

For a normal board meeting you should allow 2 hours. If there are extraordinary issues to discuss allow 3 to 4 hours. Keep things flowing and moving at a brisk pace.

Because time is limited, you should offload as much of the background information as possible so that the meeting can focus more on decision making. Prepare a "Board Package" and send it out to the directors 3 days before the meeting. A typical package will contain an agenda, draft minutes of the previous meeting, financial reports with management commentary, a navigation report fixing the company's position on it's chosen route and other relevant information. Be sure to keep the directors informed of general developments between meetings—include the directors on press release lists, product mailings, etc. It can be very annoying to a director to hear company news from an outside source.

You'll have to experiment to find the right formula for the meeting itself, but use an Agenda to keep things on track and moving. A typical Agenda will include: Approval of Past Minutes, CEO's Report summarizing and highlighting (not duplicating) developments reported in the Board Package, Operations/Marketing Report, Financial Report, Old Business and New Business.

In addition to the board itself, the meetings are often attended by members of the advisory panel, key members of the management team, like the CFO, and the company's legal counsel. Any particularly sensitive or confidential issues could be saved for a closed session that's only attended by official members of the board.

At the start of the meeting, the Chairman should check that enough members of the board are present to make up a decision making quorum. For some bizarre reason, many Chairmen still revert to olde-English language when making decisions:

> *'We have a motion to (take a decision)'*
> *'Do we have a seconder for this motion?'*
> *'All in favor say "Aye"*
> *'All those against say "Nay"*
> *'Motion approved (or disapproved)'*

Be sure to allow enough time for New Business or the "legal stuff" like approval of stock options. If the board is required to make a decision on an important issue that's quite complex in nature then you might want to ask your lawyer to carefully word the resolution before the meeting. Ask the lawyer to take care of the minutes as well—they're important legal documents and you want to make sure the appropriate information is correctly recorded and documented.

Structure a Management Team

The CEO usually pulls the head of each department together into a management team and holds regular meetings to coordinate the various operations of the company. A large proportion of the day-to-day and strategic decisions are made by this group—usually 5-10 managers. I've found that a weekly management team meeting provides a good opportunity for everyone to share their ideas and concerns, make decisions and keep up-to-date with what's going on. Personally, I try to cover all the management issues in a single session and avoid numerous time consuming meetings between each of the individual groups.

In the early stage, it's tempting to hand out grandiose titles to management team members—everyone seems to want 'Vice President' on their business cards and it's one easy way of attracting good talent to your startup. However, when the company grows up this could come back to bite you. At *IPO*, a company would typically have a couple of *executive* vice presidents and 3 or 4 vice presidents on the organization chart. If everyone other than the receptionist had vice president title, your organization chart would look a little irregular. You don't want to have to ask people to switch to more junior titles later on, so you should be very careful about giving out impressive management team titles in the early stage. To avoid title wars with employees, I ran my startups for many years without any titles whatsoever—except humorous ones like 'Big Guy on Campus' or, 'Elvis'(totally nonsensical and one of my favorites). It was great fun watching people's expressions when you handed them your business card. After the venture capitalists came in and the company grew up, we were forced to adopt more traditional titles. Fortunately we kept the fun ones as well.

In a startup, the management team gets to deal with some very difficult issues under stressful conditions. Make sure you choose people that are up to the challenge. You need them to take responsibility, make decisions and get things done—quickly. Ideally you'll find people with the experience and capacity of managing a much larger company but without the bureaucratic mentality. Choose people that are prepared to operate with restricted headcount and budget. In fast-moving and stressful situations, you need to work with team players that collaborate and support each other—there's no time for power struggles or political games.

Set Up a Bookkeeping & Accounting System

Although there's not a lot of sales revenue coming into the company at this stage, you do need a system that provides accurate financial reports and is scalable for growth. In the early 1980's I spent several years selling Unix and DOS based accounting systems to CFO's and bookkeepers that thought the electronic calculator was a new fangled device that would never catch on and thought computers were TV's with keyboards.   It was a major challenge to persuade ageing bookkeepers that the computer offered benefits over their existing ledgers, scraps of paper and quill pens. Fortunately, today things are a little more sophisticated. There's a good choice of accounting software available from vendors like Great Plains, Peachtree, MYOB, Oracle (Netledger), Intuit and Cognos. See *Bookeeping and Accounting Software*, page 395. Your accountant will surely know one package better than the rest and will have a preference that will help you make your choice.

Don't wait until it's too late—when the VC's come in to do their due diligence, you don't really want all your accounts on an Excel spreadsheet.

Hire a Head of HR

Dedicated human resource staff used to be found only in large corporations with thousands of employees. For small companies, HR was traditionally handled by the founders' wife in her spare time (yes, these were sexist companies). If you're not able to recruit and keep the very best talent in your market, you'll not make it very far on your journey from *Zero-to-IPO*. So bring in an HR specialist as soon as you can—it's a good investment even with twenty employees or less. If nothing else, it will relieve the founders and other members of the management team from having to answer the mind-numbingly tedious questions that employees have about their stock options, benefits and vacation allowance.

Prepare for a Recruitment Ramp-up

The company's ability to grow will be partly determined by its ability to recruit good staff. After you close your first round of funding, you're likely to want to aggressively step up your recruitment efforts.

Don't forget to put recruiting expenses into your business plan and operating budgets—it would be prudent to budget between $25-40,000 to hire members of the management team and between $5-20,000 for everyone else. Hiring CEO's can be a very expensive undertaking and it has its own section later in the book. See *Hire a Career CEO*, page 145.

There are various ways of finding new staff today:

✓ *Newspaper ad campaign*—some local newspapers like the San Jose Mercury in Silicon Valley can be quite effective at attracting staff at all levels. I've found it very cost effective to use a small 'teaser' classified ad inviting the reader to visit the web site for more information. I don't see much point in paying for a full page ad as all the details can be posted on the web—if the candidate can't find their way to the web site, they're probably not worth considering anyway.

✓ *Contract recruiter*—you can bring in a specialist recruiter on a contract basis to work from your office. You'll pay somewhere in the region of $50-90/hour and commit to a minimum period of something like 3 months. The good news is, as there's no commission, the recruiter is not going to try to persuade you to hire the first person that walks through the door. I prefer this approach to using outside recruitment firms and it's worked very well for my companies in the past.

✓ *Contingency recruiting firms*—these folks go out and find candidates for you without any up-front financial commitment on your part. However, you pay for it when you hire—normally between 20-25% of the employees' first years' compensation package.

✓ *Retained recruiting firms*—it can be very expensive to retain a firm to recruit on your behalf. Expect to pay 25-35% of first year's compensation for each person hired. 1/3 of the estimated fee is due up-front as a down payment, 1/3 is due on presentation of a slate of qualified candidates, and 1/3 on the employees start date. You can also expect to sign an exclusive engagement.

✓ *Postings on your web page*—as it's virtually free to add a recruitment section to your web site, it makes sense to leverage it as far as you can.

✓ *Web based recruitment services*—theoretically the Internet offers a perfect venue for matching job specifications with job-seeker resumes. In addition to the generalist sites like www.monster.com, there are sites that attract certain types of candidate: www.brassring.com, www.dice.com and www.hotjobs.com attract engineers and www.headhunter.com is popular with accountants. The cost structures vary from site to site, but you can almost guarantee that the costs will be lower than using an outside recruitment firm. See *Recruitment*, page 404.

✓ *Existing employees*—your staff can be a great source of new hires, especially if you offer a finders fee or some form of incentive for them to bring their friends and contacts into the company.

Setting Salaries

People get very emotive about salary levels. In one of my startups we soldiered on for several years with hardly any cash whatsoever—we paid the core team in stock options, buttons, IOU's and anything we could lay our hands on. No one received salaries and, strangely, the morale of the team couldn't have been any higher—we all shared a mission, our backs were against the wall and the whole team worked very supportively together. When we eventually raised our seed round of funding, we suddenly found ourselves in the unfamiliar position of being able to start paying salaries. You would have thought that the staff morale would have hit a high, but instead, a salary cat fight ensued and morale hit an all-time low. Curiously, a similar thing happened when we upgraded to smart new offices. All the employees that had been more than happy to slum it in the makeshift office above the liquor store, were suddenly upset and insulted if the window from their new luxury cubicle was facing East instead of West. So, the lesson I learned was this: if you want to keep your staff happy, don't pay them a dime and keep them in slum conditions as long as you can. Alas, this situation cannot continue indefinitely.

When salaries are a real possibility, the principle I work on is that each employee should be paid market rate for his/her specific position—using an independent yardstick there's not so much room for negotiation. Several sites like www.salary.com, www.salarysource.com, www.salaries.com and www.ventureone.com publish average salary levels for a whole range of positions and make adjustments for your specific ZIP code and other factors. Compensation packages for the CEO and some other senior executives are set by a committee made up of board members, advisors and specialist advisors, but they too are typically determined by studies of market rate levels for similar companies.

Outsource Everything that Moves

In the industrial age bigger was better. Looking back, the market conditions could be likened to a slow-moving ocean—the larger your ship, the more chance you had of weathering the storms. Today, most markets are likened to white water river rapids—only the smallest most maneuverable vehicles have any chance of survival. So you want to keep your team as small and nimble as possible. The trend in Silicon Valley is to outsource as much as you possibly can—it's easier to terminate a contracting agreement than lay off a full-time employee when you need to change direction. Employers hire only those people that are critical to the success of the company over an extended period and outsource everything else. Almost anything can be outsourced these days—product development, HR, IT, marketing, manufacturing, even business development, sales and the CEO position!

I'm sure we'll soon reach a position that a company consists of a pile of papers— business plans, legal documents defining ownership of the intellectual property and a set of outsourcing agreements. Everything else will be outsourced to specialist service providers—you'll have outsourced founders, outsourced boards of directors, outsourced CEOs, even outsourced outsourcers.

But when you walk in the office you wouldn't necessarily know that everything was outsourced—most of the staff for most of the time would still be working on-site from their cubicles. When the Internet superhighway was still a dirt track, I set up a radical new business model with a network of consultants working from home offices scattered across Europe, the U.S. and Asia. With this low-overhead, wide reaching network, we offered high tech companies an effective route to international markets. The idea seemed brilliant at the time, to me at least, but in the end it didn't work out. One of the reasons was that people are more happy and productive when they work together in the same office—at least for 2 or 3 days a week. The other reason was that the refrigerator was too convenient for some individuals who couldn't resist the temptation to snack all day long. Although the trend toward outsourcing and consulting will continue, don't expect offices to empty out, even when video-conferencing becomes part of our everyday lives.

So, to keep your core team as small as possible, you should look at outsourcing as much as you can. You'll find many high-technology outsourcing companies listed in the resource guide section of the book.

Taking Outsourcing to the Extreme

Execustaff (www.execustaff.net) is a Silicon Valley company with an interesting model. Your company retains full control of the employees in your office but Execustaff is technically the employer of record. The concept, termed 'coemployment' is becoming increasingly popular as the 'professional employer organization' acts like a huge outsourced HR department that takes care of all your employment issues including compensation, benefit programs, payroll taxes and tax filings, workers compensation and immigration. They even provide new employee orientation programs and telephone-based counseling services for employees that need someone to talk to—or scream at. Of course you pay them a percentage of the employees' salary for the service, but it can be well worth the investment if you want to spend your time building your business instead of trying to figure out what you need to do to comply with the latest labor laws.

<u>Define your Corporate Values</u>

Unfortunately corporate culture can be very ugly—at Apple the culture was once described as a cross between Disneyland and war-torn Beirut. Normally friendly people would stab their colleagues in the back at every opportunity to climb another rung in the corporate ladder. Everyone was terrified of lay-off day and the embarrassment of being accompanied out of the building with their possessions in a black garbage bag. Every company has its own culture and management style. Apple Computers' management style in many ways became a reflection of Steve Jobs' personality. Although he's mellowed a little over the years, Jobs is reported to have tantrums and launch attacks on unfortunate employees that happen to be in the wrong place at the wrong time, publicly ridiculing and often firing them on the spot. They don't have to be evil demons to incur his wrath—simply wearing the wrong clothes or accidentally bumping his car in the car park can be enough to set him off. Early managers in the company saw this and, of course, acted in the same way—

tantrums were OK at Apple. So poor management style at the top has a habit of naturally filtering down through the ranks to the rest of the company.

Unfortunately the same is not always true for good management style. The challenge with your startup is to create a positive, effective management style and corporate culture, and then have it adopted by all the new employees and managers as the company grows. This is not easy, as you may be hiring experienced managers from established corporate cultures and it's sometimes hard to teach an old dog new tricks. Somewhere along the line, you're likely to hire someone with a natural ability to upset other members of the team, without even seeming to try. They're often so focused on their own egos that they don't even realize that they're hurting other people and damaging the performance of the whole team. If employees regularly burst into tears when dealing with the same individual, it's a safe bet that there's something wrong with that individual. Your corporate values can really help you deal with this situation by defining how employees are expected to interact with each other and defining the boundaries about what's acceptable and what not. Without a well-defined set of corporate values, it's easy for these individuals to think there are no boundaries and anything goes.

When you're dealing with investors, you have to be prepared for them to make mountains out of molehills. They often pick one number out of the projections, drill down and challenge it for hours, days or weeks on end. The fact that my startup didn't have a set of corporate values became a huge issue for one investor. This became the most important issue concerning the investment and dominated two full days of discussion involving more than ten people. Following that painful experience I now make sure that the company's corporate values are published, understood and defensible.

Defining your corporate values:

1. *Review the corporate values of other companies that you respect*—they're normally published on the corporate web site.
2. *Arrange an offsite meeting with your executive team to define and agree your corporate values*—make sure everyone gets to seriously discuss the values they feel are important—and make sure that everyone fully buys in.
3. *Brainwash all existing and new employees with the corporate values*—print them up in a frame, distribute them to all staff and encourage them to hang them in their cubicles. Put them up in your meeting rooms, publish them on your web site, tattoo them on your forehead and refer to them as often as possible in all internal presentations and announcements.

I've had numerous meetings with employees of Earthlink. At virtually every meeting, someone has referred to Earthlink's corporate values. All their employees seem to know what they are and they really seem to try to live the values in everything they do. For employees, partners and customers alike, it's comforting to know that you're dealing with a company that has values and is committed to consistently living up to them. After acquiring many different ISP's and trying to meld them into a single corporation, it was vitally important for Earthlink to bring everyone together and brainwash them with the same values.

Earthlink Core Values and Beliefs

Mission: To become the leading Internet service provider in the world, as measured by number of members, member satisfaction and profitability

Purpose:
→ To improve people's lives by giving them the ability to communicate better than ever before

To enable our employees and shareholders to flourish and prosper

Core Values & Beliefs

What's important at EarthLink? We are convinced that the key to creating a truly great organization is an intense focus on the values that guide its people's actions. These are EarthLink's "Core Values and Beliefs". If we don't seem to be living up to them, call us on it!

→ We respect the individual, and believe that individuals who are treated with respect and given responsibility respond by giving their best.

→ We require complete honesty and integrity in everything we do.

→ We make commitments with care, and then live up to them. In all things, we do what we say we are going to do.

→ Work is an important part of life, and it should be fun. Being a good businessperson does not mean being stuffy and boring.

→ We love to compete, and we believe that competition brings out the best in us.

→ We are frugal. We guard and conserve the company's resources with at least the same vigilance that we would use to guard and conserve our own personal resources.

→ We insist on giving our best effort in everything we undertake. Furthermore, we see a huge difference between "good mistakes" (best effort, bad result) and "bad mistakes" (sloppiness or lack of effort).

→ Clarity in understanding our mission, our goals, and what we expect from each other is critical to our success.

→ We are believers in the Golden Rule. In all our dealings we will strive to be friendly and courteous, as well as fair and compassionate.

→ We feel a sense of urgency on any matters related to our customers. We own problems and we are always responsive. We are customer-driven.

Source: www.Earthlink.net web site.

Establish a Benefits Package

To attract good staff, you're going to have to compete with large companies that offer large company benefits. Of course you can provide some incentives and compensation packages directly—like stock options, employee referral bonuses, retention bonuses and management incentives. Other benefits need to be sourced from outside insurers and service providers:

- ✓ *Medical Plans*
- ✓ *Dental Plans*
- ✓ *Vision Plans*
- ✓ *Long Term Disability Insurance*
- ✓ *Short Term Disability Insurance*
- ✓ *Life Insurance*
- ✓ *Flex Plan Availability and Administration*
- ✓ *401k Plans*

Insurers like to service large corporations and small employers have always found themselves at a disadvantage when negotiating health insurance and other benefit packages for employees. Fortunately, it's getting easier for startups to attract good staff as a number of companies aggregate lots of small employers together to match the buying power of a large corporation.

Without a benefits director, human resource department, human resource director, or any form of benefits expertise in a small company, it can also take up a great deal of management time and energy to set the benefits package up. Like virtually every other activity, this can be outsourced to a broker that helps you identify the benefits you want and manages the whole process on your behalf. They take your requirements to the market, request bids, present to your staff and answer questions like—*'what color spectacles can I have on the vision plan?'* After you appoint your broker, you should allow eight to ten weeks to put the plans in place—three weeks for bidding and analysis, two weeks to make your choice and an additional three weeks for employee meetings and implementation.

Write an Employee Handbook

When you're the founder, sole shareholder, director and employee of your startup company, preparing and signing an employment agreement between your company and yourself is not the first thing you put on your 'to-do' list when you start work in the morning. It feels like a pointless exercise. However, as the company grows, it becomes important that each employee, including founders, signs an employment agreement clearly establishing that the company owns it's most valuable asset—the intellectual property. A technology company without full ownership of its intellectual property is worthless. After you sign the employment agreement, your invention belongs to the company—if you leave you can't take it with you.

Of course the employment agreement also has to cover all the other terms and conditions of employment—these are so numerous that they've graduated from the status of multi-page agreement to bound employee handbook. Your lawyer can provide you with an employment agreement but the handbook is more likely to be prepared in-house, with the help of some off-the-shelf templates.

Engineers, some of the most important employees in your high tech startup, are strange people. Typically the very best engineers are the most strange. One bizarre characteristic is that they work unusual hours—like vampires they often work overnight and sleep during the day. As they sleep all day and spend the hours of darkness huddled over a PC in a remote dark room, the only time you get to see them in the daylight is if you pluck up the courage to visit a Fry's Electronics superstore where whole herds of them can be spotted making all their essential weekly purchases—microchips, junk food and caffeine injected cola drinks. All the best engineers I've worked with follow this pattern. However, they've all signed their employment agreements agreeing to abide by wonderfully motivating rules like:

- *The Company is normally open for business between the hours of 8:00 a.m. and 5:00 p.m. Monday through Friday. Your supervisor will assign your individual work schedule. All employees are expected to be at their desks or workstations at the start of their scheduled shifts, ready to work.*
- *Employees are allowed a 10-minute rest period for every four hours of work or major portions thereof.*
- *Salaries and exempt employees may be required to record their time on duty using either a timecard or a timesheet. Any errors on your timecard should be reported immediately to your supervisor.*

Of course, all my employees have signed the handbook, then immediately disregarded these ridiculous terms and gone about their normal business. So what's the point in preparing the handbook in the first place? Like most things in this wonderful country, it's done to reduce the company's liability. If an employee brings a pet alligator to the office and it swallows the bookkeepers left foot, the company could be held liable and sued—unless the employees had agreed to terms in the employee handbook stating: "Under no circumstances are you allowed to bring large pet alligators into the office" or ".. you are expected to keep your left foot at least 29 inches away from the mouth of any large carnivorous animals that you may encounter in and around your cubicle". As you can imagine, as these handbooks have to protect the company from virtually every possible liability, they can become rather large—in addition to alligators, they need to cover all forms of crocodile, snakes and deadly reptiles.

It's going to be difficult to persuade anyone to sit on the board of directors unless the company has Directors and Officers ('D&O') insurance to limit their liabilities. It may be difficult to find a D&O insurer to cover you unless you have a company handbook that looks like something produced for conscripts into the military or inmates in the state penitentiary. It will cover a range of topics:

✓ *Essential legal provisions*—covers legal issues including the 'at-will' employment status and provisions for equal opportunity and harassment.

✓ *Employment policies and practices*—job duties, work schedules, meal and rest periods, timekeeping, performance evaluation, etc.

✓ *Standards of conduct*—what's prohibited, what's expected in terms of dress code, customer relations, confidentiality, etc.

✓ *Operational considerations*—employer property, employee property, health and safety, smoking, expenses, telecommuting, etc.

✓ *Employee benefits*—paid time off, holidays, leave of absence, health insurance, pregnancy leave, voting, workers compensation, etc.

The good news is that you don't have to write the handbooks yourself—there are templates available on the web and CD-ROM. Check out http://www.hrcalifornia.com/ for an example of what's available online.

Hire a Head of Marketing

The first rule of marketing in a technology startup is this: don't spend any money. The second rule: don't hire someone that wants to spend money. The third rule: hire someone that knows how to spend someone else's money. You need to keep as much of your cash as possible to build out your product—if it really has the potential to change the world, the press and analysts will get excited and you'll get valuable coverage without spending huge budgets on advertising.

However, you do need to generate awareness and recognition, stake your position in the market and start generating momentum as quickly as possible. You need a head of marketing to lead these efforts. Unfortunately these can be the most expensive people you'll ever hire.

I once hired a director of marketing with what looked like a great resume—high-level experience in lots of marquee name technology firms where he managed huge budgets. His salary was quite reasonable, but the cost of hiring him was at least $7m/year. He needed a staff of 7! He couldn't see how the company could survive unless he had a team of two people handling advertising, two people for PR, a designer, writer and someone to manage tradeshows and events. Several contractors were required to produce reports about media buying and to try to measure the effectiveness of the advertising campaigns. He then needed the services of some of the most expensive advertising and PR agencies in the world. And to cap it all off, he had to spend at least $5m on advertising. And this was never enough—he, each of his staff, and the agencies always needed more headcount and more budget! Of course, when you're a public company with a huge war chest of funds, you may need a marketing team like this, but it can quickly drain the life out of a small company.

So, take care when selecting your head of marketing! What you need is someone that knows how to squeeze blood out of a stone—or at least make a lot of noise from a small budget.

You need a head of marketing that can evangelize large, cash rich, corporations to spend *their* time and money promoting *your* product and to encourage journalists to feature your product in the media. It can be done. When our marketing budget consisted of a credit card and travel allowance, we managed to convince both Intel and Microsoft that promoting our product was a great way of promoting their own. The effect was absolutely amazing. Intel produced a TV ad featuring our product and ran it on prime time slots for several months—the total cost must have been several million dollars. Both Microsoft and Intel showcased us at their huge product launch events in front of thousands of journalists and industry VIP's. My trip to Comdex that year could not have been any easier, or inexpensive. Instead of paying for a booth, and then going through the arduous task of setting it up, I arrived at the Microsoft booth just before the public arrived on the first day, plugged in my laptop and I was in prime position for the whole show. Microsoft guided over a stream of journalists and VIP attendees and I was swamped with business cards from potential investors. Instead of having to break down the booth at the end of the show, I simply jumped in a cab and headed for the airport—they even presented me with a nice gift on my way out.

So save your cash for product development and avoid hiring a head of marketing that's accustomed to spending huge budgets. Try to find someone that relishes the challenge of exciting the press and spending someone else's money.

Appoint a PR Agency

Forget about glossy brochures and business plans. For some unfathomable reason, many otherwise normal people actually believe what they watch, read and hear from the media—so press clippings are often the most powerful materials you can provide to potential customers, investors and new hires. If you have unique technology and a product that's going to change the world, it should be of interest to the press. Even if it doesn't make front-page news, almost any coverage will provide credibility and generate momentum.

Process of Appointing an Agency

Make Appointment

Negotiate Terms

Make Selection

Take up References

Bake-Off

Shortlist Candidates

Approach Candidates

List Candidates

Set Preliminary Budget

Define Objectives

There are several web sites that enable you to post a press release and have it distributed to thousands of journalists all over the world (see *Press Release Distribution Services,* page 407). Some of them will even write the release for you—for a modest fee. PR is a simple process right? Journalists are looking for news. You send them news in the form of a press release. They copy and paste your news into their stories. The journalist is happy, the reader's happy, you're happy, everybody's happy! Somehow I actually believed this for several years—until I realized that it didn't quite work out that way. I thought I could go it alone, write my own releases, send them to journalists and generate good coverage for my product without the expense of using an agency. My press kits were sent out filled with interesting news but generated no response from the journalists whatsoever.

Then I saw the light and hired a good agency—well actually my VP of marketing hired the agency first, then I saw the light. Without paying a cent for advertising,

I've since had my product exposed to millions of customer through positive editorial stories on virtually every major TV channel, in virtually every major newspaper and magazine in the U.S., Europe and all corners of the World. My press clippings books fill a whole bookshelf with positive coverage in the New York Times, Wall Street Journal, LA Times, U.S.A Today, London Times, London Sunday Times, Time, Newsweek, Business Week, TV Guide, PC Magazine as well as literally hundreds of regional print publications. I have videotapes filled with hundreds of clips of TV news stories featuring my product from large networks all over the world including CNN, ABC, NBC, CBS and the BBC. It's the same story with radio—in depth interviews on national NPR, BBC and scores of stories on local radio stations. As a result, I'm a huge advocate of PR for startups. It's authoritative, inexpensive and, if managed properly, highly effective.

PR & Advertising

Though the lines of distinction may blur, public relations and advertising are quite different. Advertising is about creating or changing attitudes, beliefs and perceptions by influencing people with purchased broadcast time (radio, television, audio/videocassette), print space (newspapers, magazines, journals, programs, billboards), or other forms of written/visual media (fliers, brochures, bus-stop billboards, skywriting).

Public relations is about communication—communication with clients, employees, stockholders, special interest groups and, of course, the media, through which a business can communicate with the outside world. Public relations, too, influences people's attitudes, beliefs and perceptions; however, it does so through press coverage in television, radio, newspapers or magazines which, unlike advertising, is often free.

As an example of what's possible, let's look at one of my most memorable campaigns. It was orchestrated by a Seattle based agency called Waggener Edstrom. As Microsoft was its major account, Waggener had strong connections with the press and a good experience of managing consumer-oriented technology campaigns. My first press tour with Waggener in 1997 was a huge hit that generated extensive coverage for our company. In fact the account representative from Waggener was overwhelmed with the response. She told me that it was the second most successful tour she'd ever worked on—it was only bettered by the tour she arranged for Bill Gates to promote the launch of Windows95. Our second press tour together was even more successful—this one apparently even beat the Bill Gates tour according to our account rep. She may say the same thing to all her clients but it really doesn't matter to me because I was very pleased by the results—high profile national and international press coverage on TV, print and radio. One of the highlights was when

Walter Mosberg, the personal technology columnist for the Wall Street Journal authored a very accurate and unusually positive review of my product. He then went on TV to talk about the product and his column was syndicated across dozens of newspapers and publications throughout the country. The knock-on effect of this type of coverage can be very beneficial—it's one of the best ways imaginable to generate momentum. The TV spot and Wall Street Journal article were seen by several investors that were in the process of considering whether they should invest in the company—and this had a huge impact on their investment decisions. We had so many calls from Wall Street investors, asking for our Nasdaq ticker symbol, that we had to remove the telephone number from our company web site—if we'd actually had a Nasdaq ticker symbol, I'm sure the share price would have rocketed on that particular day.

So how can an agency make such a difference? Let's take the Walter Mosberg story as an example. If I'd tried to contact Walter directly, my press release is sure to have been filed away with thousands of releases from other young foolish entrepreneurs—probably in that circular open topped 'filing cabinet' in the corner of his D.C. office. It just so happens that Walter had dinner only a couple of months earlier with Melissa Gates, wife of big Bill and my account manager from Waggener Edstrom. So when the account manager called him up, Walter was at least prepared to take the call and listen the outline of our story. He liked what he heard and we arranged a short meeting and demonstration in his office. Although having Waggener as our agency provided some credibility, journalists like Walter Mosberg have to verify all their facts before they write a story. So he checked in with some of the industry analysts that we'd met up with earlier in our press tour, to establish that our story was legitimate, he then went on to contact the PR agency to request a sample product that he could thoroughly test himself. We were lucky that he found an interesting angle with which to write the story. Without having the introduction and endorsement of the PR agency or the feedback from independent market analysts, my product would never had made it onto Walter Mosberg's radar screen. I have plenty of other examples to highlight how a good agency can open doors that I would never have even known existed if I'd tried to go it alone. A good agency can be a great investment for a technology startup.

So, how do you go about finding a good agency? Here's the process:

1. Define Objectives
2. Set a Preliminary Budget
3. List Candidates
4. Screen Candidates (by Phone & Web Research)
5. Interview Short Listed Candidates
6. Request Proposals (if Necessary)
7. Take up References
8. Make Selection
9. Negotiate Terms
10. Make Appointment

The process of selecting and appointing a PR agency should take around 6 weeks.

1. Define Objectives

It will help you, the agencies and everyone else involved in the selection process if you can define, as clearly as possible, what you're hoping to achieve from your PR activities in the coming months and years.

A public relations firm is responsible for determining the way an organization is perceived by the public. The first thing to consider when choosing a firm is whether you want it to handle your company's entire public relations program or just its publicity. A firm that handles publicity sees to it that a company's products or services receive media coverage in the form of articles or radio and television broadcasts. When a firm handles public relations as a whole, its job is to help craft a company's image. Most PR firms do both but it's useful to determine how much you're asking the agency to do ahead of time.

	PR Objectives for AcmeTech Startup, Inc.
Major Objective	Company launch—introduce the company as a serious new player and quickly carve out a distinct, defensible market position.
Target Results Expected	Company launch: ✓ News stories in major industry journals ✓ News story in investor journals such as Red Herring or Upside Magazine ✓ Speaking engagements for CEO in at least one high profile industry conference and one

	investor conference.
	✓ Product launch.
	✓ TV news stories on one national and ten regional TV networks.
	✓ News stories in several national newspapers.
	✓ Radio interviews for CEO in at least 3 major cities.
	✓ Product reviews in major industry journals.
Wish List	Some, possibly impossible, targets for the agency to aim for:
	✓ CNN headline news story.
	✓ Cover of Wall Street Journal.
	✓ Cover of Time Magazine.
	✓ Cover of Fortune Magazine.
	✓ Industry awards and accolades.
	✓ Oprah show feature.
	✓ Nobel prize.
	✓ Product endorsement from the President of the United States, the Queen of England and the Pope.

It's important at this stage to decide the scope of the geographical coverage that you're looking to achieve. Regional coverage is not going to be sufficient to help you generate momentum on your journey from *Zero-to-IPO* and the decision you need to make here is whether you want international coverage or just domestic. There are very few agencies that have international coverage through wholly-owned subsidiaries but many of them have networks of overseas firms that they collaborate with on global accounts.

Almost every PR professional will advise you to issue a press release only when you have something newsworthy to say and they'll warn against being critical of your competitors or anyone else in the industry. However, my friend took a completely opposite approach—and for some unknown reason it worked. He would issue literally hundreds of releases each year, mostly announcing minor deals that the company had signed. When he was interviewed by a journalist, he would give them juicy quotes like 'the head of Yahoo is a complete bozo' or 'I'm smarter than Bill Gates'. The journalists lapped it up, he was covered extensively in the media, he

IPO'd his company and became a billionaire. So much for the conventional wisdom of PR.

You need to decide whether you're going to go for a controlled, focused campaign or whether you want to have a scattergun approach and find an agency that's comfortable with this philosophy.

If your PR campaign is a huge hit and you're swamped with calls from journalists, it's tempting to think that you no longer need to pay the agency—hey you're getting enough coverage already so why pay for more? If you do stop the agency, you should be aware that the coverage will gradually taper off and you may upset some journalists if you don't have the team in place to provide them with the information they need, when they need it—an unhappy journalist can cause you a great deal of pain! A stop-start agency strategy can have detrimental effects—so you might want to consider whether you're looking for a long-term relationship with the chosen firm.

2. Set Preliminary Budget

Here's the bad news—you can't run an effective PR campaign without a budget. When I was young and foolish I thought I could, but was proved wrong. I cut a sweet deal with the head of a large PR firm—we built their web site and they provided us with PR services in a nicely balanced trade-for-trade barter deal. It worked for them, as their site was beautifully designed and published within in a matter of weeks. But it didn't work for us because we came up against one of the fundamental laws of PR—the only clients that get any attention are the ones that pay lots of cash and make lots of noise! We had no results whatsoever—we didn't even meet with a single journalist.

Some larger agencies provide a lot of credibility and they're very effective at opening doors, however, you really don't want to be the smallest client on the agency's roster, or should I say, the smallest client budget on the agency's roster. You certainly don't want to be a barter client that's not generating any billing revenue whatsoever—you'll find yourself below the bottom of the screaming clients list. Unfortunately you'll have to come up with a real budget, shell out hard cash and have one of your team constantly chasing the agency if you're going to get any mind-share or attention.

You probably don't want to be the largest client on the agency roster either—you may be dealing with an agency that's too small to handle all your requirements, especially as the company grows and your needs develop in the coming months and years. So, technically speaking, you need to find an agency that's not too small, not too large but 'just right'. OK, that's not very technical or scientific but finding the right fit is more art than science. To gauge where you might fit on the scale, ask the agency for its minimum billing requirements.

The PR budget really depends on your company and objectives, but you're unlikely to get much attention for a major company or product launch if you're not prepared to pay the agency more than $10,000/month. For AcmeTech Startup, Inc. to achieve its PR objectives, it needs to budget at least $200,000 to cover all the external PR costs in the launch year. This may be aggressive, but compared to advertising this budget is relatively small. Executed properly, it should be money well spent.

3. List Candidates

Now you need to pull together a list of local agencies with expertise in your field:

- ✓ *Tap into the network*—ask your lawyer, accountant and members of your board and advisory panel, friends and colleagues for referrals.

- ✓ *Consult directories*—download a list of agencies matching your requirements from the web. See PR Agency Lists, page 406.

- ✓ *Dig around*—look through the publications in which you would like to have coverage; call the companies that are written about in these magazines and find out which PR firms those companies use.

4. Screen the Candidates (by Phone & Web Research)

By surfing the web site and conducting telephone interviews, you should be able to determine which agencies match your requirements in terms of industry expertise, size and whether they have the skills and capabilities that you're going to need.

The Pope's airplane lands in New York City. As he emerges, bleary eyed, from a long journey a journalist shouts: 'Welcome to our city—what do you think of all the prostitutes in New York?' The Pope, unprepared for such a question answers: 'I don't know—are there any prostitutes in New York?' Of course, the newspaper headline the following day reads: 'Pope lands in New York. First question he asks is: "Are there any prostitutes in New York?"' The journalist would claim that this is accurate reporting, but it obviously creates an inaccurate picture in the mind of the reader. If the Pope had a good PR agency, they may have prepared him for such a question by role playing and helping him find ways to answer difficult questions. One of Apple Computer's agencies had a media training program that I will never forget. As part of the training, I was to be interviewed about Apple's new PC release. I had all my lines rehearsed and was ready to answer questions on the features and benefits of the new product. The lights go on, the camera starts to whirr and the journalist fires his first question: 'Apple Macintosh prices are so high in the UK that it's cheaper for me to fly to New York first class on Concorde and buy one over there—how can you justify such a price discrepancy?' My jaw dropped, I was flummoxed—I was prepared for a different question and had no idea how to deal with this one. After a day of media training I was well prepared to answer this and any other question that a journalist with a sick and twisted mind could conjure up. So, media training is one of the services that you might want to look for in a PR firm.

Here are some other skills and capabilities that you may want to consider:

✓ *Media training*—everyone in the company that's likely to be exposed to the press should go through training to make sure they're singing out of the same songbook. They also need to learn how to control a press interview and some political maneuvers to avoid answering certain questions.

✓ *Messaging and positioning*—it's important to find an agency that can help you crystallize your core messaging and position the company and the products for the long-term as well as the short-term.

✓ *Writing*—a quick read through the agencies' press releases and other written materials should give you a good idea as to whether you like the writing style.

✓ *VNR scripting, production & distribution*—if your product has visual appeal and you'd like to pursue the opportunity of generating TV coverage, then you're going to need an agency with in-house or, more likely, a partnership with an outside group that specializes in producing and distributing video news releases (VNR's).

✓ *Radio*—like TV and VNR expertise, radio is quite a specialist skill. If you think radio could be a good media channel for you, check that the agency has the skills, resources and recent experience in this field.

✓ *Road show management*—you're likely to need expertise in this area. Alarm bells should be ringing if the agency can't point to examples of recent multi-city press tours for other clients.

✓ *Staging media events*—it's the PR firm that often organizes a huge product launch event or party.

✓ *Crisis counseling*—sometimes things go horribly wrong and you find yourself in a media spotlight. If your product accidentally gets contaminated with the Anthrax or Ebola virus and wipes out a class of cute kindergartners, expert help can come in handy when the journalists come knocking on your door.

✓ *Employee and investor communications*—as your company is young and small, you may not need these skills but they could come in handy later on.

✓ *Community relations*—if you need the local community to support you and your endeavors, you may find an agency with special skills in this field.

✓ *Research*—an agency may be able to help you research your competitors, customers or anything else that takes up lots of billing time. It can be useful if you need this information to support your business plan.

✓ *Government agency liaison*—there are a number of PR firms that specialize in government liaison. Government agency support can come in very handy for certain types of products and services.

In an effort to win your business, PR firms may exaggerate their knowledge of your industry. If you're seeking a firm with specialized experience, don't hesitate to quiz the principals about their knowledge of your field. Ask for examples of what they've done for others in your industry. To determine if they're the right size, ask for profiles of current clients and information on their minimum billing guidelines.

There are all sorts of PR agencies, some with weird and wonderful skills. They've been known to do everything from arranging meetings with world leaders to fixing up female escorts for senior executives. Without leaving your desk you should be able to narrow down your search and eliminate the ones that are unsuitable for your requirements.

5. Interview Short Listed Candidates

On paper, the agencies on your shortlist should have all the skills you need. Now you need to check them out for real and find out if there's any chemistry between the teams. To do this, you need to spend several hours together with each of the candidates—this is best achieved in the agencies office rather than your own. The agency should demonstrate, using case histories of their current clients, how it would satisfy your needs. It may help you evaluate the presentations if you use the same agenda for each meeting. Like dating, lunch and dinner are good opportunities to get to know who you're dealing with. Ask for a client list, years of experience, types of projects the firm has handled, and portfolios and any press clippings. Find out whether coverage was generated in industry trade publications or the general press (which is typically more difficult). Based on the agency's previous work, do you feel these people understand how best to "sell" your product or service?

Here are some of the questions that you need to get answered:

- ✓ *Who's the account manager and the team that you would be working with?—what are the other accounts that this team deals with?*
- ✓ *What access would you have to the agency principals?*
- ✓ *What's the firms philosophy?*
- ✓ *What's their experience of working in your industry?*
- ✓ *What reporting and measurement methods are used?*

Make sure press releases are compelling and well-written—I once interviewed an agency and found several grammatical and spelling mistakes in the first page of their sample press release. If it looks unprofessional to you, it will likely look unprofessional to a journalist. Whether you're the biggest or smallest client in the stable, you should be able to count on consistent attention to detail.

You need to make a judgment call as to whether the agency shows originality and creativity, whether they are reliable and budget conscious. No amount of chemistry and creativity can make up for a missed deadline or an estimate that's way off. Be sure the agency has not only the creative skills needed but also the time and commitment to devote to your needs.

PR firms normally have well rehearsed client pitches—don't be afraid to ask questions and drill down for detailed answers about your specific needs.

You can normally tell if there's a good fit. A good agency will express interest in getting to know you as an individual and learning more about your company. It will be good at listening and quick to learn. It will make good suggestions and react quickly to your questions and opinions. It should demonstrate the ability to anticipate what's best for your business and be prepared to disagree with you if it feels you're on the wrong track.

6. Request Proposals

After eliminating unsuitable firms from the list, ask the remaining candidates to send a written proposal. I personally don't like to waste anyone's time unnecessarily—if you've already eliminated a candidate, it's much fairer to let them know at this point rather than ask them to submit a proposal that you're not going to seriously consider.

7. Take up References

Before you make your selection, take up references from other clients. If you can set it up, try to talk to former clients as well as current ones.

8. Make Selection

Hopefully, the best choice is now obvious and it's quite simple to make your selection. Several people in your team have to work with the agency so it's a good idea to let them all feel like they're involved in the selection decision.

9. Negotiate Terms

PR firms usually charge hourly rates of anywhere from $100-$500 depending on experience, plus expenses. For a single project, the agency will likely charge a set fee to cover all expenses, with the amount of the fee depending on the size of the project and the amount of time the agency expects to spend. In a long-term relationship, which is what you're going to need, the agency will bill on an hourly basis, although it may set a minimum monthly fee. You may choose to pay a flat monthly retainer fee to ensure that you'll be able to call on the agency whenever you need to (see *Appendix 2—Getting What you Want—Negotiating the Deal,* page 313).

10. Make Appointment

The agreements are signed and you have yourselves an agency. It can be useful at this point to hold a friendly kick-off meeting to introduce the agency staff to the employees, excite them about the company and establish the basis of a working relationship. Don't burn your bridges with the agencies that were not selected – you may want to go back to them if your first choice agency doesn't work out.

<u>Launch the Company</u>

Now that your core messaging, PR firm and your web site are all in place, you're ready to launch the company and stake out your position in the market. Don't worry if your product isn't quite ready for prime time—showing a prototype will suffice at this stage. You don't launch your company by taking out full page ads. in the Wall Street Journal—this is an exercise in creating awareness and momentum with industry insiders and the press.

Working with your PR agency, you start by drawing up a press release that's newsworthy, at least for the trade journals. As with all your marketing communications, make sure that you stick with the script that was defined in your core messaging document (see *Formulate your Core Messaging and Corporate Identity*, page 87). This is the first big chance you have of establishing a brand and accurate positioning is vitally important. The story may read along the lines of: *'new company is formed to satisfy a market need that's never been effectively addressed before. Management sees huge potential for its new product line which has real advantages over the competition.'* Any supporting information you can provide about customer acceptance, strength of the management team or the investors helps establish credibility and generate a sense of momentum.

The press coverage you're looking for at this stage is news stories in major industry journals, investor publications and speaking engagements for the CEO in high profile conferences and events. If you can think of an interesting stunt or angle, you may get some consumer coverage, but most reputable journalists will wait until the product ships before they introduce it to a consumer audience—and may be more appropriate for your product launch later on.

Market research organizations typically have one or more analysts to monitor a market or specific sector. These people are very important. Before a good journalist will put pen to paper, she often requests the endorsement of a reputable analyst. As you launch the company, it's important that you meet the key analysts that cover your space and convince them that you're a real player with a right to stake your claim to a piece of this market. Make sure you're clear on the core messaging and you can defend your positioning, as they are experts and they will ask some very difficult questions. Of course, analysts should always provide an unbiased, objective analysis of the market and your company. However, don't be surprised to find the analyst double-teaming with a sales person that tries to sell you a subscription to the firms' information service. Strangely, you often get more access to the analyst and a more enthusiastic endorsement if you're a paid up subscriber. If your story is good enough you should hope that the analysts will endorse the company—regardless of whether or not you're a paying client.

As well as analysts and journalists, all industries have a set of key influencers— certain high profile individuals that people listen to and respect. They could be academics, business leaders, government officials, customers, competitors or gurus from any walk of life. Like the ripple effect of dropping a stone into a pond, these people in the center of the industry spread the word out to the people on the outskirts. If you can reach these individuals and convince them to buy in and endorse your story, you'll start to create a buzz. Your PR agency can help here but the chances are that you, and some of your staff, will have met many of these key influencers at some time in the past. So go through your contact managers to identify industry VIP's, add in lists of friends, colleagues, neighbors, everyone else you know. It can be quite effective to e-mail regular newsletters or updates to all the individuals on the list. Following up with a telephone call, of course, adds more impact to your message.

The focal point of your launch campaign should be a press tour when you go out and pitch your story to several journalists, analysts and industry VIP's in several venues across the country. It's unlikely that your company launch would make an interesting TV news story but, if you had an interesting angle, you may want to consider preparing a VNR (video news release) and have it delivered to all the TV stations via satellite. I'll cover VNR's more thoroughly when we get to the product launch phase (see *VNR—Video News Release*, page 153).

The Press Tour

It's 6.30am. You rush out of your New York hotel and jump into a waiting limo. Your PR agent, Debbie, is already in the car reviewing your schedule for the day with the driver. She and asks you if you had a good nights sleep. You're going to need it as your first appointment is a live interview on local New York radio at 7.30am and the rest of your day consists of back-to-back interviews in different areas of New York City:

7.30am—Live radio interview.
8.30 am—Interview with journalist from national newspaper.
9.30 am—Meeting with analyst that covers your space for research firm.
10.30 am—Interview with journalist from trade magazine.
11.30 am—Lunch with a well known author that's written a book about your space.
1.00 pm—Meeting with journalist from investor magazine.
2.00 pm—TV interview.
3.30 pm—Interview with freelance journalist that's written about this space before.
4.30 pm—Meeting with official from government department with interest in this market.
5.30 pm—Meeting with representative from your industry trade association.
6.30 pm—Early dinner with potential investor.
8.30 pm—Fly to Boston for the second leg.

As the car maneuvers through the traffic, you're preparing for the interview. Debbie's reading the bio she's put together on the journalist, Mike Mahoney—he's known to put an interesting spin technology stories of all types. Debbie asks you if you're awake and ready to deliver your pitch. She explains that, for radio, your message has to be very short and sweet—listeners on their rush hour commute have no patience for waffle. She tells you to pretend you're on air right now and asks you to run through the whole pitch. As you start to rehearse your core messaging script, the car suddenly scrECHes to a halt as a yellow cab decides to do a U-turn and block the whole road. Truck drivers are screaming, horns are honking and you notice that the cab driver is completely unphased. Welcome to the big city. You try to focus back in on your imaginary interview and start to deliver your story. This time you're interrupted by a call on Debbie's mobile. An important journalist has received your press pack and wants to feature your product in a story. She's on deadline to finish the story today so she needs about twenty minutes to talk to you. Your agenda is already busy so Debbie schedules a telephone interview—you'll have to do it from the car as you travel between your two o'clock to your three o'clock meetings. As you once again start to prepare to run through your pitch, the limo stops and the driver points to the glass doorway leading to the radio studio. It's 7am and you've arrived at your first appointment of the day.

After registering with the receptionist, you're greeted by a young girl with a clipboard and a copy of your press pack. She leads you to a studio and an engineer starts to put on your microphone and run some sound tests. You're asked to say something, anything into the microphone so that he can set the levels for your voice. Then the door swings open and it's Mike Mahoney himself. He says 'hi' but he's in a real rush as a big news story has thrown out their schedule for the morning. He puts the microphone in front of your nose, tells you that you'll be live on air in ten seconds and starts to look through some notes he prepared earlier. Five, four, three, two, one—you're on air talking to hundreds of thousands of busy New Yorkers. Mike makes a few introductions then fires his first question:

'How come you think you have any chance of success with this new product when so many have failed in the past?' You start to pull together your pitch presenting the company and your vision of the market but Mike stops you in mid-flow. 'Just last month I had one of your competitors sitting in this very studio with what may seem to most listeners as the same story. What makes you so different?' You pause and start to construct your answer. Mike is staring at you aggressively. The microphone is in your face screaming for you to talk to it and half of New York is wondering why there's silence on the air. The pressure is getting to you, you're blanking out. Say something… anything. You start to talk and it comes out as waffle. Soon you start to make some sense of what you're saying and remember to make a couple of important points. Your hands are sweating, your mouth is dry. Mike then suddenly thanks you for your time and wraps up the interview. You're off air. Mike wishes you success with your launch, gathers his things together and rushes out to take care of the next part of the show.

It all seems to have happened so quickly. You start to head out of the studio. Debbie asks you how you thought it went. You tell her that you found it difficult to perform so early in the morning in such a high pressure situation. She says that she thought it went OK and that these types of interviews are always difficult. Ideally, you'd schedule these radio interviews for later in the day when you've had a chance to run through your pitch a few times and warm up, but that's not always possible—especially when the journalist only works on the morning show. The limo is waiting outside, you jump in the car and Debbie starts to brief you on your next appointment. This process continues for several days, the intense meetings are only broken up by train, plane and automobile journeys to Boston, Chicago, Washington DC, LA, San Francisco and other cities.

These road shows are great opportunities to get your message out to a number of people in a very short period of time. The culmination of months of preparation, the road show is the focal point of a coordinated PR campaign involving hundreds of e-mails and phone calls.

Road Show tips:
- ✓ *Prepare thoroughly*—make sure that you're ready to pitch your message to press, analysts, customers, anyone that's prepared to listen. Don't assume you'll have much of an opportunity to run through the script in the car!
- ✓ *Use a limo and driver*—especially in New York. Dealing with cabs and cab drivers can be more challenging and stressful than dealing with journalists.
- ✓ *Have a PR specialist accompany you*—they should help you identify how your pitch can be improved and free you from worrying about all the logistics.
- ✓ *Allow ample time for travel*—anticipate traffic delays and make sure you always start and finish your meetings on schedule.
- ✓ *Arrange the most important interviews later in the schedule*—as the road show progresses, your confidence will likely build and your pitch improve.
- ✓ *Confirm each meeting*—you can expect to have several meetings cancelled or postponed. At least you'll have some warning and save yourself time if you call ahead to confirm.
- ✓ *Assume your primary demo will fail*—after laptop failures I now lug around two mirrored laptops on media and investor road shows. As my shoulder starts to collapse under the strain I try to convince myself that it's good exercise.

By the end of the road show you'll be so worn out that you'll look and feel like one of the Rolling Stones after a particularly grueling gig. But, if it goes well and you don't crack up, it could help you generate tremendous momentum in the media and elsewhere. It's also good practice for the *IPO* road show—hopefully you'll have to deal with this later on your journey from *Zero-to-IPO*.

Test the Market

One of first questions you're going to be asked by VC investors is 'how do you know the dogs like the dog food?' This comes from the time before the era of dot-com insanity, when one of the most popular VC investment categories was pet food. All type of weird and wonderful food concoctions were shipped to Sand Hill Road VC offices where hundreds of dogs and other pets were kenneled in secret underground laboratories. Studious men in white lab coats would record each dog's reaction to the latest recipe. The products that were left to dry up in the bowl were quickly rejected by the investors. The ones that the dogs consumed with gusto were considered huge market opportunities—the VC's would invest millions of dollars, the companies would *IPO*, dogs all over the world would wag their tails in glee and everyone involved would become rich beyond their wildest dreams.

Alas, the market has changed significantly—some years ago the underground pet laboratories were converted into dot-com bubble factories. Of course they've since become punishment cells for CEO's that miss their quarterly numbers. Undoubtedly all the Sand Hill Road investors you meet today will vehemently deny that there's any truth in this story—but in a moment of weakness they'll again pose that question about whether the dogs like the dog food. So how should you respond when you get the question?

- → *Best answer:* 'Yes—customers are already shelling out hard cash to buy our products'.
- → *Second best answer:* 'Yes—we've carried out independent tests that clearly demonstrate overwhelming acceptance and pent-up demand'.
- → *Wrong answer:* 'We're not sure—we think they'll like it but we don't have any proof as we haven't checked in with real live customers'.

The question comes from the basic principle that many investors don't trust their own judgment—they rely on gauging the reaction of others. But even an investor with good judgment would be foolish to back a new venture without first testing the market, so this an important milestone on the journey from *Zero-to-IPO*.

There are two components that you need to start the market testing process—your product prototype and a reputable outside research organization. Some people are impressed with statistics—*quantitative* research involving face-to-face interviews, telephone interviews and snail mail surveys produce numbers such as '*nine out of ten customers said they would buy this product*'. Others are impressed by customer reactions—*qualitative* research through focus groups and one-on-one interviews attempt to gather and summarize customer feelings, beliefs and motivations. The ideal scenario is that you show a combination of the two—statistics from a reputable independent source showing overwhelming customer demand and videotape clips of enthusiastic focus group reactions.

Often the press and industry insiders are out of touch and market research is the only way of enabling customers to have their voices heard. As the dot-com industry was crashing I designed a unique new Internet product. Based on informal chats with friends and neighbors, I knew customers wanted this product and were prepared to pay for it. However, everyone was accustomed to Internet product being free and my product and revenue model were breaking new ground. Journalists, distribution partners and industry insiders were very skeptical. So we hired a reputable research firm to go out and poll real, live customers. The analyst at the research firm said that she too was very skeptical before starting the telephone survey of 1000 customers.   87% of the customers said they would buy the product and proved her wrong and many 'experts' were shocked by the response. We then used these figures to justify our business proposition to corporate and distribution partners. These partners then went on to carry out surveys and focus groups of their own—in most cases the positive response was even higher than the 87% figure achieved in the original poll. Without market research we would never have been able to prove that customers wanted the product and were actually prepared to pay for it.

Like me, you'll likely find that customers and partners may want to conduct their own testing. Experienced marketers in large corporations often follow an online survey and focus group testing with limited product releases in the form of field trials and 'soft product launches' before they actually go ahead and commit to a full scale product release.

The Internet offers new opportunities for marketers to reach and gather feedback from customers. In addition to quantitative methods like web-based and e-mail surveys, even qualitative methods like online focus groups are available today. Transcripts are immediately available and the results can be automatically analyzed within minutes. Online research can be more cost-effective and reach more people than traditional methods—but the results may not carry the same weight.

Customers will normally tell you if your product has any chance of success. Analysts and other experts are much more likely to get it wrong. Customers can really help validate your plans and refine your product. However, you need to be very careful about bringing customers into the product design process. In theory, product design should be very simple—you ask customers what they want, then go out and build it. Unfortunately there's one fundamental reason why this doesn't work—customers don't know what they want until they actually see it. If you asked a stone-age cave man to describe his ideal form of transportation he'd probably describe a fast, friendly horse that eats very little hay. But if you give him a choice between the horse and a top of the line Range Rover, he'd surely choose the car—as long as there was a gas station nearby. Our wants and needs are quickly revised after we've been educated as to what options are available to us. If we'd asked regular customers to design all our products, we'd all be riding to work on horses today. This is because the vast majority of regular people don't have much vision. What would happen if you gave the cave man the choice between the horse and a pile of car parts? He'd choose the horse. If you told him to envision a car from all the parts, he'd hurl abuse at you as he quickly galloped off into the sunset. So don't ask customers for their feedback until you have a product or prototype to show them—and then the best way of understanding what they want is to ask them to select from a number of alternatives.

At Apple, Steve Jobs was, and is once again, the product designer. He envisions a radical new product like the original Macintosh and the iMac, pulls together a team of talented engineers and designers; brainwashes them with his vision and then humiliates and abuses them until the product is built and released. Customers fall in love with his products and buy them in huge volume—that's why, against all the odds, Apple is still in business (or *back* in business) today. When Jobs left the company in the mid-1980's he left a huge void. Without a powerful visionary leader, the company made the mistake of turning to customers to design new products. Although the Macintosh Portable was the result of a great deal of customer research, it was a big flop in the market. When researchers asked customers how long they wanted their laptop to run on battery power, not knowing the technological limitations, they responded along the lines of: '..well I work for 8 hours a day and I'd prefer not to have to plug in to a power outlet, so I'd like it to run on batteries for 8 hours… at least'. Designing to customer requirements, the Apple team built the computer around an 8-11 hour battery. Even with today's technology this thing would be pretty large but in those days it was almost the size of a car battery. So this 'laptop' became a huge monster of a machine—I know because I used to lug one to work every day. One day I lugged my Portable onto a flight from Paris to San Francisco. I found myself sitting next to Jean-Louis Gassée, the cool Frenchman with diamond earring who took over the product design responsibility after Steve Jobs left the company. He was studiously reading a huge book. I tried to put my portable under the seat in front of me but it was far too large—and this was business class. I attempted to put it into the overhead bin, but of course I couldn't cram it in there. The flight attendant started to help me. She tried to stuff the case behind a seat at the back but it just didn't fit. Jean Louis was obviously aware of what was going on but he kept his head in his book. Suddenly, when other flight attendants and passengers started debating where it could be stowed, he jumped out of his seat, snatched the computer and put it into the business class coat closet. Without saying a word he sat down and pretended to continue to read his book. Not surprisingly he was very sensitive about the size of this monster—he was responsible for designing it. Instead of asking customers what they wanted, if he'd given them the choice between a lightweight laptop with a 2 hour battery life and a huge, monster laptop with an 8 hour life, he would have been able to design and deliver a product that had some chance in the market. He'd also have discovered that most people are rarely more than a few feet away from a power outlet when they fire up their laptops. If Jobs had been involved, I'm sure that the huge 8 hour battery would never have made it past the drawing board.

The Product Development Process

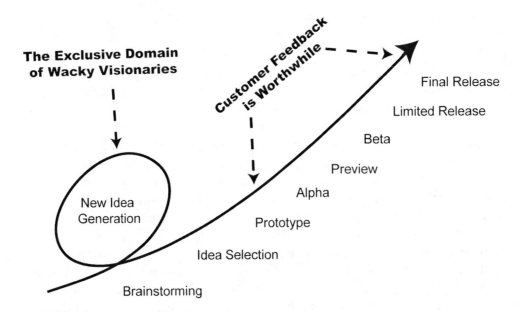

The point is this—although it's important to listen to customers, you can bring them in too early and ask the wrong questions. Don't ask customers to design your products for you—leave that to wacky visionaries like Steve Jobs. You can also bring them in too late—make sure you still have time to refine the product, adjust the price and reposition it in the market based on customer reaction

So, how do you prove that the dogs like the dog food? Although testing the market today is not as simple as putting a dish of processed entrails in front of a hungry canine, it can help you refine your product and convince investors and others that you have something that customers are actually prepared to buy.

Close your First (VC) Round of Funding

Closing the first round of funding is a landmark event in the development of any technology startup—at this point, the Fundraising Process demands a full-on assault.

The first full round of funding is typically led by a VC that agrees valuation with management, negotiates the term sheet, carries out due diligence and provides the bulk of the funds. The lead VC will normally put a partner on the board of directors, help recruit new executives and provide guidance and support to the management team. The lead VC may invite other investors to participate in the round if it feels they can add enough value. If you have a reputable VC leading the round, and taking on the due diligence and other hard work, you'll probably find a number of investors wanting to participate alongside them.

There's an established pecking order in the VC world with Sand Hill Road firms like Sequoia Capital and Kleiner Perkins Caufield & Byers at the top. Kleiner Perkins was behind such Wall Street hits as Sun Microsystems, AOL and Compaq. Sequoia was behind companies like Cisco, Yahoo and Apple Computer. With such a tremendous track record of success, these investors have the resources to open lots of doors and put you on a fast-track to IPO.

See *Selection of Prominent VC Investors*, page 399, *Investor Lists & Match-Making Services*, page 398 for links to top-tier VC's and other investors. You can research their web sites and identify partners that cover your market segment.

Ideally you want a VC that knows your industry but doesn't have any directly-competitive investments. Take a little time to understand the firms' philosophy and identify what type of opportunities it invests in—you may want to use information services like Venturewire to see how active each firm has been in recent months. Put your chosen lead VC's at the top of your list and approach them before anyone else.

Sand Hill Road

Sand Hill Road is an interesting place. It's the heart of the largest venture capital investment community in the world and the place where decisions are made to invest billions of dollars each year. It's the road where many of the largest and most successful technology companies in the world were born, or at least funded—companies like Intel, Cisco, Yahoo and basically just about anyone who's anyone in the technology sector. It's where many of the most powerful corporate CEO's in the world get their marching orders. Office rents are higher than anywhere else in the country—including New York. In 2000, Sand Hill Road and other Silicon Valley VC's invested over $32 billion in over 2000 technology startups—by comparison, only $2.9 billion was invested in the whole of Japan and $1.2 billion in Germany. The investment levels have obviously dropped since the crash, but Sand Hill Road centered investors still pumped over $12 billion into 1000 companies in 2001 (*source: Red Herring July 2002—National Venture Capital Association, MoneyTree Survey, PriceWaterhouseCoopers, Thompson Financial/Venture Economics*).

The strange thing is that I used to drive down Sand Hill Road almost every week to visit friends and the only business I was aware of was a gas station and a dental surgery—it looks like any other regular suburban residential road. The road leads from Stanford straight out to the mountains and a wilderness area so secluded that mountain lions prowl and bob cats are frequently spotted—I've seen them myself. Sand Hill Road is not exactly a financial center with thousands of middle aged men rushing around gleaming high rise office buildings in dark suits! Just set back from this sleepy road are a couple of small office developments, mostly 2 floored buildings that blend in with the local residential houses and the country club. This unassuming place is the center of the worldwide VC empire.

I'm convinced that these buildings are just the tip of the iceberg—hidden underground lie vast labyrinths of VC control centers. The partners appear innocent as they drive in to Sand Hill Road in their Porches wearing short sleeved polo shirts and jeans, but after walking into their offices they proceed into the closets where they change into their suits and cloaks, hit the transporter button and they're whisked into a huge, secret underground office complex. It's here that the new recruits learn the secret handshakes and study the Zero-to-IPO roadmaps and guides. Of course the underground labyrinth is pure fiction, something I made up to fill the time while I was sitting in a Sand Hill Road VC reception waiting for my audience with one of the local investment overlords. However, every time I drive down the road I get this sense of wonder and this niggling suspicion that it might be true. And here I am exposing all their secrets to the world. If I disappear under suspicious circumstances shortly after this book is published, you know where I am. Please, bring all your friends and rescue me by digging as deep as you can below Sand Hill Road. You'll find me in chains in a cold, dark dungeon—I'll be chained next to the former CEO of HP or one of the other companies that recently missed its numbers.

In the good old days, the Silicon Valley VC community was like a Sand Hill Road gentlemen's club—different firms would happily collaborate on deals and each partner had plenty of time to spend helping portfolio companies to grow. By today's standards, the funds were small and the deals were few and far between—one partner could provide pro-active support to 2 or 3 portfolio companies. Since that time, billions of dollars have been ploughed into these funds. By comparison, the number of partners has increased very little. The result is that the VC business has become increasingly cut-throat. Each partner spends more time investing more money in a larger number of portfolio companies—and no longer has the bandwidth to provide substantial hands-on help to any of them. Since the dot-com crash, the pressure has eased—but many partners are still overstretched. By talking to other entrepreneurs, you may want to learn how each VC operates, how much value they actually add and what resources they have in place, beyond just a huge stockpile of cash.

Your list of potential lead VC's should certainly start with the top-tier funds—but don't stop there. There are hundreds of newer funds that actively take lead positions in early stage companies, as well as well-established smaller funds.

Don't waste your time with corporate investors at this stage—they're unlikely to take a lead position—it's too much responsibility and hard work for them. Imagine the headlines if Microsoft were to take a lead position—"With $30Bn in the bank, Microsoft screws tiny technology startup over valuation". By simply participating in rounds that are priced and led by professional investors, Microsoft can avoid this type of PR—and probably ends up taking less of a risk.

Like most entrepreneurs, I struck out when I first approached top-tier firms in Sand Hill Road, so I decided to head off in a different direction and went after smaller funds, angels and corporate investors. But all paths seemed to lead back to Sand Hill Road. One smaller VC liked my story, pulled a few strings and arranged for me to present to a partners at one of the top-tier firms. He could have led the round himself but obviously thought that the company, and his investment, would have a better chance of success if he invested behind a major Sand Hill Road firm. Because they appreciate the value the top-tier firms can add, smaller VC's, corporate and angel investors often steer entrepreneurs back to the top-tier funds on Sand Hill Rd.

Your chances of success will be much improved if you can find a strong VC to lead this first round. Top-tier VC's need to own at least 15-20% of the company to make it worth their time. This can become very difficult after several rounds of funding have led to a significant number of shares being issued to other investors. So give it your best shot—the seed/early stage is possibly your one and only chance to bring in a top-tier VC and put your company on the fast-track to IPO.

Corporate Investors in your First Venture Round

At one point I had both Microsoft and Intel prepared to invest in my company on the proviso that the round was led by a top-tier lead VC. Of course, I used this as part of my pitch when approaching VC's and it was useful for getting face-to-face meetings with key partners. The lead VC I finally settled on, however, had a different view. Its approach was to invite Microsoft and Intel into a later round at a higher price—it wanted to keep all (or almost all) of this round to itself, pump up the valuation and invite in a bunch of corporate strategic investors into a later round. This is not an unusual situation—the venture investors expect the corporate investors to come in later, settle for a higher valuation and take a more passive role than a 'financial' investor. By approaching the strategic investors before the lead VC, I'd theoretically done things the wrong way around. Although strategic investors do sometimes participate in early rounds, they're normally restricted to purely financial investors.

If at First you Don't Succeed..

Ideally, you'll get a reputable investor to lead the round, set the price and possibly attract other investors in.   However, what do you do if you strike out with the top-tier VC's at the top of your list, then the second-tier VC's in the middle of the list and the angel investors at the bottom? When you reach the bottom of the list, you're presented with an interesting choice—throw in the towel or attack the list from another direction. I've personally had some success working my way back up from the bottom of the list to the top. Although I didn't get a commitment from a top-tier VC, I found that there was a good deal of interest from angels and second-tier VC's who basically said 'Gee, I like this opportunity, and I'd love to get involved if you can find someone to lead the round'. This strategy, the fundraising equivalent of passing around the hat, works as follows:

✓ *Set the share price yourself*—at a very reasonable valuation and keep the round size small.

✓ *Contact the angels and smaller investors that expressed an interest*—tell them that you'd really appreciate their involvement and, as you'd like them to join your advisory panel, you're prepared to accept an investment as small as, say, $25,000.

✓ *Pool together as many angels as you can*—even if it means lots of small investments and a large advisory panel. People will tell you that too many investors can make life difficult later on—but beggars can't really be choosers and, if you've already struck out with everyone else, you don't really have much of a choice.

✓ *Ask the angels to give you introductions to other investors*—and add these to your list. If they know their friend is investing, they're often inclined to jump on board as well.

✓ *Work your way back up the list*—updating the investors with news of the new additions to your advisory panel and any other signs of positive momentum.

Passing Around the Hat

If you're going to raise seed funds by passing the hat around a number of small investors, you're well advised to pool them together into a single entity like a partnership or trust. A company with a few large shareholders is very much more appealing than a company with many small ones—just dealing with many different investors is very time-consuming at the best of times.

Passing around the hat can be very effective at attracting the attention of VC's if you gather enough angels together that they start to create a buzz on Sand Hill Road. With the buzz and momentum, you're now in a position to re-contact the top-tier VC's at the top of the list.

Destination IPO **Early Stage**

Close Strategic
Funding

Polish your Business Plan Presentation

Go International
Appoint an Advertising or Marketing Agency

Set up a Scalable Financial Management System

Close Sales
Build a Scalable IT Infrastructure

Hire an In-House Accountant

Hire Respected Management Team
Structure Sales Agreements

Hire a VP of Sales

Form Strategic Partnerships
Publish a Corporate Web Site

Seed Customers

Launch the Company
Release the Product

Hire a Career CEO

Press all the 'Go' Buttons

Close Venture
Round Funding

Early Stage

You've closed your first (Venture) round of funding, now you have some cash in the bank, a new set of investors breathing down your neck and a long list of things you need to achieve in the coming months. The company is about to be transformed and grow out of all recognition. Hopefully, at this stage you'll feel a burst of positive momentum and a buzz of excitement. Don't be surprised if you also feel a little trepidation.

Press all the 'Go' Buttons

The cash is in the bank, the investors are looking to move ahead at lightning pace, this is what you've been waiting for. Now you can hit the 'go' button on all those projects that you've been holding off until you closed your funding. This is the time many companies start recruiting, move into new offices and buy their new hardware, software and other essential equipment. Once you start spending like this, it's sometimes difficult to figure out where to draw the line. Just remember that you're a technology startup not a luxury furniture showroom and most shareholders like to know that you're flying at the back of the plane rather than the front. The company may have millions of dollars in its bank account but it's important to keep costs under control.

Hire a Career CEO

By flicking through the pages of this book, you'll see that the list of things to do on the journey from Zero-to-IPO is pretty extensive. Many of these activities need to be carried out in parallel and almost all of them need to be done yesterday. If you tried to do it alone, you'd need a pickup truck to transport your personal organizer.

The typical technology startup is founded by a visionary from a technology, engineering or scientific background. The stereotype is Steve Jobs working from a garage in Cupertino. Not many career CEO's fit this profile—they mostly wear shoes for a start. Career CEO's are typically strong managers with experience of growing early stage companies through the IPO process and delivering quarterly results to Wall Street

I was the creative visionary who designed the cutting-edge product, founded the high-tech startup and decided I didn't need to bring in a career CEO. After designing the product, I focused on raising investment funds and brought in almost $30m. When I had the breathing space to review the product again, I was horrified. While I was out schmoozing investors, it had been hacked to pieces by successive management committees and, although the underlying technology remained strong, the finished product was a mess. So I set to work to redesign the product all over again. Meanwhile, the sales team had come up with a hare-brained idea and headed the company off on a suicidal mission. I felt like the plate-spinning performer who just managed to get one plate spinning properly, then looked around to find that another one was on the verge of crashing to the ground. I reached a point where I was exhausted running from plate to plate—I decided I needed another plate spinner. So I went out and found a career CEO. It was an unusual situation because, at the time, I had to convince the VC's and other investors that it was a good idea to bring in a career CEO. Suddenly my time was freed up to focus on what I was good at, which also happened to be what I enjoyed and what the company needed.

Naturally, Wall Street money managers buy shares in companies with CEOs that have strong track records of delivering results to investors. If the company doesn't have a career CEO with experience of running public companies in the past, and the company is still run by the visionary founder, the investors like to see a track record of good results for several years prior to the IPO. If you're prepared to take several years to establish a financial track record as a private company, like Bill Gates and Microsoft, then you could IPO with a visionary founder in the CEO position. If you're on an IPO fast-track, you're giving the company a better fighting chance if you bring in a career CEO. Lead VC's often force this issue and initiate the search.

What happens to the founding visionary when the career CEO comes in? Well, like Steve Jobs at Apple, the founder can leave the company. The problem here is that the company is probably going to suffer. If the founders head for the hills when the new CEO arrives, plates start hitting the ground very rapidly and the company loses tremendous momentum. When Steve Jobs handed Apple over to John Sculley, the company had a ten-year lead over Microsoft. Sculley and Job's didn't really hit it off and Jobs, the founder, visionary and creative genius left the company, selling all his stock—not good for public perception and momentum. Sculley did what he could to gather some momentum and tried to develop himself from a sugared drink marketer into a multimedia guru, but by the time Jobs was brought back in, Apples' technology lead had dwindled to nothing. If Sculley and Jobs had been able to work together as a team, and they'd figured out that they could license the operating system and make money, then Apple, rather than Microsoft, would be one of the most valuable companies in the world today. Instead, Microsoft could buy Apple fifty times over and still have enough capital left over to buy the odd third world country. So, it's vitally important that the founders and the new CEO find a way to work together and the passionate founder sticks around. I'm not sure who could have hit it off with Jobs—no one seemed to be prepared to take the CEO position after Jobs came back. But the company has a better chance of making it if the founding visionary stays on board and builds a working relationship with the new CEO. If one or both parties are control freaks, and they're not prepared to share some responsibilities, it's unlikely to work out and the company is sure to suffer. So personal chemistry and mutual respect with the founding visionary are important factors when selecting a new CEO. It's also important to have the visionary founder actively involved in the selection process.

Founders are sometimes shifted from CEO to 'Chairman of the Board'. This is really a ceremonial role without any important responsibilities—but most people don't know that and they think it sounds important. 'Chairman of the Board' has a ring to it. 'Chairperson of the Board' is not quite the same so I'm not going to bother using it in this book. Not because I'm a male chauvinist pig or anything—let's just assume that 'Chairman' can be male or female. 'Human' can be, so why not 'Chairman'? Hey it's only a name. OK, the Chairman technically sets the agenda for the board meetings, but that's hardly a huge responsibility is it? The point is that the founding CEO normally gets a ceremonial title and gets to focus on spinning a manageable number of plates. The new CEO is the person the investors look to for results—if any plates start crashing, it's the new CEO that has to answer the tough questions.

So, what should you be looking for in a new CEO? Someone with a strong track record of running large, preferably public, companies and an enormous rolodex of contacts. It's vitally important to choose an individual with experience of accelerating the momentum of early-stage companies where budgets are tight and things have to get done at lightning pace.

Before you start the search, it's important to form a selection team and then decide how to manage news of the search within the company. Most employees feel insecure when the company is searching for a new leader—among other things, they're worried about how the resulting reorganization will affect their own positions. If it takes several months to find the right person, the uncertainty can have a detrimental effect on employee morale and damage momentum—especially if several candidates are known to have rejected the company's offer. A great deal of momentum can be lost during the new CEO search, unless the whole search is kept totally confidential from the employees.

You can do the search yourselves or you can use a recruiter. Recruiters like Korn/Ferry and Heidrich & Struggles specializing in CEO searches of this sort. They're very expensive but they can open doors and they're sometimes quick and effective. You can expect to pay several hundred thousand dollars in cash to get the search started, and then give the recruiter a bonus of stock options when the search is successfully completed. See *Executive Search Firms*, page 402.

Before you sign the agreement to conduct the search, the recruiter will likely provide you with an impressive list of candidate names and infer that these people are already interested in the position. These will be marquee names—don't be surprised to see Bill Gates, Jack Welch or Steve Case on the list! After you sign the agreement, the list becomes somewhat different, the big names quickly disappear, and the list is filled with names of people you've never heard of, some of which are totally under-qualified for the position. Candidates are identified, called by the recruiter, sent materials, interviewed by the recruiter, interviewed by the VC's and the recruitment panel, references are followed up, offers are made, rejected, negotiated, and if you're lucky, they're finally accepted. If everything goes well, the recruitment process will take 12 weeks. If it doesn't go well, the recruiter walks away with a pocket full of cash and the company is left, at best, with nothing to show for the time and energy invested.

The other way to conduct the search is to use the network and do it directly. Pull together a list of candidates by asking your board members, advisors, investors, lawyers and accountants to go through their rolodexes and give you a list to work with, then hit the phone. This approach has worked well for me.

So, what does a career CEO cost? In terms of stock options, the CEO can normally expect to have 5% of the company immediately after the IPO. So, you take the number of shares the company has today—preference and common stock—add in the new shares that are likely to be issued in all the rounds of funding up to and including the IPO, and give the CEO 5% of that total. The stock normally vests over three or four years, and the new CEO is likely to ask for various conditions like accelerated vesting if the company is acquired.   The salary is normally relatively modest when compared to salary levels of public companies—perhaps $200-500,000 p.a.   The CEO, as with all the employees, is expected to be mostly motivated with stock options, so cash bonuses are a negotiating point but not always part of the package.

Your CEO candidate may be concerned about being thrown out or demoted if the company is acquired and she may demand a 'golden parachute'—triggering an exorbitant pay-out in this situation. Severance packages of this type are avoided in technology startups as they act as a deterrent to acquisition. Heck, most good startup CEOs will want the company to be acquired for a good price and want to be thrown out with some vested stock in the process. Who would want to buy a company that would agree to such a golden parachute anyway?   Experienced startup CEO's are motivated by stock options and they understand that private technology companies need to use cash to develop technology rather than make exorbitant payments to executives. Alarm bells should start to ring if your CEO candidate asks for a golden parachute and appears to have little interest in stock options.

When the new CEO is on board, the hand-over process takes several weeks. After introducing the new CEO to the staff, issuing the press release and making sure everything is set-up, the old CEO should physically get out of the office. One rule of thumb that's used in Silicon Valley is that the old CEO spends the first week in the office helping with the transition, the second week he/she spends one day off-site, the third week two days offsite, and from then on he/she spends only a couple of days a week working from the office. The old CEO can find a good reason to work from home, a remote office or take regular business trips until the new CEO has settled in and a new order has been established in the management team.   After a couple of months, the old CEO can spend more time in the office. At this point he/she is going to have to defer to the new CEO on strategic decisions and take deliberate steps to be as supportive as possible without getting in the way.

Release the Product—in Preview, Alpha or Beta if Necessary

Moving from a prototype to a product release is a huge milestone for the company. You can boost momentum when customers can start testing the product themselves. Up to now, you've probably been demonstrating your product prototype to investors, journalists and potential customers. You've learned where the trap doors are and you've become an expert at dancing around them. By releasing your product, you're now actually letting customers loose on their own—and there's always some inexplicable force that draws them directly towards the trap doors. As they fall through the holes, you're sure to be bombarded with incessant screaming and shouting in the form of tech support calls and e-mails. You need to fix all the trap doors before you let innocent people use your product on their own—but this is not always easy.

At what point do you release the product to the public? The answer should be simple—when it's feature complete and totally bug free. If you've developed a new drug, this is probably the way to go—I seriously don't want to discover that I'm an unwitting 'beta tester' when I pick up my prescriptions from Longs. If you're in the software or hardware business, it can be a little more complicated. The problem is that many bugs are evil and they only expose themselves to live customers. When you want them to appear in the testing lab, they become totally dormant and undetectable. As soon as you put them in front of a live customer, they spring back to life. So you're faced with this tradeoff—you want to get the product in the market as quickly as possible but you don't want to get the reputation that your products don't work.

How do you know that your new software, that works fine on your own PC, will actually work on your customers PC? You don't. Even if you tested millions of PC configurations you couldn't guarantee that you tested an exact copy of the one that your customer happens to be using on this particular day. With so many different versions of Windows, different processors, mother boards, memory chips, video cards, modems, software applications and ISP services, almost every individual customers PC configuration could be totally unique. The process of testing and releasing a software product involves iteratively growing the size of the testing group from a handful of users to the point that you've covered a statistically significant sample and you're ready to release it to the whole world.

Here's how the process goes:
1. Test the software, find and document bugs.
2. Fix the bugs.
3. Test the software and find new bugs caused by the fixes you just made.
4. Fix the new bugs.
5. Extend your testing group to include a wider range of PC configurations.
6. If your test group is less than several thousand then go back to stage 1. If your test base is substantial and there are no bugs then release the product.

Product Testing and Release Program for AcmeTech Startup, Inc. Software Products				
Product Version	**Features**	**User**	**Number of users**	**Notes**
Prototype	Real features are nice but pretty mock-ups can suffice.	Only experienced staff members—maybe 5 individuals.	5-10	*Don't demo until you've learned how to avoid the bugs.*
Internal Alpha	Limited feature set.	Only professional testers and staff.	10-50	*Prepare to be lynched if you release this version to the public.*
External Alpha	Virtually fully-featured.	Staff and insane individuals that are prepared to take the risk of loading buggy software on their PC's.	10-100	*Don't distribute if there's any chance of the software killing innocent PC's.*
Internal Beta	All features.	Only professional testers and staff.	10-50	*As new features have been added, this version can be just as unstable as the internal alpha.*
Preview	Only the features that are tested and working. Buggy features are disabled.	Investors, journalists, customers and anyone desperate to get a feel for the product.	10-1000	*This limited functionality 'preview' version can provide a stop-gap until the beta is ready for release.*
Beta	All features.	Brave (or stupid) members of the general public.	100-1000	*Be prepared to respond to lots of support calls.*
Limited Release	All features.	General public.	1000-10,000	*Make this final release candidate*

				available for a period without charge just in case some bugs have survived the beta test process.
Final Release	All features.	Everyone. Even people that are still waiting to upgrade to Windows 98.	Unlimited	*Now you have a real product and you can actually ask people to pay for it.*

* This process depends on the nature of your product, the market and your customer profile.

Not surprisingly, as a general rule, the more time and energy you invest in quality assurance the better your product will be. Some people don't seem to be able to grasp this concept. I started a software development company in the mid-1990's and our largest client had a curious stance on this—it demanded that our software was absolutely stable and completely bug free but it wasn't prepared to allow any time whatsoever for quality assurance. An unfortunate fact of life is that quality assurance takes time. Each testing iteration can take weeks—and depending on the type of product you're developing, the iteration cycles can be numerous. Quality assurance is important, so make sure that it has the appropriate profile, headcount and budget within the company—many successful companies make this a top priority.

Of course, certain bugs are more evil than others. Some bugs merely annoy customers and can be tolerated by normal people. Others can have devastating effects. Several years ago, my engineering team inadvertently created a monster of a bug that would systematically wipe your hard drive clean—block by block, sector by sector. Fortunately this bug didn't survive our internal testing process—thank goodness, I couldn't imagine taking a support call from a customer complaining that her entire hard drive had been erased.

Having worked in the software business since the '70's, I'm now convinced that there's no such thing as bug-free software. Of course engineers often believe they've created a perfect masterpiece of code and they're shocked and stunned to find it crashes, explodes or merely makes strange squeaking noises when exposed to live customers. So, if you're in the software business, you're probably going to be forced to release a product with its own complement of bugs. Of course you'll refer to them as known 'issues', 'incompatibilities' or 'behaviors'. Your challenge is to make sure that the bugs that the customers get to discover are cute and cuddly and not the nasty, dangerous, vindictive ones.

Well that's enough talk about bugs. Let's turn to the issue of actually launching your product. You have a new product to release onto the market—that's a news story that many journalists could be interested in covering if you give them opportunity. Of course your PR agency will issue a press release and probably arrange a press tour to show off your new masterpiece (see *Launch the Company*, Page 130). In addition to product reviews in your industry journals, you should aim for news stories and interviews in local and national newspapers, even radio. However, if you can come up with an interesting angle, you may want to consider a video news release (VNR). The first product I released with a video news release created hundreds of TV news stories in all corners of the U.S. and other parts of the world. I have videotapes filled with these stories. They all have the same video footage and most of them have the same narration but they're all introduced by different presenters with slightly different angles. Each of the stations downloaded our video news release from the satellite, added a nice introduction and ran it as its own news story. It's an easy way of running a story for them and it cost us relatively little. As it was editorial content, we didn't pay for any of the airtime—compared to buying TV advertising, a VNR can be a real bargain.

VNR—Video News Release

Imagine you're a TV news journalist—always on deadline and looking for your next story. It's a slow news day and you're offered a story that's interesting, newsworthy, all produced and ready to go. Like most journalists, you'd introduce the story as your own and air it. Many of the stories you see on local, even national news reports are video news releases produced by companies that are deliberately trying to get exposure.

Although it's really a PR activity, most firms, even the larger ones, tend to outsource VNR production and distribution to specialists. The whole VNR process works as follows:

1. *Select a VNR production house and distributor*—through your PR agency, your network of contacts or a web search.
2. *Write the script*—this involves collaboration with your marketing folks, the PR agency and your chosen VNR production company.
3. *Review & rewrite the script*—this is perhaps the most critical part of the process. If the story is not current, interesting and newsworthy, you're wasting your time and money—as no one's going to air it. Give it some punch.
4. *Shoot the VNR*—cameras, lights, make-up, cables, you'll find yourself in Hollywood for a day. If you're going to be on screen, make sure you rehearse, wear TV friendly clothes—and take along a good selection from your wardrobe. It will save you time and money if you plan your shots before the camera crew arrives and make sure your upstairs neighbor doesn't decide to start jack-hammer drilling on that particular day.
5. *Shoot the 'B-Roll'*—it's always a good idea to shoot more film than you think you're going to need for the VNR itself and make additional cuts of raw footage available to the newsroom production team.
6. *Edit the VNR*—work closely with the editing team to make sure you like the flow and the way the story unfolds.
7. *Review and re-edit the VNR*—have the film reviewed by PR folks, friendly journalists and normal TV viewers. Don't be afraid to go back to the drawing board if you don't think it's newsworthy enough.
8. *Sign-off the finished VNR*—congratulations; you're ready to hand it over to your chosen distribution company.
9. *Pitch the story to journalists by telephone*—a good distributor will put in calls to journalists, excitedly selling them on the story.
10. *Write a story summary*—distribute the text to interested journalists via e-mail, fax or web page.
11. *Publish a preview of the VNR on the web*—a good distributor will publish a low-

resolution version on its web site as a streaming video file.

12. *Distribute the VNR to journalists via satellite*—the complete, high-resolution version is distributed to the news studio via satellite. Sometimes the journalists request that good old-fashioned film is mailed overnight.

13. *TV newsroom adds its own introduction and makes minor edits*—if she's having a really slow news day and feeling energetic, the journalist can replace the voiceover, add B-roll and other footage.

14. *The story goes out on air*—make sure your web site URL is shown on screen so viewers have somewhere to go for further information. TV stations are normally happy to display this so that they don't receive inquiries themselves. Be prepared—your phones may start to ring at this point.

15. *Airings are tracked and recorded*—the VNR is encoded so that it can be accurately tracked whenever it's aired. You receive a report of the airings with time, place and estimated audience figures.

16. *Have fun viewing the video tapes compilations of all the airings*—be prepared for public abuse and humiliation from your colleagues and friends if you make a personal appearance on screen.

Costs

If you want to spend several million dollars on your VNR, it would be possible. You just hire Robin Williams for the voice-over, shoot your video in the Bahamas and add dramatic animations and special effects. This would likely be a waste of money. For a quality production you should be prepared to budget at least as follows:

VNR Production	$10,000+
B-Roll Production	$8,000+
Satellite Distribution and Promotion	$7,000+

Timing

When the media is filled with a big story there's no room for anything else. You wouldn't have wanted to release your VNR on September 11, 2001. On that particular day there wasn't even any room for advertising. If a major, unrelated, news story breaks and fills the airwaves, hold your VNR release and wait for a slow news day. Sometimes you may be able to piggy-back on a related story. If you were launching a car safety product on the unfortunate day that Princess Diana died, you could have expected some serious coverage.

Some news events are obviously unpredictable but others are not. We once produced a VNR about online shopping and aired it at Thanksgiving. It was picked up by stations that wanted to run stories about shopping in the holiday season. If you can tie your story into a current news event then you're much more likely to get coverage.

Seed Customers and Document their Positive Endorsements

Customers listen to customers. Journalists listen to customers. Investors listen to customers. Employees listen to customers. You need to solicit customer feedback, endorsements and testimonials as soon as you possibly can. Your first customers are guinea pigs—and they know it. They're unlikely to be prepared to pay for the privilege of being guinea pigs, so you'll probably have to distribute several seed versions of your product in the market for free—or offer a particularly sweet deal. You're looking for customer testimonials and stories that could feature in case studies on your web site, advertisements, PR articles and all forms of promotional campaigns. Many customers are keen to participate for the publicity—and the fame.

You're advised to choose your pilot customers very carefully—ideally, they're not only friendly and easy to work with, but also positive about the product and presentable in front of camera. You want to show future, paying, customers concrete examples of how the product has been successfully adopted and used by 'someone like me'—so choose seed customers that people can identify with and are typical of your target audience.

It's important that these pilot sales are successful—so you may want to appoint a team to provide support and immediately rectify the bugs and issues that are sure to arise.

The whole seeding activity is a waste of time unless you document the results and the customers' positive endorsements. Ideally, you'll come away with measurable results, written testimonials, photographs and video clips. It's valuable to quantify the effect that your product has had on the customers business—in terms of reduced costs, increased sales, etc. However, don't underestimate the effect that a picture or video clip of an ecstatic customer can have on your sales, PR and fundraising efforts in future.

Form Strategic Partnerships

In business, as well as the school yard, you tend to get respect if you hang out with large, powerful friends. If respected companies like Microsoft, IBM and Intel are prepared to endorse your product, then you'll get a good deal of momentum in the market.

Surprisingly often, corporations like these are prepared to help promote products and companies they feel showcase their platforms, provide new channels to market, stimulate new customer demand or simply help them prove a point.

Ideally, you'll sign a strategic agreement that commits your partner to ploughing valuable resources into making your company a huge success. But before you have an agreement of this type, you can leverage even a passing relationship to good effect. Most companies are interested in press exposure and they're often open to participating in a press release—this can really add credibility to your story. In an ideal world, the relationship would progress through various steps as your strategic partner:

1. Tests your product/technology and provides references, endorsements or customer testimonials for your PR and marketing efforts.
2. Features your product in their marketing campaigns—advertising, product launches, trade show booths, etc.
3. Distributes your product directly or provides access to its own 3rd party distribution channels.
4. Becomes a strategic investor in your company.

The only way to get any attention from a large corporation is to find a respected individual to champion your cause from the inside. It really helps if this individual is a mover and shaker with strong connections to various parts of the organization. Don't get stuck on seniority or titles—in fast moving organizations today, a champion in middle management may be more effective than a senior executive. Try to find a champion that's smart enough to successfully maneuver through the corporate minefields— if she steps on a land-mine, chances are that you're going to go up in smoke with her. So how do you find this champion? Basically, as with most things, it involves a combination of hard work and good luck. The hard work part is hitting the phone and setting up meeting after meeting, presentation after presentation. The good luck part is finding someone in the right position with the balls and the vision to champion your cause.

Executives in large corporations are sometimes surprisingly flattered to be asked to sit on your board of directors or your advisory panel. It can look good on the resume of someone clambering up the corporate ladder. You just need to be careful that your champion is not seen as having a conflict of interest within the corporation.

Let's assume that you've drawn up a very short list of corporations that would benefit, in some way, from your success. It may be a company that you already know well—the number of people in your industry is probably very small and the chances are that somewhere you'll find a personal contact within the corporation. Surfing their web site I found that an old Apple colleague was now running a significant chunk of Microsoft's server operations. He introduced me to people who introduced me to other people and during my first 3 day trip to Redmond I had over twenty meetings with various Microsoft groups. I flew away from Seattle with a big stack of Microsoft business cards and, although we never signed an official partnership agreement, Microsoft endorsed and promoted our product extensively over the coming months and years. That first introduction can be quite important, so you might want to ask your colleagues, investors, board of directors and advisory panel members to rummage through their rolodexes to help you find a good point of contact. On the other hand, we formed a similar relationship with Intel without such an introduction—it resulted from a cold call to their investment group and spread out to different departments from there.

For your small startup to gain respect in the market today, you're going to need to create the impression that you have strategic partnerships with large powerful corporations. With some good luck, your investment of time and energy in this effort could pay off big time in the coming months and years.

Publish a Corporate Web Site

Now that you have venture funding and you're ramping up the business, it's time to invest in polishing your web site. Customers, press, investors and potential employees often judge your company by the professional design, look and feel of your home page. The quality of your site is an important statement about who you are and what you stand for. If your web site is poorly designed, or buggy, people will assume that the same is true of your products.

Anyone can publish a web site these days at very little cost. There are even software packages and web wizards that will build a site for you in a matter of minutes. In the past few years, web surfers have become very astute—they can tell you within a matter of seconds whether your site was designed by professionals or done on the cheap. If you're not a dedicated web design firm, now is the time to hire one to create and maintain your site.

Since the Internet came along, I seem to have spent most of my life designing web sites with creative menus and navigation systems. Even working with the best designers and programmers in the business, I'm always surprised by how long it takes to make seemingly minor tweaks to a web page. Designing a whole site from the ground up is a lot of work. In fact it's so much work that my advice to you is simple—don't do it. Get your inspiration by looking at sites that have been built already. Why reinvent the wheel? Your browser will even let you see the underlying code and you can learn how the pages were built. Believe me, a lot of thought has gone into most of the corporate sites you find online today. The bugs and glitches have been worked out over several years. By learning from the underlying design of existing sites, you can benefit from years of trial, error and hard work. Ideally you can hire the agency that actually created the original, but if that doesn't work out, just hire another agency and point them at the site you'd like to emulate.

Of course you want to incorporate your own color schemes and deliver your own messages, but your site will probably share the same common components as most other corporate sites:

- ✓ *Company overview*—core positioning statements, history, mission, philosophy, etc.

- ✓ *Products*—product strategy overview, individual product brochures and sales materials.

- ✓ *Management*—biographies of the CEO, board of directors and key executives.

- ✓ *Contact details*—phone numbers, e-mail addresses, office addresses with directions, parking tips, etc. Be sure to list sales contact details.

- ✓ *We're hiring*—post descriptions of vacancies and all the reasons why this is an attractive place to work.

- ✓ *Customer service*—technical support information, frequently asked questions, software downloads, etc.

- ✓ *News*—latest press releases and news clips highlighting the company's momentum.

- ✓ *Press resources*—executive bio's, photographs, screenshots, logos and other images that journalists might want to use in articles.

- ✓ *Site search*—enable browsers to search all the contents of your site.

- ✓ *Privacy statement & legal notices*—tough new regulations force you to disclose what you do with any personal information that you collect on the site. You should hire a specialist lawyer to write your privacy policy, especially if there's any possibility that you have kids visiting your site.

You could choose an expensive advertising agency to design your site, and you'd be reasonably confident of getting a good result. On the other hand, some of the best graphic designers and web developers prefer to work as freelance agents—with an Internet connection, they can work from virtually anywhere and they don't necessarily need the resources of a large corporation to build and maintain a professional site. In fact many of the large dedicated web design agencies have gone out of business in recent years as a result of losing business to smaller, more cost-effective competitors.

Even if your site is beautifully designed and all the buttons do what they're supposed to, it could still create a bad impression if it's slow, unresponsive or the office cleaner accidentally pulls the plug on the server. Find a professional hosting company that can offer some assurance that your site will be up and running 24/7. The Internet is a pretty complex network linking thousands of ISP services over thousands of miles of cables, wireless and satellite connections. It's not uncommon for a customer at one point on the network to have problems accessing servers at another point if one of the intermediary connections is down or overloaded. This problem is not unique to customers in remote third-world countries—the guy in the next office to you may have a problem accessing your site if his ISP and your ISP aren't well connected. In fact, he may find a faster connection if he flies over to Europe. To improve the performance and reliability of your site, you may want to consider using a caching service like Akamai (www.akamai.com). Your pages will be duplicated and automatically made available on multiple high-speed servers across different ISP networks all over the world. I've used Akamai. Although it's not cheap, and it makes the content publishing process a little more complex, it can help improve the performance of your corporate site.

The whole company will suddenly appear much larger, more mature and reliable when you upgrade to a polished, professional corporate web site.

Hire a VP of Sales

Now that you have a product to sell, it's time to hire a vice president of sales. On this route to IPO, you not only need an individual with the ability to deliver results, but someone with the profile and track record to impress the heck out of investment bankers, analysts and Wall Street investors. As a rule of thumb, the most suitable candidates for this position are probably the most expensive—and this is one of those situations when it pays to hire the best you can find. Here are some of the specific characteristics you're looking for:

✓ *Experience of setting up large, successful sales operations in the past.*

✓ *Ability to direct the sales operations through several years of rapid growth.*

✓ *Propensity to work in a small, early stage startup with limited budget as well as a large, well-funded corporation.*

✓ *Business and management style consistent with the company's corporate values.*

✓ *Ability to interact with board members, investors and participate in the IPO road show presentations.*

Salespeople do not have to be experts on the product or the underlying technology—even in the most cutting-edge companies they can be teamed up with product specialists. In fact, many technology companies prefer salespeople that are focused on sales and are not prone to distraction by issues relating to technology and product development.

This is a critical role as it carries the responsibility for delivering many of the company's upcoming milestones. The VP of sales will not only have to deliver on sales today, but pack the pipeline with sales for tomorrow and answer probing questions from investment bankers and investors regarding scalability and other issues of strategic importance.

As it's such an important position to fill, many companies use the services of executive recruiters that specialize in sales and marketing positions of this type. I have had some luck placing ads in newspapers like the San Jose Mercury News and you may want to consider posting the position with one or more of the Internet recruitment sites like Monster.com. However, if you do this, be prepared to sift through lots of resumes from candidates that are less than qualified for this position.

As a Vice President or Executive Vice President position, the package will likely include a sizable chunk of stock options as well as the base salary, commissions and bonus incentives that are part and parcel of the world of sales—see *Create a Stock Option Plan*, page 95.

For more information on the role and requirements of the VP of sales, you might want to skip ahead to some of the upcoming milestones and stepping stones on the zero-to-IPO route—*Structure Sales Agreements*, page 161, *Close Sales Agreements*, page 161, *Grow the Sales Capacity*, page 180, *Deliver Impressive Sales*, page 183, *Crank up the Sales Engine*, page 194.

Structure Sales Agreements

It can take time to prepare a sales agreement, especially if you have a new technology, revenue model or distribution channel. New laws are regularly introduced to make the life of startup entrepreneurs ever more difficult—and provide continued work for the lawyers themselves. The legal hurdles are compounded when you start to do business in international markets under different legal jurisdictions.

However, you need to have the agreement in place so that when you get a real live customer, you have a contract ready to sign. It's not a good idea to go through the sales process, then hold up the deal while you prepare an agreement—the customer knows it's a guinea pig at this stage and you look like you're not ready for business.

> If you go to store, whip out your credit card, and the attendant says—'sorry, we're not ready to take your money—can you come back tomorrow when we have a cash register', you don't exactly leave in the mode of satisfied customer. Heck, they did all the hard work getting you into the store and presenting you with merchandise that you want to buy—all they had to do was to get themselves in a position to take your cash.

A well thought-out sales agreement can be an asset to your company. If it's well worded and protects the interests of both buyer and seller, it shows that the company understands the business and cares about the customer. It will take time and energy to put in place, and the lawyers are sure to charge a healthy fee, but a good sales agreement is worth the investment. You don't really have a business without one.

Close Sales Agreements

You've developed the product, released it (in some shape or form), hired a salesperson, drawn up a sales agreement—now comes the time to start closing sales with real live customers. A fundamental principle of business is that customers are prepared to buy your product for hard cash. To traditional entrepreneurs this may seem like an obvious point to make—traditional companies have a huge focus on sales from day one. However, technology companies sometimes go through several years of research and development before they have a product to sell. They become accustomed to operating a company void of sales. Their funding comes from selling the dream to investors. Switching into sales mode is not always easy—people are naturally reluctant to changing the status quo and the sales efforts can be delayed by a state of inertia.

Closing your first sale is not always easy. Human beings are often reluctant to be first, especially when there are costs and risks involved. They like to follow the crowd. This is one of the situations where you need to harness the magical force of momentum (see *Maintaining Momentum*, page 29). The first customer needs to be so overwhelmed by the positive buzz around the company and the endorsement of the seed customers, press and everyone else, that she has no hesitation in signing the order. With sufficient momentum, evidence of marked progress and positive endorsements, the first customer may never suspect that she is, in fact, the first customer.

Customers have a tendency to defer the purchase until a later date—especially in the technology business where new products, prices and features are often just around the corner. Closing your first sales means selling the product that you have available today—and closing out the order. This may sound obvious but many salespeople in the technology sector have a tendency to try to sell products that may, or may not, be available at some future date and sometimes have problems converting a technical discussion into an order.

Everyone involved in the company should feel some relief when sales revenue starts to come in. It's an important step in the process of validating the concept and building a real business.

Hire an In-House Accountant

Up to this point, you may have outsourced your bookkeeping and accounting to a part-time freelancer or an outside service firm. See *Hire a Good Accountant*, page 79, *Outsource Everything that Moves*, page 111. Now that you have real sales coming in, the demands on your accounting system are going to grow significantly. It's a good time to hire a full-time in-house accountant.

A career as an accountant in a large corporation can be quite stable and mundane. Life is certainly more *lively* in a technology startup—accountants can find themselves under tremendous pressure. An important contributor to the business planning and fundraising process, with little or no cash on hand, the accountant has to deal with employees screaming for budget and creditors screaming for payment.

At this stage, you need an accountant that's comfortable working in a fast-paced environment and isn't freaked out with cash flow forecasts that are filled with red ink. You also need to make sure that he/she is au-fait with your accounting system, communicates well with your accounting firm and is prepared to adapt to the working style of the incoming CFO (see *Round out the Management Team*, page 182). The financial systems that are put in place are not only going to have to service the demands of a rapidly growing company, but they're also going to have to satisfy the extensive due diligence process of the auditors, the investment bankers, and the SEC in the run-up to IPO. Choose carefully—your first in-house accountant has an important role to play.

Build a Scalable IT Infrastructure

The IT infrastructure is a strategic component of any business today. For a technology company that's gearing up for rapid growth, it's mission critical. Not only does the corporate network contain part of all of the intellectual property, in the form of bits and bytes, but it also provides the communication platforms that enable your staff to interact with each other and the outside world. An IT failure can have disastrous consequences—losing computer files can destroy a company's core assets today. An IT inefficiency can prevent the company from gearing up and stifle the potential for growth.

Among other things, your IT infrastructure needs to provide:

- ✓ *Communications tools and facilities*—in addition to the e-mail and instant messaging systems the companies rely upon today, Jetsons-style video conferencing can replace the need for many face-to-face meetings and is available to virtually all PC users today. Workers connected up to the office network obviously share servers, printers and other services. Using VPN (virtual private networking), all the same services are available to workers with broadband, dial-up or wireless Internet connections at remote offices and other locations—like home, hotel room, coffee shop, beach, etc.

- ✓ *Productivity tools and facilities*—the IT department normally provides and supports essential productivity software such as word-processing, spreadsheets, graphics and presentation applications.

- ✓ *Mission-critical systems*—employees can become somewhat agitated if some form of IT crash prevents them from receiving their paychecks. In addition to payroll and accounting, most companies have a number of mission-critical systems, such as customer databases, software code repositories, that need to be up and running for the business to operate.

✓ *Web site and Internet services*—the company relies upon various web sites to provide information and communicate with employees and the outside world.

✓ *Protection from hardware failure*—hardware does crash, and unless the company has a regular backup system, mirrored services and failure detection alerts, the effects can be devastating.

✓ *Protection from software crashes*—regular backups, mirrored services and failure detection systems can also help minimize the effects of software crashes. If detected quickly, by monitoring the 'heart beat' of the application, it can be auto-restarted by software or a live technician. A second identical application may be standing by—ready to take over when the first one fails.

✓ *Protection from hackers*—firewalls need to be put in place and employees need education on the use of passwords if hackers are going to be prevented from hijacking your servers, crashing them, stealing or destroying your data.

✓ *Protection from viruses*—filtering software that detects and destroys viruses has to be placed at all points of entry to the corporate network—including the e-mail server and every employees PC.

✓ *Protection from copyright infringement lawsuits*—the company can find itself on the receiving end of some damaging legal action and publicity if employees make illegal, pirated copies of software—either intentionally or unintentionally. It's usually the responsibility of the IT department to provide software licenses, make sure they're up-to-date and educate employees on what they can and cannot do.

✓ *Protection from fire, flood, earthquake and other acts of God*—even the most sophisticated backups are worthless if they're housed in the same location and that location burns to the ground in a fire, or some other form of disaster. Backup and mirrored systems have to be located at separate, and ideally remote, locations.

In many ways, the company is dependent upon the IT system and the IT system is dependent upon the IT team. The team needs to be available 24x7, working rotas, permanently leashed to the company with beepers and mobile phones. Just like software and hardware, some of the individuals in the IT team will require a backup—in case they have their own personal system crash, or fall under a bus.

The architect of the IT system needs to be able to predict the future demands of growth and design an effective and scalable infrastructure. Building an effective and scalable IT infrastructure is critical for virtual every company today—none more so than a technology startup.

Set Up a Scalable Financial Management System

Hopefully, at this stage in the journey, your accounts will have migrated from basic tools like Excel or Quicken and you'll have all the foundations of a sophisticated financial management system in place—see *Set up a Bookkeeping & Accounting System*, page 108.

Few organizations expand as quickly or experience the growing pains of a successful technology startup. If you're going to make it all the way to IPO, the accounting and financial management system not only has to handle this growth, but it also has to pass the scrutiny of the auditors, investment banks and the SEC. Here are some considerations:

- ✓ *Scalability*—based on the nature of your business, the system may need to handle hundreds of suppliers, thousands of customers and millions of transactions.

- ✓ *Flexibility*—management will require a variety of reports and analyses viewing the data in many different ways. The accounts are also likely to be recast in preparation for the IPO, see *Restate Financials,* page 211.

- ✓ *Established standard*—it's a real advantage if the system is known and trusted by the incoming CFO, the auditors and other professionals that carry out due diligence on the company, as well as new members of the finance team.

Appoint an Advertising or Marketing Agency

At this stage in the journey, the company needs effective marketing to fuel expansion and support the sales efforts. Choosing an advertising or marketing agency, you follow the same process that you did in selecting the PR agency (see *Appoint a PR Agency*, page 120).

One important objective of marketing in a technology startup is to generate momentum (see *Maintaining Momentum*, page 29). This is usually achieved through a PR-led marketing campaign that features other people praising your product. Many technology companies, especially the ones with products for business (B-to-B), can get away with virtually no advertising whatsoever—the marketing mix consists of sales, PR, events and more sales. It's not so easy if you have a consumer product—establishing your own brand and your own route to market (B-to-C) can take 10 years and cost upwards of $100m. Most venture investors know this and steer clear of consumer companies at all cost. However, it is possible to reach consumers without breaking the bank—if you can get your product marketed and sold by someone else. The B-to-B-to-C model involves persuading one or more huge corporations to promote your product and deliver it to the customer through established routes to market (see *Route to Market*, page 227).

Must-Have Marketing Activities

✓ *Consistent, powerful message*—it's important that the company has a clear identity and everyone is singing from the same songbook. See *Formulate your Core Messaging and Corporate Identity*, page 87.

✓ *PR*—you need to help the press spread the message and news of your new product and technology. See *Appoint a PR Agency*, page 120, *Launch the Company*, page 130.

✓ *Trade shows & events*—not only do events provide a valuable source of sales leads but they raise awareness for the company with industry insiders.

✓ *Web site*—you're not considered a serious business today unless you have a web site. See *Create and Launch your Web Site*, page 101, *Publish a Corporate Web Site*, page 157, *Enhance & Upgrade your Web Site*, page 197.

Must-Have Marketing Materials

✓ *Glossy product brochures*—presenting the key features and benefits in a polished and professional way. Although they're not always read or believed, they are expected.

✓ *Competitive matrix*—single-page document listing how your product competes (favorably) with the competition.

✓ *Technical white paper*—many technical buyers bypass the brochures and head directly for the white paper. See *Publish a Technical White Paper*, page 103.

✓ *Customer case studies*—people like to see concrete examples of how the product has been used in a live customer environment. See *Seed Customers and Document their Positive Endorsements*, page 155.

✓ *Corporate brief*—corporate backgrounder with overview of the company, product, technology, market, business model, competition, financing, team, etc.

✓ *Press clippings*—stories and assessments by independent journalists carry much more weight than materials written by the company.

Whether your business is B-to-B or B-to-B-to-C, the ideal marketing campaign involves a large, established corporation promoting your product—out of its own pocket. As someone else is picking up the tab, you achieve an excellent bang for your buck. However, the value of the endorsement can be immeasurable. My product was demonstrated by Bill Gates in front of hundreds of journalists and VIP's, it was the star of a huge Intel TV ad campaign and promoted center-stage on trade show booths by some of the largest corporations in the world. Other than paying some out of pocket expenses, it didn't cost me a cent. With creative thinking, plenty of schmoozing and a little luck, small technology companies with cool products and small budgets can generate momentum and make a real buzz in the market.

Nice-to-Have Marketing Activities

✓ *Co marketing*—momentum gets a real boost when your product is promoted by someone else (especially a large, respected corporation).

Nice-to-Have Marketing Materials

✓ *Video materials*—people are always impressed with lively, upbeat customer testimonials, TV press clippings, promotional pieces, etc.

If PR can't generate sufficient momentum and customer demand, and you need to appoint an advertising or marketing agency, make sure you take the following criteria into consideration:

✓ *Tight budgets*—as a pre-IPO technology company, the agency needs to understand that you're not going to start spending like Proctor & Gamble.

✓ *Partnering and co-marketing*—the ideal agency will make introductions and actively help you participate in partners' campaigns.

Branding & Advertising in Technology Startups

It's important that you have a clear corporate identity and message (see *Formulate your Core Messaging and Corporate Identity*, page 87). However, successful technology companies typically spend their funds on product development and sales activities—and spend relatively little on brand awareness and ad campaigns. There are at least two very good reasons for this:

1. *Advertising is expensive*—agencies estimate the cost of establishing a new consumer brand in the U.S. at $70m or more.
2. *Every dollar taken out of the R&D budget weakens the company's core asset*—its technology.

In the dot-com bubble years, many startups blew out millions of dollars on

Superbowl ads—before filing for bankruptcy. Back in the real world, now that the bubbles have burst, extensive advertising and brand development is again restricted to huge multinational corporations. Established technology companies, like Microsoft, Intel and Dell, spend huge budgets on advertising and have universally recognized brands today. Executives entering the technology sector from other industries like fast moving consumer goods and Hollywood sometimes need a little time to adapt (see *Hire a Head of Marketing*, page 118). I championed Apple Computer's brand for several years, however, my alarm bells start ringing when I come across a technology startup spending its cash on fancy ad campaigns.

Go International

Don't wait until you have the U.S. market sewn up before you take your first steps to go international. If you wait until you've dominated the U.S. first, you may find that the best channels and distribution partners have already been tied up by your competitors.

As 3rd Party Channel Manager for Apple Computer Europe in the late 1980's, I was the point person helping U.S. companies establish distribution and marketing operations in Europe. I became very interested in this topic and my first foray as a book author was writing about international marketing and distribution. My interactions with Apple's developers followed some common patterns. A good conversation went as follows:

> Developer: *"We don't have any distribution in Europe—who should we talk to?"*
> Me: *"Here's a list of Apple Accredited Distributors that I've scrutinized to make sure they have the marketing, financial and technical resources to properly represent your company and sell products like yours."*
> Developer: *"Do you recommend we sign an exclusive deal with one distributor or several non-exclusive deals?"*
> Me: *"Do you want your product to be well promoted and supported in this market? "*
> Developer: *"Yes, of course."*
> Me: *"Do you have the budget to open a local office and establish your own marketing and support operation here?"*
> Developer: *"No. Not yet anyway."*
> Me: *"If you were a local distributor, would you spend your own money marketing a product if you had a non-exclusive arrangement and customers could buy if from your competitor?"*
> Distributor: *"I guess I wouldn't want to pay for the marketing if I was competing with other distributors that could benefit from my promotional spend and undercut my prices."*
> Me: *"So find a strong local partner that's prepared to spend its own money to launch, market and support your product in exchange for an exclusive agreement."*

Developer: *"But what if this partner doesn't perform?'*
Me: *"Good point: You need an out-clause giving you the freedom to switch to another distributor if this one doesn't deliver a minimum level of sales."*

Many sensible developers followed this advice and successfully launched their products in the UK and other European markets. Unfortunately, several of the conversations I had with developers started out differently:

Developer: *"I took an order and signed up an exclusive distributor at Comdex last year under the impression that I was partnering with a major player. I've since found it's a mom- and pop- operation working out of a garage. My product is not being promoted, the sales results are dismal and there's no local customer support. I'm locked in to an exclusive contract for another two years."*
Me: *"Set aside a budget to hire a good local lawyer and buy yourselves out of this mess. Then go out and find another partner. Carry out some checks on your partner this time."*

I once had a meeting with a guy in the UK that had just returned from a U.S. tradeshow gripping a distribution agreement with one of the largest networking companies in the world. Not only did he have exclusive rights to sell their products in the UK market for several years but he also had the right to use the trademarked name to form a local company. How he managed to swing this deal I'll never know. Apparently it was near the end of the quarter and the company was anxious to get his order on the books. This was a multi-billion dollar company, a household name that had signed away the UK market to a small cowboy operation. It didn't even qualify as a cowboy operation—more like a cowboy with dreams of one day setting up an operation. Someone at the head office soon figured out the mistake, sent in the lawyers and ended up shelling out a huge chunk of cash to buy the company out of the contract. This mistake set the company back several years and resulted in tons of embarrassing litigation. So, although the offer of an initial order may sound appealing, don't fall into the trap of signing a distributor until you've carried out some pretty thorough checks to verify that this is indeed a good long term partner for your company.

After setting up successful channels, some developers still managed to screw things up. I had several conversations with developers that went as follows:

Developer: *"My product was achieving great success in this country until I recently expanded my distribution channels from one exclusive partner to several non-exclusive distributors. Now no one seems to be promoting or supporting the product, sales have plummeted and I'm getting lots of complaints about customer service."*

> *Me: "Unless you go ahead and open your own local office and pay for your own marketing and support, you'll have to terminate these distributors and return to an exclusive arrangement with one single partner."*

The problem was that most of these developers had successful distribution deals with multiple channels in the U.S. and they thought that the same model could be applied to international markets. They often overlooked the fact that the U.S. distributors simply fulfilled demand—demand that the developer had created through its own local marketing efforts. There's little point setting up an international distributor to fulfill demand if there's no one creating the demand—and no demand to fulfill. What these companies needed was not just local distribution, but local representation. They needed a local partner that was committed to marketing and supporting the product as well as warehousing and shipping it.

The markets today are more dynamic and sophisticated but the same principles hold true. You need quality, committed representation to establish your product in overseas markets, and this normally means building long-term exclusive partnerships. Most successful technology startups go through the following steps on their way to establishing global operations:

1. *Hire a VP of International*—make sure you don't relegate this function to a junior position. Hire someone with experience and the capacity to grow a business that's at least as large as your U.S. operation.
2. *Localize the product*—to cater to different languages, standards and tastes.
3. *Appoint a local agent*—someone to scout out all the distributors and draw up a short list of potential partners.
4. *Appoint an exclusive full-service distributor*—make sure they have the incentive to promote and support your products. Hire a point-person for liaison and treat the distributor like an extension of your sales and marketing team.
5. *Form a local subsidiary*—at some point you probably want control of some of the larger overseas markets and you have the budget to setup your own local subsidiaries and fund marketing activities.
6. *Appoint multiple non-exclusive distributors*—as your subsidiary is generating the demand, you're now in a position establish multiple channels to fulfill it.

As you probably figured by now, I'm generally in favor of exclusive distribution arrangements, however, there are some interesting alternatives. If you don't find a single partner that can provide local marketing, customer support and product distribution, you may find that you can outsource each of these functions to specialist service providers. You shouldn't have a problem finding marketing agencies, customer support agencies and box-moving distributors in most of the larger countries. In the short run, this will likely be more costly than appointing a full-service distributor, but setting up local agencies to handle each function could provide you with more control and flexibility.

You may find local investors that offer some interesting options. In the late 1980's, Symantec had a strong foothold in the U.S. market and a tremendous opportunity to bring its products into Europe. Not wanting to leave its European fate in the hands of local distributors, the company was looking to establish a European head office. There was just one problem, the company was still private and didn't have the cash to fund a subsidiary until after the *IPO*. In fact the company was trying to look as profitable as possible in the run-up to the *IPO*. The solution it came up with was very interesting. A local investor stumped up the cash to establish the local Symantec office, then built it up and sold the business to Symantec after the *IPO*. The price was derived from a pre-arranged formula based on the performance of the subsidiary. It worked out to be a win-win situation for everyone. By distributing products to the local office, Symantec achieved the benefit of accelerating international sales revenues without the costs of setting up the local subsidiary. This helped dress up the figures for the *IPO*, the proceeds of which were used to acquire the subsidiary. The local investor made a good return on its investment and everyone was happy—at least as long as the Symantec share price held up. So in addition to approaching distributors, talking to local venture capitalists and other investors may open up some interesting alternatives for you.

Tips for Going International

✓ Think global from day one.

✓ Act global and go international at the first opportunity.

✓ Appoint one or more of your best people to set up the international operations.

✓ Don't be afraid to form long-term exclusive distribution partnerships.

✓ Treat your overseas partners like part of the team.

✓ Monitor street pricing and avoid huge cross-border price discrepancies.

✓ Make sure your product is being properly promoted and supported.

✓ Listen to feedback from your international customers.

✓ Pay for localization yourself.

Along with other developers, Apple had a gray market problem in Europe in the 1980's. Compared to buying a Mac from the local dealer, it was cheaper for the customer to fly to New York on Concorde and pick one up from there. Why bother putting local distribution channels in place if you're going to force customers to come to the U.S. when they want a reasonable price? I carried out a research project to figure out what was going on. It turned out that European customers were annoyed that the street price of most hardware and software products were much higher in Europe than they were in the U.S. U.S. magazines filled with competitive price advertising were readily available in most countries and the U.S. mail order companies were more than happy to ship overseas. So, due to the huge price differential, a 'gray market' channel developed for many popular products across Europe, bypassing the 'official' distributors. After ignoring the gray market for several years, Apple and other developers finally discovered that it was damaging to their business—not only were distributors unhappy that they were losing business, but customers were surprised to find that the U.S. warranties were not honored in Europe. Many customers, upset at what they considered price gouging, turned to software piracy. After conducting several customer surveys, the message was clear— 'We're not prepared to pay these high prices, we'd rather pirate software and buy our hardware directly from the U.S.'.

The real problem was that Apple and other developers didn't adjust their U.S. discount structures or pricing models to cater for international markets. In most cases they had no idea how their products were being priced in other countries. International customers are always going to pay some form of premium over the U.S. price, especially for U.S. products, but with a little care and attention you can make sure that this price differential is kept within a reasonable range. It's important to maintain some consistency of street prices across international markets and this likely involves offering deep discounts to your distribution partners. It's customary to offer the deepest discount to your largest customers, so offering the highest discount to small overseas distributors doesn't make sense at first glance—however, your international partners need a price break to help them pay for local demand-generation and customer support activities.

As well as speaking different languages, those darned foreigners make life complicated by having different regulations, power supplies, telephones, TV's and different standards of all types—they even drive on the wrong side of the road in some cases. So another issue you need to deal with when you go international is product localization. Some products need to be almost totally rebuilt from the ground up to make them suitable for international markets and others require only a few minor tweaks. There are plenty of specialist localization agencies in Silicon Valley and high-tech cities in the U.S. and many others located in far flung corners of the world that can translate your web sites and user manuals. Depending on your product, some are capable of taking the whole localization process off your hands — for a healthy fee. Whether you handle the localization in-house or in conjunction with an outside agency, you need to be prepared to set aside some budget for this work. You can't expect your distribution partner to pay for localization unless you offer a pretty generous long term exclusive arrangement. In fact, many U.S. developers that have allowed their distributors to take care of localization have found themselves in protracted litigation over who actually owns the localized product. There's no dispute over ownership if you pay for the localization yourself—you also retain complete freedom to grow and adapt your channels in future.

Once again, vast armies of international lawyers thrive on writing contracts and litigating disputes between U.S. vendors and overseas distributors. Each country and jurisdiction has its own legal minefields to navigate and you're well advised to hire the best local counsel to handle your affairs. Letters of intent that are not enforceable in the U.S., actually have teeth in Germany and other countries. You may find some contracts very difficult to terminate, especially in the EC. I've tried using a U.S. lawyer to handle European and Asian business but I always end up shelling out for local counsel.

Whatever your industry, you're sure to have potential customers located all over the globe. In today's market, you're unlikely to attract serious backing unless you have a global perspective. If you're going to have any chance of maximizing your market opportunity, put the international infrastructure in place as quickly as you can and get it right first time 'round—fixing problems later could be very costly.

Polish Your Business Plan Presentation

At this stage in the journey, investors are accustomed to seeing a polished business plan presentation. The company is beyond the stage of a raw startup and the vision of a passionate founder is no longer sufficient to convince investors to part with their cash in the forthcoming round of funding.

Investor Information Packs

In the Internet age, you can provide investors with information in a variety of ways:

✓ *Investor information pack*—a glossy printed folder with documents, brochures, videotapes, CD-ROM, etc.

✓ *Investor web site*—a password-protected web site containing the business plan and marketing materials in PDF or Microsoft Word format, the presentation as a downloadable Powerpoint slide show (or web page format), and links to the company's home page, press stories, and other online resources that may interest or excite the investor.

As always, you'll be unlikely to get a second chance to impress an investor, so the story has to be presented in a polished, entertaining and professional way—the pitch will likely be made by the CEO with glossy print materials, impressive presentation slides and entertaining audio-video support. Here are the components you need:

✓ *Marketing materials*—corporate brief, glossy product brochures, competitive matrix, technical white paper, customer case studies, customer testimonials, press clippings. *See Appoint an Advertising or Marketing Agency*, page 165.

✓ *Business plan*—short, concise well-written document in Microsoft Word or PDF format. See *Write a Business Plan*, page 72

✓ *Videotape*—with press clippings, customer testimonials and other materials. *See Appoint an Advertising or Marketing Agency*, page 165.

✓ *Slide show presentation*—with slides on executive summary, vision & mission, objectives, technology, market, competition, product strategy, sales strategy, partnership strategy, distribution strategy, marketing strategy, management team, financials. See *Present to Investors*, page 338.

To demonstrate momentum, the following slides should be added to the presentation and given special emphasis:

✓ *Milestones and stepping stones achieved to date*—highlight evidence of marked progress and achievement.

✓ *What they're saying*—demonstrate the positive buzz in the market through examples of press coverage, analysts, customer testimonials, competitors, industry insiders and other respected experts.

Cloned Presenter

A live presentation typically involves the presenter adding a verbal dialogue to a series of slides—a narrated slide show. Companies often send out the slide show to potential investors without the narration. Many slide shows are made up of cryptic bullet points on slides—without the narration, the slides are meaningless. If you haven't done so already, it's actually very simple to record a narration and add it to your slides:

- ✓ Plug a microphone into your PC—virtually any microphone will do.
- ✓ Use the 'Record Narration' feature in the 'Slide Show' menu of PowerPoint.

The CEO or business plan presenter doesn't have to be cloned and sent out to explain the meaning of each slide in the PowerPoint slide show. Now the presentation has the narration built in—whenever the slide is viewed, the narration will be played through the PC speakers.

Close Strategic Funding

After bringing a top-tier VC in to lead your first round, you'd ideally attract strategic investors to fund your second and subsequent rounds. 'Strategic investors' are typically respected high-tech corporations with deep pockets and real marketing muscle. Not only does the investment open the way to a strategic partnership, but a respected corporate investor like this sends a strong signal to the investment community and really helps generate momentum in your industry. An ideal strategic investor for a software company might be Microsoft. To most people it means a great deal to have Microsoft on your investor list. It means that the gurus in Redmond have checked out your technology and found that you really do have something unique and valuable. It means the financial and business folks from Redmond are anticipating the company to be big success and they expect a good return on their investment. Oh, I almost forgot, it also means that they're not planning on killing you—just yet. The more respected and more selective the corporation, the stronger the signal is.

However, corporations tend to jump into the venture capital business when it's booming and slink out as soon as the market get tough. Unlike traditional VC's, their money comes from parent-company cash flows, they don't have formal venture funds that need to be maintained and they can jump in and out of the venture investing business at the drop of a hat. At the peak of the dot-com fiasco in 2000, corporations invested $4.9bn in 608 deals in the first 9 months alone (*source: Venture Economics*). Just one year later, they'd cut back to $845m in just 127 deals for the same period—a drop of over 80%. It's not surprising that corporate investors are heading for the hills—according to Corporate Venturing Report, they wrote off $9.5bn in losses in a single quarter in 2001! However, if you can pull it off, securing a strategic investor in difficult market conditions like these sends an even stronger signal to the market.

The largest corporate investors are high-tech companies like Intel, Microsoft, Compaq & AT&T. Of course, these folks like to see good financial returns but they have other reasons for investing in private startups. Over the years, Intel has invested in just about any type of product that pushes up the demand for newer, faster processors—if the company does well, Intel gets a financial reward, but it also benefits from increased demand for its own products. Another reason for a corporate investment is to open the door for a subsequent acquisition—not only do the strategic investors get a stake in the company but they get to know what's going on from the inside (especially if they take a seat on the board). Corporate as well as traditional VC's get to see thousands of business plans and they're in a privileged position to keep up to date with the latest industry and technology developments—this can be a valuable source of information for many strategic investors. So, you may want to tweek your business plan, or at least the introductory letter, to spell out where the strategic fit is with each target corporation. You certainly want to explore the fit and allude to the direct and the indirect benefits when you get a chance to make a presentation.

In your dreams, your existing lead VC brings in several strategic investors, leads a second round of funding at a nice high valuation and you suddenly find yourselves with some strong strategic investors and a war chest of cash in the bank. In the AcmeTech Startup, Inc. example, the company raises $15m at a valuation of $30m (pre-funding) and one of the strategic investors puts a friendly and impressive individual on the board or directors. As you probably figured out by now, on the journey from *Zero-to-IPO* your dreams seldom come true. Here are some of the obstacles you could encounter:

×   *Your lead VC does nothing to help you attract new investors*—some lead VC's can be very pro-active in helping their portfolio companies secure funding from strategic and other later-stage investors, but many companies have gone bust waiting for their VC's to go out and raise funds on their behalf. Guess what, it normally comes down to management to get out there and start knocking on doors. Even if you have the hottest product on the planet, strategic investors are unlikely to come knocking on your door with checkbooks in hand. You're going to have to pull together a list of investor targets, hit the phone, send out tons of e-mails and pull whatever strings you can to win the opportunity to make your pitch in front of live decision-makers (see *Appendix 3—Gathering your Provisions—The Fundraising Process*, page 325). Just make sure that someone is left running the company—when the management team is busy raising funds.

×   *Your lead VC in the first round doesn't want to participate in the second round*—this not a good signal to the other investors, even if there's a legitimate reason for the decision and it doesn't involve the investor losing confidence in the company. At this point, you need to go out and find a VC or financial investor to lead the round as strategic investors will rarely take on the task, which brings me on to my next point...

×   *None of your strategic investors are prepared to lead*—they don't want the responsibility or the hard work of fixing the price and negotiating the round. They also know that financial investors don't like to pay over the odds and they want to get the same deal.

×   *Your strategic investors don't like your lead investor*—even when they're making money, investors with humongous egos sometimes clash—imagine how ugly it gets when they're all posting gazillion dollar losses! I once thought I'd found an ideal lead—a top-tier Sand Hill Road VC. I was surprised when my strategic investor objected on the grounds that the partner had once written a magazine article that it didn't agree with. How could I have predicted that?

×   *Your lead investor doesn't like your strategic investors*—there's bad blood swilling all over the investment community. Sometimes it's just personal animosity, sometimes its deep-rooted corporate feuding.

- ✗ *Your lead investor wants to take the whole round*—after you bring in the lead investor, at the request of the strategic investors, the lead often decides that it wants the whole round. This is not unusual as most top-tier VC's need a minimum 15-20% ownership position in the company and they like to push the corporate investors out to later rounds at higher valuations.

- ✗ *Your strategic investors don't get along*—you probably wouldn't want Bill Gates and Larry Ellison on your board. Larry and Bill aren't exactly drinking buddies and it's highly unlikely that Microsoft and Oracle would happily co-invest in your company. High tech industries are filled with corporations that just don't like each other—some rivalries are obvious when the two parties are competing head-on, but there are many rivalries that are not obvious and may be difficult to predict.

- ✗ *Two or more strategic investors demand a board seat*—you can't go giving board seats to every investor. In fact, it's unlikely that you'll have more than one board seat available to represent each class of share (and each round of funding). In the AcmeTech Startup, Inc. example, the company appoints a representative from one strategic investor to the board. Of course you can create two or more board seats, but that's not really an ideal solution (see *Board of Directors,* page 54). You can try offering a seat on the advisory panel to one of the investors, with observation rights that allow the representative to attend all or part of the board meetings. You may want to try offering both strategic investors advisory panel seats instead and try to find a 'neutral' board member with whom they both feel comfortable.

- ✗ *One strategic investor demands preferential terms over the others*—as they often provide credibility, routes to market, marketing and other support, a corporate investor can add significant value above and beyond mere cash. If one investor feels it's adding more value, it may request preferential terms over the others. Of course, there are many ways to give one investor preferential treatment—even if the terms of the round appear to be identical for everyone. The investor could pay for some of its shares in cash and the remainder in 'kind', it could be provided with warrants to buy more shares in future at today's price, it could get a board seat with associated stock options. However, the other investors may object to this special treatment and ideally, you'll bring all the investors in on the same footing. One tactic you could try in this situation is good old fashioned 'charm'—you tell the investor that, although you're not able to offer preferential terms, you recognize and appreciate the contribution that it's making. This strategy, of 'sucking up' to make investors and other people feel appreciated, has of course been known to work wonders in all areas of business.

- ✗ *Your existing investors refuse to accept the terms you agree with your new investors*—a round of funding normally needs to be approved by the existing investors. If a majority of your series A investors don't agree to the terms of your series B round, you're stuck. You can't go ahead with the round without approval—if you're not in a position to raise new funds, this could kill the business. Most investors will see sense and either invest themselves or approve the new round.

Coordinating a group of strategic investors into a round of funding can be something of a challenge. When you do want them to flock together, they don't. When you don't want them to flock together, they do. Just when you get one headed in the right direction, the others seem to head in the wrong direction—it can be like herding cats. Like many milestones on the journey from *Zero-to-IPO*, a good lead VC can make a huge difference when it comes to closing a strategic round of funding with corporate investors.

Destination IPO Expansion Stage

Close Mezzanine
Funding

Appoint an Investment Bank

Turn a Profit   Start to Act Like a Public Company

Deliver Impressive Sales   Round-out the Management Team

Release Best-of-Breed Product Range   Grow the Sales Capacity

Structure a Public Company Board

Expansion Stage

Close Strategic
Funding

Grow the Sales Capacity

Management now needs to build an effective and scalable sales force. In parallel with closing sales and delivering ever-increasing quarterly results, the VP of sales has to build the foundations for a sales infrastructure that will endure for years to come.

The break down of the sales revenue can also be very important—investors are justifiably nervous about any over-reliance on a small number of customers or distributors. The ideal scenario is to balance the sales across a variety of customers, product lines and channels of distribution. This doesn't mean firing sales people that bring in large orders that would skew the figures or turning away large customers—but it does mean actively establishing a number of parallel sales efforts.

A good sales professional will develop a deep understanding of the customer buying process and create a sales process to match—this means providing information and assistance to help the customer step through each stage in the buying process. In building the foundations of a sales force, a number of questions have to be answered:

- ✓ *Organization*—are the sales territories divided by geographical region, customer type or product line?

- ✓ *Inside vs. outside sales*—does the company have an inside sales team that contacts customers through the telephone and Internet, an outside sales team out on the road or a combination of the two?

- ✓ *Channels of distribution*—how can the company establish, utilize and support alternative channels of distribution and avoid channel conflict?

✓ *International*—how can the company reach international markets (see *Go International*, page 168).

✓ *Remuneration*—how are salespeople and sales managers compensated in terms of base salary, commissions, guarantees, profit sharing, bonus and stock option programs?

✓ *Contests and incentives*—how do you use sales rallies, competitions and rewards to motivate the salespeople and encourage them to compete?

✓ *Marketing support*—how does the sales force interact with the marketing group?

✓ *Internet and automation technologies*—how can the Internet be used to streamline the sales process and provide customers with product and order-status information? Can it free salespeople from time-consuming administrative tasks?

✓ *Training*—how are sales representatives going to keep up-to-date with the latest product information, marketing promotions, sales programs, selling skills and technology?

✓ *Reporting systems*—how does the company capture information on sales activities and status reports on specific prospects? When one salesperson leaves the company, how will the replacement be able to pick up and continue the sales efforts? As the sales force grows and the reporting demands increase, many sales managers migrate from relatively simple systems like Microsoft Outlook, through more comprehensive systems like Goldmine to sophisticated online services like Salesforce.com.

✓ *Forecasting*—are sales forecasts derived from a sophisticated computer system or the back of an envelope?

Release Best-of-Breed Product Range

The primary purpose of a technology startup is to provide the world with cutting-edge technology and package it up into a product that helps customers solve a problem, do things they couldn't do before, cut costs, save time—or all of the above. This may sound a little obvious but technology startups sometimes go off track when management forgets that technology is at the core of the company and they focus attention in other areas, at the expense of the product.

What do we mean by 'Product'?

You may not be selling a complete shrink-wrap product but some enabling technology. Technology can be deployed in a variety of ways—see *How is Your Technology Deployed?*, page 73. For the purpose of this book, let's define the company's product as intellectual property, code, whatever it is that the customer buys—other than services.

The company is never going to generate sales and grow through the expansion stage unless the product is fully working and in *Final Release* state (see *Release the Product*, page 148). An 'insanely great' product will generate momentum and fuel expansion. With a 'me-too' product, the company is unlikely to excite Wall Street investors and make it all the way to IPO.

It's not enough to simply have a best-of-breed product, but you need to show evidence that it is, indeed best in it's class, from reputable, independent third parties—customers, journalists, analysts, etc. Awards are useful endorsements, but you can also compile evidence through customer surveys, articles and testimonials.

Even with a front-running position today, you need to show that you have a pipeline to stay ahead of the pack and continue to produce best-of-breed products in future. This may involve strengthening the research and development team to make sure you have the vision and leadership to stay ahead of the competition for several years to come.

Round-out the Management Team

With best-of-breed products, sales are about to flow in and the company is set to expand at a rapid pace. Many of your managers should have been in place for some time—see *Hire a Career CEO*, page 145, *Hire a VP of Sales*, page 160, *Hire an In-House Accountant*, page 162, *Hire a Head of HR*, page 109, *Hire a Head of Marketing*, page 118. In preparation for the upcoming growth, and in advance of the IPO, this is the time to round out the management team:

- ✓ *Chief Financial Officer*—ideally, you'll find an individual with a solid track record of managing public company finances who's already accepted and trusted by Wall Street investors.

- ✓ *General Counsel*—with the sheer volume and the complexity of the upcoming work, it's now expensive and impractical to leave all the legal issues to an outside firm.

- ✓ *Other executives*—dependent upon the nature of your business, the individuals you have in-place already, and the success you've achieved at reaching your milestones, you may need to strengthen the team with the addition of a Chief Information Officer, Chief Technology Officer or another senior executive.

Obviously, to manage the company's growth you need the best team you can assemble, but it's also crucial that the CFO and other key executives are up-to-speed with all aspects of the business well in advance of the IPO—the due diligence process and the road show are going to put the team under a great deal of scrutiny.

The appointment of impressive individuals can demonstrate momentum, add credibility and boost the company's standing on Wall Street as well as your industry. Many appointments, especially CFO positions, are followed by an investment-community oriented press release:

> *'AcmeTech Startup is pleased to announce the appointment of Sid Cash to the position of CFO. A seasoned professional, Mr. Cash has an impressive track record of driving technology-related companies toward growth and profitability. His expertise will be instrumental in building AcmeTech Startup into a strong, high-growth company and a successful candidate for IPO.'*

Of course, you're going to have to offer a competitive salary and benefits package, however, stock options are the primary incentive for these positions—see *Create a Stock Option Plan*, page 95. Senior positions at this stage in the company's growth are often filled by executive search firms, however, if you have the time, the connections and the bandwidth, it's sometimes more effective, and less costly, to fill them directly. See *Executive Search Firms*, page 402, *Hire a Career CEO*, page 145, *Prepare for a Recruitment Ramp-Up*, page 109.

Start to Act Like A Public Company

In anticipation of the IPO, you need to review all your records, systems and procedures and begin to think and act like a public company. If you followed the Zero-to-IPO route, the accounts and systems will have been structured under the supervision of IPO-savvy accountants and lawyers. However, it's not unusual to uncover issues that could hold up the IPO process. Several steps can be taken at this point to prepare the company for the transition from private to public corporation:

> ✓ *Review accounts and adopt GAAP accounting standards*—take particular interest in revenue recognition, allocation of software development costs, investor rights, treatment of acquisitions and mergers, employee compensation issues such as severance agreements, cheap or excessive stock option allocations. See *Carry out the Financial Audit and Due Diligence,* page 208.

✓ *Prepare to deliver annual and quarterly SEC filings*—the system needs to be established and the team needs to be prepared to produce accurate and regular reports conforming to the requirements of the SEC.

✓ *Establish corporate communications policies*—in preparation for the Quiet Period and the subsequent restrictions on who says what to whom, PR and general communications policies need to be established and employee education programs put in place. See *Go Quiet*, page 204.

✓ *Review legal agreements, licenses and issues*—pay particular attention to technology ownership issues such as assignment of third-party inventions, patent, copyright and trademark registrations.

✓ *Adopt and enforce written policies and procedures*—document the systems and guidelines that define how the company operates and how employees are expected to act.

✓ *Establish an investor relations function*—the team and infrastructure needs to be put in place for dealing with shareholders, analysts, brokers and business media. See *Prepare to Interact with Public Investors*, page 216.

Preparing ahead of time can smooth the transition and minimize the risk of nasty surprises later on.

Deliver Impressive Sales

After years of training, months of preparation and weeks of predictions and psychological warfare, there comes a time when a prizefighter stands alone in the ring. The lights glare, the crowd hushes and the bell rings. The time for posturing, chest thumping and fancy talking is over. It's time to perform. As Joe Louis once said: 'you can run but you can't hide'.

After generating momentum, creating the hype, talking the talk and achieving the milestones on the route from Zero-to-IPO, there comes a time when your startup also has to perform. It's time to deliver impressive sales. The sales pipeline has to spew out ever increasing quarterly sales results and management has to see this activity as a top priority. From this point on there will be a huge focus on sales. You can run but you can't hide.

So what defines *Impressive Sales*? This figure differs from industry to industry and company to company. What I can tell you is that you're going to have to turn a profit and impress the heck out of investment bankers and Wall Street investors if you're going to achieve a successful IPO—see *Turn a Profit*, page 185, *Are you Ready to*

IPO, page 201. With your cost structure and a spreadsheet, it shouldn't take a rocket scientist to work out what *impressive sales* means for your company.

If orders fail to materialize at this point, and you have reason to question the strength of the sales pipeline, it may be time to take your bearings and pull out your contingency plans—see *Taking your Bearings*, page 34, *Long Haul Contingency Plans*, page 59.

Delivering impressive sales should not be a problem if you've followed the route, and achieved the milestones and stepping-stones along the way—especially the ones related to building a great product and putting in place an effective sales infrastructure, see *Hire a VP of Sales*, page 160, *Grow the Sales Capacity*, page 180, *Release Best of Breed Products*, page 181.

Turn a Profit

Due to the up-front research and development costs, it normally takes some time before a technology company turns a profit—and even longer before it starts to generate positive cash flow. Investors like technology companies because they operate in new, high-growth markets and, in theory, the technical barriers to entry deter competition, lead to higher margins and huge profits—once the company is established and has a critical mass of sales. Looking at the profit and loss account for Microsoft, you'll see that the software business can be highly profitable—when your product consists of bits and bytes, the actual cost of sales can be very low. Once established, product-oriented technology companies are expected to deliver profits higher than industrial age companies, service companies and just about everyone else.

Of course, a profit and loss account that looks like a miniature version of Microsoft or Intel would be fantastic. However, pre-IPO, any profits will do—as long as they're real and not the result of a complicated accounting conjuring trick.

Turning a profit is the true sign of a healthy company. It also sends a series of important signals to the rest of the world:

- ✓ You have a product.
- ✓ There's a market for your product.
- ✓ Management knows how to sell it.
- ✓ Management knows how to support it.
- ✓ Management knows how to control costs.

    ✓ The underlying business model is profitable.

    ✓ Management knows how to run a profitable business.

    ✓ Profits are a management priority!

Appoint Investment Bank

In preparation for the mezzanine stage and the run up to IPO, you need an investment bank. And, like lawyers, you need the biggest, most expensive investment bank you can find. Among other things, investment banks provide you with access to public stock markets—they have all the secret handshakes and know how to open doors on Wall Street.

Investment Banks, also known as *Merchant Banks* and *Underwriters* make lots of money. They make money when you IPO. They make money from any secondary offerings. They make money when the company makes acquisitions. They make money if the company itself is acquired. Investment bankers have figured out one of the best get rich quick schemes on the planet. I'm not going to encourage my kids to be entrepreneurs. I'm going to encourage them to be investment bankers. Or lawyers. Or investment banking lawyers. There you go. The perfect job—an investment banking lawyer. I think I'll start brainwashing my kids with this as soon as they give up their plans to become professional soccer players. It's for their own good.

The process of appointing an investment bank is very similar to the process you would go through to appoint any form of agency; however, there is one difference—investment banks are very picky. They'll only talk to you if you've hit your milestones, you have a valuable business already and there's a serious chance of them making gazillions of dollars from your IPO or other financial transactions. Don't even bother calling if there's little chance of them making several million dollars from you in the coming months.

So, let's assume you've hit your milestones and made it to this point on the journey

Appoint Investment Bank

Negotiate Terms

Make Selection

Take up References

Bake-Off

Shortlist Candidates

Approach Candidates

List Candidates

Define Objectives

Define Objectives

Before you approach any investment banks, think carefully about what you want from the relationship. On this route to IPO, your immediate investment banking needs are pretty clear:

- ✓ *Raise the mezzanine round of funding.*
- ✓ *Underwrite the IPO.*

Following the IPO, you may want some additional services:

- ✓ *Secondary public stock offerings.*
- ✓ *Support for your investor relations program.*
- ✓ *Acquisitions*—helping you buy companies.
- ✓ *Acquisitions*—helping you sell the company.

As with all advisors and agencies, it takes time and money to switch partners, so you're ideally looking for a relationship that will endure for several years. If the relationship works well for the first phase—private placement of the mezzanine round—you'll want to continue the relationship for the IPO and beyond. However, to ensure that the terms are competitive, you may still want to open up the IPO assignment to a number of competing bids. In this scenario, you won't be guaranteeing the bank will win your IPO assignment up-front, but you can let them know that you do value long-term relationships and, if they're competitive on their IPO bid, there's little reason to go with anyone else.

Clearly defining your plans and objectives will help when it comes to approaching investment banks.

List Candidates

Investment banks come in various shapes and sizes. Wall Street investors do take notice of who you team up with—signing one of the big, respected firms like Goldman Sachs or Morgan Stanley will certainly attract attention to your company and likely provide instant credibility. Smaller banks, however, may offer a more personalized and effective service.

Pulling together names from your lawyers, accountants, board members, investors and the resource guide in the back of this book, draw up a list of candidates. See *Investment Bank Lists*, page 395. As you did when you raised funds from investors, rank them with the best candidates at the top—these are the ones you're going to contact first.

Approach Candidates

The top-tier investment banks often work with the top-tier VC's, lawyers and accounting firms—so your best way of making initial contact is through a personal introduction from one of your advisors or investors. The objective is to set up a meeting at which you can make your pitch to the bank and the bank can make its pitch to you. If you don't have too many contacts and management is busy running the day-to-day business, you may want to consider bringing in an outside consultant to act as a finder—making the introductions, setting up the meeting and guiding you through the whole partnering process.

It's important that your presentation is well prepared and polished—the banker will be assessing your presentation capabilities as well as the state of your business. The presentation should be delivered by your CEO with the support of the CFO—the same team that will be used to present to investors.

Don't be surprised to receive the red-carpet treatment if you've hit your milestones, the company is in good shape, the bankers and analyst understand where you fit in the market and they decide they want to win your assignment. You may glimpse a world of private jets, private clubs and ritzy hotels. You should get to know pretty quickly if they're interested in your business.

Shortlist Candidates

In assessing the merits of one bank over another, here are some questions to consider:

✓ *Does the bank want your business?* If it's not excited about working with you, there's little point in taking the discussions any further.

✓ *What's the banks stature?* When you mention the banks name to Wall Street investors do they react with '*Wow!*' or '*Who?*'

✓ *Can your team work with their team?* How would you feel if you were locked up with these people in close quarters for many long days and nights? You're going to spend many stressful hours with these people so you need to make sure that they're pleasant, or at least tolerable.

✓ *Who are its partners?* Can the bank assemble an effective syndicate of other banks to handle a future IPO?

✓ *What experience does the team have of your particular industry? How clued up is the analyst?* Has the bank prepared reports on your market? Has it worked with other companies in this sector?

✓ *Can it satisfy your long term needs as well as short term?* Ideally, you're forming a partnership that will continue beyond the first assignment—so you need some assurance that this bank, and the team assigned to your account, will be able to provide the ongoing services your need.

✓ *Does it have the resources to deliver? Will the bank commit an analyst to follow the company?* How well geared up is the bank to distribute your shares to both individual and institutional investors? How is it positioned to maintain visibility through analyst reports and ongoing research? How well does it do all the things that investment banks do?

Having met with a number of candidates and considered these points, you should have a good gut feeling about which ones should make it to the shortlist.

Bake-Off

Companies often put investment banks through the process of a bake-off. The candidates swoop in on private jets and essentially wait in line to pitch for the work. Companies go for the bake-off as it's a good opportunity to compare and contrast the different candidates. Board directors and CEO's secretly opt for a bake-off as it boosts their egos to see high-flying bankers grovel for their business. Personally, I wouldn't invite candidates that had little or no chance of winning the business. A bake-off is standard practice and the banks will likely be willing to participate if they want your business badly enough.

Take up References

It's always good practice to check references before making a final selection. Investment banks make no secret about the deals they've recently completed—and often use their client list as a key component of the pitch. The bankers would prefer to provide you with their own list of references, but you'll obviously get a more independent and unbiased perspective if you make your own random selection from the client list—if you're going to do this, you might want to clear this with the bank before you start making calls. In taking references, you get the most useful insights when you ask specific questions and drill down for details on areas of interest.

You can actually carry out the equivalent of an online background check of the disciplinary record of the bank through the web site of the National Association of Securities Dealers— www.nasdr.com.

Make Selection

You've met the candidates, digested the proposals, taken up references and now you should be in a position to make your selection. This is a strategic decision that normally requires the approval of the board, or at least the involvement of one or more members of the board working in conjunction with the CEO and management team.

While you still have a number of alternatives up your sleeve, this is a good time to start to negotiate terms with the selected bank—you can tell them that, assuming you can reach agreement on terms, you've decided to give them the business. Don't burn any bridges with the other candidates—your first pick might not work out for one reason or another and you may soon be looking for an alternative.

Negotiate Terms

You're looking for a long-term investment banking relationship that will likely encompass private placement fundraising of your mezzanine round, the subsequent IPO and potential merger and acquisition (M&A) activity, so you want some guidelines as to how each of these arrangements will be structured. Each deal will probably have its own contract and its own negotiation process. Typically, the private placement of the mezzanine round will be structured using the template of an amended Lehman formula—usually providing the bank with a retainer and a percentage of the funds raised (see *Lehman Formula*, page 328). The subsequent IPO will be negotiated separately (see *Assemble the IPO Team*, page 206).

Investment banks are expert negotiators. They're so good that they've had to form their own watchdog group, the National Association of Securities Dealers (NASD) to prevent them from making too much money. While virtually every other industry association in the world concentrates on helping its members make *more* money, this one concentrates on making sure its members don't make *too much*! So don't be surprised if you find the negotiation process something of a challenge. Investment banks are notorious for dragging their feet when it comes to signing any form of agreement or commitment with their clients—they often delay the signing of the IPO agreement to the evening before the IPO itself. They have also been accused of using the time between the commencement of the engagement and the signing of the contract to pick away at the deal—denying an intentional *bait and switch* maneuver, they'll likely argue that their market analysis and due diligence work has unearthed information that makes the deal significantly less appetizing than they initially calculated. This is one battle that management is probably going to have to fight on its own—the NASD doesn't really enter the scene until it comes time to IPO, and banks like to hold these negotiations behind closed doors when there are no lawyers or accountants to back you up. They also tend to renegotiate at a critical phase in the process when management is feeling most vulnerable.

So, brace yourself for a fun negotiation process. After you've reached agreement, write down the agreed terms in the form of a letter of intent. It's also a good idea to set a date for signature of the final agreement and agree on guidelines regarding conditions that might lead to terms being modified between the signings of the letter of intent and the final agreement.

Appoint Investment Bank

For most investment banks, the assignment starts with the signing of the letter of intent. Your objective at this point is to get the investment banking team up to speed as quickly as possible—getting in their faces and chasing them up will help your assignment take priority over those of other clients.

<u>Close Mezzanine Funding</u>

In the run-up to IPO, a mezzanine round of funding not only strengthens the balance sheet by boosting the cash on hand, but also provides a valuable boost to momentum. Often arranged by the investment bank, the mezzanine round sends a signal to Wall Street that the company is preparing for IPO—with the endorsement and participation of respected investors. Mezzanine funds can be used to cover the cost of restructuring in advance of the IPO, boost the pipeline of sales and raise awareness through marketing programs. If it's large enough, it can also provide a contingency fund in case the IPO is cancelled or postponed.

Literally meaning 'middle', a 'mezzanine' usually refers to a bridge or connecting level between two floors of a building. To create confusion, the term is used to describe various financial scenarios—*mezzanine capital* describes funding that bridges the gap in a company's capital structure between equity and senior debt and *mezzanine loan* refers to a commercial real-estate loan, similar to a second mortgage. In this book, *mezzanine funding* is used to describe a round that bridges the gap between venture funding and the IPO.

In the capitalization table for our imaginary company, AcmeTech Startup, (see *Setup your Capitalization Table*, page 93) we assume that the mezzanine round is structured as a $20m sale of series C stock (equity). This is typical of how many of these rounds are structured; however, mezzanine rounds often feature debt as well as equity. Of course, the downside of raising the funds through equity is that it dilutes the ownership position of the other shareholders. The downside of taking the funding as debt is that it weakens the balance sheet—at a time when the company's financials are about to come under tremendous scrutiny. If the funding is arranged in the form of debt, it is usually accompanied with some form of equity participation (or 'kicker'), frequently in the form of options or warrants to buy shares at preferential rates in future. The wide range of financial instruments and structures available to mezzanine investors is beyond the scope of this book, however, the section on *Raising a Bridge Loan*, page 262, provides an example as to how a loan can be arranged with equity warrant coverage.

To set the stage for the IPO, it's important that the mezzanine investors are well known and respected on Wall Street, or wherever it is that public investors hang out these days. Mezzanine investing attracts different types of investors, as it's typically more lucrative than investing in public companies, or IPO's, and less risky than early stage venture capital. As well as arranging the funding with specialists mezzanine funds, venture investors, insurance companies and corporate investors, investment banks often participate through their own in-house funds (see *Hiring a Professional Fundraiser*, page 327 and *Appoint Investment Bank*, page 186). This private placement funding may be a good opportunity to cement the relationship with the investment bank in advance of your IPO.

At the mezzanine stage, it's important to assemble investors that are unlikely to sell the stock at the first opportunity—the ideal investor will hold the stock for several years beyond IPO. A mezzanine shareholder dumping stock on the public markets can jeopardize investor confidence and trigger a Wall Street sell-off of your stock.

As you're now only a matter of months away from *IPO*, your investment bank will be in a position to compare the company's performance with existing public companies, and help set a valuation that's based on current public share prices in your sector. The company is still private, and the stock is hardly liquid, so they're sure to take the public market valuation and apply a discount. A mezzanine round valuation of $50-100m is not unusual for a technology company, but the price really depends on the current climate on Wall Street—and this is somewhat difficult to predict (see *What's it Worth? Valuing the Company*, page 301).

Destination IPO **Mezzanine Stage**

IPO

Prepare to Interact with Public Investors

Set the Share Price

Present the IPO Roadshow

File Registration Documents with the SEC

Draft the Prospectus & other Documents

Carry out the Financial Audit & Due Diligence

Assemble the IPO Team

Go Quiet

Brace the Company for the IPO Process

Take Decision to IPO

Enhance the Web Site

Appoint Marquee Names to the Board

Crank up the Sales Engine

Mezzanine Stage

Close Mezzanine
Funding

Crank up the Sales Engine

Going into the IPO process, the company should have a market leadership position and a strong pipeline of sales. At this point, the foundations for the sales team should have been built and the company should have been delivering impressive sales for some time (see *Grow the Sales Capacity*, page 180, and *Deliver Impressive Sales*, page 184). In a normal IPO market, the sales should be sufficient to turn a profit (see *Turn a Profit*, page 185) and impress investment bankers and Wall Street investors (see *Are You Ready for IPO?* page 201).

Wall Street investors like quarterly sales results that are not only impressive but also predictable. A pipeline that's packed with orders will enable management to accurately forecast the sales results several quarters out. Analysts are extremely impressed by companies that consistently deliver on their sales forecasts. They also like to plot sales results as smooth lines rising from the bottom left to the top right of the chart—they get nervous when they see one quarterly result that doesn't fit a regular pattern (even if it's higher than they expect). The ideal scenario is that you structure your sales agreements in such a way that you have some flexibility regarding how the revenues are recognized and spread across various quarters—this not only helps smooth out the chart but also helps make future quarters more predictable.

Predictable Sales Results

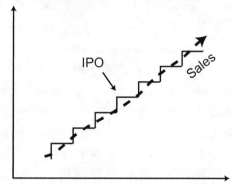

You need a solid pipeline of sales that will deliver growing sales results through the IPO and several quarters beyond. A good use of the funds raised in the mezzanine round is to invest in growing the sales team, adding new channels of distribution, improving marketing support and funding various efforts to boost the sales capacity. This is not a good time to allow management distractions to cause a dip in results—it's time to throw everything you can into the sales effort.

Appoint Marquee Names to the Board of Directors

In advance of the IPO, this is the time to expand the size of the board from five to seven members—see *A Team for the Long Haul*, page 54 (*Board of Directors* section). The magic number doesn't *have* to be seven—you could have five, nine or even eleven but seven is what most investors have come to expect. Obviously, what the board *does* is important, but at this point, it's crucial to consider how the board *looks*—especially to Wall Street investors. Ideally, in advance of the IPO, you'll be able to appoint marquee names to the board—individuals that are already well known and respected by public investors. This is what you're looking for in your new directors:

- ✓ *Independence*—independent directors, without direct affiliations with the company, or any potential conflicts of interest, are expected to provide unbiased guidance and better protect the interest of shareholders.

- ✓ *Track record*—public investors like to invest in companies directed by individuals with track-records of building successful businesses and making money for investors in the past.

✓ *Ability to work with the team*—a friendly and functional board is more effective (and fun). Pulling together a group of marquee names doesn't automatically mean you're assembling a functional team. A good Chairman will help mould a team, but you need to search for individuals with compatible chemistry. The last thing you need at this stage is a dysfunctional board.

✓ *Willingness & ability to commit time*—you need board members that regularly attend meetings and are active participants in the business.

✓ *Specialist skills*—board members can bring valuable insights into management, finance, marketing and other valuable areas of expertise.

✓ *Experience*—many investors like to see you appoint veterans that have served on other public company boards and have successfully directed other companies through similar phases of growth.

✓ *Overall good judgment*—the board is going to make decisions that have the potential to make or break the company. You can't get a PhD in good judgment but it's probably the most important characteristic you can find.

Directing a Public Company

Boards have more responsibility and are more visible than ever before—sophisticated investors pay attention to the boards' roster and value the shares, in part, on the profile of the board members. The Nasdaq and other stock markets also set certain standards for corporate governance that you need to be aware of when structuring and operating your board.

The primary function of a public company's board is to oversee the management of the company and to make sure the company acts in the best interests of its shareholders. At a minimum, directors are expected to show loyalty and diligence to the company by attending meetings (quarterly meetings are the standard), keeping informed on issues relevant to the company's activities and remaining responsive to the needs of shareholders. Besides these basic monitoring roles, directors should act as mentors, helping to guide the company's management in their own specific areas of expertise.

Board Committees

Forming specialist committees enables directors to channel their expertise into specialized areas and produce a more functional board. At the very least, the company should establish the following committees:

✓ *Audit committee*—each of the major stock markets require that all listed companies have an audit committee. The audit committees' job is to oversee (in conjunction with the independent auditors) the accounting and financial controls of a company, the financial reporting process and the internal audit function. The Nasdaq stock market actually requires the audit committee to have a minimum of three members and be comprised of independent directors only.

✓ *Nominating committee*—the nominating committee is responsible for the long-term health of the board, and is charged with recruiting potential candidates to fill initial board positions and vacancies

✓ *Compensation committee*—this group advises the Chairman and board on matters related to compensation and is responsible for establishing an overall compensation policy for board members and key executives.

Recruiting and Remunerating Board Members

By asking individuals to join your board of directors, you're asking them to take on a huge responsibility. In the wake of the Enron, Worldcom and other financial disasters, the whole world seems to be taking an interest in the subject of corporate governance. You can expect the regulations to become increasingly strict and I'm sure that we'll see increasingly harsh punishments for directors of companies that get into trouble and end up harming customers or investors.

So, today's directors are offered increasingly competitive compensation packages in exchange for their board participation. Generally, companies don't offer separate compensation packages to management directors who are already paid as employees, however, outside directors expect compensation packages that include:

✓ *Annual retainer.*

✓ *Per-meeting fee.*

✓ *Expense reimbursement.*

✓ *Stock options.*

As they come in to the firing line when things go wrong, board members are keen to make sure that the company has Directors & Officers (D&O) Insurance to help shield them from personal liability when things go wrong.

Enhance & Upgrade your Web Site

A public technology company is expected to be represented in cyberspace by a highly polished and professional web site. At this stage in the journey, you should already have a site that you're proud of—see *Publish a Corporate Web Site*, page 157. However, the audience will expand in the run up to and beyond the IPO—coming under the scrutiny of bankers, analysts, public investors, government bodies, competitors and psychopathic hackers. Even if you have the best corporate web site on the planet, there are at least two major enhancements are likely to be required in preparation for the IPO:

> ✓ *Investor relations section*—the web site acts as an important information source on the company and a valuable communications vehicle for investors. See *Prepare to Deal with Public Investors*, page 216.

> ✓ *Comply with SEC and other restrictions*—as a private company, there are relatively few restrictions regarding the disclosure of information on the web site and elsewhere. This is not the case for public companies, or IPO candidates, that come under extremely tight regulations regarding what, when, how and to whom certain information is disclosed. See *Go Quiet*, page 204, *Regulation Fair Disclosure*, page 218.

As a public technology company, the web site takes on an expanded role, is much more visible, addresses a larger audience and is judged by a higher set of standards.

Take Decision to IPO

Shares and share options in private companies are not very liquid—this means it's virtually impossible to sell or exchange them for anything that you can use to actually buy anything. Yes, this means that they're practically worthless. In most scenarios, you only get to sell your shares if the company goes through an IPO, or is sold—in a *Cash Flow Sale* or *Asset Sale*. As a result, investors refer to IPO and acquisitions as *liquidity events* and *exit routes*—they enable investors to convert shares to cash and get their money back out.

The IPO maneuver, for most technology companies, means raising funds by selling shares to the public, through a listing on the Nasdaq or one of the other major stock markets. Costing several million dollars, the process requires the support of an underwriter working in conjunction with legions of accountants and lawyers.

At *IPO*, all the company shareholders effectively exchange their preference and common shares for stock that can be traded on one of the public markets—such as the Nasdaq or New York Stock Exchange. Most private investors consider *IPO* to be the ultimate exit route as it traditionally provides the highest valuation, and gives them the flexibility of selling the shares whenever they like—all shareholders are not forced to sell at the same time as might be the case in an acquisition. (Having said that, don't get the impression that you'll be able to offload all your shares the day after the IPO—this is rarely the case and you'll likely be restricted from selling shares for a year or more.)

Taking the decision to IPO is an enormous step for any company. It normally requires the approval of the shareholders as well as the board. In a bull market, the costs and headaches associated with IPO are normally outweighed by the benefits of high valuation and access to capital. In a bear market, there may be little point in incurring the cost of directing the company along this arduous route—it may still result in a low valuation and fail to provide access to any capital at all.

IPO—the Benefits

A well-timed and well-executed IPO can boost momentum by providing the company with a war chest of cash and a glittering new public company image. As well as providing a route for the founders, employees and investors to sell some, or all, of their shares, the IPO can provide the company with real market credibility. To customers, competitors and investors alike, an IPO means the company has passed the rigorous checks and balances imposed by the SEC (Securities Exchange Commission), the stock exchange, the underwriters and the most expensive lawyers and accountants on the planet.

IPO—the Financial Costs

There will be little interest in your IPO unless it raises a reasonable amount of cash—you won't even appear on the radar screen of many investment banks unless you're raising $25m or more. For a successful IPO, you should expect to budget a couple of million dollars at least. Some of the costs are relatively fixed, others, like the underwriting fee, vary with the size of the deal:

Estimated Cost of Going Public on Nasdaq

Offering Value	$25,000,000	$50,000,000
Total Shares Outstanding	5,880,000	5,880,000
Item	**Estimated Fee**	**Estimated Fee**
Underwriting Percentage	7%	7%
Underwriting Discounts & Commissions	$1,750,000	$3,500,000
SEC Fees	$9,914	$19,828
NASD Fees	$3,375	$6,250
Printing and Engraving	$100,000	$100,000
Accounting Fees & Expenses	$160,000	$160,000
Legal Fees & Expenses	$200,000	$200,000
Blue Sky Fees (for Small Cap Market)	$25,000	$25,000
Miscellaneous	$34,200	$34,200
Nasdaq Entry Fees	$63,725	$63,725
Nasdaq Annual Fees	$11,960	$11,960
Transfer Agent & Registrar Fees	$5,000	$5,000
Total	**$2,363,174**	**$4,125,963**

Source: *Going Public* , Nasdaq

IPO—the Other Costs

In addition to the financial costs, there are a number of 'hidden' costs associated with IPO including:

- *Distracted management*—instead of running the business, the CEO and other crucial members of the management team will spend most of their days talking to lawyers, accountants and investment bankers. Then the road show will take them out of the office for weeks. If the business doesn't run itself, you'll need replacements to step in or step up to cover the top executives in their absence.

- *Structure, systems and bureaucracy*—to conform with the stringent reporting requirements of the SEC and satisfy public investors, several departments of the business will have to be restructured, new systems established and bureaucracy introduced at various levels. This may involve additional headcount and budget requirements from various departments including accounting, PR and investor relations.

Are you Ready to IPO?

There are real dangers in attempting to IPO before the company is ready. If there's little interest in the shares, the IPO could be withdrawn leaving the company with nothing but a huge stack of legal and accounting fees. If the pipeline of sales is weak, investors may participate in the IPO, then dump the stock later on when less-than-impressive results are announced (see *Crank up the Sales Engine*, page 194). When your shares are dumped, the price plummets, the stock gets de-listed from major league markets like the Nasdaq, and drops to one of the minor leagues where it trades alongside other penny shares. It's branded as one of the bottom-feeders of the public markets when the stock fails to make the regular pages of financial publications like the Wall Street Journal and is listed on the pink sheets instead. This is a big blow to momentum—it doesn't exactly help create a positive buzz around the company or attract new customers, investors or employees. It's then very difficult (virtually impossible) to shed the stigma attached to being one of bottom-feeders of the public markets, reverse this negative momentum, and drive the stock back up to the top. So, don't IPO until the company is ready and the timing is right.

The qualifications and conditions required for a successful IPO are not fixed. In fact, they change with the state of the economy, the state of your specific industry and the current mood on Wall Street. However, since the bursting of the dot-com bubble, it's back to business as usual in many respects and the first thing you need is a real business if you're planning an IPO. Then you need to complete each of the milestones along the seed, early and expansion stages of the zero-to-IPO route (see *Zero-to-IPO Milestones*, page 58). If you've hit the milestones, you have a solid pipeline of sales for several quarters and the climate on Wall Street is favorable, it could be time to explore the possibility of an IPO with your investment bank. Don't be surprised if you receive conflicting advice from different banks—a second tier bank may tell you that you need sales of $10m a *year* to qualify for IPO whereas a top-tier bank sets the bar at $10m a *quarter*. They'll obviously look at your profitability and the sales pipeline, but they'll also take an interest in other factors such as the mix of sales coming from products and services—public investors tend to favor product companies over service companies as they're considered more scalable.

Listen carefully to what the bankers and analysts have to say. It's not really in the interests of the investment bank to underwrite the IPO if the company is not quite ready—especially if you're asking them to do it on a firm commitment basis (see *Assemble the IPO Team*, page 206).

No More Shortcuts

Instead of going through the rigors of the IPO, it used to be easier to buy a company with a public stock market listing already. Corporations, with no real business at all, were formed with the sole purpose of completing the SEC filings and being sold as public shells for private companies. This shortcut, often called 'reversing onto the market' offered a popular route for many years—thousands of companies have made the transition from private to public in this way. This route effectively bypassed the IPO controls of the SEC as the maneuver was not viewed as a new listing on the market, simply a change in ownership of a company that was already listed.

In 2000, the SEC decided to take action. It said that private companies reversing onto the market in this way would be subject to the same checks and balances as those going through IPO. The route is still there—if you have a few hundred million dollars to spend, you can buy a real public company to obtain a public listing—however, there's little point as you'll still have to go through the rigorous controls of the SEC. The shortcut was effectively closed—probably for good.

IPO—Which Shares to Sell?

Which story do you think sounds the most appealing to public investors?

> *A. "We're issuing new shares for sale through IPO in order to raise cash for the company to fund its growth."*
> *B. "We're pursuing an IPO as the founders and private investors are anxious to offload their shares by selling them to the public."*

Story *B* understandably fails to hit the mark for most incoming investors—it creates the impression that the rats are deserting the sinking ship. So, an IPO typically involves creating new shares to sell to the public.

IPO—How Many Shares to Sell?

The number of shares issued is normally relatively small. At some point in their careers, investment bankers often discover that, for the most part, share trading obeys the fundamental economic principles of supply and demand—they figure out that dumping a huge volume of stock onto the public market will lead the share price to drop (see *Economics 101—The Laws of Supply & Demand*, page 301). Anyway, to maintain a strong share price, the bankers figure that they should sell a small percentage of the company at IPO, allow the management team to establish a track record and some trust with the public investors, then slowly offload more shares over time. Founders, employees and other shareholders may be anxious to raise cash by selling some of their shareholding on the public markets but it's in their interests to hold off until a stable market for the shares has been established—usually several quarters or years following the IPO.

On the one hand, the underwriter wants the number of shares traded at IPO to be kept to a minimum as this helps maintain a healthy price. On the other hand, the bigger the IPO, the higher the underwriters commission—and they typically don't like deals smaller than $20m. So, a typical IPO may involve raising in the region of $25m for the company by selling 2m new shares through underwriters at, say, $12.50 each. A stock split is usually required before the IPO to get the shares into this price range—don't worry, the re-pricing is purely cosmetic and shouldn't adversely affect your shareholding or that of anyone else.

IPO—What if it Goes Wrong?

After paying all the costs, a successful IPO can deposit in excess of $20m in the company's bank account. On the other hand, the company could emerge from an unsuccessful IPO with nothing but a pile of legal and accounting fees. A failed IPO for a company with positive cash flow simply means putting expansion plans on hold. A failed IPO for a company that's burning up cash can mean a severe cash crisis leading to imminent shutdown, even bankruptcy.

The distraction of the IPO process can lead management to forget to take its bearings, fail to identify a looming cash crisis and fail to take appropriate evasive action as the company slips through the scramble, survival and freefall zones (see *How a Cash Crisis Develops*, page 252). Just in case the IPO is withdrawn, management should prepare a number of contingency plans (see *Long Haul Contingency Plans—If IPO becomes Unattainable*, page 60).

The contingency plans should include:

- ✓ *Raising funds through a private placement.*
- ✓ *Selling the company*—see page 351.
- ✓ *Eliminating the burn rate by cutting or slashing costs*—see *Slowing your Descent— Cutting Costs*, page 264.

The IPO preparation involves assembling a team of investment bankers, lawyers and accountants, preparing a prospectus and carrying out extensive due diligence. The good news is that the preparation work can come in handy if you're forced to raise funds through a private placement or sell the company before it runs out of cash. Ideally, your investment bank will help draw up these contingency plans and alert management the moment it gauges potential problems with the IPO. It will then be able to switch from IPO mode into private placement and/or M&A mode.

Brace the Company for the IPO Process

Now that you've decided to direct the company on this arduous ascent to IPO, you need the involvement and support of the employees as well as the management team, board and investors. This journey requires a coordinated team—a slip by one individual can throw the whole ascent in jeopardy. Everyone in the company needs to understand that it's not business as usual—many of the ground rules they've operated by in the past are about to change. Before you go any further, there are some important messages that you want to get across to the team:

- ✓ *Identify 'Destination IPO' and map out the route*—it's important that they understand what's involved in this process and are prepared for the challenges that lie ahead. Heck, buy them all a copy of this book!

- ✓ *Distracted management*—ensure they're not surprised to find empty desks where managers used to be. Make sure they understand that the IPO process will tie up key members of the management team for days, weeks or months on end. When managers are unavailable, you'll need people to step up, take the lead and make decisions to maintain momentum throughout this difficult process.

- ✓ *Strangers snooping around the office*—in the coming weeks, the underwriters, accountants and lawyers have to collect a great deal of information. They'll likely need help and support from the employees.

- ✓ *More structure, systems and bureaucracy*—get ready for more procedures, documentation and a much more regimented management style. Private companies have tremendous flexibility in the way they operate. Public companies don't.

- ✓ *Restated finances, re-priced shares*—in preparation for the IPO, the companies' financial statements are likely to be recast and the shares restructured. Don't worry—this is normal.

- ✓ *Keeping quiet*—make sure everyone understands what they can and cannot say. Especially in the quiet period, it's important that this message is spelled out and there's no confusion. One slip of the tongue could upset the SEC and the whole IPO process could be suspended.

- ✓ *Stick to the script*—when they do have to communicate with the outside world, make sure the employees are all singing out of the same songbook.

Go Quiet

The IPO process thrusts many technology companies from the relaxed sunshine of Silicon Valley into the hustle bustle of Gotham City. Or New York City. Whatever.

They enter a whole new world complete with a real-life Batman and Robin tag team that's hell-bent on setting rules, catching the bad guys and cleaning things up. Created by Congress in the aftermath of the 1929 stock market crash, the Securities Exchange Commission (SEC) plays the role of Batman and the National Association of Securities Dealers (NASD) does an excellent impersonation of Robin. If you want to survive in this city, don't go around breaking the rules—Batman and Robin can get very upset.

This particular Batman is obsessed with what you say. Tell lies and he freaks out. He even gets upset when you tell the truth– if you're telling it to too few people or your telling it in the wrong way. In this world, it's best to keep quiet until you figure out what you can say and when you can say it. In fact, just to get you used to keeping quiet, a period of complete silence is required from the time that you contemplate the IPO until after the filing with the SEC, and then only limited offering information may be released. Everything must be kept quiet on a strict 'need to know' basis. Nothing can be said to the outside world that could affect your business affairs or a market for your stock.

What's the Point of the Quiet Period?

The SEC is interested in protecting public investors from basing buy/sell decisions on inaccurate or misleading information. In the absence of a quiet period, the SEC would have little control over how companies communicate with investors in the run up to IPO. If the company goes quiet, investors are forced to look to the prospectus for information on the company. The prospectus goes through rigorous SEC controls and investors have some level of assurance that it provides an accurate picture of the company with a balanced view of the risks involved. The quiet period prevents the company from bypassing the controls of the SEC, communicating with investors and hyping its stock.

During this period, management is strictly bound by the information contained in the prospectus. Most written communications regarding the IPO itself will simply contain the name of the issuer, the title of the security and the amount of the offering and a brief description. Cynical journalists claim that the Quiet Period is just a convenient excuse for CEO's and managers to avoid answering difficult questions about the company in the run up to IPO. Cynical investors claim that it's used by investment banks to save the juiciest deals for large institutional investors.

If you're accustomed to promoting your company, hyping the products and generally spreading the good vibes, you could go crazy in the quiet period. Virtually all forms of communication can get you in trouble—speeches, press releases, brochures, advertising, web publishing, e-mails, online chat rooms, even conversations with your spouse.

Oh, one more thing about the quiet period— it technically doesn't exist. But neither do Batman and Robin, technically speaking. When it did exist back in the 1930s, before the advent of the Internet and 24-hour cable-television financial news, the quiet period was, in fact, quiet. A would-be investor was unlikely to run across information about a company anywhere but in the prospectus. Things have changed—when a company files to go public today, it creates a commotion of cable-TV chatter, message-board speculation and financial-news coverage online and in print. Millions of people who have never seen the prospectus may make investment decisions based on information they pick up from these sources. Frequently, it's bad information.

Investor communications have changed since the 1930's and, sooner or later, Batman is likely to bring the regulations and conventions regarding Quiet Period up to date. Meanwhile, in the Quiet Period you're well advised to listen to your lawyers—just go quiet.

Assemble the IPO Team

Making your debut onto Wall Street and the public markets is very difficult unless you get the right introductions and hang with the in-crowd—the team with all the connections, the secret handshakes, golf club memberships and matching sets of old school ties. To many public investors, the value of your stock will have a direct relationship to the stature of the team you manage to assemble. Your IPO is unlikely to attract any attention if you turn up at Wall Street with an unknown team—the company will be likely perceived as a second-rate mom-and-pop operation. This is a prime example of when you need to hire the most expensive bankers, lawyers, accountants and advisors you can find.

As with any team, it's important that all members establish a good channel of communication and work well together—this is another reason for choosing experienced advisors. Over the years, the prominent bankers, lawyers and accountants have worked together on many occasions and established good working relationships as a result. They've also established important channels of communication and familiarity with other individuals critical to this process like investors, the SEC and NASD.

The IPO team includes the following members:

- ✓ *Management & board members*—the most visible members of the IPO team are the CEO and CFO. It's important that these individuals make a positive impression with public investors. Other members of the team, such as the VP of Sales, will likely participate in the road show and other meetings. The CFO can coordinate the whole IPO process. However, companies often find it more effective to appoint an executive to act as full-time project manager. Board members and significant investors are also likely to participate in the process—specifically in the selection of the team and approval of the overall strategy.

- ✓ *Investment bank (underwriter)*—perhaps the most crucial member of the team, the investment bank takes on the responsibility of underwriting the offering and managing much of the IPO process.

- ✓ *Law firm*—of course, you need a specialist firm of IPO lawyers that's familiar with the underwriting process, dealing with the SEC, NASD Regulation (NASDR), and the state securities commissions regarding prospectus approval. An experienced lawyer will not only ensure that proper procedures are observed but will hopefully prevent inordinate delays by anticipating and addressing potential issues before filing.

- ✓ *Accounting firm*—the accountants will clean up and restate the balance sheet, prepare and review financial statements and provide endorsements in the form of comfort letters. Following the Arthur Anderson collapse, the association of a big accounting firm, and the implied endorsement through a comfort letter, may not carry as much weight as it once did, however, it will certainly carry more than that of a small, unknown firm.

- ✓ *Underwriting syndicate*—the investment bank is likely to spread some of the risk by bringing in a syndicate of underwriting partners.

- ✓ *Others*—printing of the prospectus and other official documents pertaining to the IPO is a specialist business—make sure you select a printer with experience in this area and the facilities to print sufficient quantities under tight time constraints. It's also important that your PR firm and other agencies are accustomed to working with clients in the IPO process—for example, they should be familiar with the constraints imposed during the Quiet Period.

It's important to factor that the process of selecting and appointing an agency takes a good deal of effort and several weeks, or months, to complete.

If you followed the zero-to-IPO route by the book (this book), you'll be prepared for this moment—your CEO, CFO, lawyers, accountants and investment bank will have been in place for some time.

See *Hire a Career CEO*, page 145, *Hire a Good Startup Lawyer*, page 77, *Hire a Good Accountant*, page 79, *Round out the Management Team*, page 182, *Appoint an Investment Bank*, page 185.

Advisor Selection Process

Make Appointment

Negotiate Terms

Make Selection

Take up References

Bake-Off

Shortlist Candidates

Approach Candidates

List Candidates

Define Objectives

Negotiating the Underwriting Deal

There are basically two alternative arrangements with the underwriter—*best efforts* and *firm commitment*. In a best-efforts arrangement, the investment bank is saying 'we'll try to sell your shares—but no guarantees'. Under a firm-commitment arrangement, they're saying 'we'll pay you in full, in advance, for all the shares offered. It's then our responsibility to sell them on the market'. A firm commitment is like money in the bank—however, underwriters are often reluctant to actually sign the agreement until they have buyers already lined up to take the shares off their hands (this could be the evening before the IPO).

Of course, given a choice, the underwriter will opt for a best efforts arrangement. As with any negotiation, you're likely to get a better deal if you have a number of investment banks competing for the business—especially if you put them through a bake-off (see Appendix 2—Getting What you Want—Negotiating the Deal, page 313). It's safe to assume that the underwriters' commission will come out at 7%.

Carry Out the Financial Audit and Due Diligence

This is the point that investment bankers, lawyers and accountants descend on the company, rifle through all the filing cabinets and meet with seemingly everyone involved in the business—including management, employees, suppliers, creditors, distributors, customers, even competitors! The goal of due diligence is to fully understand your business, identify the risks and problems the company is likely to face and assure that the information provided to investors in the prospectus is accurate and complete.

Following the Enron collapse and other accounting scandals, let's hope that the accountants, bankers and lawyers are consciously looking for ways to find and expose the skeletons in the closets—as opposed to looking for ways to hide them. To this end, they have to investigate any cause for concern regarding the financials, technology, management integrity, adverse market trends and litigation. Issues that are of little concern to a private company can become reasons for alarm in a public company—for example, potential litigants can crawl out of the woodwork when they hear news of the IPO.

You will be asked to provide the due diligence teams with a seemingly never-ending list of documents and materials such as:

- ✓ *Annual and quarterly financial information for the past three years*—income statements, balance sheets, cash flows and footnotes, planned versus actual results, management financial reports, breakdown of sales and gross profit by product type, channel & geography, current backlog by customers, accounts receivable aging schedule, quarterly financial projections, revenue by product type, customers and channel.

- ✓ *Management and personnel*—organization chart, historical and projected headcount by function and location, summary biographies of senior management, including employment history, age, service with the Company, years in current position, compensation arrangements, copies (or summaries) of key employment agreements, benefit plans, incentive stock plans, significant employee relations problems (past or present), personnel turnover and key unfilled vacancies.

- ✓ *Capital structure*—current shares outstanding, schedule of all options, warrants, rights and any other potentially dilutive securities with exercise prices and vesting provisions, summary of all debt instruments/bank lines with key terms and conditions, off balance sheet liabilities, capital losses.

- ✓ *Financial projections*—detailed income statements, balance sheets, cash flow statements, major growth drivers and prospects, assessment of financial stability, risks associated with foreign operations (e.g., exchange rate fluctuation, government instability), industry and company pricing policies, economic assumptions underlying projections (different scenarios based on price and market fluctuations), explanation of projected capital expenditures, depreciation, working capital requirements, external financing arrangements and assumptions.

✓ *Other financial information*—summary of current federal, state and foreign tax positions, including net operating loss carry forwards, analysis of general accounting policies (revenue recognition, etc.), schedule of financing history for equity, warrants and debt (listing investors, dollar investment, percentage ownership, implied valuation, etc.).

✓ *Products*—descriptions of each product within each market segment, major customers and applications, historical and projected growth rates, market share, speed and nature of technological change, timing of new products, product enhancements, cost structure and profitability.

✓ *Customer information*—list of numerous representative customers by product—including contact name, address, phone number, product(s) owned and timing of purchases. List of strategic partners (contact name, phone number, revenue contribution, marketing agreements), revenue by customer (name, contact and phone number for any customers accounting for a significant percentage of revenue), brief description of any significant relationship severed within the last two years.

✓ *Competition*—description of the competitive landscape within each market segment including market position and related strengths and weaknesses as perceived in the market.

✓ *Marketing, sales, and distribution*—overall strategy and implementation, discussion of domestic and international distribution channels (including any VARs, Systems Integrators and OEMs), positioning of the company and its products, marketing opportunities and risks, description of marketing programs, examples of recent marketing/product/public relations/media coverage, status and trends of major customer relationships, prospects for future growth and development, sales pipeline analysis, principal avenues for generating new business, sales force productivity model, sales quotas and compensation models, sales cycles, analysis of feasibility of marketing budgets.

✓ *Research and development*—description of the R&D organization, strategy, key personnel, new product pipeline, development status and timing, cost of development, critical technology dependencies & risks, joint R&D efforts, participation in industry associations, dependence on outside licensing and patents, patents currently held by the company.

✓ *Legal*—pending lawsuits against the company (details of claimant, claimed damages, brief history, status, anticipated outcome, and name of the company's counsel), pending lawsuits initiated by the company (detail on defendant, claimed damage, brief history, status, anticipated outcome, and name of the company's counsel), description of environmental and employee safety issues and liabilities, safety precautions, new regulations and their consequences, lists of material patents, copyrights, licenses and trademarks, summary of insurance coverage (and any material exposures), summary of material contracts, history of SEC or other regulatory agency issues or disputes.

✓ *Other company information*—business plan, list of board members, meeting minutes, employee manual, list of all stockholders with shareholding, options, warrants or notes.

Phew! Collecting all this information and preparing all this documentation is a huge undertaking. The next phase involves answering gazillions of questions, verifying and cross-checking facts, helping the lawyers and accountants drill down into the minutia and defending many of the assumptions. A time-consuming and demanding process, due diligence can't be avoided—it's a crucial step on the ascent to IPO.

Restate Financials

In the process of investigating the financials, there's a good chance that the accountants will find reason to restate the accounts for previous years. Perhaps the accounts didn't adhere to GAAP (Global Accepted Accounting Principles), or they find some intra-company transactions, compensation arrangements and relationships involving management or the board that might be appropriate for a private company but must be eliminated from the statements of a public company. So, it's not unusual to see a new set of profit and loss accounts, balance sheets and other financial statements for several years prior to the IPO.

At the completion of the due diligence process, you'll need to prepare a memorandum for the SEC summarizing the steps that have been taken to ensure that the information provided in the draft prospectus is accurate and complete—so remember to keep track of all the activities including meetings and visits.

Draft the Prospectus and Other Documents

At the center of the IPO process is the prospectus, also known as the *registration statement, S-1* or *red herring*—the 'red' part of red herring dates back to the days when a large, 'Pending Approval' notice was printed on the cover of the draft prospectus in red. Where the herring came from is anyone's guess. Technically, the red herring is a draft prospectus—as it hasn't yet been approved by the SEC. This is the whole point of the prospectus—it has to be approved by the SEC and NASD (working as a Batman and Robin tag team), before it can be distributed to potential investors. SEC regulations govern the contents of the prospectus and the NASD, in its capacity as the self-regulatory securities industry association, checks to see that the underwriters haven't earned too much money.

Since it's the only information that the law allows to be disseminated about a public offering, the prospectus is a sales brochure disguised as a legal disclosure and liability disclaimer document—see *What's the Point of the Quiet Period?*, page 204. If the prospectus were a pure selling document, it would surely qualify as one of the very worst selling documents ever produced. I think the designer behind the look and feel of the prospectus was the same individual behind the design of uniforms for police women—a designer with a talent for making anything appear ugly and unglamorous. Void of any form of color or graphical appeal, the prospectus is filled with text. If you actually read the text, it's scary! It's deliberately written in a way to scare investors away—a tremendous proportion of the document is devoted to identifying all the potential risk factors that could adversely affect the company. What do you expect—it's written by lawyers!

> **If you see an ad like this in this months' glossy magazine, it's safe to suspect that it was written by a former prospectus writer:**
> 'Morning Flakes, Breakfast Cereal—some people have said it tastes OK, however, before buying this product at your local supermarket, please take a little time to review the associated risks. Morning Flakes could cause an allergic reaction and excruciating pain. After eating this product you may become repulsive to the opposite sex. It may explode, killing your whole family. The manufacturer cannot be held responsible if your house is overrun by evil axe wielding homicidal maniacs when you are eating Morning Flakes.'

After reading a prospectus, you certainly come away with a very clear picture of all the risks associated with the company. In addition to the regular business risks that you come to expect, this company could be affected by nuclear war, plagues of locusts, alien invasions, drought, floods, disease—the list is endless. It's almost impossible to understand how anyone investing in an IPO could ever complain that the risks were not clearly identified in the prospectus. How on Earth could the dull, scary prospectus continue act as a sales document? The answer is that over the years, investors seem to have developed an immunity to it– they're accustomed to the cautionary tone and simply ignore it.

Usually, the entire IPO team is involved in developing the prospectus. In conjunction with the financial audit and due diligence, the process normally takes in the region of 6-8 weeks. The law firm is primarily responsible for drafting the narrative, while the accounting firm will prepare the financial statements and the investment banker will supply the underwriting details. In addition to a detailed description of the company's business, the prospectus is required to contain a description of the management structure, compensation figures, and details of any transactions between the corporation and the management. The names of principal shareholders and their level of ownership should be included, as well as the company's audited financial statements. Then there's the Management's Discussion and Analysis ('MD&A') of the company's operations and financial condition together with information on the use of proceeds, effect of dilution on existing shares, dividend policy, and capitalization. Finally, the prospectus should describe the underwriting agreement, including whether the underwriting will proceed on a 'firm commitment' or 'best efforts' basis and outline details regarding all forms of compensation and the investment banking firms involved.

It's in everyone's interest to make sure that the information contained in the prospectus is accurate and complete. The company, its corporate officers and board of directors are liable for any inaccuracies or omissions (biff!, bang!, kapow!—you don't want to incur the wrath of Batman and Robin).

File Registration Documents with the SEC

Now it's time for Batman and Robin to give their formal approval. Since investors feel they were duped by the likes of Enron and Worldcom, the SEC and NASD are now under increased pressure to apply even more diligence to this process.

If there are no insurmountable problems, the review process can take three to six months, but there are no guarantees. The SEC can, and will, extend its review until fully satisfied—in conjunction with the NASD, they can sit on the files forever.

Here we're assuming that you're planning to trade your stock on one of the major national markets, like the Nasdaq or the NYSE. If you're planning on trading on a smaller, more regional, exchange, you're likely to be forced to have the offering reviewed according to state 'blue sky' laws. These can be quite stringent and complying with the regulations in each state is not cheap.

The SEC and NASD do not review an IPO for its soundness as an investment— they leave that to the investor. Some state security commissions do but this shouldn't affect you if you're listing on the Nasdaq or one of the other national exchanges.

Prospectus Review by the SEC

Batman is obsessed with disclosure—the SEC reviews the prospectus for accuracy and adequacy of any information that may affect investment decisions. IPO's tend to be scrutinized more closely than secondary offerings because then have not previously been subject to such careful analysis.

The SEC's role in the regulation of IPO's, as with corporations generally, is primarily in the area of disclosure. The Division of Corporation Finance, within the SEC, will review the prospectus for the accuracy and adequacy of 'material facts'—information that would affect investment decisions.

Once reviewed, you should receive a letter from the SEC listing any deficiencies that need to be addressed. You can reply in writing or request a pre-filing conference with SEC staff. If the SEC finds the prospectus to be inaccurate, incomplete or misleading, it can require that the company re-circulate an amended version.

It can be difficult to predict which parts of the prospectus Batman will object to. He'll certainly take a good look at the discussion of the operations, the financial results (management discussion and analysis) and the company's liquidity and resources. The SEC often questions or objects to the way that certain accounting principles have been chosen in preference to others—especially when it comes to reporting revenue. It's also interested in making sure that there's adequate disclosure of risk and is likely to scrutinize the management compensation.

The SEC requires public companies (except those that are very small or overseas) to file prospectus, periodic reports, and other forms electronically through EDGAR (Electronic Data Gathering, Analysis and Retrieval System www.sec.gov/edgar.shtml). Anyone can access and download this information for free.

Prospectus Review by the NASD

Robin is concerned with fairness. While Batman is checking the accuracy and completeness of the prospectus, Robin is checking that the underwriters haven't made too much money—that the terms of the arrangement are fair to the company (and its investors). The guidelines used to measure what's fair and what's not are known as the 'NASDR Corporate Financing Rule' or the 'NASDR'.

The NASD looks at the whole underwriters' compensation package, including the cash, stock, stock options, warrants, and contractual post-offering investment banking services, then makes a determination of fairness. The guidelines are not restricted to the underwriters—any compensation paid to finders, (someone who locates an underwriter), financial consultants (who often advise on financial statements, the size, price of the offering and other financial matters) is also to be monitored and approved by the NASD. Of course, a 'firm commitment' arrangement carries more risk than 'best efforts' and the NASD understands that this arrangement qualifies for a higher reward. Underwriters are also expected to receive a higher percentage of an IPO compared to a secondary offering.

If it finds that the proposed compensation and arrangements are unfair or unreasonable, the terms of the underwriting deal will have to be re-negotiated and the prospectus amended. Although the NASDR guidelines are confidential, you can request pre-filing advice before drafting the prospectus.

Approval

The SEC will not declare an underwriting effective until NASDR has concluded its review and issued a comment letter expressing an opinion of 'no objections' to the proposed compensation and arrangements. When it is satisfied, the SEC will declare the prospectus 'effective upon request'. The preliminary prospectus should be circulated to potential investors at least two days before the effective date, then the final version can be printed.

Present the IPO Road Show

In the weeks running up to the IPO, the underwriters drag the CEO, CFO and other key members of the management team out of the office and parade them in front of potential investors and analysts in key cities across the country. The purpose is to generate investor interest in the company and essentially pre-sell blocks of shares in advance of the IPO.

The road show consists of a fairly elaborate formal presentation on the company's operations, financial condition, performance, markets, products and services—and enables investors to meet face-to-face with management. There are breakfast meetings, lunch meetings, dinner meetings, group meetings, one-on-one meetings, investors meetings, broker meetings, underwriter sales force meetings, meetings about meetings, meetings within meetings. The whole process is very stressful, demanding and exhausting—for a taster see *The Press Tour*, page 132.

Road shows are normally conducted before the prospectus has met the approval of the SEC and the NASD—so the company is still in the quiet period. The meetings are conducted in a bizarre cloak-and-dagger tone—the shares are not technically for sale, and investors are only allowed access to information contained in the official prospectus (which isn't yet official). 'Pending Approval' status is stamped prominently on the front cover of the prospectus (in red, fish-smelling ink)— announcing that the IPO is just a possibility and does not constitute an offer. You're not even allowed to use words like 'buying' or 'selling'. This wacky situation would charm any Batman and Robin storyline.

It's at, or following, these meetings that institutions, and brokers, let the underwriters know whether they're interested in buying shares in the IPO. The underwriter gathers these commitments in a 'book' and it's at this point that the viability of the IPO can be more realistically assessed.

Set the Share Price

Normally the offering is priced just before the underwriting agreement is signed, on the day before the IPO. There are many, many ways of valuing a private company. Most of them are meaningless. The true value of the company is the price that informed buyers are prepared to pay—but this can be difficult to predict. At IPO, the company's shares (or some of them) are openly traded and market forces—supply and demand—set a price. As market forces set this price, it can be argued that this is the first true valuation of the company and its shares. Predicting what this price will be means predicting the actions of Wall Street investors—some of the most unpredictable entities in the known universe.

There are a number of different and conflicting forces at play in the process of pricing shares for IPO (see *Valuation Techniques for IPO*, page 312. The company wants to set the price as high as possible, to maximize the proceeds of the share sale, the underwriter wants to set the price low enough that all the shares are sold, and the investor wants to see an early rise in the price after trading opens.

In the dot-com bubble years, stocks could leap 50 percent, 100 percent or even higher on the first day of trading. Since, many stocks have plummeted from the moment trading begins. If the price is set too low and goes through the roof on trading, privileged investors, who got in at the offering price, make out like bandits—and the company receives only a small fraction of the proceeds it might otherwise have had. If the price is set too high, the company takes home a lot of money, but its stock could quickly plummet below the offering price as trading continues, resulting in negative publicity and unhappy investors.

Fortunately, after gauging investor interest at the road show, the underwriter will have a feel for what price the market will bear and make a recommendation price per share for management approval. For years, underwriters used a general rule of thumb: Value the deal so that the stock will jump about 15 percent on the first day of trading. This can be more of an art than a science.

Prepare to Deal with Public Investors

There's little point paying millions of dollars to go public if you're not going to invest in an effective investor relations program. Even the best company can fail to attract public investors if it fails to communicate with them in an effective and professional way.

In advance of the IPO, you need to establish an investor relations function. The first step involves building a communication channel connecting the company with the investors and the investment community at large. The second step is to articulate corporate messages that carefully positioning the company, the market, the products, the competition and the direction it's headed in future—see *Formulate your Core Messaging and Corporate Identity*, page 87. The third step is to use the channel to regularly deliver results, news and communicate with individual investors and the investment community at large. Obviously, today much of this can be achieve through the Internet.

It's important that management understand that the investor relations program will require headcount, operating budget and continued support beyond the IPO—an investor relations group is a permanent fixture for a public company. Once a basic investor relations program is established, you can continue to support the fair market valuation of the stock price by working to:

✓ *Present the stock as an attractive investment product*— explain why your stock is appealing when compared to the multitude of alternative investment opportunities out there.

✓ *Establish a following of analysts*—analysts are the key link to the investors, providing research, recommending stocks and overseeing transactions.

✓ *Create a balanced base of different shareholders*— the ideal shareholder buys in volume and holds—the market gets jittery whenever people start to sell. Most public companies want a well-balanced shareholder base of individuals as well as institutional shareholders such as mutual funds, value investors and growth investors. Although individual investors are usually expected to be more loyal than institutions, bear in mind that many individuals invest in stocks through mutual funds.

✓ *Harness the broker network*—brokers are your direct link to individual investors selling stocks and an extensive array of other financial products. They serve customers representing all demographics—men and women of all ages, occupations, portfolios and income levels.

✓ *Set the stage for further fundraising initiatives*—after the company is known and appreciated by the investment community, it's easier to raise cash from secondary stock offerings or bond issues.

Regulation Fair Disclosure

The SEC is interested in providing a level playing field for all investors, making sure that one investor is not provided with information that is not available to another. When you disclose information to an analyst or investors, you must then make that same information available to the public. 'Intentional' information must initially be made available to the public. 'Unintentional' information, perhaps disclosed in discussion with an analyst or investor, should be made available to the public within 24 hours or before the next market opens. The intent of Regulation Fair Disclosure is that material information should be available in a timely manner to the investment community at large. This means full and fair disclosure of such information distributed as widely as possible, so individuals have access to it at the same time as the financial analysts and institutional money managers.

Measuring the Success of an Investor Relations Program

Here are some of the metrics you can use to track the effectiveness of your investor relations program:

- ✓ *Price to earnings ratio*—you can track how the company's P/E (share price vs. earnings) ratio compare to the industry average, whether it's increasing or decreasing over time and whether it's following the industry trend (see *Valuation Techniques—Earnings Multiple*, page 303).

- ✓ *Number of new shareholders*—the company can track the number of new individual, institutional and other shareholders.

- ✓ *Number of total shareholders*—you can monitor trends to figure out how the shareholder base is growing or shrinking. Metrics like the number of investors, growth levels and the break down of institutional vs. individual investors can provide an insight into how the company is perceived on the market.

- ✓ *Average trading volume*—trading volume can be tracked as a barometer of market sentiment regarding the company and industry. Low volume is common when the number of shares on the market (the float) is small and the stockholders have a strategy to buy and hold. Unusually high volume may indicate that rumors are circulating about the company or the industry.

- ✓ *Analyst following*—it's important to track how many analysts are following the company. You might want to distinguish the influential, respected analysts from the rest—and distinguish the analysts with a positive attitude about the company from the ones that just don't 'get-it'.

Retail Shareholders

Don't snub the small guys. Individual investors can hold on to your stock through good times and bad. Holding your stock for years on end, they can be the most loyal or stubborn (or some would say 'stupid') shareholders you can find. It's important to make these small individual investors feel significant to the company. They appreciate clear, honest and timely communications, and the corporate web site may be the best platform for making this possible. They watch your web site, listen carefully to your press releases and corporate statements—although they no longer hang onto the every word of the brokers and analysts, they can still be heavily influenced by the media.

Institutional Shareholders

The biggest institutional shareholders can be the most rewarding and the most troublesome. It's important to open up a communication channel directly with management. CEO's and CFO's often visit large institutional shareholders in person. It's in the company's interests to answer troublesome questions one-on-one rather than in the public arena of a shareholders meeting. In addition to one-on-one meetings, it's possible to gauge the mood and concerns of these and other investors through surveys and monitoring online newsgroups.

Some companies welcome new institutional investors with a telephone call and a package of information. This is an opportunity to tell the investor that he/she is appreciated, drill home the core messages and refer the investor to the web site and other channels of communication that make up the investor relations program.

Establishing a Following of Analysts

Although recently maligned by scandals and concerns of conflicts of interest, many analysts remain highly influential and their attitude can have a profound impact on the performance of your stock.

Regulation Fair Disclosure (see above) restricts you from providing privileged information to analysts, or anyone else, without making it available to the investing public. It's important to make sure the analyst understands your market strategy, positioning and how the company should be measured—to make sure that it's not judged by inappropriate ratios or standards.

You're not only restricted in what you say to analysts, but what you say about analysts. Making comments about analyst forecasts and reports as your comments can be interpreted in a lawsuit as being 'entangled' with the forecast or even 'adopting' it. Your best advice is to avoid reviewing analyst forecasts all together—if you can resist the temptation.

Conflicting Interests

Analysts advise investors on which stocks to buy and sell. Analysts work for investment banks that make money by selling the stocks for their client companies. Analysts also have their own stock portfolios—and sometimes buy shares in private companies prior to IPO. An analyst report slamming a company can immediately trigger a sell-off and the stock price to plummet. How can analysts offer a fair and balanced view of the market and provide investors with reliable, independent advice when presented with such a conflict of interests? This question is not only being asked by investors that lost their shirts in the dot-com crash, but also by the SEC, the media, the White House and society at large. Questions are also being asked of accounting firms that audit the books for companies that are also important paying clients—accounting firms like Arthur Anderson with clients like Enron and Worldcom. Where are Batman and Robin when you need them? Hopefully, these conflicting interests will be removed and, in future, investors will be able to rely on information provided by analysts and auditors.

Effective communication, within the constraints of the Regulation Fair Disclosure, helps analysts accurately analyze the company and helps get the message, and good news, out to the investment marketplace. Here are some initiatives to consider:

- ✓ *Analyst group meetings*—make sure your presentations are well planned and prepared, schedule time for questions and answers and provide impressive information packs for the attendees to take away.

- ✓ *Company tours*—organized visits to company headquarters or facilities.

- ✓ *Analyst trade association and specialty group meetings*—speaking at these events is a good opportunity to raise your profile within the analyst community.

- ✓ *Analyst prospecting*—target particular key analysts for office visits and presentations by corporate officers.

Harness the Network of Stock Brokers

Many individual investors buy stocks through brokers, and listen to the brokers' advice. In return, the brokers often place their trust in analysts and sales managers. You can help raise the profile of your stock with brokers by providing them with short, interesting selling points about the company through e-mail, snail mail, even live presentations to the sales managers.

Interacting with Market-Makers

Market makers actively trade in specific shares—they stand by ready, willing and able to buy or sell at publicly quoted prices. Acting like wholesalers, market makers quote buy and sell prices to brokers. They often compete with each other to provide the best prices on the shares in which they trade.

As they have an influence over other investors, it's important to make sure that any market-makers trading in your stock are kept up-to-date with all the latest company news and information. This can be achieved through e-mail, telephone calls and trading room visits.

Of course, the fair disclosure regulations prevent you from disclosing any information to market makers that's not available to the public, but it can have a significant effect—once you disclose the information to the market maker, he/she effectively becomes an insider and is prevented from trading the company stock until the information is revealed to the public. Stopping the market maker from trading your stock is not really the result you're looking for!

Leveraging the Media

For a technology company, PR is probably the most effective way of getting news about your product and company out to the market (see *Appoint a PR Agency*, page 120). When the company is public and you're under tight restrictions about what you can say, whom you're allowed to say it to and when you're allowed to say it, dealing with journalists becomes even more of a challenge.

Public investors read newspapers, books, magazines, watch TV and listen to the radio. Like everyone else, they react to momentum. If you can generate a positive buzz about the company in the media, it's sure to attract investors and strengthen the share price.

It's in your interest to supply journalists with company news and juicy quotes. However, for a public company, disclosing information to journalists is like walking a tightrope—one slip and you're in serious trouble. Make sure that everyone talking to the press, acting as a company spokesperson, is fully aware of Regulation Fair Disclosure and what can and cannot be disclosed. Say too much and you're sure to upset the SEC.

News Releases

News releases are used to disclose company information to the investing public. In fact, they're a crucial component of the disclosure process under Regulation Fair Disclosure. You're considered to have made a good faith effort at disclosure when you send a release to the following:

✓ *Major national newspaper*—Wall Street Journal, New York Times, etc.

✓ *Major regional newspaper*—in the city where the company has its headquarters.

✓ *Major news wires*—Dow Jones, Reuters, Bloomberg, etc.

✓ *Paid news wires*—PR Newswire, Business Wire , etc.

You'll also want to send news releases to regular press, and list it on other wires such as the Associated Press and United Press International, business information services such as Standard & Poor's, business magazines, trade publications and regional and local newspapers. News releases can also be sent directly to analysts following the company's industry, as well as institutional investors. It's important that you inform the financial community regularly of the company's performance—including promptly reporting all forms of 'material developments'. Whether you're delivering good news or bad news, preparing the market will help maintain the company's credibility and preserve relations with the investment community.

Web Site

You want a web site that not only provides investors with an effective communication channel but also creates a positive and professional image for the company. Investors can come away with a negative image if the site is out of date, poorly designed, unreliable or painfully slow. Most public investors will never visit your offices or meet your staff. The web site is their only interaction with the company—so make sure they find what they're looking for and make the experience a positive one.

Investors increasingly look to the company's web site for news and information. The web site provides a convenient and immediate channel of communication directly connecting investors and the company. By this point, you should have been acting like a public company for some time and the investor relations component of your site should be well established (see *Enhance and Upgrade your Web Site*, page 197).

Conference Calls

Regular conference calls, normally timed to coincide with earnings and major new releases, have become an important part of the communication channel connecting public companies with their investors. Anyone can dial in and listen to major investors, analysts, and journalists ask questions of the CEO, CFO and other company executives. The calls are often recorded and made available on the Internet—so you can now listen to these thrilling dialogues whenever you like!

Internet Message Boards

Internet message boards have flourished in recent years and provide a forum for investors and the general public to chat and exchange information about a public company and its stock. The idea is brilliant—any investor with an Internet connection can participate and share information.

Like any public forum where the participants are anonymous (you can create a new screen name within seconds), many of the postings are junk. Message board provide an opportunity for disgruntled employees to launch vitriolic attacks on the company, spread malicious rumors about individual managers and for competitors (and anyone else) to trash the company and its stock. Anyone can say virtually anything– and get away with it.

Under the fair disclosure rules and the guidelines of the SEC, management has to be very careful about participation in these public forums. However, after sifting out the junk, message boards can offer a useful source of feedback on investor sentiment and concerns.

<u>Go Public—The IPO Itself</u>

Congratulations! After the prospectus has the approval of the SEC & NASD, the stock can start trading on the chosen public market. You finally made it! As of today, the company is no longer an independent private entity—it's now transformed into an independent public entity. In the context of this book, you've reached your destination! For many, it's a time to breathe a sigh of relief and celebrate.

Unfortunately, the state of relief is likely to be temporary—with analysts, the SEC and public investors breathing down your neck, life may just be getting harder instead of easier. And don't take the celebrations too seriously– a former colleague of mine worked as a lawyer on an IPO that went tragically wrong. In celebration, the CEO went out and bought himself a Ferrari, crashed, killed himself and triggered a sell-off on the very day the stock started trading. Hmm, now that I've dampered the excitement, let's look at how the process works in the run up to, and beyond the IPO:

✓ *1-10 days before IPO*—the company issues the press release, the accountants deliver draft comfort letters and the underwriters form the syndicate and place the tombstone advertisement announcing the offering.

✓ *1 day before IPO*—the management and underwriters set the shares price, the underwriting agreement is signed (eventually), the final prospectus is filed by the lawyers, it's printed by the printers, the SEC declares the offering effective and the NASD issues a declaration of no objections.

✓ *Day of IPO itself*—trading in the company's shares begins!

✓ *3 days after IPO*—the company provides investors with shareholder certificates, the lawyers deliver opinion letters and the underwriter provides the company with the proceeds in the sale

✓ *Up to 30 days after IPO*—the company continues to provide additional certificates and collect additional funds, the lawyers update the closing documents, the accountants issue more comfort letters and the underwriter starts to analyze the stock, perhaps preparing a research report.

✓ *Many months after the IPO (usually about 12 months)*—management, employees and pre-IPO investors can start selling stock on the public market. If you're a founder, this is likely your first opportunity to sell shares and options, however, the stock price can plummet if insiders start to sell at the first opportunity.

To maintain the momentum from the IPO, the ideal scenario is that you release a series of good-news press releases in the following weeks and months. This will help the investors develop a comfort level around the company and the stock.

When I told my friend, a scientist, that I was writing a book about the journey taken by a technology startup company, his only comment was that he hoped it had a happy ending. Well, this is about as happy as it gets—the company is now public, founders, investors and employees can trade stock on the public markets. Of course, this is where a new journey begins. Let's hope that one has a happy ending as well.

Switching to Destination Cash-Flow Sale

After setting out to take their startups from *Zero*-to-*IPO*, many entrepreneurs find themselves on a journey from *Zero*-to-acquisition. In fact, statistically, the journey is much more likely to end up with an acquisition than an *IPO*. There are many reasons for this—the most obvious being that most markets can only support a small number of competitors, and these companies swallow up all the smaller new entrants.

Many startups start to look for an acquirer when they discover that they're off track and an *IPO* is no longer a realistic option. But it's not unusual for companies with real *IPO* prospects to choose to sell out instead. After my friends' company completed its successful *IPO*, I was astonished to find that many of the management team regretted that they'd chosen to *IPO* instead of selling the company. These were folks that had become multi-millionaires virtually overnight (on paper). The whole

IPO process had been too painful and the disclosure requirements were tedious. The team felt that its freedom to make decisions and react to rapidly changing market conditions was severely constrained by quarterly reporting requirements and constant scrutiny from Wall Street analysts. Heck, because of the *IPO*, they'd even been forced to circulate an employee handbook that outlawed swearing in the office!

Why is a merger or acquisition often more appealing than an *IPO*?

- ✓ *Liquidity*—if you choose to *IPO*, you'll likely be restricted from selling any of your shares for a significant period of time—normally several months at least. When you do sell your shares on the public markets, you risk triggering a sell-off from other shareholders, especially if you're still considered to be a company insider. On the other hand, the day you close on an acquisition, your bank account could see a nice deposit of cash. Would you prefer to hold hard cash or restricted shares that you may be able to sell at some point in the future—if the market holds up? If cash today is appealing to you, an acquisition could be the way to go.

- ✓ *Flexibility*—there's relatively little flexibility in the structure of an *IPO*, but it may be possible for an acquisition to be structured to meet your personal needs and minimize your tax liability.

- ✓ *Valuation*—you're likely to get the best company valuation from an *IPO*, however, it may be possible to get 80% of that valuation from an acquisition. When you're dealing with the whims of Wall Street investors, there are of course no hard and fast rules. In bull markets as well as bear markets, Wall Street actually values many companies lower than they would be valued by a strategic acquirer (see *What's it Worth?—Valuing the Company*, page 301).

- ✓ *Synergy*—a strategic acquirer may offer complementary technology, a valuable distribution channel and established customer base. The theory is that the whole is greater than the sum of the parts—one plus one makes three and all that..

- ✓ *Lower risk*—after the Wall Street crash of 2000, several companies that had been readying themselves for *IPO* found themselves scrambling to raise private funds to stay afloat. Many had previously turned down offers of acquisition and decided to shoot for an *IPO*. *IPO* turned out to be a risky journey that resulted in the untimely death of many a company. Wall Streets' gyrations are highly unpredictable, especially when it comes to *IPO*'s. Unless your idea of fun is taking your life savings with you on a night out to the casino, an acquisition can be a much more sensible alternative.

✓ *Quicker & easier*—as you'll see below, an acquisition is not an entirely painless process, however, it can be a breeze when compared to preparing the company for *IPO*.

✓ *Management flexibility*—CEO's and managers of public companies often feel as though they're working in shackles. Reporting to a parent company can be easier than reporting to Wall Street.

✓ *Personal liability*—the idea of an *IPO* is that the company can sell shares to a large number of unsophisticated investors. When the share price heads south and these investors lose money, they often claim investor fraud and blame the company for not disclosing some relevant piece of information. You could also face personal liabilities related to disclosing accurate and full information in an acquisition, but as the acquirer is considered a sophisticated investor capable of conducting its own due diligence, you're not considered as accountable.

In an ideal world, one of your strategic partners will approach you out of the blue with an enticing bid to acquire your company. This does happen but don't hold your breath as you wait—most entrepreneurs find that they have to go out, target potential acquirers and actively sell the company. If you do receive an unsolicited bid, don't just accept it, even if you think it's generous—the buyer will be expecting to go through the negotiation dance and immediate acceptance may raise some suspicion (see *Appendix 2—Getting What you Want—Negotiating the Deal,* page 313*).* Express your interest, bring in some specialist help and discretely approach other potential acquirers. If there's one buyer interested in your business, chances are that there are other interested parties out there, many of whom will be more likely to improve their offers in the face of competition. Ideally, you'll get into an auction situation with two or more companies and you'll see the initial offer price increase significantly. Sellers that accept an unsolicited bid seldom recognize full value for their businesses (see *Selling the Company*, page 351).

There are good times and not so good times to sell your company. The ideal time is when the buyers are buying and the company is up-trending. The worst time is when you're in trouble and the buyers are heading for the hills. Positive momentum like sales growth, the closing of distribution partnership deals and the release of a new product can really increase the level of interest and value.

Chapter 4—The Short Sprint to Destination *Asset Sale*

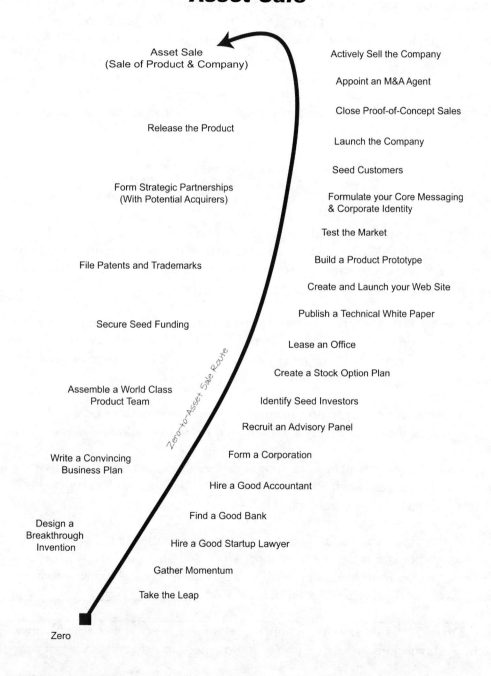

Asset Sale
(Sale of Product & Company)

Actively Sell the Company

Appoint an M&A Agent

Close Proof-of-Concept Sales

Launch the Company

Release the Product

Seed Customers

Formulate your Core Messaging
& Corporate Identity

Form Strategic Partnerships
(With Potential Acquirers)

Test the Market

Build a Product Prototype

File Patents and Trademarks

Create and Launch your Web Site

Publish a Technical White Paper

Secure Seed Funding

Lease an Office

Create a Stock Option Plan

Identify Seed Investors

Assemble a World Class
Product Team

Recruit an Advisory Panel

Form a Corporation

Write a Convincing
Business Plan

Hire a Good Accountant

Find a Good Bank

Design a
Breakthrough
Invention

Hire a Good Startup Lawyer

Gather Momentum

Take the Leap

Zero

Zero-to-Asset Sale Route

New technologies and inventions are best created by small, independent developers, however, they are best commercialized by large organizations with deep pockets and established routes to market. Some small developers grow into large corporations taking the route from Zero-to-IPO, but for many this is not possible, or doesn't make sense. The short sprint from *Zero-to-Asset Sale* is a completely different route—it involves building a company to sell from the ground up with the focus on creating assets and packaging them in a way that best appeals to a corporate buyer.

At its most basic level, there are only three components to a successful business: a great product, a market of paying customers and a route to market that connects them together.

Building a great product can take a couple of years of focused research and development. Building an effective route to market can take decades. Building a market of willing customers is something best left to the Gods—even Bill Gates has little influence over this component.

Whatever your product, there are sure to be a number of existing companies out there with established routes into your market. Even if your product is unique and way ahead of the pack, your target customer is certain to have some form of existing trading relationship with other suppliers. So here's an idea:

> **Focus your startup on building a great new product and combine it with another company's established route to market.**

Your product should benefit from your undivided attention, and your partners' route to market is probably much more established than anything you're likely to build yourself within the time frame available.

This idea is certainly not new. However, it's an idea that's sure to become increasingly popular as it grows ever more costly and time consuming to build new routes to market from the ground up. For an online technology trading exchange that's frequented by technology buyers check out www.tynax.com.

Route to market = distribution channel + sales force + brand name + executive team + administrative system + everything you need to deliver the product to your customer.

Building a New Office Block

Property Developer Approach

1. Figure out what sort of office block is most attractive to a prospective buyer.
2. Buy the land, negotiate planning permission, etc.
3. Hire outside contractors: architects, project managers, engineers, builders, etc.
4. Construct the building.
5. Contract with a realtor & put the property up for sale.
6. Sell the asset at a profit.

Traditional Silicon Valley Approach

1. Buy the land, negotiate planning permission, etc.
2. Design a T-shirt.
3. Hire the most expensive CEO in the business. Offer him an option to buy one of the floors, when completed, for a few cents.
4. Recruit an executive management team, board of directors, board of advisors, armies of clerks and underlings. Offer each individual an option to buy a room for a few cents if they stay on board.
5. Hire a huge sales and marketing team.
6. Build a floor of the building.
7. Issue a press release.
8. Host a party.
9. Design a new T-shirt.
10. Launch a web site.
11. Spend gazillions on a nationwide ad campaign.
12. Create a new business to occupy this completed floor.
13. Bring in new investors. Raise more funds.
14. Remind the building team to complete another floor.
15. Go back to step 6—and continue until each floor is complete or you run out of cash.
16. Pretend you're not interested in selling the property. Play hard to get & wait for a buyer to find the property and make an offer that's too good to refuse.

In real-estate, it's not unusual for a developer to build a new house or office block with the clear objective of simply selling it as soon as it's complete. They often have no intention of generating any form of income whatsoever from the property—other than selling the whole asset for a lump sum.

Unless they're prepared to go through a complete brainwashing and reprogramming process, I wouldn't recommend that Silicon Valley investors venture into the property development business. Property developers, on the other hand, may be able to bring a refreshing new approach to the process of developing new technology products and bringing them to market.

The property developers approach to building a technology company:

1.   Figure out what sort of product and business unit is most attractive to a prospective buyer.
2.   Form the company, the founding team and design the product blueprints.
3.   Hire outside contractors: design architects, project managers, engineers, etc.
4.   Construct the product.
5.   Contract with an M&A firm & put the product up for sale.
6.   Sell the asset at a profit.

Thinking like a property developer, you're unlikely to embark on the long haul from *Zero-to-IPO*—you'll plot out a quick sprint route from *Zero-to-Asset Sale*. You'll focus on building an asset and packaging it up to appeal to a potential acquirer.

The Zero-to-IPO Strategy

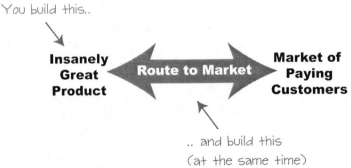

The Zero-to-Asset Sale Strategy

The technology is usually dependent on a team of designers, engineers and product support staff—they become an important integral piece of the asset. The company can be viewed as simply a wrapper or a vehicle to sell the product. So that it doesn't obstruct the sale of the product, the company 'wrapper' should be as thin and disposable as possible—so don't hire teams that a buyer is not going to need and avoid making long-term commitments like multi-year leases on office space.

To execute this strategy effectively, you may need to cleanse your mind of the conventional wisdom that you can't build a valuable company without strong sales and profits. In fact, on this route, you're not building a viable business at all—you're simply building a valuable asset. The asset incorporates the product, the underlying technology and the dependent team—the product team.

Congratulations—you reached the part where this book starts to get weird! To prepare yourself for this route, you may want to start by ceremoniously burning all your traditional business books—and start reading up on the real-estate market.

Back-of-a-Napkin Travel Plan for the Short Sprint from Zero-to-Asset Sale

Team
Team Members & Responsibilities

A small, fast moving, self-sufficient product development and support team can be most effective here.   You need a team that's prepared to target Asset Sale as opposed to IPO. Be warned – many VC's have aggressive return on investment criteria that may prevent them from targeting Asset Sale.

Provisions
Budget & Resources Required

If you carefully ration out the funding, you may be able to make it to an asset sale with a single round of funding, especially if the team can survive on modest levels of sales and supplement the funding with service revenues.

Taking Bearings
How to Fix your Position

It's easy to wander dangerously off course even on a short journey. Keep a keen eye on your cash position, track your progress and regularly seek reality checks from independent outsiders.

Plotting your Route

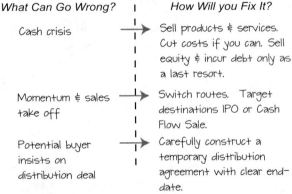

Asset Sale

Target Destination
Where do you Want to Be?
Plan to sell the technology, and other assets, at a healthy profit.

Starting Point
Identify Starting Position
Earth-shattering invention or technology ("Zero").

Release the Product

Gather Momentum

Seed Funding

Zero

Product Prototype

Maintaining Momentum
How to Keep the Wagons Rolling

You'll have to encourage the team to continue to push ahead in spite of the constraints imposed by limited funding. Learn how to whip them into a frenzy of enthusiasm and constantly keep the dream alive.

Contingencies

What Can Go Wrong?	How Will you Fix It?
Cash crisis	Sell products & services. Cut costs if you can. Sell equity & incur debt only as a last resort.
Momentum & sales take off	Switch routes. Target destinations IPO or Cash Flow Sale.
Potential buyer insists on distribution deal	Carefully construct a temporary distribution agreement with clear end-date.

Destination Asset Sale

Would you buy an unprofitable business that was consistently burning up cash, bearing in mind that after the acquisition, the cash that was burning was the cash in your pocket? It doesn't sound like a very appealing proposition. However, in the technology sector, it is possible to sell a company that's unprofitable and cash-flow negative. In fact, it happens all the time.

Imagine you own a national chain of pet stores with millions of regular customers. You discover that a revolutionary new recipe for dog food has been invented (probably in that secret underground laboratory beneath Sand Hill Road, Menlo Park). Evidence shows that dogs relish the taste of this particular recipe and wolf it down with gusto. It also has miraculous properties—just one meal will cure any canine illness, restore dogs to the prime of health and make the pets more loving and friendly towards their owners. You figure that every dog owner in the world would want this particular brand of food! Of course, this product would sell well on the shelves of your stores, however, if you could acquire it on an exclusive basis, you'd attract customers from your competitors stores as well—they'd have to come to you as you wouldn't make it available elsewhere. If you could buy exclusive rights to this product, you figure you could double the size of your business in 6 months, deliver humongous profits and your share price would go through the roof. You need this product! However, your competitor, and deadly enemy, is also hankering to buy it. The recipe is covered by patents, trademarks and all forms of protection—it's definitely unique. Depending on how much you bid, either you, or your competitor, will get to win the prize and buy this product on an exclusive basis—it's a winner-takes-all scenario. The recipe was developed by a team of 10 nutritional scientists and belongs to a small company that they formed for this purpose. Although it's been thoroughly tested, the product has not yet been commercialized and the business is burning up cash at the rate of $250,000 each month.

Does this sound like an appealing acquisition? How much would you pay? Clearly, this product is of strategic importance to your company. If you buy it, you get to dominate your market and expand your business. If you don't, you'll lose your customers to your competitor and struggle to compete. Of course, the $250,000 per month cash burn is not too appealing, but this should not prevent you from buying this company. There's much more at stake than a $250,000 per month burn rate. Combining this new product with your routes to market would boost your business and, in the long run, could be worth billions of dollars in sales and profits. You'd be crazy not to pay a good price for this company, put its development team on your payroll with non-compete employment contracts and get to own the winning recipe outright.

In many ways, the dog food inventors have been very smart. Instead of taking on the cost and responsibility of building their own chain of stores, they focused all their attention on building the product. This meant that they could avoid having to hire a large team, keep costs under control and steer clear of raising multiple rounds of funding. After creating the product, all they need to do is prove that the dogs like the dog food, protect the recipe from infringers and shop the product, and company, to a list of existing players with established routes to market.

The Company as a Disposable Wrapper for the Product

In this scenario, the company is simply a wrapper for the product, the intellectual property, and its supporting team. On acquiring the product, the buyer is likely to dispose of the wrapper—including all the employees that are not directly involved in designing, building or supporting the product and any non-product related costs and commitments, such as office leases.

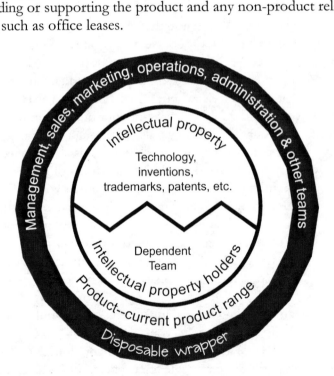

To dress the company up for sale, the wrapper needs to be as thin and disposable as possible. Typically the thinner the wrapper, the lower the burn rate—and that's a good thing when it comes to selling your company.

In an *Asset Sale*, the buyer often disposes of the whole company wrapper on acquisition—it likely has its own management, sales, marketing and operational teams in place. However, based on the circumstances, it could decide to keep some, or even all of these teams. In some cases, it may even dispose of the current product range and use the intellectual property, with the core product team, to create a new breed of products. There may be instances where the buyer is only interested in acquiring the technology itself—without any staff whatsoever. However, the intellectual property often resides in the minds of the core product team and is virtually worthless to anyone else. To make the deal appealing to a buyer, the wrapper should be as thin and disposable as possible, and you need to be flexible when structuring the deal with a potential acquirer.

Targeting Asset Sale from the Outset

If you were a property developer, you wouldn't raise any eyebrows if you started out with a plan to build an office complex with the sole purpose of selling it for a profit as soon as it was constructed. As a high-tech entrepreneur, when you take this route, you're effectively saying the following:

> *"We have no intention of building a viable stand-alone business."*
> *"We have no intention of building our own route to market."*
> *"We have no intention of creating a sales and marketing operation that will do anything more than prove that there's a market of paying customers."*
> *"We have no intention of ever making a profit."*
> *"We have no intention of ever turning cash-flow positive."*
> *"We plan to sell the company as soon as the product is developed and the market is proven."*

After you've helped them up from the floor, you should be able to convince sensible investors and other team members that this plan makes good business sense.

Or maybe not. I can understand why people have a problem with the notion of building a business that has no intention of turning a profit, however, I'm forever surprised when I come across investor resistance to a business plan that targets a sale of the company. Without an *IPO* or sale of the company, shares in a private company are virtually worthless. Rather than target a sale of the company and drive towards it, many Silicon Valley insiders believe it's better to limp around aimlessly in the hope that a huge, friendly, deep-pocketed buyer will track them down, make them an offer that's too good to refuse and buy them out. They're really hoping for an acquisition but they don't want to plot out a route that will take them there directly. In some cultures, like Japanese, selling the company is considered the sign of weak management. Likewise, many U.S. managers and directors see it as a failure or a weakness to admit that they want to sell the company, so they never put the wheels in motion to start the sales process. Personally, I don't see anything wrong with targeting an acquisition and structuring the company to achieve this goal.

Mergers and acquisitions are very much more common than *IPO*'s and it's a more likely exit route and destination for most technology startups—so it's a mystery to me why so many CEO's fail to take the steps necessary to make the company look appealing to a potential buyer.

One common misconception is that targeting a sale means putting a 'FOR SALE' sign outside the office and letting everyone know that you're up for grabs. This is not the case. You may be targeting a sale and creating a business plan to reach this goal several years before you actually engage an M&A team and start the process. You could be targeting a sale before you actually design the product. Indeed, unless you're in a fire-sale situation, you don't want to advertise the fact that the company is targeting a sale—this could introduce unnecessary uncertainty within the customer base and employees. If you read the section on *Selling the Company*, page 351, you'll see that this information should be kept confidential from all but a small, select team.

There should be no stigma attached to selling the company, creating an exit route for the investors, providing a stable home for the employees and putting some real muscle behind marketing the product.

The 'Buy vs. Build' Cap

If you're simply selling your product as an asset, you're sure to come up against the buyer that asks 'why should I pay you more for this product than it would cost me to build it myself?' The assertion is that the valuation of the asset, and the company is capped at the bare cost of reverse engineering and rebuilding the product using the buyers own, or a contract, development team.

Of course, the value of the asset is somewhat less than you'd achieve from an *IPO* or *Cash Flow Sale*, however, it could be significantly higher than the bare build cost. Yes, it is a smaller pie, but you should be able to retain a much larger share for yourself—as the short sprint is a much less costly route requiring a smaller team, and a smaller number of investors, there are fewer people to share the sale proceeds.

Build vs. buy cap? What build vs. buy cap? If you plan this properly, you're not selling a product—you're selling a unique business opportunity.

Breaking through the build vs. buy cap:

- ✓ *Time to market multiple*—technology markets move quickly and the window of opportunity for this product may be open for only a fleeting moment of time. Building a copy of your product will certainly take time, lots of hard work and management attention—by the time it's finished, the window of opportunity may have slammed shut. First mover advantage can make all the difference between failure and success.

- ✓ *Momentum multiple*—there goes that 'M' word again! A product with momentum is worth significantly more than the product on its own. With good PR you can whip the market up into a frenzy of enthusiasm for your product and position it as the clear leader in its space, even before the product is officially released. Large, established companies sometimes struggle to create the energy and enthusiasm that comes from a small, focused team. A positive buzz in the press, the customer base, the employees and the market as a whole may be possible with a modest budget, however, it can boost the value of the company significantly.

- ✓ *Auction fever*—I recently sold a camera lens on eBay that I had used for over a year and was out of warranty. Believe it or not, there were 16 bids for this used product and the final 'winner' paid almost the current retail price—he could have ordered a brand new product, with warranty, for just a few dollars more. The reason behind this apparent insanity is *auction fever*, a long-time member of the *ego* family of dangerous diseases. The fever can strike anyone—after they get into the bidding race, rational decision-making goes out the window and the process becomes an issue of 'winning' or 'losing'. If you can get two or more competitors into an auction environment to buy your company, you may be able to gently play them off against each other and create the perfect conditions for auction fever.

If you read the appendices, you'll start to appreciate how a good M&A intermediary could help negotiate the price upwards way beyond the imaginary build vs. buy cap. Professional negotiators often use a figure of 3 or more for the time to market multiple—so, if the build costs are, say $5m, the value is at least $15m after applying the multiple. With positive momentum and auction fever, who knows how far the price could reach. It may not be an *IPO* valuation but the return on investment from a *Zero-to-Asset Sale* strategy would certainly look very appealing to a property developer and almost any normal investor.

A Short Sprint Team

The direct route from *Zero-to-Asset Sale* is new to some, and may be considered unusual. If you take this route, it's vitally important that the whole team understands and buys into the plan. Fortunately there's a sure-fire way to make sure that everyone is fully synchronized with the plan. Founders, investors, employees and everyone involved should hold hands, skip around an open fire outdoors at dawn and recite the *Asset Sale* mantra in a low guttural tone (dress code: bare feet, headbands and white cotton tunics).

The *Asset Sale* Mantra

We're heading for Asset Sale,   *Advertising's not for us,*
That's the place for us,   *No babies will be kissed,*
We're building a product,   *Our marketing is just to prove,*
That we'll all be proud of.   *Our customers exist.*

As soon as it's complete,   *We'll never ask for budgets,*
We'll sell it to a buyer,   *We'll never wonder why,*
We'll never turn a profit,   *The place is filled with engineers,*
Suits we'll never hire.   *And no one wears a tie.*

Budgets will be tight,   *We'll never lay down roots,*
Investors very few,   *We know that we'll be sold,*
That leaves more to share,   *We're looking for a nest egg,*
For the likes of me and you.   *For when we all grow old.*

Ritual recital of the mantra on the third Tuesday of every month will ensure that there's no confusion about the company's destination, the route you're following and the factors for success. (Now you know just how low I'm prepared to stoop in an attempt to make a point and liven up a dull topic!)

The point is that you're in for serious trouble if half the crew is pushing the company toward *Asset Sale* and the other half is planning on building a profitable business and pushing it towards *IPO* or *Cash Flow Sale*.

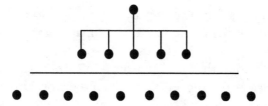

Fortunately, the team you need for this short sprint is much smaller and more manageable than the team you would choose for the long haul to *IPO*—good news when you come to buying the cotton tunics. In fact, to minimize the burn rate, avoid having to constantly raise new funding from outside investors and make the company more appealing to potential buyers, you really have to keep the team as small as you can. Think long and hard before you hire anyone that's not directly involved in designing, building or supporting the product—the salary and related costs will increase the burn rate and they're unlikely to be retained by the acquirer after the deal is closed.

Founding Partners

You may feel there's safety in numbers but it's in your interests to go it alone for as long as you can before bringing in any partners. Make sure you read the section on *Founding Partners, Page 28* before bringing in partners and telling your friends or colleagues about your idea.

Directors

On this route, you're not building a board of directors to impress Wall Street or anyone else outside the company. The role of the board is purely functional—to take care of the corporate governance issues and direct the company along its chosen route. The ideal size of the board is an integer larger than *Zero* and smaller than two—this is a short sprint strategy and a small board makes quick decisions.

	Startup	*Post-Investment*
Founder	✓	✓
Investor		✓
CEO		✓

If your investor demands a board seat and wants to bring in a CEO, you're going to have to extend the board to 3. Anyone else with interest in joining the board should be steered toward the advisory panel.

Advisory Panel

As always, there's little to lose and a great deal to be gained from creating an advisory panel. As your board is going to be kept very small, the advisory panel can play an important role in helping steer the company. Some decisions that you take in the course of running the business will make the company more appealing to a potential buyer and take you a step closer to successful sale. Others will take you a step further away. In addition to the usual culprits (see *Recruit an Advisory Panel*, page 79), you may want to consider putting an expert from the world of M&A (mergers and acquisitions) onto your panel—this could help you take your bearings and determine whether you're on track and heading in the right direction.

Zero-to-Asset Sale CEO, Executives & Management Team

The CEO that you need to lead a company from *Zero-to-Asset Sale* knows how to deliver a great product as quickly as possible with a small team and a tight budget. To do this, the CEO has to understand the product inside out, deliver inspirational presentations and demonstrations and motivate a team of cranky designers, developers and engineers. Good project management and planning skills are always important, as well as the ability to drive toward a goal, build momentum and keep the wagons rolling when the going gets tough. There's no replacement for good judgment, drive and charm.

It may be nice to have a CEO with experience of raising funds from investors and selling companies, but this work can be assigned to outside agents and intermediaries. You certainly don't need a CEO with an impressive track record on Wall Street, experience of spending humongous budgets and building empires of sales and marketing staff. You don't have the budget to hire a career CEO—in fact you don't want anyone on the team with an accomplished track record of growing teams and spending money. Many a good technology company has been destroyed by a big spending CEO. On the *Zero-to-Asset Sale* route, the ideal CEO is prepared to make the coffee, accept a relatively low salary, fly coach class and stay in cheap motels to set an example and help contain costs.

You don't need layers of managers and executives to build a great product—there's probably no room for them in your garage anyway. In fact, by adding staff that are not directly involved in designing, developing and supporting the product, you're increasing the burn rate and making the company less attractive to a potential buyer. So, your executive and management team should be kept as small as possible—in some cases a good CEO may be all you need.

Why Budgets are Tight on the Route from *Zero*-to-*Asset Sale*

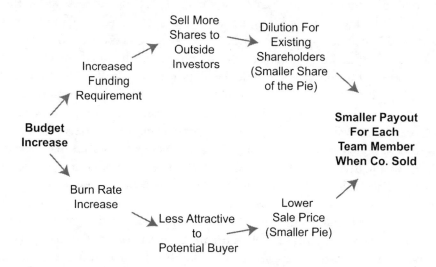

Zero-to Asset Sale Investors

When you bring in an investor, you usually get a lot more than just cash. You normally receive plenty of advice—whether you want it or not. If you're on the *Zero-to-Asset Sale* route and your investor won't join you in reciting the *Asset Sale Mantra*, you could find yourselves pulling the company in opposite directions.

If you're going to have any chance of making it along the route from *Zero-to-Asset Sale* you're going to have to avoid venture capital investors that specialize in guiding companies along the alternative route to *IPO* (unless they're prepared to don the tunic and join you at dawn on the third Tuesday of each month). As well as encouraging you to ramp up your costs, build your own sales and marketing operation, and raise more capital, the traditional VC investor is unlikely to be prepared to accept the type of payout that results from an *Asset Sale*. Many have a model that depends on at least some of their portfolio companies reaching *IPO* and their shares hitting pay dirt. As the outside investors get preference shares, they get to decide whether to accept, or decline, an acquisition offer to sell the company. An acquirer could make an offer to buy the company that's acceptable to the founders and employees but it doesn't meet the aggressive return on investment requirements of an outside investor. At this point you realize that your common stock is virtually worthless—typically, the preference shares held by the outside investor are the only shares with a vote when it comes to selling the company. As common stockholders you don't even have a say!

I recently met a very interesting company with hot technology that had successfully boot-strapped its startup phase by licensing its intellectual property and selling consulting services. With a killer product, a proven market, healthy sales and a strong client base, this company had already made excellent progress along the route to *Asset Sale*. It had no outside investors, no preference shares—all the common stock was held by founders and employees. The team was content to be aiming for *Asset Sale*—they figured they could sell out within 18 months and share about $50m between around 10 founders and employees—not bad at all! To achieve this valuation they felt they needed a cash injection from outside investors to invest more heavily in their product development. So they were seeking funds from venture capital investors as well as some of their corporate clients. On the surface this appears to be a pretty healthy situation, however, there's possibly a major flaw in this plan. The outside investors, as preference shareholder, will of course, get to veto any future offer of acquisition. The top-tier venture capital firms they were talking to were all interested in *IPO*—they had no interest in targeting *Asset Sale*. With existing routes to market and billions of dollars in the bank, their existing clients were also potential investors and the most likely ultimate acquirers of the company. By selling shares to a corporate client, they would be giving full control over the future sale of the company to one of the potential buyers. This would seriously restrict the company's ability to sell to another corporate buyer. The venture investor would ramp things up, bring in a new management team, and steer the company toward *IPO*. The corporate investor would block the sale to one of its competitors and awareness of this situation could prevent the company from creating an auction environment between a number of bidders. By bringing in a venture capital or corporate investor, the founders were effectively losing control of the sales (M&A) process and cutting off the route to *Asset Sale*. Unless they could bring in a different type of investor that was comfortable to target *Asset Sale*, their new investor would block their chances of selling the company for $50m.

So, when targeting *Asset Sale*, you may want to avoid traditional venture capital and corporate investors. What we really need is a new breed of *Zero-to-Asset Sale* investor that's prepared to chant the mantra, help their portfolio companies build great products, dress the companies up for sale and then help find a suitable buyer. Perhaps they'll come from the property development business? More likely, they'll emerge from the pool of angels and venture capital investors that wake up to the fact that the *Zero-to-IPO* route is no longer the Holy Grail that it was in the dot-com days and that there is an alternative route.

The *Zero-to-Asset Sale* route actually holds a number of attractions for an investor:

- ✓ *Clear exit route*—as the whole team is targeting selling the company from the outset, there's little mystery regarding how the investor is going to achieve a return on its investment.

- ✓ *Fast sprint*—the process of building a great product, then selling the company can take as little as 24 months, and sometimes even less. In the time it takes to guide one company all the way to *IPO*, an investor could complete several journeys from *Zero-to-Asset Sale*.

- ✓ *Small investment*—a large proportion of the funds that investors plough into companies goes into building a route to market. Career CEO's, advertising budgets and sales teams certainly don't come cheap. Funding a bunch of techies to build a product is comparatively inexpensive.

- ✓ *Smaller, more manageable team*—a traditional seed round may be all the company needs to carry it through the short sprint to *Asset Sale*. Many an investor would relish the prospect of being the sole shareholder working with a relatively small, manageable board and management team.

- ✓ *Low burn rate*—when times are tough, it's much easier for a company with a low burn rate to avoid shutting down and navigate its way out of trouble.

OK, this route doesn't offer the glitz and glamour of the *IPO* but for investors that are interested in seeing good returns, more quickly and with lower risk, the *Zero-to-Asset Sale* route can offer a refreshing and attractive alternative. I expect more investors to specialize in *Zero-to-Asset Sale* investments in the coming years.

The Route from Zero-to-Asset Sale

In the early stage, this route shares some of the milestones and steps with the route from *Zero-to-IPO*.

This is a short sprint strategy—there's a limited window of opportunity for you to hit the milestones, build the product and get it up for sale. Delays cost money and allow competitors to catch up.

Zero-to-Asset Sale Milestones

1. *Design a Breakthrough Invention*—the journey starts with a breakthrough idea, technology or invention.
2. *Write a Convincing Business Plan*—reflecting the fact that you're not building a viable stand-alone business, this is not a *regular* business plan. Instead, you need to describe the product, how it solves your customers' problem, how it

beats the competition, why it would be appealing to a potential buyer and how much funding will required before the company is sold.

3. *Assemble a World Class Product Team*—you need to pull together the core product designers, scientists and engineers. If you don't have the funds to hire them, and they're not in a position to take stock for salary, get a commitment from them to join when you close your funding.

4. *Secure Seed Funding*—ideally from investors that can help guide the company along the route to *Asset Sale* (some VC's and corporate investors should be avoided on this journey—see *Zero-to-Asset Sale Investors* page 241.)

5. *File Patents and Trademarks*—to protect and defend the company's major asset—its intellectual property.

6. *Form Strategic Partnerships*—with large, respected corporations that have an established route to your market. Bearing in mind that a strategic partner is potentially the ultimate acquirer of the company, take care in structuring these partnership and distribution agreements (*see Distribution Trap, Page 245*).

7. *Release the Product*—complete the product development, release the product to customers and close some early sales. This validates the product and proves that the market exists.

8. Asset Sale—sell the company bundled with the product and supporting team.

Short Sprint Contingency Plans

Of course, the journey from *Zero-to-Asset Sale* doesn't always go as smoothly as you'd hope. Assuming there are no fundamental problems with the product, or the development process, the most likely obstacle you're likely encounter on this journey is a *Cash Crisis*—running out of cash before the product is complete. It's quite possible that a potential buyer with an established route to market insists on a distribution deal instead as a cheaper and lower-risk alternative to buying the company. If you don't handle this carefully, you could be led into the *Distribution Trap*. On the other hand, you may be surprised to find that the market takes off, you gather momentum, reach your milestones with ease and even start to generate respectable sales—this is time to consider changing routes, start building a viable stand-alone business and heading for *IPO*.

Cash Crisis on the Short Sprint to Asset Sale

Before starting any form of small business, it's important that you brush up on your survival skills and read the chapter on the *Slippery Slope to Shutdown* (page 251).

As you're not even trying to generate sufficient sales revenue to support this company, and you're keeping your outside investment to a bare minimum, the probability of encountering a cash crisis is pretty high. Here are the steps to take in this situation, in order of preference:

1. *Cut costs, slash costs if you have to*—the priority is to protect the product from cost cutting and try to maintain the core product development team. Offer stock-for-salary deals and other incentives before cutting the core product team (see *Cutting Costs*, page 264, *Slashing Costs*, page 273).
2. *Generate revenue from service work*—you can generate revenue by hiring your staff out on an hourly or daily basis. Rather than being a distraction, the ideal scenario is that the team comes out of the project with ideas and intellectual property that you can use to enhance your own product. In addition to finding clients, you'll have to set up a time and billing system and ask staff to keep track of their hours.
3. *Raise funds from outside investors*—a new issue of preference shares, bridge loan & debt. Remember—the more your raise, the less the founders and employees get to share out of the proceeds from the ultimate sale of the company.
4. *Sell the company in a hurry*—as a last resort, you could shop the company to potential buyers (see *Selling the Company in a Hurry*, Page 372).
5. *Shutdown*—once the cash crisis is terminal, orderly *Shutdown* is a better alternative than *Bankruptcy*, especially if there's any chance of a restart (see *Making and Elegant Descent—Orderly Shutdown*, page 291).

Potential Buyer Insists on Distribution Deal (Distribution Trap)

Beware the Distribution Trap. An existing company with an established route to your market is likely to be interested in selling your product. Signing a distribution agreement with you is sure to be a much cheaper alternative to buying your company. Many distribution agreements should come with a financial health warning: *"Signing this agreement could kill your chance of ever selling your company."* With a renewable or perpetual distribution deal, you could be leasing your product out to a potential buyer indefinitely, providing them with no incentive to buy it outright— and even if your product meets with success in the market, your investors could be forced to wait decades for a return on investment. When you decide to focus on building a great product and forget about building your own routes to market, you're giving up the notion of building a viable stand-alone business and effectively cutting *IPO* and *Cash Flow Sale* from your list of destinations. That leaves only *Asset Sale*, *Shutdown* and *Bankruptcy* as places your startup could go. If you sign the wrong sort of distribution agreement, you might as well cross *Asset Sale* off your list as well—

your distribution partner already has access to the product, doesn't need to buy the company and the distribution deal locks other potential buyers out as well.

The Effect of Signing the Wrong Distribution Deal

The financial health warning shouldn't necessarily be placed on all distribution agreements—a well structured deal could actually act as the first step in the process of selling the company to your distribution partner. If the owner of the route to market demands a distribution deal and can't be persuaded to buy your product (and company) directly, make sure you structure the distribution agreement as a 'try-before-you-buy' deal with a firm termination date that forces them to buy the company or lose the product.

Momentum & Sales Take Off

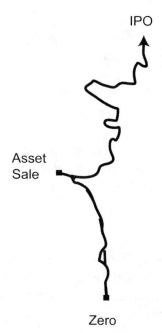

IPO

Asset
Sale

Zero

When you start to find customers lining up outside your door waving dollar bills and trying to buy your product, it's time to wonder whether you've chosen the best route for your company. You're sure to find a number of interested buyers if you want to proceed with an *Asset Sale*, however, there may be sufficient momentum to switch routes and head for *IPO*. There are no real obstacles to you switching routes—all the steps that you've taken on the road to *Asset Sale* have been heading you in the right direction and there's no need to backtrack over previously covered ground. *Asset Sale* is well within your reach—*IPO* is a longer, riskier journey with a potentially bigger reward at the end. This switch is difficult to reverse—see *Switch to Cash Flow Sale*, page 60, so it's worth taking a little time to consider your options—see *What's the Best Route for You and your Product?*, page 43.

Reaching Destination Asset Sale & Cashing Out

In the past, many companies have reached *Asset Sale* by accident—after attempting and failing to build a viable stand-alone business with its own in-house sales and marketing operation. As a result, some people still unfortunately equate *Asset Sale* with 'Fire Sale'. Large investment banks and other financial intermediaries have been reluctant to represent companies in *Asset Sale* situations and prefer to concentrate on larger *Cash Flow Sale* deals.

This is beginning to change. Entrepreneurs are beginning to realize that new technologies are best invented by small independent teams but best marketed by large corporations with deep pockets and existing routes to market. They're beginning to build technologies to sell and target *Asset Sale* from the outset. To many new entrepreneurs, destination *Asset Sale* means cashing out—and making a significant profit. The business model is pretty straightforward—build new products and technology at low cost and sell them to large corporations. *Build Cost Plus* is one of the few techniques you can use to put a value on your technology (see *What's it Worth?—Valuing the Company*, page 301).

Although *Asset Sale* doesn't necessarily mean selling the whole company, it follows the same process (see *Selling the Company, the M&A Process*, page 351) If you want to actually reach the destination, and close the deal, you're going to need to pick the best team you can find:

- *M&A intermediary*—specialists in this field are few and far between. Ideally, you need a small, independent M&A agent focused on technology *Asset Sale* deals or a dedicated online match-making service.
- *Negotiator*—if the negotiator doesn't come with your M&A intermediary, you may want to hire the services of a good lawyer with a proven track record of closing deals or a professional M&A negotiator.
- *Accountant*—you need someone to provide accurate financial information but the numbers are a secondary consideration in an Asset Sale deal and the firm doesn't necessarily have to need to have the support of a marquee-name firm.

Dressing the Company up for Asset Sale

In a *Cash Flow Sale*, the buyer is acquiring the business as a going concern. A cash flow buyer is interested in the company's financial performance and the true state of the sales pipeline. In an Asset Sale, the sales pipeline doesn't yet really exist—and cash is flowing out instead of in. An Asset Sale buyer is concerned with issues like the technology and how it could be incorporated into the product line, the development team and how it could be integrated into the organization, the burn rate and how it might be slashed.

Dressing the company up for an asset sale involves maximizing the value of the asset, minimizing its cost and helping the buyer figure out how it might be able to commercialize the technology at a profit. There's little point in heralding the strength of the management, sales, marketing and administration teams, if the buyer sees them as liabilities to be disposed of when the acquisition is complete.

In an Asset Sale situation, the sales materials need to cover the following issues:

- ✓ *Core messaging and positioning*—a short, accurate and impressive product description and positioning statement will help the buyer understand and value the asset for sale.
- ✓ *Primary application*—this helps the buyer identify the target market and understand how the technology could be productized or otherwise delivered to customers.
- ✓ *Other applications*—describe additional markets and products in which the technology could be deployed.
- ✓ *Problem solved by the technology*—identify the problem that the technology is designed to solve, its associated costs and implications.

✓ *How the technology solves the problem*—here you can explain the approach taken to solve the problem.

✓ *Competitive advantage*—describe why the technology is superior to the competition.

✓ *Development status*—here you can explain where the product is in the development cycle (prototype, internal alpha, external alpha, internal beta, external beta, preview, limited release, final release, etc.)

✓ *Localized languages*—many buyers are global corporations interested in delivering the technology into various markets. Let them know if you've localized the technology into other languages like French, German, Japanese and Swahili.

✓ *Platforms supported*—buyers of software products obviously need to know which operating system platforms are supported. If the buyer is a UNIX shop and the software runs only on Windows, this needs to be communicated sooner rather than later.

✓ *Development platform*—technology buyers are interested in the platform and development tools that have been used to build the technology. If you have software written in Java rather than Visual Basic, you might want to focus on selling it to a company like Sun rather than Microsoft.

✓ *IP ownership status*—obviously, a potential buyer needs to know whether the seller owns all components of the technology for sale, components are licensed from third parties and whether there's any dispute over ownership.

✓ *Deal structure*—if you have a strong preference, it can be helpful to let the buyer know whether you're selling the company with the technology, selling the technology asset on its own, an exclusive or non-exclusive license.

✓ *Technology dependencies*—this is where you identify 3rd party platforms, tools and products on which the technology relies.

✓ *Patent status*—buyers are understandably interested to understand if the technology is patentable, and the current status of patent filings.

✓ *Team dependencies*—describe the team members, if any, that a buyer would need to hire, or contract with, in order to successfully deploy the technology.

✓ *Current location*—identify the city where the team is currently located.

✓ *Team mobility*—if the buyer is in New York, the team on which the technology relies is in Barcelona and is not prepared to relocate, this could hold up the deal. So, it will be useful to indicate whether the team is prepared to relocate across town, to another city, another state or another country.

✓ *Sales status*—sales revenues are always welcome—even small revenues can validate that the market actually exists. Whether you're pre-sales, have paying beta customers, paying seed customers or volume sales are already rolling in, the buyer is sure to want to know where you are in the sales process.

✓ *Sales generated to date*—if you don't feel comfortable disclosing actual sales results in your prospectus, you can refer to a category like 'six figure sales have been generated since the product was released 3 months ago'.

✓ *Technical white paper*—a serious buyer will want to dig into the technology, understand what it does and how it works. Obviously, you don't want to give away any trade secrets, but you do need to help the buyer make an intelligent evaluation of the technology.

Chapter 5—The Slippery Slope to Destination *Shutdown*

It would be a little shortsighted of me to write a book for startup technology entrepreneurs that failed to address the one situation they're most likely to encounter—cash crisis. You may have the best team, product and technology in the world, but the company is sure to hit the rocks if it runs out of cash. You're going to have to learn how to avoid and escape a cash crisis if you're going to have any chance of success as a startup entrepreneur.

Companies can run out of cash and die at virtually any stage of development. You'll notice that I created Startup Island with steep slopes surrounded by shark-infested seas—wandering off track at any point can put you on the slippery slope to *Shutdown*.

After a crash, its not unusual for the management and board of directors to claim to be the poor innocent victims of a cash crisis that crept up and blindsided them. Of course, looking back, we can all spot the warning signals, but in the heat of the moment, these signals are often undetected, or ignored. It is possible to find yourself blindsided if you don't take your bearings on a regular basis. When you know where to look, it's not difficult to detect a distant or looming cash crisis.

After reading this chapter, you should be armed with a better understanding of how you can find yourself heading for cash crisis and a variety of strategies and ideas to help you navigate the company through this difficult terrain. We start by analyzing how the cash crisis develops, how momentum transforms from a magical force into a deadly menace, and we break the process into several phases—the *Scramble Zone*, *Survival Zone*, *Freefall Zone* and *Shutdown Zone*. An important part of *Taking your Bearings*, page 34 is figuring out whether you're *On Track* or in the *Scramble Zone* or one of the other zones on the slippery slope. In this chapter, we investigate how you can react when you take your bearings and detect a distant or looming cash crisis and provide action plans for each of the zones.

Navigating the slope involves climbing back on track by raising money from investors in an *Up Round* of funding, a *Down Round*, or a *Bridge Loan*. It also involves slowing your descent by *Cutting Costs* or *Slashing Costs*. We also identify some radical maneuvers such as *Switching Destinations*, *Reinventing the Company*, *Warm Restart* and *Cold Restart*—all aimed at reversing the slide and boosting momentum.

Finally, when all else fails, we figure out how to make an elegant descent—navigating to an orderly *Shutdown* instead of a messy *Bankruptcy*.

Slippery Slope to Cash Crisis

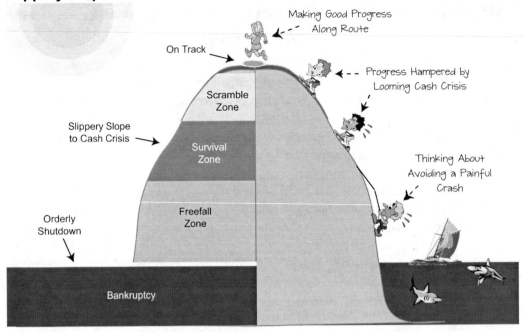

How a Cash Crisis Develops

An unfortunate fact of life is that technology startups burn through cash. It takes time and people to develop a product and bring it to market. Time and people cost money and a technology startup is in a seemingly endless race to raise new cash from investors before its existing cash burns out. You don't raise funds overnight—the process usually has a gestation period of around 9 months. A cash crisis develops when the cash burns out more quickly than management's ability to raise funds (see *Step 2) Are you On Track or the Slippery Slope to Cash Crisis?*, page 40).

On Track

With more than 9 months cash, fundraising efforts are under way and you're on schedule to comfortably close a round of funding or sell the company before the cash burns out.

Cash flow worries should not slow your momentum and you should make good progress in hitting the milestones and stepping stones along your chosen route.

Scramble Zone

At your current level of fundraising activity, you don't have the time to close a round of funding or sell the company before the cash burns out. You still have a positive bank balance but a cash crisis is looming.

After living hand-to-mouth through the seed stage, you may be forgiven for feeling a sense of security when you have several months of cash in the bank. At this point, it can be tempting to focus all efforts on building a killer product and ease off the process of raising new funds, however, if you fail to accelerate fundraising efforts now and start to cut costs, you're putting the company's survival in danger. Momentum has a tendency to slow as you take your focus off building the product and other activities and start the scramble to raise funds.

Survival Zone

Accelerated fundraising or M&A efforts are now unlikely to avert the cash crisis. The crisis is still probably survivable if you act quickly to lighten the load, cut the burn rate and buy the company more time.

Momentum stalls as people realize that the company doesn't have sufficient time to close new funding before the cash burns out. The cash crisis becomes a major distraction—team members become so pre-occupied that they forget to continue to hit the milestones and stepping stones.

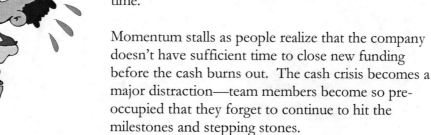

Freefall Zone

There's a lack of traction in the fundraising process. Although the company has several months cash in the bank, people start to realize that it would take something close to a miracle to close funding or sell the company before the cash burns out.

Fearing an impending crash, key team members start to bail out, word gets out on the street that the company is in trouble and the investors start to head for the hills. The remaining employees spend time polishing their resumes and the company goes into a state of paralysis. The company goes into freefall as the cash crisis moves from 'survivable' to 'terminal'.

Shutdown Zone

With a planned descent into the *Shutdown* zone, you could reach the safety of an orderly *Shutdown* and move on to your next startup. If you handle things carefully, you may have the option to re-launch—see *Cold Restart*.

If you leave it too late or you don't prepare a shutdown plan, the company is likely to sink into *Bankruptcy*—brace yourself for the assault of the angry creditors!

On Detecting a Distant or Looming Cash Crisis

After taking your bearings, detecting a distant or looming cash crisis and fixing your position somewhere on the slippery slope, you're faced with an interesting range of options:

a) Ignore your findings and blindly soldier on.
b) Spend valuable time trying to figure out where and why you went off track.
c) Point fingers to apportion blame.
d) Become despondent and do nothing.
e) Prepare a plan and take action to cut costs, raise funds and get back on track.
f) Produce a hockey stick sales forecast so the crisis magically disappears.
g) Attack the navigator.

If you selected e)—congratulations! You get to continue on the journey with at least a chance of success. If you selected one of the other options—congratulations, you're an ideal candidate to work in a large corporation where people sometimes get away with making stupid decisions. You could be there sooner than you think—your startup is heading for *Shutdown* or *Bankruptcy* as soon as its cash burns out.

Many companies seem to select option a) in conjunction with f)—they make a few tweeks to the sales spreadsheet, take little or no action to avert the crisis and end up crashing, in spectacular fashion. To understand why they do this, scientists have been forced to put a number of small innocent animals into pans of water and boil them alive. It's rather drastic action, I admit, but it would be much more expensive to boil up real, live, corporate executives—and they'd make more of a mess.

Don't Try this at Home

Rumor has it that if you put a frog in a pan of cold water on the stove and turn up the heat, it will stay put while the water gradually heats to a boil. At some point, the frog becomes a tasty form of hot, green slime.

Why doesn't the frog jump out of the pan when it figures out that the water is getting progressively warmer? There are at least two reasons—denial and inertia. The frog initially goes into a state of denial convincing itself that the water is still cool. Then it goes into a state of inertia—*'well the water does seem to be getting a little warmer and I probably should take some action but I'm busy right now—I'll deal with that problem later.'*

Faced with a looming cash crisis, the frog's distant cousin—the corporate executive—often exhibits the same behavior. In a bizarre quirk of nature, human beings (and frogs) often go into a state of denial when faced with unpleasant news—they choose to hide from the truth. I can't figure out why natural selection has allowed this characteristic to endure throughout the ages. Unfortunately, in business this state of denial, combined with inertia, a resistance to any form of change or fluctuation in status quo, often leads management to delay taking evasive action until it's too late.

So, what can be done if the CEO and board of directors choose to ignore a looming crisis and blindly soldier on? The first thing to do is alert them to the crisis and make sure they're aware that some people that care about the company are concerned. If they can't be gently coaxed out of this state of denial and inertia, concerned employees and shareholders may have to resort to some form of intervention. A confrontation with lots of emotional screaming and shouting may shake them out of their complacency—or get a number of people fired. Heck, they're going to lose their jobs when the company goes bust anyway, so what do they have to lose?

On detecting a distant or looming cash crisis, it's important that management prepares a plan and takes immediate action to cut costs, raise funds and get back on track. The basis principle is this—the closer you get to running out of cash, the more aggressively you need to accelerate your efforts to raise funds, sell the company, maintain momentum and cut costs.

Scramble Zone Action Plan

You're in the Scramble Zone when your cash is likely to burn out before the current fundraising and M&A activities conclude—so the priority here is to accelerate the fundraising efforts. However, there are a number of additional issues to address.

Scramble Zone Dash Board

1. **Accelerate Fundraising Efforts**—by injecting energy and resources into the process of raising funds (see *Appendix 3—Gathering your Provisions—The Fundraising Process,* page 325). Make sure you have an active, effective fundraising team—you're now in a race against time. Your fundraising efforts are not yet desperate and you still have the time to *Raise an Up-Round* (page 260).

2. **Commence M&A Efforts**—in case you fail to raise funds before the cash burns out, this is a good time to start the process of *Selling the Company* (see page 351). This doesn't mean putting a 'For Sale' sign outside the office—you can pick the M&A team and prepare to sell the company without informing the staff or the outside world. A potential investor is often a potential buyer so the fundraising and M&A activities can be readily combined.

3. **Cut Costs**—hopefully the looming cash crisis will be averted by accelerating the fundraising process and bringing in more cash, however, this is a good time to *Cut Costs* (see page 264)—especially obvious, non-essential costs.

4. **Fix your Position Regularly**—Take your bearings (see *Taking your Bearings,* page 34) and track your progress on a monthly or quarterly basis.

5. **Maintain Momentum**—it's important that you take action to counteract the tendency for momentum to drop—*Spread the Good Vibes* (page 32) and *Plot the Route Ahead* (page 33).

6. **Prepare for More Radical Maneuvers**—like *Reinventing the Company* (page 276), *Slashing Costs* (page 273), *Warm Restart* (page 280) and *Switching Destinations* (page 275) before you actually slip into the Survival Zone.

<u>**Survival Zone Action Plan**</u>

You're in the Survival Zone when accelerated fundraising and M&A efforts are unlikely to avert a looming crisis—so the priority here is to buy more time by cutting costs. However, you need to run several important activities in parallel—if you're going to have any chance of survival.

Survival Zone Dash Board

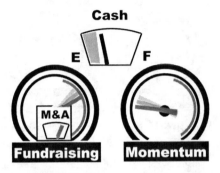

1. **Accelerate Fundraising Efforts**—you can't slacken off on the fundraising efforts while you take radical steps to cut costs. It's time to inject even more energy, add outside agents to the fundraising team, call in favors and pull as many strings as you can to drive toward a quick closing of funds. If you're lucky, you'll be able to close a *Up-round* (page 260) however, expect investors to take advantage of your increasing desperation and negotiate better terms for themselves—this means that you could be forced to accept a *Down-Round* (page 260) or even a *Bridge Loan* (page 262).

2. **Accelerate M&A Efforts**—this is the time to press the button to start the process of *Selling the Company in a Hurry* (page 372).

3. **Cut Costs or Slash Costs**—the earlier and the deeper you can cut costs, the more time you'll be able to buy. So, in addition to *Cutting Costs*, this is the best time to *Slash Costs* (page 273).

4. **Fix your Position Regularly**—*Take your Bearings* (page 34) and track your progress on a monthly or weekly basis.

5. **Take Radical Momentum Maneuvers**—to prevent the menacing effects of negative or freefall momentum, you need to encourage an upbeat team and continue to show marked progress by hitting milestones and stepping stones on your route. As always, continue the gentle maneuvers like *Spreading the Good Vibes* and *Plotting the Route Ahead*, but this is the time to take some of the more radical maneuvers like *Switching Destinations*, *Reinventing the Company* and *Warm Restart*.

6. **Prepare for More Radical Maneuvers**—before you enter the Freefall Zone, get ready to *Slash Costs* further. If you haven't yet taken radical maneuvers like *Switching Destinations*, *Reinventing the Company* and *Warm Restart*, this is the time to prepare to carry them out.

Freefall Zone Action Plan

You're in the Freefall Zone when you have less than 4 months of cash and it would take something of a miracle to close funding or sell the company before the cash burns out. When you find yourself in this position, your priority is to buy more time while you work for a miracle and take action to avoid a painful crash.

Freefall Zone Dash Board

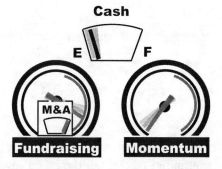

1. **Accelerate Fundraising Efforts**—the team is tired and stressed out but you can't let it show—it's important that you work flat out to close some funding as quickly as possible. In view of your weak position, investors are sure to negotiate a *Down-Round* or *Bridge Loan*, however, you can still push for *Up-Round*—miracles have been known to happen!

2. **Accelerate M&A Efforts**—hurry with your parallel efforts to sell the company (see *Selling the Company in a Hurry,* page 372).

3. **Slash Costs**—the company is in freefall, you have only a matter of months or weeks to continue before you crash into the *Shutdown Zone*—you have to *Slash Costs* to buy more time for that miracle to take place.

4. **Fix your Position Regularly**—*Take your Bearings* and track your progress on a weekly or daily basis.

5. **Take Radical Momentum Maneuvers**—momentum is in freefall, everyone is bailing out and this is your last chance to shock the company back into action. Continue the gentle momentum maneuvers like *Spreading the Good Vibes* and *Plotting the Route Ahead*, but now you have to take some of the more radical maneuvers like *Switching Destinations*, *Reinventing the Company* and *Warm Restart.*

6. **Prepare an Orderly *Shutdown* Plan**—this is time to take action to avoid a messy *Bankruptcy* (page 295) by planning an elegant descent to *Orderly Shutdown* <u>before</u> your cash runs out. You can also start thinking about the possibility of a *Cold Restart* (page 285).

Climbing Back on Track—Raising Funds

Climbing back on track means putting cash in the bank. The cash could come from a miraculous upturn in sales, the pixies, friendly aliens from another planet or you could go out and raise funds from investors—see *Fundraising Process*, 325. In my experience, raising funds from investors is your best bet.

Raising an 'Up' Round

If you can demonstrate momentum and you don't leave it too late to start the fundraising process, you should be able to attract a number of potential investors and raise funding at a higher valuation than the previous round. As the share price goes up, intelligent investor types refer to this as an 'Up' round.

Raising a 'Down-Round'

In the ideal world, your company valuation is on a constant rise and each successive round of funding closes at a higher price than the last. However, the world is not always ideal and you may have to agree to accept a 'down-round' that sets the share price lower than one or several of the previous rounds. There are a myriad of reasons why your valuation could drop from one round to the next, and some of them, like general market conditions, may be out of your control.

As existing shareholders aren't always ecstatic about the share price going down, and you can't complete the round without shareholder approval, the process of closing a down-round can involve more steps and take more arm twisting and negotiation than an up-round. For these reasons, down-rounds can take a little longer to complete—and this is unfortunate as management often agrees to a down-round when the company desperately needs an injection of cash.

Some down-rounds can be quite severe. After the Wall Street crash, one company that I was involved with was forced to take a round of funding that was one tenth of the previous share price. This type of severe down-round is affectionately known as a 'cram down'—a term borrowed from *Bankruptcy* litigation. Although the company had hit some important milestones and closed some nice deals, the investor effectively reduced the company's valuation by 90%. Management had little choice but to accept the terms as the financial environment had soured almost overnight and you couldn't exactly say there was a bunch of investors lining up to throw money at any company. The new share price was set below every one of the previous four rounds and this was not particularly good news for any of the existing shareholders. Valuation is not the only thing to worry about in a down-round—the investor can demand very aggressive liquidity preferences and other forms of priority treatment over the other shareholders. In the post-crash environment, it was not unusual for investors to demand liquidity preferences of 2, 3 or even 4 times —so they stand first in line from the proceeds of a future acquisition and take 2, 3 or 4 times their investment out before passing any remaining funds on to the shareholders following them in the line.

Of course, the employees and other common stockholders stand at the very back of the line. Disgruntled employees can be potentially more damaging than disgruntled shareholders and it's important to make sure that a down-round doesn't demotivate the team. You may need to come up with some sweeteners to keep the staff from heading for the hills when they realize that their ownership has been diluted in a cram down situation. This could be a good time to carve out a bonus plan for the active employees that effectively lets them push into the front of the line and share a percentage (typically 5-10%) of any sale proceeds between the employees and the management team before the proceeds are handed to the preference shareholders.

Before you can close any round of funding, you're likely going to need approval from each class of preference shareholder. So, if you're working on a series C round of funding, you're going to have to get approval from a majority of the series A and series B investors. If the majority of the A investors approve but the majority of the B investors disapprove, you can't go ahead with the round—most companies are structured in such a way that you need the approval of every class of shareholder. Investors sometimes block down-round deals. Fortunately, most investors realize that this can kill the company if there are no alternative deals on the table, and they often come to their senses after a little persuasion.

The chances are that your existing investors will have the right to participate in future rounds of funding, at least to maintain their percentage share of the company ownership. Be warned—down-rounds also usually trigger a re-pricing of shares issued in previous rounds as well. So, although they're not investing in the new round, you're likely to find yourself issuing shares to existing shareholders as well as the new ones. So a down-round can have a real impact on your capitalization table and you may find that you end up with many more outstanding shares than you anticipated. This, of course, means dilution for the founders, employees and everyone else.

Raising a Bridge Loan

A bridge loan can span the gap between two rounds of funding. Timing is the reason that most companies turn to bridge funding—either they don't have enough time to negotiate the valuation and complete the due diligence or they want to buy more time to hit certain milestones and pump up the valuation before they close a round.

Lenders such as Sand Hill Capital, Silicon Valley Bank, Venture Banking Group and Imperial Bank (recently acquired by Comerica Bank) specialize in bridge financing. Of course they need some confidence that there's a subsequent round of funding to bridge to, otherwise the loan can hardly be called a 'bridge', more like a road to nowhere. They're normally introduced to the company by top-tier VC's that want to buy more time for negotiations and due diligence. For later-stage companies, the bridge can be provided by an existing investor as a lifeline to help the company reach its next round.

The bridge lender doesn't immediately become a stockholder of the company but buys a promissory note that converts over to stock with the next round of funding. Although they may get the secret handshake, a nod or a wink from their VC friends, the bridge lenders rarely get any form of firm guarantee that the next round will actually close—and deals have been known to fall apart in the valuation negotiation or due diligence process, so bridge lenders need some sweeteners to encourage them to invest earlier and take on more risk than the other investors in the round. The tastiest sweetener is normally a warrant—an option to buy more shares in future at a favorable pre-agreed price.

If you don't have a term sheet from a reputable investor, and some assurance that it's preparing to lead a round of funding in the next 90 days or so, you could be wasting your time looking for a loan from professional bridge lenders. Remember—it's a loan designed to buy enough time to close a real round, not an alternative to venture funding.

Example Bridge Loan Structure

✓ *Promissory note converting to shares at the next round of funding.*

✓ *Warrant coverage of 20-50%*—20% warrant coverage in first month increasing 5% per month with a cap of 50%. The warrant coverage increases each month—so the company is encouraged to close the round of funding as quickly as possible. Instead of warrants, it would be possible to offer the bridge lender a discount on the price of the round but this would mean that the company would be issuing shares of different prices in the same round—this is normally avoided as it complicates the calculation of liquidity preferences later on.

✓ *Automatic conversion*—if the next venture capital closing does not occur prior to the maturity date (12 months), the note can be converted into common stock at a relatively low valuation.

✓ *10% loan interest*—as each day goes by, the amount of interest owed to the bridge lender grows. That's the way interest works. If the interest were paid in stock, this would mean the capitalization table changing on a daily basis—that's too complicated for investors to handle. So interest is normally paid in cash.

✓ *Security*—none. The loan is not normally secured against the company's assets. Hey, the conversion into stock and the warrant coverage should be enough for anyone!

It's not impossible for an existing investor in a distressed company to use a bridge loan as an opportunity to push the other shareholders out of the picture, take control of the company or take ownership of all the assets. The bridge can be structured in such a way that the investor can demand repayment of the loan at any time. If the company can't repay, it can be forced to turn all the assets over to the investor—including the intellectual property, the cash, customer contracts, anything of any value. The investor can then restart a 'clean' new company that it owns outright—see *Cold Restart with Asset Transfer,* page 289. Other shareholders are left with shares in a company that has a balance sheet that doesn't exactly appear very balanced—it has plenty of liabilities but no assets.

As well as bridging the company to it's next round of funding, the bridge loan can be used to bridge the company to an acquisition. A distressed company with a valuable product can offer a very appealing opportunity to a bridge investor. The investor provides a loan with an aggressive liquidity preference, flips the company (sells it) and takes a huge chunk of the proceeds. This can be a profitable activity—imagine a bridge investor providing $1m to a distressed company that has burned through the $20m it raised in previous rounds. Imagine this investor demands a liquidity preference multiple of 4—meaning it receives the first $4m proceeds from any sale. It then sells the company for just $4m and walks away with a 300% return on its investment. The investors that provided the previous $20m walk away with nothing. It does happen, especially in the new, new economy. Bridge investing in conjunction with mergers and acquisitions can be a profitable business!

It's expensive, but if you need to buy a little time before your next round, a bridge loan could be a useful source of short-term funding for your technology startup.

Slowing your Descent—Cutting Costs

You're running out of cash—with every dollar you spend, you're taking another step down the slippery slope to cash crisis. You can slow your descent by cutting costs. The deeper you cut, the slower you descend. The slower you descend, the more time you buy to raise funds and take action to avoid *Shutdown*.

Cutting costs can only go so far without damaging the company. Slashing costs involves reinventing the company, stripping out product lines and cutting back to a skeleton team.

Cutting Costs

Salaries and other employee-related costs make up a huge percentage of the cost structure for any technology company, so lightening the load normally starts with a reduction in headcount. Only the smallest, most streamlined teams will survive tough times and difficult terrain.

Headcount Reduction

In some countries, like France and Germany, the employment laws are designed to deter companies from laying off staff. By comparison, laying people off in the U.S. is relatively painless and inexpensive—especially if the company has an 'At-Will' employment policy (make sure this is one of the first documents you receive from your lawyer).

Laying people off is an unpleasant activity for everyone involved. You don't exactly set out in business with the view to hire people then lay them off. This is not a skill you really want to perfect, however, the way the headcount reduction is handled can have a profound effect on the morale of the team and the future prospects for the whole company.

<u>*Objectives*</u>

Of course, the primary objective of the headcount reduction is to cut costs, however, if the process is poorly handled, it can demoralize the team, create freefall momentum and throw the company into a dangerous death spiral.

<u>Objectives of a well-managed layoff process:</u>

✓ *Cut costs.*

✓ *Minimize the pain inflicted on departing staff.*

✓ *Maintain momentum in the remaining team.*

✓ *Avoid lawsuits and material damage.*

A disgruntled former employee can be a dangerous beast. The vocal types have been known to run around the office shouting '*No one's safe here! You'll be next!*' The physical types have been known to start throwing punches, files, laptop computers and other forms of everyday office weapons. The quiet types have left the office secretly scheming to hack in to the network. Postal workers sometimes return armed to the teeth. The Internet provides a new platform for disgruntled employees to air their grievances and inflict damage on the company—in addition to the large commercial web sites specifically designed for this purpose, former employees often create their own sites, chat rooms and newsgroups.

A layoff can convert an upbeat team making marked progress into a down beat team in a state of paralysis. A single layoff is bad enough for moral, but a series of layoffs sets a worrying pattern for the remaining team—often with disastrous effects. Making a positive effort to maintain momentum and retain an upbeat team is critical. If handled properly, the layoff process can be remarkably smooth, even uplifting. I was touched when an employee, that I hardly knew, hugged me and gave her undying support for my company and it's mission before clearing her desk and leaving the office. It's always sad to see good people go but it's nice to know that they leave with a positive attitude toward the company and the remaining team.

Cost-Cutting Process

Take Decision to Reduce Headcount

Appoint Cost-Cutting Team

Draw up Stay/Go Lists

General Cost-Cutting

Termination Follow-Up

Complete Preparations

Termination Interviews

Take Decision to Reduce Headcount

The decision to reduce headcount is normally taken by the board of directors. Management is then given its instructions—*'Cut costs by, say 30%, before the end of the month'*—and starts to implement the process.

One large layoff is much better than a series of small ones. A single, definitive layoff that's well handled by management, and well understood by the employees, allows the remaining staff to continue to work with at least some sense of security—they don't automatically flood their resumes onto the street. With a second layoff, they see a worrying pattern starting to emerge. After a third layoff, the remaining employees naturally assume it's just a matter of time before they're laid off themselves. This is when the company goes into freefall momentum—progress is paralyzed as the employees spend time polishing their resumes and interviewing for new jobs. So, don't be squeamish when it comes to fixing the scale of the cut in headcount– make a single cut, make it as large as you can and do it quickly.

You can probably cut very much deeper than you think. People are very much more adaptable than machines. Let's assume you find your car is burning too much gas—so you decide to lift the hood and pull out several parts of the engine that look like they're gas thirsty (you're not a mechanic but you decide they're the noisiest parts, the dirtiest parts or the ones that are the easiest to remove). When you turn the ignition key, you find that the car doesn't quite operate effectively—it probably doesn't work at all. The engine is a finely tuned system with each component playing an important role. Take one component out, like the spark plugs, and the whole system fails.

Now imagine you removed the spark plugs, turned the ignition key, nothing happened for a few seconds, then you started to hear a little noise, and miraculously the engine started to sputter to life. After a couple of minutes, the engine is firing on all cylinders. Lifting the hood, you're amazed to find that the cylinder head has miraculously morphed itself and grown a spark plug. So has the distributor cap. The remaining components have figured out that they can't operate without spark plugs, and they've adapted themselves—building spark plugs of their own.

Auto-makers are a few years away from having technology like this. However, this is exactly the way the company operates following a layoff. Rarely does the company grind to a halt because critical tasks that were previously carried out by now-departed individuals are no longer performed. We humans are remarkably adaptable—especially when we collaborate in teams. Remove an individual and other team members pick up his/her tasks and responsibilities. Even if the manager doesn't officially reassign duties, team members have an amazing ability to identify the critical tasks and take the responsibility of performing them. Teams are extremely resilient in this way.

Some individuals do have unique skill sets and they may be impossible to replace—with another individual. However, the same set of skills, or a workably similar set can almost always be found in a team. Worried that the company would grind to a halt when certain individuals leave a company, I've been repeatedly surprised to see how quickly the remaining team members adapt and fill their roles. (One chilling conclusion to draw from this is that however, great you think you are, you're not irreplaceable. It may be impossible to find an individual with your exact skill-set, but all your skills could be found across the various members of a team—especially in times of crisis when people are forced to adapt to survive.)

So, when taking the decision to cut payroll, the board should provide management with the direction and the mandate to make a single, decisive layoff, to make it quickly and to manage it in a professional way.

Appoint Cost-Cutting Team

With the directions and mandate from the board, the CEO appoints a team to manage the headcount reduction and cost-cutting process. A team size of around four is ideal—a large team of more than five can be unwieldy to control and a small team of less than three can fail to represent a balanced range of perspectives.

As well as representing the financial, HR and legal perspectives, the team also has to take into consideration issues like team morale and maintaining momentum.

At this point, no one really knows which names will be on the Stay/Go lists. The only names that are sure to be on the *Stay* list are the members of the cost cutting team themselves. This is another good reason for keeping this team relatively small. It can be convenient and tempting to use the whole management team as the cost cutting team, however, highly paid management team members are sometimes the most cost-effective individuals to lay-off.

Making decisions about who's laid off and who gets to stay is a very responsible job. You don't want anyone that's prepared to use his/her position on the team as an opportunity to settle an old score or use the process to political advantage.

Draw up Stay/Go Lists

Preparing a Stay/Go list in the run up to a layoff can be one of the most unpleasant business activities you can undertake. However, it has to be done—so the best thing you can do is to plan carefully and do it well. In addition to each individual's role, performance and salary, a wide range of factors have to be taken into consideration.

- ✓ *Survival spirit*—following the layoffs, the *Stay* team needs to be capable of picking up the duties of the departing individuals, quickly developing into a balanced, fully functioning team. It should be made up of individuals with the spirit to collaborate, bounce back after the layoff process and tough it out. The *Go* team should include people that bring down the morale of the team and cannibals—individuals that lash out at colleagues when the going gets tough.

- ✓ *Target destination*—the whole process needs to be looked at in the context of the overall objective of the company. If the company is looking to reach *IPO*, what are the skills that it's going to need for the journey? If the company is driving toward an acquisition (*Cash Flow Sale* or *Asset Sale*), what type of team will make it more attractive to an acquirer?

- ✓ *Loaded cost of employment*—a marketing manager may have the same salary as a sales representative, but the cost of employment is considerably higher if the marketing manager needs an expensive advertising budget to be effective. A sales representative may have the same salary as an engineer but travel and other expenses push the overall cost of employment considerably higher.

- ✓ *Core value*—if the company's major asset is its product and intellectual property (IP) then the core product team and the intellectual property holders (the individuals with the IP between their ears) are central to the company's value.

For a technology team going through a cash crisis, engineers and product-related individuals are often very much more valuable than sales and marketing folks— especially if the company is driving toward an *Asset Sale* (see *The Short Sprint from Zero-*

to-Asset Sale).   An acquirer is likely to buy the company for its product, and the supporting product team—it's unlikely to buy a technology company for its sales force.

Every group that has one or more of its team members removed will suffer some form of trauma.   The fewer the teams that experience the trauma the better.   So, following this line of thinking, it would be better to remove a whole department rather than take one or more heads from every department.   In fact, this is very true.   The other thing to consider is the location—leaving one location fully intact and closing down a remote office altogether can minimize the trauma on the Stay team.

After drawing up a preliminary list, it's important to gather input from the various managers whose teams are affected.   *The board has instructed the management to go through a headcount reduction process.   We need to cut the payroll from your group by $X , and this is our first attempt at a Stay/Go list.   It's your group and we want to make sure you're involved in the process.   Can you think of a better way of achieving this cost reduction?'*   It's important to make sure that the whole process is kept under wraps until the layoff itself—leaks can be very damaging to morale.

Complete Preparations

Even after you've finalized the Stay/Go lists, it can still take several days/weeks to complete preparations before the actual layoff itself.   These preparations include:

- ✓ *Fix the layoff date*—often the finance department likes to select the date to coincide with a payroll period.
- ✓ *Paperwork*—you're going to need signed terminations letters, agreements and other forms of paperwork.
- ✓ *Checks*—for severance, salary, vacation pay and expenses.
- ✓ *Schedule the termination agreements*—book the meeting rooms, and make sure the appropriate managers are available to participate.
- ✓ *Anticipate questions and issues*—some questions are not impossible to predict— some (like *'why me?'*) can only be answered in person, others (like *'what about my health insurance?'*) can be answered in a Q&A document.

Finally, make sure you're on the right side of the law—have the paperwork checked by a lawyer and ensure that everyone involved in the process is fully briefed on what they can and cannot say in the termination interview and beyond.

Termination Interviews

If you have to be laid off, you really don't want to be informed by e-mail, hear it on the company grapevine, read it in the newspaper or arrive at the office to find that your key card has been deactivated and you're locked out. You want to be told to your face in a termination interview and have the opportunity to ask questions.

> Termination Interview Do's:
>
> ✓ *Show respect.*
>
> ✓ *Show compassion.*
>
> ✓ *Explain that it's not personal.*
>
> ✓ *Keep it brief.*
>
> Termination Interview Don'ts:
>
> × *Don't crack jokes, card tricks or otherwise make light of the situation.*
>
> × *Don't seize the opportunity to be vindictive.*
>
> × *Don't get drawn into a debate.*

If the termination interview is handled well, the laid-off employee will leave the room feeling good about himself, feeling good about the company and feeling that the process was handled in a professional way. A smooth termination interview could proceed as follows:

1. Enter the room. Sit down. Make eye contact.
2. Management: *'I'm afraid that we have to let you go as part of a cost cutting exercise.'*
3. Give them time to digest the information.
4. Management: *'It's nothing personal. In fact, you've been a wonderful member of the team and I feel like we've failed you.'*
5. Go over the paperwork.
6. Ask if you can answer any questions.
7. Thank them with a handshake.

If you suspect that the individual may be extremely upset and you may want to diffuse the situation a little before you enter the room by setting the scene and saying something like 'I'm worried that you're going to be very upset about what I'm going to say'.

You really want to keep the meeting small and personal—restrict the number of attendees to the employee, the HR representative and possibly the employees' manager. If you suspect the employee has the potential to pursue legal action, it's a good idea to have a second person from management to witness the proceedings. If the individual is potentially prone to violence, choose someone large and muscular.

On his way out, following the termination meeting, a disgruntled employee can inflict damage on the company, and upset the remaining team. For this reason, large corporations often have a security guard escort the individual from the termination meeting to his desk, hand him a dustbin liner in which to deposit his personal belongings, prevent him from talking to his co-workers, demand his key card and escort him out of the building. How disrespectful and humiliating is that? For heavens sake, you might as well strip him naked, tar and feather him, and parade him through the office in handcuffs. It may be an idea to ask some of the remaining team to keep an eye open for anyone that appears upset or disruptive, but give them the time and space to clear out their desks and say their goodbyes in peace.

Follow Up

Following the layoff, it's time to boost the morale of the remaining team. In my experience, the best way of achieving this is an all-hands company meeting.

Example CEO Talk at the Post-Layoff Company Meeting

'I'm sorry to have to report that today we were forced to lay off a number of employees. This is never pleasant and I'm sure that many of us are sad that the company had to take this action.

As part of a cost-cutting measure, the board of directors asked myself and the management team to make this headcount reduction. The strategy was to make one single, decisive cut—there are no plans to make layoffs a feature of working for this company. Rest assured—there are no further cuts planned or envisaged at this time.

We put a lot of work into making the layoff process as smooth and painless as possible. Unfortunately, in a layoff like this you lose some excellent people. This was no exception. I know I'll miss many of the people that left today, and I suspect that many of you will as well.

Cutting costs and lightening the load will make the company more healthy and help us to achieve our milestones and objectives. (Talk about where the company is going and how it's going to get there. Identify specific milestones and stepping stones.)

I'm going to need your help to make this layoff process worthwhile. A smaller team means that we all have to take on more responsibility. I'm going to have to wear several hats, and many of you will be asked to do the same. Please help your manager in the process of reassigning tasks. If you spot a dropped ball, pick it up and bring it to your manager's attention. Let's pull together and make sure this layoff doesn't get anyone down.

The investors and the board of directors have full confidence in what we're doing. With your support, I'm sure that the company is going to continue moving forward and making progress. In fact, I'm very excited and enthusiastic.

I'm happy to answer any questions you have right now. My door is always open if you have any concerns or there's anything you'd like to discuss.'

If you're not careful, it's very easy for a company to go into freefall momentum and a state of paralysis following a layoff. So, you may want to have a follow-up talk with the managers and tell them how critical it is to maintain morale, encourage an upbeat team and keep the wagons rolling.

General Cost Cutting

The objective of the exercise is to make a meaningful reduction in the burn rate without damaging the company's assets, distracting or demoralizing the staff. The first place to look for significant savings is in the marketing budget. Sometimes, significant savings can be made here without affecting the overall performance of the company or the morale of the team. It may be possible to cut back on expenses— flying coach class and avoiding fancy restaurants can help in real savings but it also has the effect of drilling home to employees how important it is to economize.

In deciding where to cut, you need to be careful and selective. Since the layoff, you may have more office space than you need. However, moving offices is a major upheaval and a real distraction—perhaps you could sublet instead. Cutting back on snacks, drinks and employee treats can have a demoralizing effect on the whole team—and offer little in the way of savings.

Slashing Costs

People are capable of adapting and filling the gaps left by departing colleagues, however, this can only go so far. If you slash the size of the team, say from fifty to fifteen employees, you can't expect to continue in business as usual. Making radical cuts in the size of the team can be done, but it involves going back to basics and reinventing the company.

See *Reinventing the Company*, Page 276.

Slashing costs is not always a depressing activity. It can be an opportunity to refocus the company on its core business, reposition the company in the market, drop unprofitable product lines, re-think the marketing strategy and draw up a new business plan.

Running on Fumes

It's sometimes possible to radically cut costs and run the company on little more than fumes for a period of several months. As well as holding off the creditors, the challenge in this situation is to prevent the core technology team from heading for the hills—a technology company without its technology team is pretty much worthless. Some tips for running on fumes:

- ✓ *Communicate with creditors*—meet them, explain the situation and maintain open communication. Take the lead, arrange to meet face-to-face, use a little charm and regularly check back with news and updates as they develop. It's important that creditors feel you're honest and reliable in this situation—so make sure you follow through on promises. You may be surprised by how supportive creditors can be in this situation—even office landlords have been known to wait for their rent.

- ✓ *Communicate with staff*—regular meetings, unrestricted access to information and an open-door policy will help allay their fears.

- ✓ *Stock-for-salary deals*—you can pay staff in shares instead of salary. They'll probably still be eligible to pay tax on the income if you pay them in preference shares, so the way to avoid this is to use common stock. However, the employees common stock may be worthless—see below.

- ✓ *Liquidity preference carve out*—it's impossible to incent the staff to stay with the company if their common shares have little or no hope of ever having any value. When the company is sold, the employees have to stand in line behind the investors (see *Liquidity Preference*, page 342) . If the company is sold in a fire-sale situation, there's usually nothing left for employees after the investors have taken their share. To incent the staff to stick around, you need to get the investors to agree to a carve out for the current employees— effectively the current employees get to the front of the line when it comes to sharing the proceeds of a company sale, take a percentage of the proceeds before the investors get their hands on the rest.

- ✓ *Loan out staff*—if you can't pay them until you close a round of funding and you don't want them to go get a permanent job elsewhere, you may be able to loan them out on a temporary basis and have their salaries paid by someone else.

Radical Momentum Maneuvers

Switch Destinations

It's easy to lose your will to push ahead when you know deep down that your target destination is impossible to reach. At this point, the best course of action is to switch destinations—to a destination that it won't take a miracle to reach.

Question:	*When is a good time to Switch Destinations?*
Answer:	*The moment you realize that your current destination is unattainable.*

It can be unsettling and destructive to switch destinations so you don't want to make a switch unless your original destination becomes unattainable and you find it impossible to generate momentum along your current route. You certainly don't want to switch destinations on a regular basis but don't be afraid to take this action when pressing ahead becomes pointless. At this point, the best possible course of action is to ceremoniously burn your old travel plan, switch destinations and draw up a new one. A new travel plan is quite an undertaking—it means a new route, new milestones, new team, new provisions, contingency plans. Everything can, and often *should*, change.

After completing the bulk of the journey from *Zero-to-IPO* you may find that *IPO* is no longer a realistic option, possibly due to forces outside your control—the *IPO* market may have crashed and burned or your particular sector may no longer be flavor of the month on Wall Street. If the company has positive cash flow, there's no urgency to raise new funds and you could sit it out and wait until the *IPO* climate improves. Alternatively you can forget about *IPO*, switch your target destination to *Cash Flow Sale*, dress the company up for sale, start the M&A process and take all the steps necessary to have the company acquired as a profitable going concern.

If you have to drop the objective of *IPO* when the company is still burning cash, you don't have the luxury of time to hang around and wait for the market conditions to change. You either raise more funds and continue on your journey or you switch from targeting *IPO* to targeting *Asset Sale*—this can involve a good deal of backtracking and radical change. In this scenario, it often makes sense to strip the company down to just the components, that an acquirer is likely to want—a smaller, more product-focused team with a low burn rate is understandably more appealing to a buyer.

On the other hand, after setting out on the Short Sprint from *Zero-to-Asset Sale* you may find that the market takes off and you start to generate tremendous momentum. When customers start lining up to buy your product and investors start a knocking on your door, building a viable stand-alone business may become a real possibility and it could be time to consider switching destinations, targeting *IPO* or *Cash Flow Sale*. This can be a radical transition that involves a new route, larger team, serious VC investors and career CEO.

Alas, things don't always go this well and you may find that you can't gather the momentum to hit your milestones and you find yourself off track, with a measly bank balance and cash flowing out much more quickly than it's actually flowing in. In a survivable cash flow crisis, you can cut the costs (perhaps *slash* the costs), target *Asset Sale*, draw up a new travel plan and raise more investment funds. At one point a survivable cash flow crisis becomes a terminal cash flow crisis, and this is when you actually *target* and drive the company toward an *Orderly Shutdown*. At this point *Orderly Shutdown* is a much better destination than the only alternative—*Bankruptcy*.

If you don't target another destination and drive towards it with full speed, *Bankruptcy* is where you're likely to end up. Switching destinations and drawing up new travel plans can be a painful and costly process—but sometimes it has to be done. Be brave—make the switch as quickly and efficiently as you can.

Reinvent the Company

A fundamental problem with your product, strategy or business plan will always prevent the company from making progress and hitting its milestones. Even if the strategy, product and business plan were perfectly matched to customer requirements yesterday, a shift in the market could cause a major mismatch today. Sometimes, the only way to boost momentum is to go back to basics and reinvent the company. As well as repositioning the company in the market, this is often the best maneuver to fundamentally restructure, and slash, costs.

Question:	When is a good time to Reinvent the Company?
Answer:	When there's a fundamental problem with the product, the strategy or the business plan.

Reinventing the Company

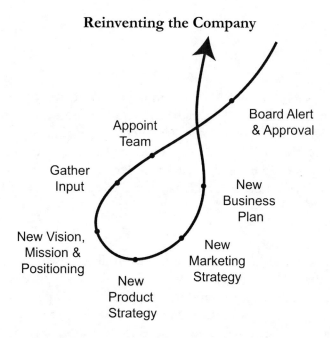

<u>Board *Alert* *and* *Approval*</u>

A radical maneuver like reinventing the company requires approval and full support from the board—it also helps to win the backing of other investors and advisors. Board meetings can be dull, predictable affairs. They're certainly livened up when management, or someone else, alerts that board that the company has a fundamental problem that cannot be solved without going back to basics, re-examining out who we are, what we offer and what we're doing here.

You may be lucky enough to have a proactive board that approves such a maneuver without making much of a fuss. However, board members are not immune to complacency and inertia, and you may have to resort to shock treatment to kick them into action. One of my most memorable board meetings was when I deliberately shocked the board members and advisory panel into approving a complete reinvention of the company. This was the first meeting after closing an eight figure round of funding and the attendees were coming along expecting to hear the CEO lay out his plans for the future and defend his record. What they heard was my forecast that the whole dot-com business was going to collapse like a house of cards and that this company would be dead within six months unless it took radical action to get back to its roots as a technology business. There were plenty of drained faces and gaping mouths, but the shock treatment worked.

If nothing else, alerting the board of a fundamental problem will always liven up an otherwise dull afternoon. Like all major decisions, it helps if you've done some behind-the-scenes twisting of arms beforehand and you have some support going into the meeting.

Appoint Team

The board appoints a team to conduct a comprehensive review of the market, the company and return with a report of its findings and recommendations. It's important that this team is capable of looking beyond the company's existing business operations and question all the theories and assumptions. Ideally, this team could be led and facilitated by an impartial outsider with expert knowledge of the process, however, it could be led by a creative and open minded CEO or member of the board.

Gather Input

When I first went through this process, I decided to interview people from all levels and all departments of the company just so that they'd be supportive and feel part of the process. I was taken aback to find that some of the best perspectives and ideas came from the most unlikely sources. Don't be surprised to find that the most valuable insights and perspectives aren't gained from the executive team but from that young spotty faced engineer and the quiet clerk in the accounts department. Sometimes, the people at the bottom of the organization chart have a strong grasp on the product, the market and a good deal more common sense than you'll find at the top. The opinion and ideas of customers and other knowledgeable company outsiders can be equally valuable—it's important that many different voices are heard as part of this process.

New Vision, Mission & Positioning

The video games market has always been restricted to a small number of competitors—there's simply not enough room for a number of competing platforms and standards. Sega was a major player in the early '90's competing with Nintendo for top spot in the games platform market. Sony came into the market in the late '90's, took the top spot and Sega found itself competing for second position. When Microsoft entered the market, someone at Sega obviously decided it was time to go through the process of reinventing the company. Compared to Sony and Microsoft, they discovered that Sega was financially weak and faced a real threat of being the 4th player in a market of 3. However, the games market continues to offer tremendous growth opportunities, and the company had real strengths in its game development expertise and global channels of distribution. The board took the brave decision to pull out of the platform business and reinvent itself as a software publisher. The company's core strengths could be leveraged in a way that was less costly, less risky and had more chance of success. This decision may well have saved the company. The jury is still out on whether Sega will be a runaway success in its new guise, however, as a result of this radical maneuver, the company survived dangerous market conditions and at least gave itself a fighting chance.

Reinventing the company often reveals a case of mistaken identity. After leading it through the process, one business that I was involved with realized: *'We're not a media company, we're a technology company!'* This led to a radical new product strategy, new marketing strategy, new business plan, cost structure and organization chart and ultimately saved the company from a quick, painful demise.

It's this type of insight that you're looking for when you create your new vision, mission and company positioning. A clear assessment on the company's strengths, weaknesses, opportunities and threats, an insightful vision of where the company is headed, some creative brainstorming ideas and perspectives and a preparedness to take radical measures.

New Product Strategy

After reinventing itself as a software publisher, Sega obviously had to drop its hardware product line and come up with a new product line and strategy. Another company that I was involved with rationalized five products into one. Reinventing the company often has far-reaching implications on the company's product line.

It's tempting for companies, even small startups, to respond to different customer and market demands by creating new products. This may simply involve a repackaging of existing technologies, however, the process of testing, debugging, managing and supporting a wide range of products can be extremely resource intensive and costly. As a result, it can be healthy for any company to go through the exercise of rationalizing of the product line, culling products and lines that don't meet market needs. This can also be a highly effective method of slashing costs and refocusing the business.

New Marketing Strategy

Reinventing the company can have a profound effect on the marketing strategy. One startup that I led through this maneuver cut its marketing costs from a million dollars a month to a few thousand—and actually increased its market profile in the process. This was achieved by reinventing itself as a *Business-to-Business (B-to-B) company as opposed to Business to Consumer (B-to-C)* and relying on its huge distribution partners for marketing and promotions.

The new marketing strategy doesn't necessarily involve slashing costs, but it should involve communicating the company's new positioning in the market and getting more bang for your buck.

<u>*New*</u> <u>*Business*</u> <u>*Plan*</u>

In addition to gathering together the new financial projections, the new business plan will articulate the new corporate positioning and strategy to key company insiders. In times of change such as this, an articulate and up-to-date business plan is more important than ever.

Warm Restart

Progress will slow if the current team is weighed down carrying too many passengers and baggage from the past. When you feel your company starting to grind to a halt, wouldn't it be nice to hit the 'control-alt-delete' keys, *Shutdown* and restart like you can with your PC? As you go about your daily business, your PC inadvertently accumulates tasks and processes that unnecessarily clog up its memory and processor, slowing everything else down. A good restart cleanses out all this junk and releases valuable resources for the use of your new applications. Similarly, in business you sometimes feel as though you've accumulated unwanted shareholders, creditors, disgruntled employees and all forms of unwanted baggage. Well, it can be possible to hit 'control-alt-delete' a couple of times, restart your business, shed the excess baggage with the back-seat passengers and start afresh. However, restarting a business is not quite as straightforward as restarting your PC—and if you get it wrong you can find yourself in the state penitentiary instead of the local PC repair store.

> **Warm Restart**
> Let's define a warm restart as a radical restructuring of the existing company that boosts momentum and releases valuable resources without losing customer contracts or other relationships. Although the maneuver involves sweeping internal changes, they can be imperceptible to customers and the outside world. The objective of a warm restart is to give the company a fresh lease on life without losing any existing market momentum.

Troubled companies saddled with debt, lots of bickering investors and other liabilities are often affectionately referred to as the 'living dead'. A restart can sometimes be the only way to breathe new life into your company when you find yourself in this situation. One of my friends has been with the same company for over 15 years. We used to joke that it was the oldest high-tech startup in the world. Although it's the same team selling the same technology to the same customers, technically it's not the same company. Every couple of years they used to go through a complete restart and reappear again under a different guise. After ten years of warm restarts, cold restarts and all forms of reincarnations, the endurance and creativity of the founders finally paid off and the latest manifestation of the company is now a respected market leader with a healthy Nasdaq stock price.

Restarts don't always have a happy ending. Another good friend that's been through several restarts has vowed never to go through this painful process again. I've been through various forms of restarts myself—sometimes they're absolutely the only way forward, but I think I'll try to avoid them in future.

Question:	*When is a good time for a Warm Restart?*
Answer:	*When the company is weighed down with unnecessary baggage, there are too many passengers and the current team has little incentive or motivation to succeed.*

Warm Restart

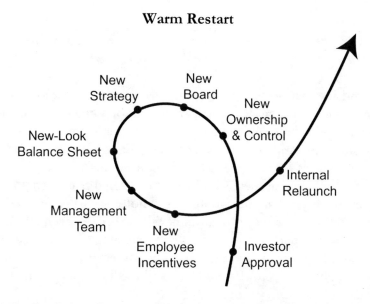

Coming out of a warm restart, the company could have new ownership and control, a new board of directors, new executives, new management team, new strategy, new business plan, even a new-look balance sheet. With expert advice, planning, and a little luck, this can all be done without upsetting customers or losing any traction in the market.

Investor Approval

The board of directors can tear up the business plan and set the company off in a new direction. The management team can replace the employees, the CEO can replace the management team, the board of directors can replace the CEO, the shareholders can replace the board of directors, new shareholders can replace old shareholders and virtually every component of the company can be removed and replaced in a restart situation. But who gets to press the restart buttons and decide which components are going to be removed and replaced? At the end of the day, ultimate control rests with the shareholders—not the common shareholders like the founders and employees of course, as their shares normally carry virtually no weight whatsoever, but the top of the chain of command usually ends with the investors through their ownership of preference shares.

So, ultimately, the investors are the only people that get to press the restart buttons and restructure the whole company. This can present something of a problem if the investors are also considered to be excess baggage. The ideal warm restart will transfer some ownership and control from old investors to new investors, key executives and employees—the people that the company needs the most moving forward.

> *'As an investor, we'd like you to agree to a restructuring that's intended to rid the company of excess baggage—oh, and by the way, you're some of the excess baggage that we want to get rid of.'*

It's hardly surprising that persuading investors to agree to a restructuring that positions them as excess baggage and cuts them out of some of the potential upside can be something of a challenge, but a new investor that's prepared to provide a lifeline to a distressed company can present the old investors with a simple choice— let the company shut down or agree to a restructuring that reduces their ownership and control. Well aware that there's nothing to be gained from a shut down, and figuring that even a large share of nothing is still nothing, many investors will agree to a restructuring that gives the company a new lease on life, even if it means they have a reduced level of participation. So when financing a distressed company, an investor has a good opportunity to carry out a warm restart, releasing the company from some of its obligations to shareholders, and creditors, and giving the new team something of a fresh start.

New Ownership & Control

You really don't want to have to go ask the old shareholders to relinquish any of the preferences they paid for when they bought their shares, as this will likely result in lots of kicking and screaming. Fortunately with a new round of funding, all they need to do is accept that the new class of preference shares, issued to the new investor, has priority over the old classes of preference shares—more control to decide who sits on the board, and first claim over any funds resulting from an acquisition (through the famous 'liquidity preference' clause, page 342). To provide incentives to the current executive and management team, you can ask the shareholders to carve out a bonus plan providing a share of any profits or the proceeds of an acquisition. In this way, the old investors can find themselves agreeing to give up a piece of the pie to new investors, key executives and employees—the people that the company desperately needs moving forward.

New Board of Directors

In the U.S., significant investors normally ask for one seat on the board, sometimes two. After several rounds of funding, the board can accumulate a number of investor representatives, each with his/her own perspective and agenda. Inertia can set in, existing board members can become reluctant to change and it's often impossible to implement a warm restart without making radical changes to the board.

Early-round investors and their board representatives are often considered excess baggage. New investors will often make their investment contingent on a restructuring of the board—*'we'll invest on condition that we put our own people on the board, and that some, or all, of the existing board members resign'.*

New Strategy

The *Warm Restart* is designed to boost momentum by shedding excess baggage. It's not a necessary part of the maneuver to draw up a new strategy, but with new ownership and control, it's normally a good time to make minor tweeks or major changes to the strategy. In fact, when radical change is required, the *Warm Restart* can be carried out in conjunction with *Reinventing the Company, page 276.*

New-Look Balance Sheet

When a company loses momentum and progress grinds to a halt, it's just a matter of time before it burns out of cash and heads for *Shutdown* or *Bankruptcy*. Savvy shareholders and creditors are aware of this and are sometimes prepared to make sacrifices to contribute toward the success of a warm restart process.

If the existing shareholders and creditors are not exactly volunteering to give the company a break, often an incoming investor has the leverage to twist their arms— 'If I don't invest, this company will likely go bust and your shares and notes will be worth nothing.. I'm prepared to invest if you make a contribution and reschedule the debt and approve a cram-down of the shares.' Whether it's considered arm twisting or a gun to the head, it is an effective strategy that's often used with success.

In a distressed situation, the share structure and the liabilities on the balance sheet can sometimes be restructured, shedding baggage from the past and lightening the load for the existing team.

New Management Team

A warm restart doesn't necessarily require changes to management, but it's sometimes more effective to have a new strategy implemented by a new team—the old team may not have the appropriate skills or it may be simply resistant to change. Often an incoming investor will demand these changes—sometimes they demand sweeping changes, like a new CEO and management team, other times the changes they demand may be relatively minor.

The whole idea of the warm restart is to shed some of the baggage from the past and give a boost to momentum. To make this effective, it's vital that the team is upbeat. It's important that the employees are not demotivated and downbeat as a result of the changes in management. Sometimes this means making no changes at all, other times it means making a clean sweep, bringing in new blood and energy.

New Employee Incentives

Stock options are not much of an incentive if they're worthless and the employee knows that it's unlikely that they'll ever have any value. This is often the case after the company has closed several rounds of funding—as the employees have to stand in line behind the external investors when the company is sold (see *Liquidity Preference*, page 342). The employees get to share in the remainder after the investors have had first pick of the spoils—in many cases, this means the employees coming away with nothing. As a result, the stock options held by employees in many private technology companies are absolutely worthless—whether they're vested or not. To provide an incentive to employees, the shareholders often agree to a carve out for the active common stockholders. A percentage of the proceeds from the sale of the company, say 10%, is given to management and the currently active employees. What this means is that the employees effectively push in line ahead of the investors when it comes to dividing up the spoils of a company sale. This can provide a major incentive for employees and can be instrumental in boosting momentum.

In addition to injecting some potential value in the stock options, a warm restart may be a good time to review the other benefits and employee incentives including bonus plans and sales commissions.

Internal Re-launch

To gather momentum coming out of a warm restart, you can arrange a series of *Rah-Rah* sessions to rally the troops. At the very least, you're going to need a company meeting to announce the change in strategy and answer questions from employees that, by this time, are likely wondering what the heck's going on. I like offsite meetings—it's a little more costly to take the team out to a hotel or conference facility but it certainly grabs attention and eliminates the regular office distractions.

The restructuring activities and the resulting changes are internal to the company and a warm restart can be totally invisible to customers and the outside world—so an external re-launch may be unnecessary.

The team should come out of the internal re-launch meetings in an upbeat frame of mind, enthusiastic about the company and its new strategy, clear about the route ahead and the role that each individual has to play.

Question:	*What if word gets out on the street that the company has troubles and it loses customers and market momentum during the warm restart process?*
Answer:	*In addition to the Internal Re-launch, you can carry out an External Re-launch to reposition the company and regenerate momentum in the market. Some warm restarts are warmer than others!*

Cold Restart

When your PC grinds to a halt and ctl-alt-delete fails to initiate a warm restart, you often have to switch off the power, wait for the noise of the fans and hard drives to subside, then power back up. Although the PC normally comes back up, there's no guarantee that it will—some of us have learned that the cold restart maneuver can harm hard drives, losing valuable data and cause other forms of damage to the PC.

Similarly in business, you can shut down, wait for the screams to die away, then restart an entirely new company. In this way, the product inventors and founders can shed the baggage of the old company and start completely, or almost-completely, afresh.

Cold Restart
Cold restart is a corporate reincarnation that involves shutting down the old company, forming a new company and starting over.

The *Cold Restart* involves killing the old company and performing a miraculous reincarnation. In fact, the reincarnation is not very miraculous at all—it's a surprisingly simple legal maneuver that law firms orchestrate on a regular basis. However, launching a new company is a difficult and time-consuming undertaking that involves rebuilding every component of the business. Restructuring and re-launching the old company, through a *Warm Restart*, can be a much less painful way of achieving a similar result.

Question:	When is a good time for a Cold Restart?
Answer:	If the company is weighed down with unnecessary baggage, there are too many passengers, the current team has little incentive to succeed and a Warm Restart is not possible.

The business journals are filled with stories of unscrupulous executives closing down companies, buying up all the assets for pennies on the dollar, then forming new corporations with the same team, same core product, even the same office space and furniture. The law courts understandably frown on this practice. On the other hand, the courts are normally understanding that former employees of defunct companies have to earn an income, and this often involves forming new companies in the same line of business.

Cold Restart

Shutdown Old Company

It's always good advice to aim for an *Orderly Shutdown* (page 292) rather than a *Bankruptcy* (page 295)—never more so than when you're planning a *Cold Restart*. Although you're technically forming a new company, the creditors, shareholders and employees from the old company are not going to disappear into thin air—especially if they were significantly out of pocket or otherwise hurt by the *Shutdown*. Law suits are the last thing you need when you're starting a new business.

Form New Company

If you want to start a new company, and avoid law suits from disgruntled shareholders, creditors and employees, it's important that all ties with the old company are completely severed and that none of the old company's assets or resources have been transferred to, or used by, the new. As always, it's a good idea to hire the most expensive lawyers you can find to advise you through this process. You'll be advised to make certain that you don't violate any non-compete agreements or pass the new company off as the old one. There are some gray areas that you need to be careful of. Any idea or invention that you had while you were still with the old company probably technically belongs to that company, especially if there's any documentation or evidence of it's existence while you were still employed there.

New Board of Directors

Forming a new company is a great opportunity to put in place a small, manageable board—see *Form a Board of Directors,* page 105. To avoid stalemate, the board should always have an odd number of directors—and some say that three is too many! The advisory panel can be a much larger and more effective resource—see *Recruit an Advisory Panel,* page 79.

New Strategy

A new company needs a new strategy and a new business plan. This is a perfect opportunity to get something out of the painful experiences from the old company and capitalize on the lessons you learned.

New Balance Sheet

A new company starts life with a new balance sheet. A *Cold Restart* is a sure-fire way of losing liabilities and other unwanted baggage—of course you also lose ownership of the product and other assets in the process.

New Management Team

The new company's shareholders appoint the board of directors, the board of directors selects the CEO and the management team. This team can, of course, be made up of individuals that were on the management team of the old company. It could also be a great opportunity to appoint a new CEO and build a new team—see *Structure a Management Team,* page 107.

<u>*New Employee Incentives*</u>

To attract employees to the new company, you're going to have to draw up new employment contracts, *Create a Stock-Option Plan* (page 95) and *Establish a Benefits Package* (page 116).

As the old company developed and attracted new investors, the employees saw their share of the pie get progressively smaller. In theory the pie was getting bigger, but in practice it became progressively smaller—at the point where the old company was shut down, the pie was little more than a crumb! Well a new company means a new pie—so you're probably now in a position to issue stock options that provide a real incentive to the staff. This is one of the major reasons that the cold restart has real potential to boost momentum!

Health Warning

Employees that are terminated from a company can usually continue to receive health insurance coverage through COBRA. This is not the case if the old company is shut down or the insurance policy terminated—until they take new jobs, former employees may well be devoid of health insurance!

It's surprisingly easy to hire the old employees into the new company and establish identical health insurance, 401K and other benefits—the benefits providers are more than willing to sign up the new company with similar packages and terms to the old one. However, after paying their social security payments through the old company, the employees may have to pay them all over again for the new company, then claim the excess back at the end of the year. But hey, what can you expect from a government body?

<u>*External Re-launch*</u>

The old company has shut down, or at least started the process of shutting down, and this information is in the public domain. If customers, competitors and journalists haven't yet heard the news, they soon will—news like this spreads through the grapevine at a rapid pace! At some point the new company will be launched onto the market, this means you have to *Formulate your Core Messaging and Corporate Identity* (page 87), *Appoint a PR Agency* (page 120) and *Launch the Company* (page 130).

If the old company successfully achieved an *Orderly Shutdown*, and its memories continue to enjoy a good reputation in the market, you may want to position the new company close to the old one. The new company could resemble the old, but make sure that they're not so similar that it's easy to confuse one for the other.

If the old company was not shut down in an elegant way, it may well have a negative profile in the market. In this case, you may want to distance the new company as far away as possible from the old one. A messy *Bankruptcy* (page 295) understandably leaves a bad taste in the mouths of almost everyone involved and it may be prudent to allow a little time for people to cleanse their palates before launching the new company (yup—there's another metaphor for you to digest!). A new story, positioning and messaging, new logo and graphics, new business cards, web site, brochures and new faces on the team will help provide some differentiation.

It's important to quickly generate positive momentum—don't forget to *Spread the Good Vibes* (page 32), encourage an upbeat team, *Plot the Route Ahead* (page 32) and engineer some early wins as the re-launch works best when surfing on a wave of positive momentum (there's another—just to keep you on your toes!). People will surely refer to the problems associated with the old company, but you need the team and the whole market to differentiate the old company from the new one, get excited about the new company's buzz and look to the future instead of the past.

Cold Restart with Asset Transfer

In the process of a *Cold Restart*, assets are often legitimately transferred from the old company to the new one. These assets include the products, stock, all forms of intellectual property including software code, patents and trademarks, fixed assets such as office equipment and contracts such as customer agreements and office leases. Anything of any value can be classified as an asset and transferred to the new company.

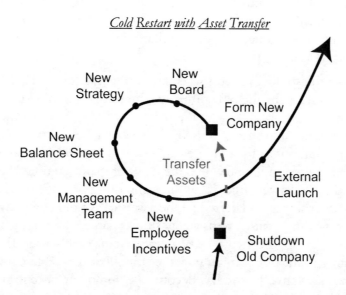

Cold Restart with Asset Transfer

You may wonder how all the liabilities can be left with the old company and the assets transferred to the new one—it doesn't exactly seem very fair on the creditors and investors in the old company! There are actually several different scenarios that can make this possible including:

✓   *The assets were offered by the old company as security for a loan or investment*—bridge loan or other investors in the old company take ownership of the assets when the old company fails to repay its loans or meet the obligations it agreed to when accepting funding. The assets are legally transferred to the investor or lender, they then form a new company, transfer the assets in and perform a *Cold Restart*.

✓   *The assets are sold to the highest bidder*—an important part of the *Shutdown* process for the old company is to liquidate the assets and distribute the proceeds to the old company's creditors and shareholders. In industrial age companies, real tangible assets such as real-estate, plant and equipment could be auctioned off to raise funds that would go at least part-way towards paying off the creditors. It's a very different story for technology companies in the information age—there are rarely any tangible assets to sell, and the intellectual property, often in the form of patents, software code and data, is totally unusable and worthless when parted from the team that created it. The auction of the assets is often a lonely affair—with the original product designers and engineers as the only realistic buyers. You don't have to be an economist to figure out what happens to the price when your target market comprises one single buyer—it's hardly a complicated supply vs. demand scenario! Actually, negotiations with only one buyer and one seller can become quite interesting. One day, perhaps, insolvency law will come out of the industrial age.

✓   *Spinout*—in the spinout process, the new company is created as a clean investment vehicle by the old company—investors will more readily invest in a company free of baggage from the past. The old company is not dissolved but continues to hold shares in the new company—the new company is effectively spun out of the old one. Investors in the old company continue to have an interest in the new one, the new company is more likely to attract funds and it is relatively free of law suits and other baggage from the past. The new company is transferred all the assets of the old company and carries on business—often with a remarkably similar name. A spinout from AcmeTechStartup, Inc. may well be named AcmeTechStartup II, Inc. Since the bursting of the dot-com bubble, the spinout structure, in combination with a *cram-down* investment, has become a common occurrence in Silicon Valley.

Question:	*When is a good time for a Cold Restart with Asset Transfer?*
Answer:	*Whenever the assets are available and affordable for a Cold Restart.*

There are numerous other ways in which the assets from the old company can be transferred to the new company in the process of a *Cold Restart*. A good lawyer will help you through this minefield—for a healthy fee, of course.

Making an Elegant Descent—Orderly *Shutdown*

For an orderly *Shutdown* you need 3 things: a shut down plan, cash and time. If you leave it so late that you don't have all 3 of these ingredients you may find yourself facing a *Bankruptcy*.

Shutdown Zone

As the management team of Enron will attest, bankruptcies can be messy—very messy. As a member of the board of directors or the management team, bankruptcy could mean trouble. Trouble comes in various forms spanning nuisance calls from disgruntled employees and creditors through to losing your credit rating, your house and all your personal assets. Very few people actually go to jail as the result of a messy bankruptcy, but I highlight the possibility here to drill home the message that people get hurt when the company struggles on instead of shutting down while it still has sufficient cash in the bank to discharge its debts. The creditors are not the only people to get hurt — a whole bunch of individuals, including the board of directors, management, employees and shareholders, can be hurt in more ways than one.

Orderly Shutdown

As well as minimizing the pain and suffering inflicted on creditors and other people associated with the company, an orderly shutdown leaves the reputations of the management team and the board of directors intact. In fact, in my opinion, navigating the company through a cash flow crisis and implementing an orderly shutdown is an achievement that should actually enhance your resume.

Orderly Shutdown

Let's define an *Orderly Shutdown* as a managed dissolution of the company that involves discharging all the outstanding debts. The shareholders may lose their stakes as the shares become worthless, however, all the creditors are paid off before the company is dissolved.

Following an orderly shutdown, you should be free to attempt some form of restart or safely sail away to your next startup and your next adventure.

Prepare Shutdown Contingency Plan

It's good practice to have a shutdown contingency plan prepared, possibly by the CFO, well in advance of any potential cash flow crisis. If anyone questions why you're preparing to shut down the company, you can respond that it's standard procedure to have a contingency plan and doesn't reflect the state of the business or the confidence of the management team and the board of directors.

The shutdown plan identifies a transition team, estimates the shutdown costs, forecasts the shutdown trigger date and lays out a roadmap and timeline for the various steps in the process.

Investigation Date

You need to fix a date, probably 2-4 weeks in advance of the shutdown trigger date, that you start to investigate the realistic likelihood of an imminent injection of cash.

At this point it's a good idea to alert the board, the shareholders and the staff that the company is a matter of weeks away from starting the shutdown process. This can flush out potential investors and provide them with a sense of urgency. It also ensures that people associated with the company are fully informed, and not unduly surprised, when the decision is taken to shut up shop. You may assume everyone is aware of the seriousness of the situation but shareholders often claim to be shocked when they hear the news—and furious shareholders can hamper a smooth shutdown process.

Shutdown Trigger Date

Technology startups normally have only one form of liquid asset—cash. Each day the company continues in business, more cash is burned up. The shutdown trigger date is the point at which your cash is just sufficient to cover the shutdown costs.

$$\textit{Cash on Hand} = \textit{Shutdown Costs} \rightarrow \textit{Shutdown Trigger Date}$$

When calculating the shutdown costs, make sure you include salaries and layoff packages for employees, legal, accounting and consulting fees, outstanding taxes, secured loans, credit lines and the cost of running a skeleton crew to liquidate the assets. Then add a pool to cover unexpected expenses.

This date can normally be estimated with some accuracy several months in advance when you prepare the shutdown contingency plan. With your cash position, burn rate and estimated shutdown costs, it doesn't take a genius to work out the date at which your cash position is only going to be sufficient to cover the shutdown costs.

When this date arrives, you're going to have to inform lots of people about the shutdown in a very short space of time—you may want to prepare a list of phone numbers and e-mail addresses in advance. As well as informing shareholders and other people associated with the company, don't forget to put close family on the list—one entrepreneur that has been through this process reported big trouble when his mother heard the news of the shutdown from someone else.

Curiously, instead of this being a black day, entrepreneurs often report a huge sense of relief the moment they make the decision to shut down—for many it marks the welcome end to a long struggle.

'In the Vicinity of'.. Jail

As a director of an insolvent company, you can find yourself in legal minefield if the creditors are not paid off and you find yourself heading for *Bankruptcy* instead of *Orderly Shutdown*. Directors of solvent companies are responsible to their shareholders—creditors' rights are strictly defined by their contracts. As the company becomes insolvent, or it reaches the 'vicinity of insolvency', the directors' responsibilities change—they become accountable to creditors. Some courts deem they're answerable to both creditors and shareholders.

There are two ways of staying on the right side of the law:

1. *Pay off the creditors, avoid Bankruptcy & stage an Orderly Shutdown.*
2. *Understand precisely when the company passes from solvency to insolvency, or the 'vicinity' of insolvency and act accordingly.*

In the industrial age, courts used two main methods to determine if a company was solvent or insolvent:

✓ *Equity approach*—a company is insolvent when it is unable to pay its debts as they become due.
✓ *Balance sheet approach*—a company is insolvent when the value of its liabilities exceeded the value of its assets.

In the information age, when assets consist of bits, bytes and patents, virtually all startup technology companies can be classified as insolvent under the balance sheet approach. If you thought that was confusing, the measures determining when the company is in the 'vicinity of insolvency' are even more vague. In fact, the courts make the assessments on a case-by-case basis, looking at a variety of factors including:

✓ *Increase in burn rates.*
✓ *Decrease in cash or cash flow.*
✓ *Status of liabilities.*
✓ *Status of receivables.*

As you can see, it's not exactly simple to figure out when the company passes from solvency to insolvency, or the 'vicinity' of insolvency. It's a legal minefield that you're best advised to avoid. Play it safe—pay off the creditors when you have the chance.

Appoint Transition Team

The layoff process will likely be managed by the company's HR representative. The company's CFO, or another executive with a strong grasp on the financials, will stay on board after the other staff are laid off and work as part of a team that manages the whole shutdown process. Hopefully, you've saved up enough money to pay for a big name accounting firm and a lawyer that specializes in this field. Not only do you have to make the right moves at the right time, but the shareholders and creditors will feel more relaxed if they feel the process is designed and endorsed by a reputable team of professional advisors.

Layoff Staff

After laying off virtually all the staff, the HR representative then gets to lay himself/herself off as well (see *Headcount Reduction*, page 264). As an at-will employer, the company is unlikely to be forced to make huge severance payments to departing employees—in fact, it's probably not obliged to provide any severance pay at all. However, it's hardly fair to lay off an employee without any form of severance. Remember—the objective of an orderly shutdown is to prevent people getting hurt and preserve the reputations of the management team and board of directors.

Liquidate Assets

The creditors are going to be paid off so this is not a bankruptcy situation and management can sell the assets in just about any way it sees fit—it's not being monitored by a trustee or creditor committee. Actually, management is still responsible to the shareholders, and they're going to want to see that the assets were disposed of responsibly. The objective is obviously to raise as much money as possible from the liquidation.

Pay off Creditors

The difference between an orderly shutdown and a bankruptcy is that the creditors are paid of in full and the company is closed down without leaving any outstanding debt. Any cash remaining after everyone has been paid off can be distributed among the shareholders.

Bankruptcy

In your first shutdown situation you may be tempted to struggle on beyond the *Shutdown Trigger Date*—you resist shutting down because it's a sign of failure, you still believe in the dream or you simply don't know when to shut down or how to do it. Second time around, after your release from the state penitentiary, you'll probably be much more aware of the pitfalls and more likely to start the shutdown process while you still have the time and the money to do it in an orderly fashion.

> **Bankruptcy**
> For the purposes of this book, let's use the term *Bankruptcy* to describe the process of shutting down a company when there are insufficient funds to discharge all the outstanding debts—one or more creditors remains unpaid after the assets have been liquidated and the proceeds paid out.

If you have a low burn rate, little or no debt, a realistic prospect of quickly closing a round of funding or generating sales revenues you may be able to push the shutdown date back a little—but the longer you stretch it out, the more chance you have of finding yourself in a messy bankruptcy situation.

The official shutdown process starts with the filing of a Chapter 7 petition with the court. If you're simply shutting down and liquidating the company, you file Chapter 7. Chapter 11 is the way to go if you plan to continue to operate the business, but you need breathing room and relief from creditors to allow management to reorganize the company.

File Chapter 11

In Chapter 11 the business typically remains in operation with the goal of repaying creditors through a court-approved plan of reorganization. The plan is basically a contract with your creditors as to how they will be repaid, and from what source. There's no outside trustee appointed in Chapter 11, the management team continues to run the company taking on the same responsibilities as a trustee. However, this doesn't mean that management is left unchecked—its actions and decisions will be monitored by a number of outsiders including the creditors, the examiner and the United States trustee. The creditors often form a committee and hire lawyers to 'consult' with the management team and 'assist' in the formulation of the plan—they'll investigate any questionable payments and activities.

Reorganization

Chapter 11 provides some relief from creditors so that you can prepare a reorganization plan and have it confirmed by the court. This plan could involve *Cutting Costs, Slashing Costs, Reinventing the Company, Warm Restart*—or a combination of several maneuvers aimed at cutting costs, generating revenues, liquidating assets and paying off debts.

Chapter 11 filings often lead to shutdown, occasionally followed by a *Cold Restart*, however, sometimes the reorganization works, there's a miraculous turnaround and the company re-emerges as a viable stand-alone business.

File Chapter 7

On the filing of a Chapter 7 petition, the court appoints a trustee to sell the company's assets, and then make distributions to creditors. In most Chapter 7 cases, the business has already stopped operations, or stops once the case is filed. The Chapter 7 process can take 3-4 months.

Appoint Trustee

Once the Chapter 7 petition is filed, a trustee is appointed to supervise the bankruptcy—this is the point that management effectively relinquishes control and it's role shifts to assisting the trustee. Be prepared to provide detailed information and answer plenty of questions. Dealing with the trustee can be a strain, but the relationship can be eased with cooperation. After working through a difficult shutdown process, a CEO recently told me he received a box from the trustee—when he opened it up, he found a Christmas gift and a thank-you note.

Creditor Meetings

Creditors meetings are opportunities for creditors to gather information and ask questions of the management team and the board of directors. As people are not normally happy about losing money, these are not the type of affairs where people start singing and dancing on tables. Facing angry creditors can be likened to swimming with sharks in a feeding frenzy.

It's important to make careful preparations for the meeting. As well as gathering the financial information that the creditors are going to grill you on, it's essential that you're well briefed on the legal implications of what you might say. One school of thought says that the best way of diffusing anger is to answer questions as completely and directly as you can—refusing to answer, or being economical with the truth, may be a good idea from a legal perspective but it can antagonize the creditors unnecessarily.

Liquidate Assets

The primary role of a Chapter 7 trustee is to liquidate the assets and maximize the return for the creditors. Normally this means selling all the unsecured assets, however, the trustee can pursue lawsuits and continue to operate the business if these activities have some likelihood of increasing the proceeds of the liquidation. The trustee can also set aside payments that were made to creditors before he was even appointed—if he feels they provided preferential treatment to one creditor over the others.

For a technology company, liquidating the assets usually means selling the office furniture and equipment and trying to find a buyer for the intellectual property. In the aftermath of the dot-com crash, Silicon Valley has been the home to some very high profile auctions of company equipment and assets—it's a good opportunity for many to snoop around the offices of once high-flying Internet companies and buy PC's, furniture and office equipment at knock-down prices.

Distribution to Creditors

The trustee distributes the proceeds of the liquidation to the creditors in accordance with strict laws and regulations defining how the money is to be shared. The trustee's commissions and other administrative expenses are paid first, followed by payment of priority debts (often taxes), and the remainder goes to general unsecured creditors.

Jail?

People have been known to go to jail as the result of a messy bankruptcy. You're unlikely to go to jail but your house and other personal assets could be on the line if you really screw things up. Here are some sure-fire ways of getting yourself into trouble:

- *Spending money that belongs to the Inland Revenue Service*—these folks get a little upset when they don't get paid and they'll bypass the company and go for your personal assets. They can do it and they will if you spend any payroll taxes or other tax dollars that happens to be sitting in the company's bank account.
- *Spending money that belongs to your employees*—in addition to payroll tax withholdings, the company may be holding cash that's been deducted from employee salaries for pensions, savings plans and other benefits. Although it's in the companies' bank account, this money doesn't belong to the company, so it's out of bounds for any other purpose.
- *Buying anything on credit when it's unlikely the company will be able to settle the debt*—be very careful about buying anything on credit.
- *Paying off one creditor at the expense of the others*—it's tempting to pay off the little mom and pop creditors with your last few dollars and leave the big ones high and dry. As with any other payments you make at this stage, take advice and be very careful.

You really want to avoid getting into any of these situations and you want to make sure your creditors, employees and shareholders are aware that you are dealing with matters in a clean and professional way. In selecting the financial and legal advisors for the company, you'll gain credibility if you go for the biggest and most well-respected names.

This is the point that you regret signing your name on any loan guarantees—the cost of repaying personally guaranteed loans or leases will likely come out of your own pocket. But there could be an upside—if you can think of any reason why you'd like to personally own lots of PC's, photocopiers and other office equipment that the company had acquired through loans secured on your personal guarantee. It's good advice to hire an independent consultant to help guide you through the process and save your own hide—even if you have to pay the fees out of your own pocket.

If you can act before the *Shutdown Trigger Date* and implement an *Orderly Shutdown* instead of *Bankruptcy*, you'll likely be free to sail on to your next startup.

Appendix 1—What's it Worth? Valuing the Company

I spent half of my college days majoring in economics. For some reason I loved it. Probably because the school of economics attracted better looking girls than the computer science department, where I spent the other half of my time. Until I checked out the electronic engineering course, I was under the impression that computer science attracted the dullest girls on the whole campus. Anyway, back to economics. One of the first things you learn in economics is that price is driven by two factors—supply and demand. Excess supply forces the price down. Excess demand forces the price up. The supply of attractive girls on an electronics engineering course is so low and demand so high that competition among the guys is fierce. Sorry, there I go again. In a perfect proof of the laws of supply of demand, cute girls in the engineering school are not cheap dates—much more costly and hard work than those from other departments, like the school of arts, where they can be found in more abundant supply. Or something like that—I was obviously distracted during my economics classes.

Economists take many years creating complex models and theories; children take a few minutes exchanging trading cards; they all reach the same conclusions:

Economics 101—The Laws of Supply & Demand
- ✓ **The real price is what a buyer is actually prepared to pay.**
- ✓ **The price will tend to rise when you introduce additional competing buyers.**
- ✓ **The price will tend to fall when you introduce additional competing sellers.**

The supply/demand pricing model works best when there are gazillions of buyers and sellers competing in an open market with a common currency. It tends to fall apart when there are very few buyers or sellers and when natural market forces are restricted—and strange things happen to prices. If there's just one seller and multiple buyers, the seller tends to win—and set an extremely high price. Monopoly situations like this are now regulated by consumer advocates the world over. When there's just one buyer and multiple sellers, the buyer tends to win—and, you guessed it, the price drops through the floor. So, who wins and what happens when there's just one buyer and one seller? Like a husband and wife fighting for the TV remote control, the outcome is totally unpredictable. Not. The wife will almost always end up watching her program and the buyer will almost always end up setting the price.

> ### <u>Increasing the Price—the Golden Rule of Valuation</u>
> The best way to increase the price is to increase demand, by introducing additional competing buyers. The best way of introducing buyers is to make marked progress in your sales efforts and create a positive buzz around the company (See *Fundraising Process*, page 325, *M&A Process*, page 351).
>
> *'Marked progress and a positive buzz'—isn't that how we defined Momentum?*
> *..that 'M' word is getting everywhere.*

In this chapter we'll look at various valuation techniques—some more complicated than others. Before we do, let's bear in mind that whatever you're selling, shares in your company, your technology or the company itself, the real price you achieve will ultimately depend on your ability to create an auction environment with a number of competing buyers. If you're selling shares, the valuation will depend on your ability to bring in investors. If you're selling the company, the valuation will be driven by your ability to attract a number of competing acquirers.

> ### Pre- and Post- Money Valuations
> *Pre-money* refers to the valuation of the company immediately before the investment and *post-money* is the valuation immediately after the investment. In the case of AcmeTech Startup (see *Setup your Capitalization Table*, page 93), the company is valued at $10m pre-money for the series A round, then $8m is invested, leading to a post-money valuation of $18m.

Many of the valuation techniques that you'll find in the business school libraries today were formulated in the industrial age when tangible assets, like land, property and machinery, were relatively easy to sell and estimate a fair market value. Valuing bits and bytes, patents, expertise and ideas in the information age is not so straightforward. The balance sheets of information-age companies represent very little value if traditional valuation methods, like book value and liquidation value, are employed. Research and development costs are often expensed, and it's not easy to put a value on the real assets of the company, like intellectual property, customer base, distribution channels, sales leads, strategic alliances and staff.

There's very little to list in the asset column and the balance sheet has little bearing when it comes to finding the real value of a technology company today. However, there are a number of techniques available to value technology companies today. The easiest technology companies to value are the large, mature corporations with years of financial history and shares that are traded on the public markets. True market forces come in to play when large numbers of investors buy and sell shares on the stock market—so the market value of a publicly traded company is arguably the most accurate valuation metric you can find. On the other hand, how do you put a value on a small, immature private company with virtually no financial history at all? You have to revert to looking outside at the valuations of similar companies and apply simple rules of thumb. As the company matures, its financial performance can be analyzed and more sophisticated valuation techniques can be employed.

Valuation Techniques for Technology Companies

	Seed Funding	Early Stage Funding	Expansion Funding	Mezzanine Funding	Cash Flow Sale	Asset Sale	IPO	Stock Market
Rule of Thumb	✓	✓				✓		
Discounted Cash Flow			✓	✓	✓			
Build Cost Plus						✓		
Return on Investment	✓	✓	✓					
Comparable Deals	✓	✓	✓	✓	✓	✓	✓	
Revenue Multiple				✓	✓		✓	
Earnings Multiple				✓	✓		✓	
True Market Forces								✓

Valuation Techniques—True Market Forces

The forces of supply and demand produce a market price when a company's shares are feely traded on a stock market. Simply multiply the current share price by the number of outstanding shares and you have a valuation for the company.

Share price = $10/share.
Number of outstanding shares = 1m.
Company valuation = $10m.

Of course, people will argue that the stock market is less than a perfect example of true market forces, but it's as close as we're going to get for valuation purposes, so let's pretend that it is for the time being.

Valuation Techniques—Earnings Multiple

In this model, the company valuation is based entirely on its earnings performance.

> *Company's earnings (for last 12 months) = $10m.*
> *Average Price/Earnings ('P/E') ratio for (public co.'s) in this industry sector = 20x.*
> *Company valuation (public company) = $200m.*
> *Company valuation (private company) = $150m (after applying liquidity discount).*

The price/earnings ratio for the industry is calculated by comparing the valuation of public companies (using the *True Market Forces* method above). If all the companies in the sector generated a total of $100m in earnings and the total market value of these companies is $2Bn, the multiple is calculated at 20—the ratio of price to earnings.

Liquidity Discount

A private company is normally valued lower than a public company. This is because its stock is not tradable; it's not liquid and is therefore less valuable to an investor. A liquidity discount, normally of 25-33%, has to be applied when comparing private companies with their public brethren.

Valuation Techniques—Revenue Multiple

This works by comparing the company's revenue with the revenues of public companies. You then calculate how the revenues relate to the known valuations of these public companies:

> *Company's revenues (for last 12 months) = $10m.*
> *Average revenue multiple for (public co.'s) in this industry sector = 8x.*
> *Company valuation (public company) = $80m.*
> *Company valuation (private company) = $60m (after applying liquidity discount).*

In this example, the total revenue of all the public companies in this sector during the last 12 months was $100m and the total valuation of these companies (using the True Market Forces of the stock market) was $800m. So the revenue multiple for this industry is calculated at 8x revenue.

Valuation Techniques—Discounted Cash Flow

Instead of looking at historical financial performance, this method involves valuing the company based on projected cash-flows for several years ahead. Essentially, this technique says that the company is worth the cash flow it will generate in the coming years, after discounting to acknowledge that projected future cash flow is not exactly the same as cash in the bank today. Typically you use a 3 year projection and discount the cash flow by something in the region of 30% (each year) to reflect the associated risk and volatility. You can use 4 or 5 year projections—if you can realistically project out that far. It's important that you don't forget to use the after-tax cash-flow figure as cash flowing to Uncle Sam's is of little use to the company.

> *Projected net cash flow, year 1 (after tax) = $1 m.*
> *Projected net cash flow, year 2 (after tax) = $2 m.*
> *Projected net cash flow, year 3 (after tax) = $2 m.*
> *Discount rate = 30%*
> *Discounted cash flow projection, year 1 = $1 m / (1.30) = $0.77 m.*
> *Discounted cash flow projection, year 2 = $2 m / (1.30)² = $1.18 m.*
> *Discounted cash flow projection, year 3 = $2 m / (1.30)³ = $0.91 m.*
> *3 year cash flow = $1 m + $2 m + $2 m = $5 m.*
> *3 year discounted cash flow = $0.77 m + $1.18 m + 0.91 m = $2.86 m.*

This is a good valuation technique for companies that have highly predictable cash flows and accurate projections—characteristics seldom found in the technology sector!

Valuation Techniques—Build Cost Plus

Before acquiring an asset, a buyer will usually make a build vs. buy calculation and estimate how much it would cost to build the asset using its own team and resources.

> *Asset valuation = buyers build cost.*
> *Buyers build cost = fully loaded cost of 5 engineers, & project manager for 24 months = $2m.*

In this scenario, your company is considered to be worth no more than what it would cost the buyer to rebuild your product by hiring an in-house research and development team. However, a good negotiator will point out that when this internal development project is complete, in 2 years time, the market will have changed considerably—and the opportunity will be long gone. In this situation, it's not unusual to apply a time-to-market multiple to recognize the momentum generated to date and come up with a reasonable valuation:

> *Asset valuation = buyers build cost x time to market multiple.*
> *Buyers build cost = $2m.*
> *Time to market multiple = 3x.*
> *Asset valuation (after applying time-to-market multiple) = $2m x 3 = $6m.*

Remember—you use the buyers build cost for this valuation. The build cost of a large corporate buyer in Silicon Valley might be $2m, however, a bootstrapped startup working out of a garage may have completed the development at a considerably lower cost—especially if it has some of its team in India, China or some other low cost development center. *The Build Cost Plus* valuation technique for technology assets can offer considerable profit potential for developers—building an asset for $1m and selling it for $6m is not bad business if you can pull it off.

Valuation Techniques—Comparable Deals

This method is highly complicated. You look around to see if any similar private companies have been recently sold and compare your valuation with theirs. OK, it's not really very complicated at all, however, it does rely on finding comparable companies out there—and this may be unlikely if you're pioneering a new market.

> *Private company identical to yours just sold to an identical buyer for $10m.*
> *Your company valuation = $10m.*

Of course, it's not exactly easy to find two companies that are identical, so adjustments have to be made. Liquidity discount adjustments (see *Earnings Multiple*, above) should always be made when comparing private and public companies:

> *Public company identical to your private company has market valuation of $100m.*
> *Your private company valuation = $100m less the liquidity discount (say 25%) = $75m.*

Many investors and corporate buyers subscribe to information services like VentureOne to monitor the current market valuations. When I last checked, the VentureOne service was only available to 'investors and strategic partners', but your lawyer or one of your advisors may be able to access the information and use it to help you with your negotiations. If that doesn't work, you may be able to find out the valuations your competitors negotiated through bribery, corruption and champagne lunches. However, you get hold of it, this information could be highly valuable to you in your negotiation discussions.

Valuation Techniques—Return on Investment

The beauty and intrigue of this method is that a value is placed on the company with little reference to the market, the technology, the team, milestones achieved or momentum generated to date. In fact, the only information an investor requires from the company is a copy of the Capitalization Table (see *Capitalization Table*, page 93). With this information, details of the amount of money they're investing, the value of the company at a point in the future, say 3 years from now, and how much they want their investment to be worth at that point, the investor works out how much of the company they need to own today—and from here they can determine the current company valuation.

3 Years From Now

Company valuation is estimated at $100m (based on Comparable Deals, Earnings & Revenue Multiples).

Total number of shares outstanding is estimated at 20m (after allowance for future rounds of funding).

VC wants 15% of company at this point—so this translates to 3m shares with value of $15m.

Today

In order to achieve 1000% (10x) return on investment, the VC needs to buy 3m shares today at a $1.5m.

With 10m shares outstanding today (before shares are sold in later rounds), this values the company at $5m.

When negotiating with lead VC's, it's important to understand where they're coming from. The top-tier Sand Hill Road firms are looking for a substantial share of the company—normally in the region of at least 15-20%—otherwise they just can't afford to get involved. They're also looking for huge potential returns like 1000% over 3-5 years. Although it seems to have little relationship with the company, the milestones achieved or momentum generated, the *Return on Investment* technique is commonly used by investors in seed and early stage companies.

Valuation Techniques—Rule of Thumb

Repetition leads to familiarity and individuals that are doing a large number of deals, like investors and corporate buyers, develop a rule of thumb—an awareness, conscious or unconscious, of what seems to be the market rate for companies at various stages of growth. If you knew what your investor or potential buyers rule of thumb table looked like, you'd be able to short-circuit the discussions, however, they don't print it out, and they're often unaware of its existence until they're presented with a valuation that oversteps the range they feel comfortable with.

Example Investor Rule of Thumb Valuation Table

	Seed Stage	Early Stage	Expansion Stage	Mezzanine Stage	Asset Sale
Fair Momentum	$1-3m	$3-10m	$5-15m	$50-100m	$0-1m
Good Momentum	$5-10m	$5-15m	$10-50m	$100-300m	$0.5-4m
Excellent Momentum	$5-15m	$10-30m	$15-100m	$200m+	$2-10m

* *Pre-Money Valuations*

Valuation Techniques—Weighted Average

In the ideal world, you'll enter negotiations armed with a report that values the company using each of the relevant techniques listed above, then takes a weighted average of them all to produce a figure that carries some credibility. Credibility may be enhanced if the report has been produced by a reputable firm of lawyers, accountants or M&A advisors. It's further enhanced by the thud factor—a thick, detailed, well presented report can grab attention. However, all credibility will be lost if there are any errors or miscalculations.

Valuation Techniques for a Seed Stage Company

In the seed stage, the company probably has revenue and earnings of zero. You don't have to be a mathematical genius to figure out that in this case, the *Revenue Multiple* and *Earnings Multiple* techniques will also value the company at zero. It's advisable to use other valuation techniques when you negotiate your seed funding—starting out at zero is not recommended.

Playing the Discounted Cash Flow Game—for a Company with Very Little History

Your investor may want to play the discounted cash flow game. Valuation of the company based on its future cash flow projections can be a useful tool for more mature companies with solid and predictable revenue and profit projections—however, for a seed- or early- stage company it's almost entirely meaningless. Nevertheless, if the investor wants to play this game, you're probably going to have to play along, so you need to know how it's played. It goes like this:

1. You both pretend that your business plan projections are meaningful and realistic.
2. The VC works out the future cash flow projections, estimates a future valuation and then discounts it to produce a valuation for today. The valuation is lower than you want.
3. You dispute the aggressive discounting formula they used and produce your own valuation that's a little higher than what you'd be willing to accept.
4. You enter into meaningless technical discussions about appropriate discount rates and future valuations.
5. You both ignore the calculations completely, revert to the *Return on Investment*, *Comparable Deals* and *Rule of Thumb* techniques.
6. You pick a number between your estimate and their estimate and try to agree on that.

Of course, your professional advisors love this game. In fact, I suspect it was invented by Silicon Valley lawyers and accountants as a way to increase billing hours.

Discounted Cash Flow is obviously the way to go—produce humongous estimates of your future profits, discount them back to today's value and you have a lovely valuation. All you need now is for investors to take the valuation seriously. It may be possible to dupe your uncle Orville or your lotto-winning neighbor that a discounted cash flow valuation is reasonable; however, a sophisticated investor, or anyone with any sense, will laugh in your face—before showing you the door. I learned this the hard way. In preparation for an investor meeting, my accountant prepared a $70m discounted cash flow valuation for my seed stage company and sent me off to lead the negotiations—like a lamb to slaughter. What was she smoking? Fortunately, the investors resisted the temptation to throw me out of the building and our negotiations focused on the rule-of-thumb valuation technique. I came away with the funding and a valuation of $5m. The accountant was quite impressed—she knew the $70m figure was ridiculous—but she failed to mention this detail to me before I was sent into battle. Not only did the unrealistically high *Discounted Cash Flow* valuation damage my credibility with the investors and jeopardize the whole deal, but it affected morale within my team—the other team members had been convinced that $70 was a reasonable figure and were initially disappointed with the outcome.

With little or no history to work from, the only valuation techniques that make sense in the seed stage are *Return on Investment, Rule of Thumb* and *Comparable Deals*. In fact, seed rounds are often completed without setting any value at all—the money is invested as a loan that converts over to equity when a valuation is fixed by the lead VC investor in the next round.

Valuation Techniques for an Early Stage Company

Valuations resulting from the *Discounted Cash Flow* model are obviously dependent on the cash flow projections for the upcoming years. If it's going to take several years for the company to turn cash flow positive, the *Discounted Cash Flow* model will value the company at something resembling nothing—and some investors will try to use this to their advantage.

You're sure to meet resistance from Sand Hill Road investors if your business plan projections don't show the company growing to *IPO* candidate stage within 3-5 years. If you're not projecting profitable revenues of at least $10m/quarter within this period, the discounted cash flow analysis may raise serious questions about the plan.

Once again, *Return on Investment, Rule of Thumb* and *Comparable Deals* are the only techniques that make any sense for an early stage company.

Valuation Techniques for Expansion Funding

Comparable Deals and *Return on Investment* techniques are often used for expansion stage companies, however, as the company starts to generate sales, financial projections and *Discounted Cash Flow* valuations begin to carry some credibility. New investors trying to get a stake in the company also tend to offer higher valuations than existing shareholders. So, when it comes to your strategic round of funding, you're well advised to have the round led by an outside strategic investor—if you have a choice. A strategic investor, like a large corporation, will normally accept a higher valuation than a financial investor, like a VC.

Valuation Techniques for Mezzanine Funding

As the company is now only a matter of months away from *IPO*, your investment bank will be in a position to compare the company's performance with existing public companies, and use *Revenue Multiple* and *Earnings Multiple* techniques to set a valuation that's based on current public share prices in your sector. The company is still private, and the stock is hardly liquid, so they're sure to take the public market valuation and apply a discount. There's a lot more history to go on and this does make the valuation calculations much more reliable, however, the price very much depends on the current climate on Wall Street—and this is somewhat difficult to predict.

Valuation Techniques for Cash Flow Sale

To sell your company in a *Cash Flow Sale*, it obviously needs to have cash flowing in an inward as well as an outward direction. This means you need to have sales and, ideally, profits. With sales, you can use the *Revenue Multiple* technique, with profits, the *Earnings Multiple* technique comes in to play. As always, you can refer to *Comparable Deals*. With relatively believable cash flow projections it's not unusual to use the *Discounted Cash Flow* method. A professional M&A firm will use the most flattering techniques, take a *Weighted Average* of them all and produce a detailed valuation report.

If the company is public, an acquisition price will be somewhat based on its current share price. *True Market Forces* will help set the company valuation—but this is not the end of the story. It's not unusual for an acquirer to pay a significant premium over the current stock market share price to take control of the whole company rather than buy a small number of shares.

The Golden Rule (see *Increasing the Price—the Golden Rule of Valuation*, page 302) applies and the best way of increasing your valuation is to bring in additional competing buyers. Some buyers are prepared to pay more than others—a strategic buyer that's interested in the technology, patents, teams, distribution channels and other components will likely pay much more than a financial buyer that's solely interested in the cash flow. The ideal scenario is that auction fever takes hold with a number of strategic buyers that are head-on competitors with bad blood between them and plenty of ego in the board room.

Valuation Techniques for Asset Sale

By definition, if sales were flowing in, and the company had a financial history to make a song and dance about, your target destination would be *Cash Flow Sale*. In an *Asset Sale* situation, the company has little, or no, cash flowing in an inward direction—for one reason or another, the sales and marketing operations are often insufficient to bring in revenues. This means all the cash flow based valuation techniques, like *Revenue Multiple*, *Earnings Multiple* and *Discounted Cash Flow*, are somewhat inappropriate.

Many technology assets are worthless without a core team. In an *Asset Sale* situation, the acquirer is forced to take on the team and pick up the associated burn rate. The *Build Cost Plus* technique values the company purely based on the cost of reverse engineering its technology asset, however, a high burn is not exactly attractive to a buyer and can significantly reduce the price it's prepared to pay. Don't be surprised to find that a savvy buyer makes an adjustment to the *Build Cost Plus* valuation to factor in the cost of taking on the team.

The valuation in an *Asset Sale* always depends on the negotiation process (see *Getting What you Want, Negotiating the Deal*, page 313) and, true to the economic laws of supply and demand, with only one buyer, you can expect the price to fall to whatever that buyer wants to pay.

Valuation Techniques for IPO

As soon as the company's stock is traded on an open exchange, its valuation is effectively set by *True Market Forces*. Hopefully, savvy investors set the valuation using metrics like *Revenue Multiple* and *Earnings Multiple*; however, a host of other factors including greed and fear come into play. A matter of days, or hours, before the IPO, the company's underwriter has to assess valuation and fix an opening share price (see *Set the Share Price*, page 215). It's important that this is done accurately—a miscalculation here can be damaging to the company's profile.

The Golden Rule (see *Increasing the Price—the Golden Rule of Valuation*, page 302) applies to public as well as private companies—the price is dependent on the company's ability to attract competing investors to buy the shares. An effective investor relations program can help (see *Prepare to Deal with Public Investors*, page 216).

Appendix 2—Getting What you Want—
Negotiating the Deal

Whether you're raising funds from investors, selling the company to an acquirer or selling products to customers, you're sure to have to go through a negotiation process to close the deal and get what you want. It's important to understand the process, assemble a savvy team, and be aware of the deal killers—in many cases you'll find yourself up against seasoned or professional negotiators that know every trick in the book.

The Negotiation Process

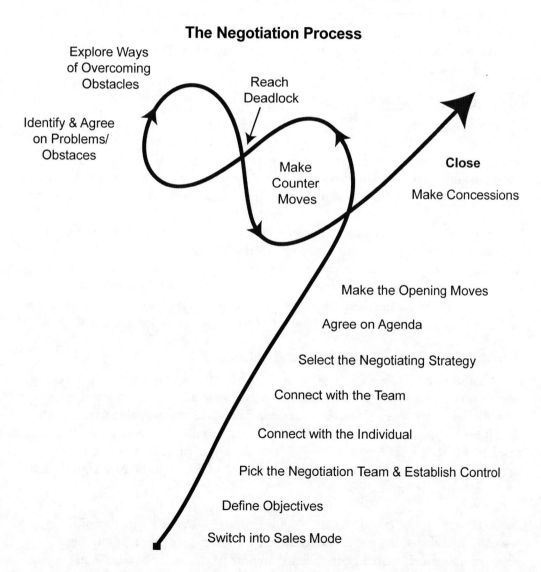

Explore Ways
of Overcoming
Obstacles

Reach
Deadlock

Identify & Agree
on Problems/
Obstacles

Make
Counter
Moves

Close

Make Concessions

Make the Opening Moves

Agree on Agenda

Select the Negotiating Strategy

Connect with the Team

Connect with the Individual

Pick the Negotiation Team & Establish Control

Define Objectives

Switch into Sales Mode

No two negotiations are the same—some go through many iterations of counter moves, others need very few; some reach deadlock, others progress to close with hardly a hitch; some take months, others take a matter of minutes. Nevertheless, there is a common process that virtually all negotiations follow.

Switch into Sales Mode

A negotiation is not a scheduled event that occurs as you sit face to face over the boardroom table. All communication between buyer and seller can be categorized as negotiation—including a "how's it going?" chat in the elevator, a shrug, or a wink of the eye. It's important that everyone on your team that might come into contact with the other party is aware of this—and switches into sales mode before stray comments are allowed to do any damage. The sales mode continues throughout the negotiation process—any opportunity to talk to the other party is a chance to sell and enhance your position.

Define Objectives—Where Are We Going?

If you don't know where you're going what chance do you have of ever getting there? In the negotiation process, targeting your destination means defining your objectives—and distinguishing the 'must-haves' from the 'nice to haves'. It's important that your appointed negotiator is clear on what you want and what you're prepared to accept before you actually get into serious discussions.

Expect less—get less. The challenge in defining your objectives is to aim high without overshooting the mark. It can be difficult to figure out what you really want from the deal, especially when you have to satisfy the needs of several members of the team. It can also be very revealing. However, it's worth taking the time to get this right—the whole negotiation process can be accelerated if both sides come into the discussions with a clear understanding of what they're looking for.

Pick the Negotiating Team & Establish Control

Large teams don't make good negotiators. In fact, the smaller the team, the better your chance of success. Pick a point-person to handle all negotiations and brief your team to make sure that all questions and inquiries about the possible terms of the deal, however, informal and innocent, are deferred to this lead negotiator. It's vital that he/she has a clear understanding of the objectives of your side. In the fundraising process, the lead negotiator is often the CEO. In the M&A process, it's often the agent or intermediary.

A good lead negotiator will quickly establish control—making sure that all discussions between the parties are channeled through this single point. One negotiation is much more effective than multiple parallel negotiations—an experienced negotiator on the opposing team will exploit any evidence of disagreement on your side.

The lead negotiator is likely to be supported by lawyers, accountants and other members of the team—and will regularly have to check back with management, the board of directors, major investors and anyone else on your side that might have a bearing on the deal. A good-guy bad-guy tag team (see *Negotiating Tips & Techniques*, page 320) can be highly effective. The good-guy is often the CEO or company insider, the bad guy is often the agent.

As always, it's vital that you have a good lawyer on the team. Lawyers can participate in, and sometimes lead the negotiations. They often play the part of the bad guy—many of them are naturally gifted and well suited to this role. Based on the personality of the lawyer, it can be safer to keep him/her out of the process until the business terms have been agreed and the letter of intent has been drawn up. Lawyers that are poor negotiators can introduce legal issues that complicate and confuse the discussions and create unnecessary friction between the parties. After the terms have been agreed, and the letter of intent has been signed, the role of the lawyer is essential to the successful completion of the deal.

Connect With the Individual

In his classic ancient book, The Art of War, Sun Tsu, the acclaimed Chinese author recommends that we take the time to understand our enemy before going into battle. Empathy is a valuable asset when it comes to negotiations—you'll gain an advantage if you can put yourself in the other person's shoes and see things from his/her perspective. This will help you select the most appropriate techniques and predict how he/she will react to your moves. It will also help if you create a positive and respectful relationship as well as an open, two-way channel of communication.

As well as personality type, other factors such as culture, gender and age can have a major bearing on how the individual reacts to various negotiation techniques. Each individual is unique, driven by a distinct set of beliefs, traditions, preferences, motives, wants and needs. Believe it or not, men and women often react to the same situation in different ways. So do people of different generations. When I was working in the European head office of Apple Computer, my colleagues were drawn from many countries and cultures and I observed the interactions with an amused fascination. The Americans would arrive at meetings eager to make decisions and would soon become frustrated with their French colleagues—who were there to explore and debate. Every culture has its own characteristics. Sake and karaoke bars are an integral part of the deal-making process in Tokyo—negotiators from Japan and many other countries would never dream of doing business with anyone they haven't socialized with and feel they know on a personal level.

Your position in the negotiations will be enhanced if you know how the individual handles confrontation and responds to emotional displays. A gauge of the individuals' ego can be very useful—as this can block many deals (see *Some Deal Killers to Look out For*, page 321). On the other hand, if you play to his/her ego, you can use it to your advantage.

In a friendly chat on his first meeting, the negotiator representing the buyer, in an M&A deal I was involved with, bragged that he had recently bought a yacht at a bargain basement price. Of course he then went on to play hard-ball and demand a bargain basement deal. Sounding out the individual beforehand can provide a valuable indicator of what you'll be up against and prepare you for the upcoming negotiations.

Connect With the Team

In addition to the lead negotiator, you're likely to be facing a team comprising management, board members, investors, lawyers, agents and intermediaries, as well as individuals playing the roles of business and technology analysts. Connecting-with and selling-to each and every member of the team is essential—as one dissenting player could block the whole deal. It's important to understand the decision making process the team follows, where the power lies, and how the members interact. Don't be misled by titles—the real power in companies often lies with individuals that are not officially on top of the organization chart.

Partners in venture capital funds are often unable to make investment decisions without winning approval from an investment committee—normally made up of other partners. Sometimes these committee meetings are held behind closed doors; sometimes startups are invited along to present. Even though a partner is championing your cause, don't be surprised if the committee fails to approve the deal—this is not unusual. Corporate acquirers sometimes go through a similar committee process—if they don't have a dedicated acquisition committee, this role is taken on by the board of directors.

Understanding the process, identifying, connecting-with and selling-to each member of the team will increase your chances of closing the deal.

Select the Negotiating Strategy

Now that you have a connection and understanding with the opposing team, you should be able to predict how they'll respond to different negotiating strategies and techniques. Expert negotiators have a whole selection of strategies to choose from. Some are based on pushing the opposing team to get what you want; others are based on pull—attracting them to your position. Based on the circumstances, you may go for the good-guy/bad-guy technique, play hard to get, start haggling, lay all your cards on the table or keep them close to your chest.

Obviously, you need to pick a strategy that you can carry off and feel comfortable with. Take care here—your choice of whether to bully, brainstorm or barter could have a profound impact on how the negotiations proceed.

Agree on Agenda—How Are We Going To Get There?

Whether you call it an agenda, a project plan, program or schedule, if you lay out some form of roadmap with clear milestones and deadlines, you may be surprised by how willing people are to follow it. Agreeing on an agenda up front may be the best way of generating and maintaining momentum in the negotiation process. This can also be an opportunity to set some ground rules and responsibilities. It doesn't have to be a formal process—an informal chat in the back of a cab and a few notes on the back of an envelope may be all you need.

Make the Opening Moves

All the preparations are complete; now it's time for each side to make its opening move. M&A experts often recommend the seller postpone the opening move and the discussion of price for as long as possible. The theory is that this gives the buyer time to get to know and appreciate the company. It also provides you with more time to listen to and understand the buyer, research comparable company valuations and generate more momentum in sales, product development and other areas.

You're unlikely to get what you ask for in your initial request, so it's a good idea to make your opening demand somewhat higher than the final figure you're prepared to accept (see *Define Objectives—Where are we Going?*, page 314). This will give you some room to haggle and make concessions later on.

Whether you're selling part of the company to an investor or the whole company to an acquirer, there are two schools of thought on when and how you disclose your opening price:

1. *Seller suggests the initial price*—if you're not in an auction situation and you've done enough listening to understand what the buyer is looking for, you can put your stake in the ground, present your valuation calculations and outline how you'd like to see the deal structured. This can work well in situations where you suspect the buyer would open the bidding with an extremely low-

ball offer that you don't even want to discuss. Of course, with this strategy, you run the risk of setting a price lower than the buyer is prepared to pay.

2. *Seller waits for the buyer to suggest a price*—expert negotiators often recommend waiting for the buyer to make the opening offer. When the opponent shows his/her opening hand, you have a better idea of what you're dealing with. In some situations, especially when there's an auction environment with a number of competing buyers, the buyers' opening offer may be higher than the seller expects. This strategy can also buy time to establish a relationship and prevent premature termination of the discussions if the two parties' opening offers are far apart.

The strategy you adopt will also be driven by your personal style. My approach is to try to short-circuit the discussions and give my opening price when the seller requests it. However, I'm not a professional negotiator, I'm not very patient and I personally don't play cat and mouse games at all well. Your style and that of your team will be likely very different and it's important to do what you personally feel comfortable with.

Make Counter Moves

From the Turkish Bazaar to the swish offices on Sand Hill Road, the haggling process has been around for thousands of years. The buyer starts low, the seller starts high. Both sides then concede ground in a series of counter moves that pull the two sides closer together until a point is reached that everyone finds acceptable.

Offers and counter offers are not always official documents. They're often comments, or hypothetical suggestions like 'well, if we were to find ourselves in a situation like this, we may respond in this way'.

Reach Deadlock

Sometimes, the two parties fail to make sufficient progress toward a mutually acceptable deal and the move-counter move cycle grinds to a halt. It can be tempting to disengage at this point, however, think carefully before you do (see *Disengage without Burning your Bridges*, page 324).

Identify & Agree on Problems/Obstacles

Make sure you don't walk away without identifying the obstacles that are holding up the negotiations and reinforcing your belief in the ultimate value of the deal.

> *"You're saying that you can't live with a valuation over $10m and we're not in a position to drop below $15m, so we've reached a stalemate. Another obstacle appears to be the structure of the deal—you're looking for a three stage payment schedule and we want a*

single payment up front. Would you agree with this assessment? Have I missed anything?"

The ability to listen and reflect can come in very handy at this stage (see *Negotiation Tips & Techniques*, page 320).

Explore Ways of Overcoming Obstacles

The best negotiators are great listeners with a creative approach to overcoming deadlock and engineering win-win situations. By introducing alternative currencies, there are many ways that a deal can be structured to make it more appealing to a buyer without necessarily giving up ground on issues like valuation (see *Introduce Alternative Currencies*, page 323). This may require a good deal of brainstorming and thinking outside of the box.

Make Concessions

In my experience, win-win deals are the most lasting. Everyone wants to walk away feeling like a winner after the deal has been agreed. Sooner or later, the losing side in a win-lose situation will inevitably find a way to sabotage the deal.

To create a win-win situation, it can help if you hold something back until the end—then make some sort of concession to close out the negotiations with everyone feeling good about the outcome. 'Straw men', deal demands that you're secretly prepared to concede, are deliberately created by experienced negotiators—and they're often the trigger required to close out the deal. Just make sure you don't make the concessions without first putting up a realistic struggle. This move must at least appear to be genuine.

Close

Professional salespeople have a variety of techniques designed to close a deal and transform a discussion into a binding agreement. They generally involved begging, bullying and various forms of bribes. Whatever it takes, the deal is not done until the contract is signed (and the cash is in the bank).

Don't you just hate it when you make a deal with someone only to find that he comes back later with the fateful words 'oh, I forgot… just one more thing…'? No one likes to deal with this, and you run the risk of derailing your discussions if you don't make sure that you have all the deal points on the table when you reach agreement with the buyer. Once you've struck a deal, you'll ideally move to the contract without adding new terms or changing any of the terms that have been agreed.

Negotiation Tips & Techniques

Before you enter into important negotiations, it's worthwhile arming yourself with some basic tips and techniques. In recent years, a whole management training industry has developed around this field of negotiation—with books, seminars, videos and training courses available to suit various tastes and budgets. It's hardly surprising as the difference between success and failure in business negotiations can be enormous.

Listen

One of the most important assets of a good negotiator is the ability to listen and understand the position of the other party. Asking open ended, probing questions and listening carefully to the response will allow you to gauge where the other party is coming from. This will help you structure a win-win deal. Remember, you have two ears and only one mouth. The more it's kept closed the more time you have to listen—and the less time you have to put your foot in it.

Reflect

You do have to open your mouth from time to time, partly to show that you've listened carefully and understand the other sides' position.

> *'So what you're saying is ….'*

You can prove that you've heard and grasped what the other party is saying without necessarily agreeing with or endorsing it.

As well as raising the level of common understanding, active listening and reflecting can prevent people making the same point over and over again. When they hear that you've got it, they'll usually move on. I've tried it on my kids and it works quite well. Like anyone else, kids can go into an infinite loop when they're making a point that they feel passionate about:

> *"I want an ice cream. I want an ice cream. I want an ice cream.."*

The most effective way of stopping it (without immediately buying an ice cream) is:

> *"So, what you're saying is that you'd really like an ice cream."*

You've shown that you've listened and understood. They've stopped repeating the demand. Now you can make your point:

> *"And what I'm saying is that you can't have an ice cream now as you're having your lunch in a few minutes."*

Now that you know what they want, you can use it as a bargaining chip to get what you want:

> *"If you eat all your lunch and clean up your room, you'll get an ice cream this afternoon."*

In a complex negotiation, as well as stating that you've heard the other sides' position, it often helps to document your understanding in writing.

Some Deal Killers to Watch Out For

✓ *Ego*—people often allow personal interests to take precedence over the successful completion of the deal. Sometimes they're unprepared to make concessions in the negotiation process; sometimes they block the deal as the result of a personal dispute or argument with an individual on the opposing side.

✓ *Focusing on single currency*—the seller wants a high price/valuation. The buyer wants a low price. The parties fail to find an acceptable middle ground and walk away without attempting to break the deadlock by introducing currencies other than price (see *Introduce Alternative Currencies*, page 323).

Watch the Clock

The clock becomes a crucial consideration in many forms of sports events—like soccer, football, basketball, hockey, etc. The team that's in the lead will do what it can to let the clock tick away. As it does, the position of the team that's behind grows progressively weaker.

Time can radically alter our expectations. In January, the management and directors of one company that I was involved with was raising funds at a $70m valuation—and adamant that this was absolutely the lowest price it was prepared to accept. By February, with the cash crisis looming, the price had dropped to $30m. In March, the management turned down an acquisition offer of $3m. In September the company was sold for $1m. Fully aware of the falling expectations, the buyers and investors were in no hurry to close any form of deal and used the clock to their advantage.

Time is almost always against you when you're in a startup. Especially, when the company is burning up cash, you'll find yourself fighting the clock as well as the other party. Of course, investors and acquirers know this and they'll use it to their advantage. For your startup, there are essentially two ways of combating this form of time terrorism:

- *Target a close date, draw up a roadmap to get there and maintain momentum along the way–* ideally, you'll get all the parties to agree and buy in to an agenda up-front, project manage to keep things moving, police the deliverable dates and drive towards completion.
- *Introduce additional competing buyers*—competition creates a sense of urgency.

In many startup negotiations, one side is racing against the clock and the other side is happy for time to tick away. Unless someone takes responsibility for maintaining momentum, the negotiation process can grind to a halt. If you're representing the startup, this responsibility rests with you.

Charm

Like me, you've probably walked away and killed deals when you've lost trust or respect in your opposing party. The negotiations have more chance of making progress if they're conducted in an honest, reasonable and pleasant environment. It's amazing how charisma and a sense of humor can diffuse the most difficult and confrontational situation. Some people are naturals—born with outstanding interpersonal skills like the gift of the gab. Others are totally devoid of charm and, if they fail to develop it, often struggle to get what they want.

Keep it Professional

Although often very tempting, it's advisable to avoid exchanging insults, getting into fist-fights or otherwise alienating any of the members of your opposing team. One disgruntled individual can sabotage the whole deal—believe me. I had one deal that fell apart at the twelfth hour because I allowed myself to lash out in retaliation to antagonism from one of the opposing team.

It's also important to respect confidentiality and non-disclosure agreements. You really have to be careful here. I signed a confidentiality agreement with one potential acquirer that called me up a couple of days later threatening legal action—claiming that our side had breached the agreement. The negotiations broke down at this point. I discovered that one of my board members had mentioned the deal to the individual that had originally introduced the two parties—discussions within the company and the board were OK, but as soon as news of the deal reached someone outside the company, this constituted a breach. Of course, we were under the impression that the person that brokered the deal in the first place was aware of what was going on, but this was not the case—and the acquirer was concerned that this particular individual was a blab-mouth. So, respecting agreements and keeping it professional can make the difference between failure and success.

Emotional Displays

Human beings are remarkably sensitive to displays of emotions such as aggression, tears, despondency, affront, disappointment and anger. Emotional displays are highly potent weapons that can trigger extreme reactions. Use them with extreme caution—they can backfire.

Good Guy/Bad Guy

The bad guy pushes for concessions, often using emotional displays of anger and aggression. A regular feature of TV detective shows, this technique has been use for centuries by expert negotiators in all walks of life. The good guy gently encourages for the same concessions and maintains the relationship between the two parties.

You don't really want to break the relationship with investors or acquirers during the negotiation process—as you may have to work with these individuals for years to come. The good guy/bad guy arrangement can work quite well in this situation—the bad guy is the outsider that disappears after the deal is complete; the good guy is the company insider that sticks around as part of the team.

Introduce Alternative Currencies

Two children are squabbling over a toy. It's a classic Win:Lose situation—one toy, one winner, one loser. You rummage around and find another toy. You make a big deal out of how special and valuable this toy is and cut a deal—one child gets this toy, one gets the other one, then perhaps they switch. Parents have used this technique to resolve disputes for years. What's happening is that the children are initially in a stalemate situation as they're squabbling over one toy—a single currency. By finding the second toy, the parent is introducing an alternative currency. This is the only way of converting this Win:Lose situation into one of Win:Win.

Many business negotiations reach stalemate when the discussions are focused on a single currency—normally price or valuation. The introduction of alternative currencies can break the deadlock. Alternative currencies come in various forms:

- *Strategic currencies*—offering to structure the deal in a way that's more tax-efficient or otherwise beneficial for the other party can enable them to make concessions over price. Offering access to sales and distribution channels, marketing support or other currencies can have a similar effect.
- *Financial currencies*—stock, options, and warrants are currencies that could be offered instead of, or in addition to cash to sweeten a deal.

- *Emotional currencies*—when one investment deal I was working on reached stalemate over valuation, I started looking around for alternative currencies. I realized that the other party was looking for recognition of its contribution to date. Deadlock was broken when our side expressed its appreciation and gratitude for the other sides' efforts. Emotional currencies cost very little (in terms of cash at least) and can be very effective.

The introduction of alternative currencies can break the deadlock and convert a win-lose situation into a win-win.

Disengage Without Burning your Bridges

Expert negotiators often suspend discussions and walk away from the negotiating table. Sometimes it's done for genuine reasons—they feel the two parties are too far apart and are not making sufficient progress to bridge the gap. Sometimes it's simply a tactic to make a point and win concessions. When you disengage, it's important to take care that you don't burn your bridges in the process—do it in such a way that negotiations can be resumed at some point in future.

Appendix 3—Gathering your Provisions—The Fundraising Process

Raising money for your startup is not a black art, a magic trick or a secret gift that's bestowed on the chosen few. Successful fundraising is not restricted to the educated, the young, the beautiful, the cool or the famous. It's a process that takes planning, hard work and more than a little luck.

The Fundraising Process

Close Round of Funding

Complete Due Diligence

Sign Term Sheet

Negotiate & Agree Terms

Present to Investors

Listen & Respond to Investor Feedback

Approach Investors

Prepare to Approach Investors

Create Investor Info. Packs

Identify Target Investors

Formulate the Pitch

Appoint Fundraising Team

Fundraising doesn't happen overnight. There's a gestation period of around 9 months. The process of raising a round of funding, selling your company or having a baby all take around the same length of time. All three processes are kicked off in a similar way—with the creation of a 'team', they then go through several distinct phases and, after one or more 'near-death' experiences, they all conclude with some form of painful, stressful event.

Fundraising Process	Takes in the Region Of	
Appoint Fundraising Team	2	weeks
Formulate the Pitch	4	weeks
Identify Target Investors	2	weeks
Create Investor Info. Packs	4	weeks
Prepare to Approach Investors	2	weeks
Approach & Present to Investors	12	weeks
Negotiate & Agree Terms	3	weeks
Sign Term Sheet	1	week
Complete Due Diligence	4	weeks
Close Round of Funding	1	week
The whole fundraising process	**35**	**weeks**

Unfortunately, the fundraising process doesn't always conclude with the closing of a round of funding—it often concludes with the company running out of cash and shutting down. You're going to have to inject a tremendous amount of energy and perseverance to prevent the process from grinding to a halt.

Appoint Fundraising Team

An effective fundraising team requires a variety of skills and team members play a number of roles:

- ✓ *Team leader*—co-ordinates the activities and keeps the wagons rolling.

- ✓ *Pitch person*—makes the introductory calls and presentations whipping investors into a frenzy of excitement.

- ✓ *Info. coordinator*—diligently pulls together the business plan and other components of the information pack then responds to information requests.

- ✓ *Diplomatic negotiator*—has the charm and wisdom to push for the best terms without alienating the investor.

- ✓ *Pedantic lawyer*—helps negotiate terms and prepare contracts.

This doesn't mean that you need a dedicated team of five—one individual can wear several hats and take on a number of these roles, especially in an early-stage startup. There are no hard and fast rules as to who wears each of these hats—in some companies, the CEO is the pitch person, in others, it's the visionary product designer (the pitch person is rarely the CFO—although he/she will play a more prominent role in the later stage rounds).

As the process develops, different roles take on varying levels of responsibility and importance:

Fundraising Activity	Primary Responsibility
Appoint Fundraising Team	*Team Leader*
Formulate the Pitch	*Whole Team*
Identify Target Investors	*Info. Coordinator*
Create Investor Information Packs	*Info. Coordinator*
Prepare to Approach Investors	*Info. Coordinator, Pitch Person*
Approach & Present to Investors	*Pitch Person*
Listen and Respond to Investor Feedback	*Whole Team*
Negotiate & Agree Terms	*Negotiator, Lawyer*
Sign Term Sheet	*Negotiator, Lawyer*
Complete Due Diligence	*Info. Coordinator*
Close Round of Funding	*Negotiator, Lawyer*

The fundraising team is normally made up of company employees and insiders; however, you're well advised to choose an outside attorney as opposed to a staff lawyer—an experienced and active specialist in fundraising transactions will be up to speed with the latest deal trends have an arsenal of ammunition to combat the more aggressive investor demands. The lawyer not only guides the company through the legal minefield but also plays a vital role in the negotiating process—often working with the negotiator in a good-guy, bad-guy tag team.

Hiring a Professional Fundraiser

Most early-stage investors like to deal directly with the company and don't like the idea that a chunk of the money that they invest will be paid to a financial intermediary instead of going into growing the business. However, professional fundraisers can sometimes open doors and bring in capital that you couldn't bring in on your own, especially if you're new to the fundraising business.

Investment banks are normally brought in to arrange mezzanine rounds of funding in excess of $10m. They like to deal with these large, mostly corporate rounds, acquisitions and *IPO*'s where they can make a fortune by taking a percentage on the transaction. When these large lucrative deals are thin on the ground, the investment banks will sometimes lower their standards and actually take an interest in raising capital for early stage companies.

I once hired an investment bank to help raise an early stage round. They helped me focus the presentation materials and then took it out to their investor list—which was mostly made up of corporate investors they'd worked with on mezzanine rounds in the past. As this deal was a little early for the corporate investors, they didn't have much luck. They did set-up a meeting with a corporate investor but, on balance, their contribution appeared to be a waste of time and retainer fees. I realized that I couldn't rely on them to raise funds and decided to target the lead VC's myself. After two weeks of my e-mails and phone calls, I'd personally set up face-to-face meetings with ten top-tier lead VC's. We agreed to terminate the investment banking agreement and move on.

A couple of months later, we had a call from the banker, saying that he had a wealthy investor that was interested in meeting with us—he'd asked them if they had any deals he might like to invest in. I arranged the meeting, presented the plan and he wired me $1m that very afternoon. He then went on to help me raise a further $5m from his own network of contacts. So, looking back, the investment bank hadn't been such a waste of time after all.

In addition to the large investment banks, there are a number of smaller financial intermediaries that prey on technology startups helping prepare materials and hook them up with VC's and other investors. Fundraising is a difficult business and they can be quite choosy in selecting the startups they're prepared to represent.

Lehman Formula

Professional fundraisers normally ask for a monthly or up-front retainer but their primary source of compensation is the commission, or as it is sometimes euphemistically referred to, the "success fee"—it's paid when, and only when, the transaction is completed. For many years, the generally accepted standard for computing the intermediary's commission has been the so-called "Lehman formula". This formula prescribes a fee equal to 5 percent of the first million dollars in purchase price, 4 percent on the second, 3 percent on the third, 2 percent on the fourth, and 1 percent on the purchase price in excess of $4 million.

Although the Lehman (or 5-4-3-2-1) formula is still widely used today by many firms, a number of variations, and even some new creative approaches to fee structure, have become more common, especially in smaller early-stage deals. As early stage investment funds have dried up, many intermediaries ask for a flat percentage somewhere between 5-10% of the funds raised.

With startups desperate for funds, some intermediaries can demand very aggressive terms. I was shocked when I received a proposal from one firm—in addition to the retainer and the success fee (based the Lehman formula) they also wanted warrants to buy 7% of the company at *IPO* (at the current share price). If I'd signed this deal, it would have turned off all subsequent investors—the fundraiser would have been the largest shareholder at *IPO*. So, even if you're desperate, you need to be very careful that you don't cut a deal that will jeopardize the company's long-term prospects.

If the intermediary is going to put any effort into helping you raise funds, you're going to have to give them some form of exclusivity. However, if they don't deliver, you need to make sure you retain the option of raising funds yourself, without paying the intermediary a commission. Make sure you restrict the exclusivity to specific investors that they introduce and set a firm time limit after which the exclusivity expires.

An active and effective intermediary can bring structure to the fundraising process and provide introductions to investors that you would never reach on your own. If you don't have the resources to put together your own in-house fundraising team, and you find a good team of specialists prepared to take on the assignment, it can be worth the expense.

Formulate the Pitch

Investors are inundated with gazillions of crackpot proposals. If you're going to have any chance of making it past first base, you're going to have to write a compelling business plan (see *Write a Business Plan*, page 72) and condense it down into a one page summary and a 30 second sales pitch.

The pitch is a quick summary of the business plan and the parameters of the round. For example:

Stage & Space	*"We're an early stage startup based in Palo Alto..*
Category	*.. in the biotech widget space..*
Competitive Advantage	*.. with patent-pending technology from Stanford..*
Simple Product Description	*Our product will provide a cure for green monkey disease (or whatever).*
Momentum	*The prototype has been recognized as a leader by the New York Times and endorsed by the Biotech Widgets Association.*
Target Destination	*The company will become an attractive acquisition target within the next 18 months.*
Round Parameters	*We're planning to close a $5m round in the next 8 weeks.*
Investor Profile	*I've contacted you as we're looking for a respected lead investor and a specialist in this space."*

The one pager, that also doubles as the executive summary of the business plan, needs to go into a little more detail on each of these topics and provide a concise explanation as to why the investor should invest in this opportunity in preference to one of the myriad of alternatives.

Sometimes, minor adjustments to the pitch can have far-reaching effects. For example, investors can be very sensitive to the precise wording you use to describe the category. After the word *'portal'* was first used by a consulting company, it suddenly became a hot buzz word in investment circles. Although anyone with any sense could see that the business model was fundamentally flawed, all the VC's were jumping on the bandwagon—for a while there, VC's were hell-bent on investing in portals of every shape and color. I actually had one VC partner tell me that he liked my business but couldn't invest because I hadn't described it as a *'portal'*. He actually agreed to invest if I told him it was a *'portal'*, without making any changes to the business plan or the underlying business.

If you have any friends in the investment world, you may want to solicit some friendly feedback on your pitch, and make sure you're using the latest buzzwords, before approaching real-live investors.

Identify Target Investors

Investors are specialists—approaching a later-stage investor with an early-stage deal is probably a waste of your time. If you're in L.A., there's little point in approaching a Seattle-based investor that refuses to look at deals outside the Seattle/Tacoma region. If you're in the web services space, don't waste your time chasing investors that focus exclusively on biotech. If you're looking for a lead, don't contact investors that only follow.

You're sure to be rejected when you start to approach investors—so get used to it. However, if you do your homework and draw up a list of target investors that specialize in deals that match your profile, you can at least keep the rejection quotient to a minimum.

Here's how you compile your list:

a) Meet with your lawyer, accountant, bank manager, and any other contact that's plugged in to the financial community. Ask them to take out their Rolodex and give you the names and contact details of all the investors that may be interested in your opportunity.

b) There are a number of good investor lists available online today for you to tap into—you'll find several of them in the *Resource Guide,* page 398

How long should your list be? 10 is probably too few and 100 is probably too many—40-60 might be about right, but you might not need them all at the outset as you'll hopefully get new introductions as you work through the list. When you start approaching investors, even if they're not interested in investing themselves, don't forget to ask them if they know of any other investors that might be a better fit for this opportunity. This could add some very targeted names to your list. In this way, your list will be constantly evolving with new names being added and existing names being crossed off.

It's important that the investors, founders and management team all target the same destination. If the plan is to build out the product and dress the company up for *Asset Sale*, you want to avoid an investor that's hell-bent on steering all its portfolio companies toward *IPO*. There may be enough in an *Asset Sale* to satisfy the needs and ambitions of the founders, but not enough to make this option of any interest to venture investors—and they're the ones that get to approve any potential merger and acquisition deal. Likewise, you don't want an investor that's pushing for *Asset Sale* if you're planning to build a viable stand-alone business and drive toward *IPO*.

You're going to start at the top and work your way down the list. So put the most appealing and prestigious VC's at the top and call them first. They like to have the feeling that they're getting first look at a new opportunity. They're naturally deterred if they hear that the deal has already been shopped around and rejected by a number of their competitors.

When you find a good investor candidate, take the time to check out its web site, look at the profile of its portfolio companies and study the background and expertise of the various partners.

Create Investor Information Packs

Before making a decision to invest in your company, an investor (especially a lead VC) is going to need to gather a tremendous amount of information on the company. The process is sure to go more smoothly if you have these materials prepared beforehand. As a minimum, your investor information pack will consist of the following:

- ✓ *Business plan*—with concise executive summary and general parameters of the round (see *Write a Business Plan*, page 72).
- ✓ *Cover letter and e-mail*—to accompany and introduce the plan itself.
- ✓ *Presentation*—entertaining 15-20 minute slide show. This will normally be presented in-person, however, with Microsoft PowerPoint it's very simple to record and add a voice narration to each slide (see *Cloned Presenter*, page 175). It's also very easy to convert the presentation to a web site.

Personally, I think the most efficient way of providing this information is to make the whole pack available online through a password-protected web site. You provide investors with the web site address and the password, allowing them to browse at their own pace and drill down for more information on a specific topic. Many investors will appreciate this, however, some are sure to object, demanding a printed version to be sent my snail mail or a digital copy sent by e-mail. You'll find very little consistency in how investors operate and how they react to your pitch. One of my investors refuses to accept any paper whatsoever, even brochures, and will only accept digital files—he gets upset if I leave a brochure in his office. Another refuses to read e-mail or use a PC at all.

Obviously, all your materials should be consistent in the message, the story and the look and feel. Make sure you stick with consistent fonts and color schemes in all your documents and presentations—if you haven't yet had the chance to hire artists and define your corporate identity, you can use regular templates from software applications like Microsoft Word and PowerPoint.

The more polished the materials, the greater your chance of success—especially in the later rounds when the company has little excuse for errors or tacky presentation. To find the errors, and cover your back, it's a good idea to have the information pack checked by your lawyer, accountant and other experts with an insight into the fundraising process.

Prepare to Approach Investors

When you place that first call to the investor on the top of your hit list, you'll leave a voice-mail message, send an e-mail and receive a call from the managing partner within a matter of hours, asking you to come in for a presentation to the investment committee that very afternoon. OK, this is wishful thinking. In fact there's virtually no chance of this happening at all, but how would you feel if it did—and you screwed up because your presentation wasn't polished and ready for the big time? It's important that you have the pitch down pat, a polished presentation and all your materials are ready to go before you start to approach investors. If you reached this stage in the fundraising process, you should have the following materials at hand:

 ✓ *Clearly formulated pitch*

 ✓ *Target investor list*

 ✓ *Investor information pack*

However, until you add the following, you're still not ready to contact investors:

- ✓ *Introductory voice-mail script*—introducing yourself, the company and telling the investor that the plan is on its way.

- ✓ *Follow-up voice-mail script*—the objective now is to fix up a presentation.

- ✓ *Contact management system*—to keep track of the status of each investor on your list.

When you put in your voice-mail message, you want it to be smooth and polished. You don't want it to come across as disjointed with lots of 'Ums' and 'Ers' You may think I'm crazy, but I suggest you rehearse your script into a tape recorder before making the call. Of course, it needs to sound upbeat, clear and concise. I recommend the same rehearsal process for the presentation—running it through several times with a video camera and a stopwatch until it's sufficiently short and sweet.

Sample Introductory Voice-mail Script

Introduction	*"Hi, This is John Doe from AcmeTech Startup.*
Mutual Contact	*Mark Ray from Arthur Anderson (or Enron, or some other highly reputable organization) gave me your name and suggested we talk.*
Stage	*We're a seed stage startup based in San Francisco..*
Category	*.. in the optical security space.*
Simple Product Description	*Our product provides the most secure protection and intruder alarm system on the market.*
Competitive Advantage	*The company was founded by Professor Albert Plank, the Nobel prize winner and recognized leader in this field.*
Momentum	*The technology was recently featured on CNN TV and we already have a purchase order from the White House.*
Round Parameters	*We're closing a $15m round at the end of March.*
Why We're Calling	*We're looking for an investor with strong links in the defense industry and I know this is your expertise.*
Next	*I've e-mailed you an electronic copy of our business plan—if you'd like a hard copy, just let me know. I'll follow up in a couple of days when you've had a chance to review the plan.*

Sample Follow Up Voice-mail Script

"This is John Doe from AcmeTech Startup. You may remember I was introduced by Mark Ray and you received a copy of our business plan a couple of days ago.

Things are really starting to take off here—we're generating some real momentum. I'm actually going to be passing by your office on Tuesday next week and I'd love to have the opportunity of dropping by to give you a 20-minute presentation if you can squeeze me into your calendar."

Contact Management System

Now you need a system for keeping track of the telephone calls and contacts with each of your potential investors. The ideal tool would be contact management software like Microsoft Outlook or Goldmine, but you may be more comfortable with a spreadsheets, word-processors or the back of a large envelope. The point is that you have an up-to-date status report on every contact on the list – with details of all conversations, e-mails, letters and other forms of communication.

Approach Investors

How to approach investors:

✓ *Ask your lawyer, accountant, or mutual contact to e-mail or call the investor*—giving her a heads up that you'll be getting in touch with an interesting opportunity.

✓ *Make the introductory call*—using the introductory voice-mail script (like the example above).

✓ *Send an e-mail with the business plan as an attachment (Windows version of Microsoft Word or Adobe Acrobat PDF's seem to be the preferred file formats)*—the covering e-mail should be about half a page long and reiterate the same pitch as the introductory call. Don't forget to highlight your wins and the momentum you're starting to generate.

✓ *Wait a couple of days*—give her a chance to read it.

✓ *Make your follow-up call*—and try to setup a face-to-face presentation.

How NOT to approach investors:

✓ *Don't leave more than one voice-mail with the same message*—my father does this sometimes and it drives me nuts. He calls, I'm not around, he leaves a message. Then he calls again, leaving the same message. He can do this five or six times over! When I get home and listen to all his messages one after the other, I get the impression that he's absolutely desperate, and mentally deranged.

✓ *Don't freak out if a living, breathing person actually picks up the phone*—you'll be expecting to leave a voice-mail message and you may be a little shocked when you find yourself speaking to a live investor. One of my VC friends told me that when he picked up the phone, the caller was so surprised that he asked him to put the phone down again so that he could call back and leave a voice-mail. My friend obviously thought this was hilarious and didn't take the subsequent business plan at all seriously. So, however, unlikely it is, be prepared to talk to a real human being. If she picks up the phone, you should make sure you cover all the things you were planning to say to the voice-mail machine (without sounding as though you're reading it verbatim).

✓ *Respect her time*—don't keep her on the phone and ramble on about the details of your business. Your objective is to set up a face to face presentation—this is a much better platform to sell the opportunity. She'll appreciate you respecting her time and will be more inclined to take a serious look at the plan and arrange the meeting.

✓ *Don't let the investor get conflicting calls from your colleagues*—make sure all your colleagues know what to do if an investor makes contact. I had a top-tier VC call me back at my office and somehow the message was picked up by my VP of sales who went ahead and called the investor back, treating it as a sales call without checking in with me. By the time I spoke to the investor, he was totally confused.

Investor Don'ts

✓ *Don't ask them to sign NDA's*—they can't, so it's a waste of time asking. Just asking can show that you don't know how to play the game. However, don't share your 'secret sauce' recipe or detailed strategy—especially if the investor is aligned with one of your competitors.

✓ *Don't keep secrets*—as your mother told you, they'll come back to bite you sooner or later.

✓ *Don't talk valuation early*—postpone these discussions until late in the process.

✓ *Don't expect quick decisions*—you'll only get frustrated.

✓ *Don't argue*—if, after hearing your pitch, they say they're not interested, just thank them for their time and move on. There's nothing to be gained and a great deal to be lost by arguing.

Be prepared—investors can be very opinionated, dismissive and challenging to deal with. Sometimes they deliberately try to derail your pitch or just interrupt you to see how you respond—your best asset in the fundraising process may be a good sense of humor!

Investor Pitch Events

In the dot-com years, herds of VC's and other investors have packed into conference events organized by publishers like IDG (Demo Conference), Red Herring and Upside magazine. Normally held in fancy hotels with plenty of free wine, food and entertainment, investors sit and listen to presentations from selected 'hot' startups. Investment banks hold similar events for public and later stage private companies.

If you ever get a chance to present to a group of investors, make sure you go for it! It's the perfect opportunity to create a real buzz in the investment community. The ideal scenario is this: your room is packed, late arrivals are forced to stand at the back, you deliver a well practiced, whiz-bang, presentation, following which a line of investors forms to collect your business card. This has all the key ingredients required to demonstrate momentum and excite investors. Firstly, by being invited to present in the first place, you have some validation—you're now officially a 'hot startup'. Secondly, the excitement in the room is contagious. Thirdly, it creates an atmosphere of competition among the investors.

On the other hand, a poor presentation in a half-empty room with an obvious lack of audience interest could hamper your fundraising efforts for some time. So, as always, preparation is vital:

✓ *Select the best venue*—ideally you want a small room that's easily accessible. Try to avoid having a room so large that it appears half empty.

✓ *Practice your presentation until your message is clear and concise*—lock yourself in a hotel room with a video camera for several hours before the presentation.

✓ *Buy a stopwatch*—you need to be able to time your presentation to within a few seconds.

To liven up the proceedings, there are various formats for the presentations. One format is the 'Gong'. You stand on stage and give your presentation to a panel of investors—any one of them can hit the gong when they've had enough. You really want to finish before you get 'gonged'. Here's the trick—finish your presentation early. You always get the chance to do the bulk of your pitch—in fact the gong almost always goes off in the last minute. If your presentation slot is 6 minutes, wrap it up at 4 minutes and 45 seconds. You have to be precise here, so make sure you practice with the stopwatch to get it right. If you go on too long you're sure to get the gong. With good timing you can deliver your concluding statements and the audience has no idea that you deliberately closed it early.

At investment bank events, public company CEO's like Steve Jobs and Larry Ellison present to Wall Street investors. The format is usually a 30 minute session with a 15 minute presentation from the CEO followed by a 7 minute presentation from the CFO (the remaining 8 minutes are spent eating ice-creams, or something like that). Afterwards the presenters and audience retire to a separate room for a question and answer session. There are often free slots available on the agenda that can be allocated to private companies—to get a spot you really need to be able to pull strings and lobby the analysts and bankers that cover your space.

For the startup events run by magazine publishers, it's normally a journalist that selects the companies to appear. To get on the agenda, you really need your PR agency to set you up with an opportunity to pitch to the journalist, well ahead of the conference. Your story needs to be new and interesting if you're going to have any chance of making the cut. You may be invited to take a demo station or booth at the event—this can be a good investment as it enables investors to find you and gives you a chance to talk one-on-one.

You'll find a list of some of the best investor pitch event in the resource guide—they offer a great opportunity for you to quickly generate a buzz and momentum in the investor community.

Remember—Investors are Human Too

Investors are attracted by an upbeat team that's making progress and creating a buzz. This is one of the benefits of generating positive momentum. Although they claim to invest based on the merits of the team and the business opportunity, I suspect that a large number of investment decisions are driven by investors that simply gauge the reaction of others. If other investors are excited, they become excited themselves. If they hear anyone sounding alarm bells, they head for the hills, knocking each other over on the way out. Each investor that ever funded one of my companies did so on the basis that the convoy was heading to the promised land, filled with excited passengers and, unless they jumped on board, they'd be left behind. Of course, I didn't tell them this—but it's my impression of what they were thinking as they clambered on board.

Excitement and fear are contagious emotions. The first thing I do if a plane hits turbulence is look at the face of the nearest flight attendant. If I saw the flight attendant panic, I'm sure I'd start to panic myself. A flight attendant could surely have some fun here:

> *When he feels a little turbulence, he rushes down the aisle to attract attention, looks anxiously out of the window at the wing, puts his head in his hands, tightly straps himself*

into his seatbelt and nervously shouts 'there's no need to panic, everything is under control!' before adopting the crash position with his head between his legs.

This is sure to fill any passenger with fear. The reaction of other passengers could fill you with fear as well—if you hear blood-curdling screams coming from other passengers, you're sure to be alarmed. If you consider that you're the flight attendant and all your investors are passengers, then your job is to maintain a level of positive excitement until you reach your destination. If any passenger starts to panic, you need to lock them in the restroom for the remainder of the journey, drug them or find some way to have them accidentally disembark the plane mid-flight

Investors also like to be wanted. They like to feel that you're not just after their money. Tell them that you want them to join you on your journey because you admire their team and the resources they've assembled together. Be specific.

They're also competitive. They like to win—especially if that means pushing other investors out of the way to take the prize. You'll be in a much stronger position if you can create a situation where several investors feel they're competing to get into a round that's 'oversubscribed' (see *Increasing the Price—the Golden Rule of Valuation*, page 302).

Present to Investors

Don't assume that the demo-gods will smile on you when you get the opportunity to present to an investor. You have to assume that whatever can go wrong WILL go wrong. My experience is that whatever could go wrong DID go wrong:

- × *Hackers brought down my site minutes before my live demo.*
- × *I plugged my laptop into a digital phone line and blew up the modem.*
- × *Instead of giving me a 128k connection, my wireless modem delivered 1k performance.*
- × *The investor kept interrupting and wouldn't allow me to get into my presentation.*
- × *There was supposed to be a projector in the room but it mysteriously disappeared the night before.*
- × *The investor fell asleep.*
- × *My car was stuck in traffic and I arrived late.*
- × *I arrived early but it took an hour to find a parking spot.*
- × *I arrived at the office on time—only to find that the firm had moved to a new address.*
- × *I apparently rang the wrong doorbell so the investor didn't know I was waiting outside.*
- × *My tire blew out on the freeway on the way to the meeting.*
- × *I was completely drenched in a thunderstorm and arrived soaking wet.*
- × *My prototype software crashed in a particularly embarrassing manner.*
- × *I spilled coffee all over my clothes minutes before the presentation.*
- × *A virus screwed up my laptop.*
- × *My laptop had a hardware failure and wouldn't even boot.*

× *There were no meeting rooms available so the presentation had to take place in the lobby.*

× *Some of my colleagues were not singing from the same songbook and confused the investor with comments and answers that were certainly not part of the pitch.*

× *I installed my software on the investors own PC, it crashed, destroying some of his work.*

If you're lucky, you'll have only one or two of these problems to deal with. If you're unlucky you'll have all of them together on the same day. Here are some tips to help you prepare:

✓ *Always take at least two laptops loaded up with mirrored demos in case one goes down—* this is also a good body-building exercise.

✓ *In case your laptops both explode without warning, be prepared to deliver your presentation on one of the investors own PC's—*have the files available on CD-ROM and downloadable from a web page.

✓ *Always plan to arrive early, very early, for your appointment.*

✓ *Arrange to have access to the room at least 30 minutes before the meeting so that you can have everything set up by the time the meeting starts—*you don't want to be crawling under desks playing with cables when the investors are trying to ask you questions.

✓ Don't ever rely on being able to establish a live Internet connection.

✓ Brief your colleagues beforehand to make sure everyone's singing from the same songbook.

✓ *Run through your whole presentation beforehand—*lock yourself in a room with a video camera and a stop-watch if you have to.

✓ *Make sure you have all your materials—*don't forget print-outs of the presentation, business plans and brochures.

Plan for your investor presentation to take about twenty minutes and allow time for Q & A. Make sure you make your pitch and cover the following key points at the very least:

✓ Your Vision & Mission

✓ The Team

✓ The Market

✓ The Problem Facing Customers Today (and its costs and other implications)

✓ How your Invention Solves the Problem

✓ Your Technology Advantage

✓ Competition

✓ Revenue Model

Your mission is to cover all these points in the session, even if the investors make numerous concerted effort to derail you. If you're just starting to talk through the first slide on the vision and mission and the investor asks a question like 'what's the revenue model?' there are two ways of dealing with this. You could stop what you're doing and answer their question, or you could tell them that you'll be covering the revenue model in a couple of minutes and carry on with your pitch. My advice is to take the second option—stay with your presentation and don't allow yourself to get derailed. Maintain control and keep the presentation on track. It's easier to do this if you start out by showing an outline of your presentation, so that they know what you're planning to cover and when to expect it.

You rarely get a second chance to give an investor presentation—so make sure you're prepared to give your first chance your best shot.

Listen and Respond to Investor Feedback

No one really likes rejection, but you're going to have to develop a positive reaction to it as you go through the process of calling potential investors—you're sure to have many doors slammed in your face.

Before raising almost $30m million in funding, one of my startups was rejected by over 50 VC's for one reason or another. I didn't get too despondent because there seemed to be no consistency or pattern to the investors' reasoning. I was also spurred on by stories of other entrepreneurs like Sandy Lerner and Leonard Bosack who founded Cisco System in 1984. Over 70 VC's in the Valley reportedly rejected their business plan. At one point in 1986, Lerner went back to work as a corporate data-processing manager to raise some cash. Finally Don Valentine of Sequoia Capital backed Cisco and his $2.3 million investment went on to be worth over $150 billion—conclusive proof that the first 70 VC's were dead wrong!

Many of the investors that reject your plan will also be dead wrong, but once they've made up their minds, there's little point in arguing with them—it's better to just move on. However, if there is a strong pattern and consistency in their reasoning, you need to listen and adapt. Adaptation may be as simple as strengthening the plan or polishing your pitch or it could mean taking radical steps like Reinventing the Company (page 276). Don't be afraid to go back to the drawing board if there's a fundamental problem—this will be much quicker and less painful than getting another batch of rejections.

Negotiate and Agree Terms

Be prepared to negotiate the valuation alongside some other, possibly more important, components of the term sheet (see *What's it Worth?—Valuing the Company*, page 301, *Getting What you Want—Negotiating the Deal*, page 313). The negotiations will typically revolve around the precise definition of the 'preference' component in the term 'preference shares' and the steps that the investors are demanding to take to recover their money if the company stumbles en-route to *IPO*.

Since the bursting of the dot-com bubble, VC's have had a tough time and they're imposing tougher terms on new companies. Once again 'Cash is King' and they're in a strong position to negotiate very aggressive terms before handing greenbacks over to a startup. In addition to liquidity preference, ratchets and redemption rights, there are a string of additional terms such as right of first refusal, indemnity, shareholder protective rights, supermajority provisions, board seats and protective rights that are likely to become part of the negotiation.

As a founder or employee, you'll likely have 'common stock'. Common stock is not quite the same as preference shares—it's missing that important 'preference' prefix. Try this elementary math test: if, through founders stock or stock options, you own 10% of the company, and the company was sold for, say, $10m, how much would your stock be worth? If you said $1m then you're almost certain to be wrong! Very wrong—so wrong that instead of buying a house in Atherton, you'd be renting an apartment in East Palo Alto. Most likely, all $10m would go to the preference shareholders. Together with the other common shareholders you'll stand in line behind the preference shareholders and get nothing at all.

That's because almost all term sheets these days include a liquidity preference clause, also called 'participating preferred'. This and other clauses are designed to minimize the downside to the investor if the *IPO* is not achieved. At *IPO*, the preference shareholders convert to common stock and lose all their preferences—this is the only time that all the shareholders are going to find themselves on a level playing field. Before *IPO*, there are several terms that you're going to have to negotiate with investors. Some of them you may be forced to accept—or they may be deal-breakers. Some of them you should be able to negotiate and have removed, others you may achieve a workable compromise. It's worth taking the time and effort to understand the terms in the term sheet and work with a good lawyer to negotiate a deal that doesn't demoralize the management team, scare off potential acquirers or investors in future rounds.

Preference Share Agreements

As a founder or employee you'll likely be issued with common stock. The investors will receive a different class of share called 'preferred stock' or 'preference share' that provides them with certain privileges over 'commoners' like yourself. Investors like to have different classes of share to reflect the belief that their cash injections are more valuable than the sweat-equity investments of the founders and employees. Up to the point of *IPO*, the two classes of shares can be priced very differently. The price of the preference shares will increase as the company's valuation grows, and the common stock will follow but at a much lower level. Preferred stock is priced by market forces—the price that investors actually pay for the stock, based on the company valuation. The common stock price is set by the board of directors, normally within the following guidelines:

	Common Vs. Preference Share Price
Price guidelines in early stage company	Common is no less than 10% of preference share price
Price guidelines in run-up to IPO	Common is no less than 80% of preference share price
Price at IPO	Preferred shares exchanged for common shares. Price parity.

As well as providing an opportunity for investors to achieve preferential terms, the price differential helps you and the other common shareholders avoid tax liability on paper gains in your common stock. This is very valuable as you want to avoid a tax hit on shares that are theoretically valuable but effectively worthless—even if they have a paper value, you're highly unlikely to be able to sell your common shares until some time after the *IPO*.

As you'll see later on, your lead investor will probably request more preferences than you want to give up and you're sure to get into some heavy negotiation on this topic. However, you want to be prepared to complete your paperwork quickly once you finalize the term sheet and it's a good idea to have your lawyer draft up a preference share agreement beforehand. If you can, use this as the starting point of your term sheet discussions.

Liquidity Preference or Participating Preferred

What the investors are saying here is that, if the company is acquired or liquidated, they want to get their money back first before sharing the remaining proceeds with the founders and employees—they're buying their shares with hard cash, darn it, and you're only paying in blood, sweat and tears!

Let's take AcmeTech Startup Inc. as an example of a company on the journey from *Zero-to-IPO*. As you'll see, AcmeTech Startup raises a total of $43m in its series A, B and C rounds of funding. Of course, these are all preference shares. Now, let's imagine that the lead VC agreed to a liquidity preference paying Series A investors all their cash back before then sharing the remaining proceeds with the common shareholders—employees and founders. It's safe to assume that this same clause was demanded by the later series B and C investors. Now let's assume that Mega Tech Inc. decides to buy the company. Let's look at different buying price points and see how the funds are distributed:

AcmeTechStartup, Inc.	Cash Invested	Shares Held	Shareholding %			
Acquisition Price				$ 40.00	$ 50.00	$ 60.00
Common Stock[1]						
Founder Stock		2.50	9%	$ -	$ 0.61	$ 1.49
Employee Stock Options		5.00	17%	$ -	$ 1.22	$ 2.97
Career CEO		1.55	5%	$ -	$ 0.38	$ 0.92
Total Common		9.05		$ -	$ 2.22	$ 5.38
Preference Shares						
Series A (including Angel round)	$ 8.00	6.00	21%	$ 12.28	$ 9.47	$ 11.57
Series B	$ 15.00	7.53	26%	$ 15.40	$ 16.84	$ 19.47
Series C	$ 20.00	6.02	21%	$ 12.32	$ 21.47	$ 23.58
Total Preference Shares		19.55	100%	$ 40.00	$ 47.78	$ 54.62
Total Preference Investment	$ 43.00					
Notes						
1 -- Assumes all common stock is vested						

Selling the company for $40m means that the CEO, founders and employees get nothing, nada, naff-all, absolute Zero, zilch. In fact, if the company is sold for $43m or less, all the proceeds go to the preference shareholders. As you'll see from the table, if the company were sold at $50m, then $47.78m goes to the preference folks and $2.22 is shared between all the commoners. At a $60m acquisition, the commoners share grows to a 'whopping' $5.38m, almost 9% of the total.

The investors would say that this provides a good incentive for the management team to achieve *IPO* or get a very good price for the company in an acquisition. This is true, but it starts to have a negative effect on all shareholders if the company is worth less than the amount of cash invested. At this point, there's no incentive for the CEO, founders or employees to sell the company for, say $40m. It would probably be in the interests of the preference shareholders to sell at $40m but it's going to be difficult to do this if there's nothing in it for the management team. The management team members can see that the only possibility of ever trading their stock certificates for any form of cash, is to *IPO*—even if it's a one in a million chance. Management, probably common stockholders, may be prepared to bear the risk when the preference folks would prefer to minimize their losses and sell the company. So the management and shareholders may be heading for different destinations.

If the company finds itself in this position, it's not unusual for the management team to negotiate a carve-out for the active employees under the heading of 'Staff Retention Plan'. Former employees that have vested stock and since left the company are not necessarily included in this group. What this means is that some, or all, of the employees jump the line and get in front of the preference shareholders when the company is sold. Some of the proceeds of the sale would be given to these common shareholders, possibly in the form of an employee bonus, then the balance would be given to the preference folks. This is a good solution to keep the current staff and team incented, but it's difficult to negotiate this up-front in the term sheet. You don't really want to be discussing such a bleak scenario as a negative return on investment with the VC's—they may read it as a lack of belief in the company and its prospects. You may be better advised to negotiate the management carve out later on. Equitable solutions have been found in the past.

In the AcmeTech Startup example, let's imagine that the CEO starts to look for buyers at $60m but finds that there are no takers. Then one buyer comes back with an offer of $40m. The preference shareholders vote and agree to accept this offer. Under the terms of the liquidity preference, they get to keep all the $40m. All the paperwork is prepared, but before the deal is actually closed, the employees revolt and decide to leave the company en-masse. Without the team, the deal is dead, so the preference shareholders pull together a staff retention package that involves carving out a share of the sale for the common shareholders, or at least the key employees. Another scenario is that the acquirer gets cold feet when it's realized that there's no incentive for the staff to stick around for the acquisition—there are cases where the acquirer demands a change in the liquidity preference clause before agreeing to sign. In the interests of closing out an important deal, many issues are open for negotiation—and concessions can be won!

Back to the term sheet—if the VC is not prepared to drop the liquidity preference clause, you could offer a formula that's a little more appealing for the common shareholders. The formula could be to repay the preferred, then pay the common, *then* both share in the upside. In the AcmeTech Startup example, the common shareholders would still get nothing, if the company was sold for $40m, but they would get a reasonable share of a $50-60m sale.

You're now expecting a liquidity preference clause in the term sheet, and hopefully you know what this means. Don't be surprised to see that instead of demanding all their cash back before sharing the proceeds of a sale with common shareholders, the VC demands two or three times their cash back before sharing anything with the commoners. As the VC's have suffered in recent months and years, the terms have become increasingly tough for entrepreneurs.

The Dreaded Ratchet

A *ratchet* always sounded to me like an instrument of torture. The *full ratchet* sounded like the ultimate in pain and suffering. I imagined being summoned to a meeting with my lead VC on Sand Hill Road, where I'm interrogated for missing my milestones. I find myself bound and led off to the subterranean dungeons with the words 'take him to the punishment chamber—give him the full ratchet'. When I plucked up the courage to find out what a ratchet actually was, I was somewhat relieved. It's simply a cunning ploy by investors to protect themselves from dilution—at the expense of the founders.

At a liquidity event such as *IPO*, merger or acquisition, the preference shares convert over to common stock—usually it's a 1-to-1 ratio where one preference share buys one common share. Effectively, if the company raises new money at a lower price, an anti-dilution clause kicks in that drops the conversion price and gives the preference shareholders more common for their money. The ratchet and weighted average are two of the most common formulas used to decide exactly how much more common stock they actually get.

Let's take AcmeTech Startup as an example. See *Setup your Capitalization Table*, page 93. Let's say since closing the $8m series A round at $1.33/share, the company had stumbled and was struggling to raise it's series B at a reasonable price. A new investor offered to come in with, say $2m at $1.00/share.

With the full ratchet formula, what the investors are saying is: 'if you drop the price within, say 12 months, then we get our share price dropped to the same figure'. In the case of AcmeTech Startup, this would mean that their 6m preference shares would buy 8m common shares instead of 6m. So the existing 'A' round investors get an additional 2m shares—that's a lot! The series B investor is paying $2m for their 2m shares but the series A investor in this example is getting the same number of shares and paying nothing at all.

With the weighted average formula, the 6m series A shares convert over to 6.2m common shares. So, in this scenario, the ratchet formula gives the A investors an additional 2m shares and the weighted average gives them 0.2m—the difference is a factor of ten!

In this scenario, the series B investor would be very unlikely to invest if the full ratchet was in place, and the management team and employees would likely resent the level of dilution.

This is another important issue and, as a common shareholder, you should try to negotiate a weighed average formula wherever possible. If it's really a deal-breaker for the investor, and there are no alternative sources of funding, you may want to try offering a compromise that provides them with the ratchet only if they invest in the new round. It's a pay-to-play offer that forces previous round investors to invest in the new round in order to qualify for the anti-dilution rights.

OK, the ratchet isn't quite the instrument of torture that I'd imagined but it can be pretty painful for the founders.

Two Traunch Deals

Instead of injecting their cash into the company in a single lump sum, many investors today are providing part of the money up-front and tying the investment of the balance to the company achieving a series of milestones. An investor may be saying:

> .. *'you tell me you'll have three strategic partnerships by the end of the year. I believe you. I'll put in half my investment today and the other half will come in at the end of the year when your three deals have been signed. By the way, if you don't get the deals signed, then I'm not committed to coming in with the second half of the investment. Also, if you don't hit this milestone, the company valuation will be lower than projected and, as compensation, even though I'm not investing any more money, I want to be issued with more shares.*

In theory, this may appear to be a good structure—the investor benefits from the risk reduction and the management team has a good incentive to stay focused on hitting the milestones. There are problems though. In a single traunch deal, the cash is invested up-front and this provides more financial stability. This security can be vital for attracting customers and employees alike. If the company has only a few months before it's next injection of funds, and that injection is contingent upon hitting certain milestones, there's a higher chance of the company going belly-up and this uncertainty could scare away some of the key people that the company needs to attract. Another problem is that startup companies sometimes need to react to radical changes in the market—and they need to be able to turn on a dime. If this is the case, a milestone may become redundant within a matter of months.

If you can't negotiate a single traunch deal, you need to be very careful about selecting milestones that are realistic and allow the company some room for maneuver in a volatile market. Unrealistic milestones can demoralize the team and halt momentum.

Redemption Rights

Imagine you invested $10m in eSomeStupidIdea.com, Inc. in March 2000. The bottom drops out of the market and it's obvious that this investment is only going to fail. The company still has $9m of your money in its bank account. You're forced to sit and watch as the management team burns through your money. Many investors have been through this experience in recent years and they now demand the right to force the company to buy back their shares, even paying a premium.

If a series A investor demanded these redemption rights, then it could be very difficult for the company to attract investors for series B and subsequent rounds. The series B investor could say *'I want to invest to build this company, I don't want my money being used to buy out the series A folks.'* Not only can redemption rights block the company from attracting future investors, but it often prevents banks and other lenders from providing credit facilities.

Although redemption rights may appear attractive to investors on the surface, there's a good argument that they're not healthy for the company in the long run.

Co-Sale Rights

This clause protects the investor from the founder selling his/her own shares, heading for the hills and leaving the other shareholders high and dry (one example of a mixed metaphor is nothing—I'm working on getting four or more in the same sentence). As a founder, even if someone were interested in buying your common stock, co-sale rights would restrict you from selling it. With co-sale rights, you're not allowed to sell any of your shares without offering investors the opportunity of selling their shares at the same time.

As founder and CEO of a hot Silicon Valley startup I received a term sheet with co-sale rights from a top-tier lead VC, I pushed back on this clause because I was planning to sell some of my common stock to raise cash to put a deposit on a house. The VC responded by saying they wanted the co-sale rights but they would invest more cash into the company so that the company could provide me with a venture loan, secured against my shares, to buy the house. From my perspective, the deal seemed too good to be true. If the share price went up in value after *IPO*, I could sell some shares, pay off the loan and keep the profit. If the share price went down, I kept the loan—the only security was attached to the shares. Of course, the deal *was* too good to be true. The VC had figured that I would be so keen to do this deal that, at the last minute, I'd consent to slash the company valuation—the one we'd already agreed to and written up in the term sheet. As it worked out, I told the investors to take a hike, not a very smart move looking back, as I lost the venture loan and I had to go out and find alternative investors virtually overnight—but at least I could stick to working with investors I felt I could trust.

Sign Term Sheet

There's little point in doing any work on the definitive agreement until you have full agreement on all the major terms written down in the form of a term sheet. If the term sheet is not properly thought through, the company's chances of success can be seriously jeopardized in the long run. Getting a signed term sheet from a lead VC is a major milestone. Once the term sheet has been agreed, a good VC will stick to the terms in the definitive agreement.

Complete Due Diligence

Before handing over large chunks of cash, many investors, especially lead VCs, need to make sure that the team, the company and the technology are real and legitimate. Can you imagine the embarrassment if the whole operation were a fabricated scam to part VC's from their stockpiles of cash? That's obviously very unlikely, but all investors are scared of screwing up—they have a responsibility to their own investors and they'll do whatever they can to cover their backs.

One of the most important roles of the lead investor is to carry out due diligence. This is one of the reasons that you shouldn't make any claims that you can't back up. Gather all the information they need and answer all their questions with a smile. This may feel like a laborious process but it's nothing compared to what you're going to go through when you prepare for IPO (see *Carry Out the Financial Audit and Due Diligence*, page 208).

The investor may use its own staff or hire third party consultants to review the company's finances and legal documents. There's also likely to be a 3rd party evaluation of your technology by a 'technical expert'. Don't be surprised if this 'technical expert' knows nothing at all about your particular technology, especially if you're working on the cutting edge of your field—you may need to provide some education here. Don't be surprised if your staff, customers and strategic partners receive due diligence calls. The key founders and management team will likely have to provide personal references. Among other things you can expect detailed background checks on your credit record, educational qualifications, and police record. Some VC's hire former police interrogators to conduct interviews with key members of the team.

Close Round of Funding

Don't be surprised when you experience several 'near-death' experiences in the fundraising process. It's not over 'till the fat lady sings—or until all the funds are in your bank account. It may seem obvious that you need to actually close the round out—but with so much going on, the closing can find itself repeatedly deferred to a later date.

The more investors coming in to the round, the more difficult it can be to close. Have you ever noticed how penguins huddle together on an iceberg? Nervously looking at the sea, they're tempted to swim but no one has the guts to take the first leap. In this way, they can flock together on the iceberg for some time. Then one penguin accidentally slips on the ice and splashes into the water, this triggers all the others to follow. Then there's a mad rush to dive in—no one wants to be left behind. Like penguins, investors flock together and often exhibit the same behavior—they don't want to be first to commit and they don't want to get left behind, so they all wait for the trigger and jump in together.

According to your fundraising agreements, you often need to close the whole round out before you're in a position to spend any of the cash. If four out of five investors wire their cash into your bank, you'd be tempted to start spending—especially if the company is under financial pressure. However, depending on how your fundraising agreement is structured, you may be restricted from spending a cent until the fifth and final investor stumps up its cash and the round is closed out. Like closing a sale or closing on a house purchase, the process needs to be carefully planned and executed. It can be useful for all the lawyers and finance folks involved to agree a set of milestones running up to the actual closing. Your lawyer may take on the role of project manager, making sure all parties know what they're expected to do and policing the deadlines.

After the round has been officially closed, many companies take a moment to celebrate the achievement—this is an important milestone. Print a T-shirt, issue a press release, have a party, whatever turns you on, but don't go too wild—you need all your senses about you as you embark on the next stage of this journey.

Appendix 4—Selling the Company—The M&A Process

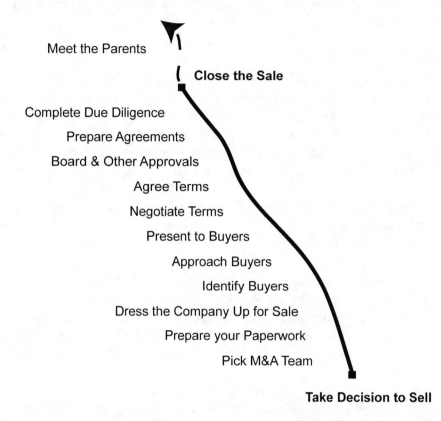

Meet the Parents

Close the Sale

Complete Due Diligence

Prepare Agreements

Board & Other Approvals

Agree Terms

Negotiate Terms

Present to Buyers

Approach Buyers

Identify Buyers

Dress the Company Up for Sale

Prepare your Paperwork

Pick M&A Team

Take Decision to Sell

Companies have been bought and sold for centuries and a sophisticated merger and acquisition (M&A) industry has developed to cater to the needs of buyers and sellers in all lines of business. The process is well established (it's actually changed very little during this time) and has a gestation period of about 9 months from commencement to close (don't they all?).

Some deals have been known to close quicker than this—but when starting out, it's impossible to predict how long the whole process will take for your company, with any degree of accuracy (see *Selling the Company in a Hurry*, page 372). Some of these activities, like the selection of the intermediary and the preparations to sell the company, are under your control and it is possible to estimate how long they will take, however, as soon as potential acquirers are involved, the timing is somewhat out of your hands. Some acquirers are geared up to move more quickly than others. The buyer is likely to be a public company with fiduciary responsibilities to conduct due diligence checks that force it to drag out the process for several months. Unless you work hard to maintain momentum, the whole process can easily grind to a halt.

In reality, several of the activities run in parallel—the buyer often appoints one team, or individual, to carry out a business evaluation and another to carry out the technical evaluation.

Take Decision to Sell

Before you embark on this part of the journey, it's important to make sure that the key members of your team, including the CEO, founders and investors, are in some agreement over where you collectively want to go and what you want to achieve by selling the company. In fact, you're likely to require the approval of the board and shareholders with certain rights, before a sale could be completed. So, it's a good idea to align the team and set realistic expectations before you go any further.

This is a decision that should not be taken lightly. As well as making sure that the key shareholders and the board of directors are on the same page, there are some other considerations to bear in mind:

- *Management distraction*—selling the company is a demanding activity that is sure to tie up several members of the management team for several months. Entrepreneurs often report their companies grinding to a halt after the team has become obsessed with a pending sale. It's important to maintain momentum in the every-day business operations while the M&A process if going on.
- *Stress*—there's a great deal at stake and the process can be highly emotional. In fact, behind the death of a loved one, selling the company ranks up there on the stress meter as one of the most nerve-racking events of an individuals life—alongside selling a house, childbirth and buying a pair of shoes from Foot Locker.
- *Timing*—choosing when to sell can be crucial. The best time is when the company is up-trending—making marked progress and there's a positive buzz in the marketplace (showing positive momentum). It also helps when you're offering to sell what the buyers are looking to buy. By investigating what buyers are looking for, you can start to make your company more attractive well before you actually put it up for sale—this could involve changing your revenue model, product strategy, cost structure and making other structural changes that would make the company a more appealing proposition.

- *Budget*—the cost of engaging the M&A firm, preparing the paperwork and dressing the company up for sale, cannot be ignored (see *Appointing an M&A Firm/Intermediary*, page 353).

Pick M&A Team

You obviously need to assemble an effective team to take care of the process of selling the company. However, putting a 'For Sale' sign outside the office could have an adverse impact on your customers and employees. It's generally not advisable to let all the employees know that the company is up for sale—the sales process can be a major source of distraction to employees that are unnerved by the prospect of change and wonder if the next suit to walk through the door is their next boss. You need your employees to keep focused on running the business—with a little care and planning, the process can be kept quiet from all but a small team of insiders. Bearing this in mind, the team might comprise:

- *CEO, CFO & other core management team members*—your CFO or accountant will have to be involved in the sales process, as well as your in-house attorney—but keep the inside team as small as possible.
- *Lawyer*—once again, it's important to hire the most expensive and experienced lawyers you can find. Poor lawyers can upset the buyers, mismanage the sale or screw up the deal in a multitude of ways.
- *Accountant*—there's a good deal of work for accountants in the M&A process. The accountant is normally very active in estimating valuation, preparing the paperwork, structuring the deal and providing due diligence documents. This often involves recasting the numbers and providing advice on tax issues. A well-known and reputable firm can add credibility to the numbers (see *Hire a Good Firm of Accountants*, page 79).
- *M&A firm or intermediary*—see *Appointing and M&A Firm/Intermediary*, below.

<u>Appointing an M&A Firm/Intermediary</u>

Like selling your house, you can go it alone or you can use an agent. There are brokers and financial intermediaries out there that specialize in selling technology companies in all stages of development. It's obviously less costly to go it alone and no one is going to know the company better than you do yourself. However, there are some good reasons for going with an intermediary:

- ✓ *Expert negotiator*—it's always a good idea to assign sensitive negotiations to a professional (see *Getting what you Want, Negotiating the Deal*, page 313

✓ *Heat shield*—an agent will not have the same emotional attachment to the company as you do yourself. This can help cool down heated conflicts in the negotiation process.

✓ *Good guy/bad guy*—this is a tried and trusted negotiation technique that's difficult to pull off on your own, unless you have a personality disorder.

✓ *Higher price*—a good intermediary will help you justify and push up the valuation. They are experts at opening up the number of buyers and creating an auction environment with a sense of urgency and pressure.

The cost of using an intermediary can be significant. In fact an investment bank would be looking to make $2-3million on any deal and would not normally consider getting involved if it couldn't see the potential to walk away with at least $1m. Of course, in addition to the large investment banks, there are other players that are often prepared to take on smaller deals. In the peak of the dot-com boom, the major investment banks were only prepared to look at companies that could realistically be sold for several hundred million dollars. Since the crash and the fizzling out of the *IPO* market, they have become much more humble—they're now competing for much smaller deals and even relatively small acquisition candidates can attract the attention of the once-elite investment bankers.

Company Valuation	Intermediaries	Success Fee	Monthly Retainer	Notes
Under $10m	Business Broker	3-10%	$0+	For tiny businesses like retail stores. Not suitable for tech startups.
$5-200m	Major investment banks Boutique M&A firms Regional investment banks Commercial banks Attorneys Accounting firms Freelance agents	2-5%	$5-10k +	Up-front fees and minimum success fees are not unusual.
$200m +	Major investment banks	1-2%	$0+	Retainer is negotiable for very large transactions

The formulas for calculating the success fees can be quite sophisticated. The Lehman Formula (*See Lehman Formula*, page 328) is still widely used but many agents now go for a sliding scale—like 8% on the first $2m, 6% on next $2m and 4% on all proceeds beyond that. Just in case you end up selling the company for peanuts, you can also expect them to demand a minimum success fee—this could be anything from $50-500,000. Remember, success fees are only paid when an offer is accepted and closed. You're probably going to have to sign an exclusive engagement with a minimum period of 12 months if you want a high level of commitment from the intermediary.

Let's say the success fee and the retainer adds up to 5% of the value of the sale—this can be really expensive. However, the benefits can easily outweigh these costs. An agent should be able to increase the sale price by much more than 5%. By introducing multiple suitors, creating an auction environment and professionally handling the negotiation process, it's not out of the question for a good intermediary to increase the sales price by 100%, or even more.

If you were going it alone, without the help of any form of agent or intermediary, the process could become a huge distraction and leave management with little time to run the company. Even if the sales process doesn't actually lead to a sale of the whole company, it can lead to the sale of specific assets and open the door to business development, partnering and minority investment deals.

Most professional agents are in a much better position to handle the sales process than you are yourself. They have lists of thousands of potential buyers with specific company and industry research information. This is their business and they know how to approach buyers, make an effective pitch and help them understand the company's value. Many buyers will take a call from a reputable investment bank but you'd find yourself in a voice-mail void if you approached them directly. Although it's not exactly unbiased, a valuation estimate from an intermediary, with lots of experience in this field and comparable data points, may carry more weight than one prepared by the company itself.

Having gone through the M&A process myself several times, and made almost every mistake in the book, I'm convinced that the benefits of hiring a good M&A advisor can easily outweigh the costs. Looking back I see that some of my M&A deals that fell apart could have actually closed if they'd been handled differently.

So, if you've decided to engage a financial intermediary to help you sell the company, how do you go about the selection process? It's simple—you put calls into Goldman Sachs and Morgan Stanley, they dispatch their top teams in private jets to present you with their credentials and compete in a 'bake-off' to win your business. You select the one you prefer, sign them up and you're off. The big banks are accustomed to competing in beauty contests to win lucrative *IPO* and M&A deals, whether they'll fire up the corporate jet for your business depends on the size of the deal. A potential buyer is more likely to take a call from Goldman Sachs or Morgan Stanley than they are from a smaller, unknown business broker—so going with one of the big boys could open up your list of potential buyers.

On the other hand, smaller boutique agents can typically give you more attention, especially if you're not exactly a billion dollar company. The nice thing about dealing with the smaller boutiques is that you can get the personal attention of the senior partners and your account is not destined to be handled to some less seasoned associate.

Here are some things to consider when selecting an intermediary to help you through the M&A process:

- ✓ *Team*—it's important that you feel comfortable with your chosen team. You're going to be working with them very closely in the coming months and these people are going to representing you and your company to potential buyers.

- ✓ *Network*—a good intermediary has a strong database of buyers and personal contacts. Don't restrict the search to one region or even one country—many companies are eventually sold to foreign buyers.

- ✓ *Technical and creative capabilities*—the ability to produce an accurate and defensible valuation is very important. So is the ability to come up with creative ways to structure a deal to meet the needs of both buyer and seller.

- ✓ *Market and industry expertise*—ideally, the team will know your market. If it doesn't, it should be able to learn very quickly. Up-to-the-minute information on how deals in other markets are being valued and structured will also come in handy.

- ✓ *Sales and presentation skills*—a good intermediary will understand and present your business in its most favorable light and have excellent follow-up and organizational skills.

- ✓ *References*—listen carefully to the feedback from lawyers and accountants as well as clients.

When you've made your choice, be prepared for a thorough going-over. Your chosen intermediary will need to gather a great deal of information from you in the coming weeks.

Prepare your Paperwork

In addition to preparation of the sales materials (see *Sales Materials*, below), the M&A process involves a tremendous amount of paperwork:

- *Due diligence documents*—see *Carry out Financial Audit and Due Diligence*, page 208.
- *Budgets & forecasts*—the numbers should be defensible. Avoid hockey-stick sales forecasts.
- *Valuation reports*—see *What's it Worth? Valuing the Company*, page 301.

The idea is to make it easy for someone to come in and buy the company. Ideally, you ship a pre-prepared set of binders over to the buyer; the paperwork is accurate, up to date and provides the buying team with everything it needs. In reality, this is unlikely to happen, but it's certainly a goal worth aiming for.

A serious buyer is likely to request an audit or send in its own bean counters to give your books a thorough inspection. Don't be afraid to recast your financial forecasts and reports to put them in the format that buyers are familiar with. This normally means making the figures look like those of a public company in the same market. Often adjustments are made to make the selling company's reports match the financial profile of the buyer.

Recasting the numbers can work to your advantage and help make the company look like a more attractive proposition. When you're not planning on selling the company, you probably look for ways to defer or minimize your revenues and earnings to reduce your tax liability. However, the opposite is true when you're trying to make the company look like an appealing acquisition—don't hide profits if that's what you're trying to sell.

If your paperwork is a mess it reflects on the rest of the business. Unrealistic projections, miscalculations, typos are a turn off to a buyer. It can hamper your prospects if you're scrambling to prepare documents at the last minute.

Dress the Company Up for Sale

Dressing the company up for sale involves preparing the selling materials and carefully positioning what you have to offer a potential buyer. This can be quite straightforward if your sales and marketing materials are up to date (*see Formulate your Core Messaging and Corporate Identity*, page 87). On the other hand, making the company more appealing to a buyer could involve a major restructuring and cost-cutting exercise that could take several months, or even years.

Hiding skeletons in closets can be quite difficult and time consuming. Unfortunately, all the skeletons are going to be found sooner or later, so you're advised to leave them out in the open. In fact, the best advice is to show the skeletons to your buyer. Timing can be quite important here—point them out too early and you run the risk of scaring the buyer away before he/she's had a chance to appreciate all the positive things the company has to offer. Pointing them out too late can shock the buyer and create an atmosphere of mistrust.

Selling Materials

A buyer that already knows the company well may not need a prospectus or any other sales materials to spark an interest in an acquisition. For everyone else, the selling materials are important, sometimes critical. Sellers and their agents sometimes put a great deal of time and money into the preparation of a glossy prospectus. It can be money well spent. I've sold companies in situations where I've been convinced that the sales materials made a significant contribution. Some buyers are impressed with glossy sales materials, others are not.

The size and nature of the deal can have an impact on the materials required—selling a large, established company in a *Cash Flow Sale* can be very different from selling technology in an *Asset Sale* (see *Dressing the Company up for Asset Sale*, page 248).

The information you provide, and the way that you position and deliver it, can have an impact on the buyer. The buyer can get the information through fax, mailed binders or a password protected web site. If you're serious about selling, I suggest you provide the materials in various formats and let the buyer choose the one it prefers. A typical information pack might include:

✓ *Teaser*—you only have a few seconds to grab someone's attention in a letter, fax, web page or e-mail, so make sure that your core messages are properly presented and highlight all the reasons that the company would be attractive to a buyer. You may want to customize the message to appeal to each individual prospect.

✓ *Executive summary*—try to keep it short (4-6 pages is ideal) yet provide an impressive overview that leaves the reader with a good understanding of the business. Weaving a story through the document can help keep the reader flowing through each of the sections:
   o *Overview*—short introduction that carefully positions the company.
   o *Background*—the company history and results.
   o *Market opportunity*—market growth statistics and projections.
   o *Sales model*—target customer, distribution channels, sources of revenue.
   o *Competitive position*—summary of how and why the company beats its competitors.
   o *Products & technology*—core competencies, current and future product overviews.
   o *Summary*—review how and why the company is poised for success.

✓ *Company slideshow*—as always, make sure it looks pretty and keep it short and sweet. Use an artist or artist-created template for the graphics and practice with a stop-watch to keep the presentation to no more than 20 minutes. As always, rehearsing with a video camera can help polish the pitch.

✓ *Financial memorandum*—this is a pack of financial information containing historical statements and reports, year-to-date figures, revenue analysis organizational charts and resumes of key personnel.

✓ *Competitive analysis*—details of each competitor's strategy and product line and how they compare.

✓ *Customer testimonials*—as well as written endorsements, photographs of happy customers and video clips can make an impact on a potential buyer.

Identify Buyers

Now that you've figured out what you have to offer a potential buyer and your sales materials are ready, it's time to draw up lists of potential buyers. What you're ideally looking for is a strategic buyer that can leverage your company and its products in ways that you couldn't as a stand-alone entity. Calculating that 1+1=3, a strategic buyer can justify a higher price than a purely financial buyer. List the most obvious strategic buyers, but don't stop there—many companies are eventually acquired by players where the fit is not immediately obvious.

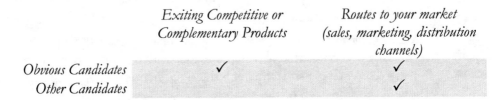

	Exiting Competitive or Complementary Products	*Routes to your market (sales, marketing, distribution channels)*
Obvious Candidates	✓	✓
Other Candidates		✓

According to the Golden Rule (see *Increasing the Price—the Golden Rule of Valuation,* page 302), you need more than one buyer if you're going to prevent the price dropping through the floor. In fact, you may be surprised by how large your list could grow—a good intermediary should have a database listing thousands of known buyers across several sectors. In drawing up your lists, include competitors, technology partners, companies with synergistic and complementary products, companies selling to the same customers, large corporations interested in diversification, companies interested in the same distribution channels, distributors, private investors, even employees.

The Internet is an excellent medium for reaching a wide base of buyers. Web-based intermediaries may be able to introduce you to serious buyers that you would never think of contacting directly.

Approach Buyers

Once the preliminary work is complete, the selling process begins. This involves hundreds of phone calls, e-mails and Fedex packages intermingled with feelings of rejection, frustration and the rare sensation of triumph. It's not a good idea to conduct this work in the middle of your office—it can be very unsettling for employees to overhear these phone conversations. If you're going it alone without using an outside intermediary, you might want to carry out this work offsite or in a private office. An intermediary could help you complete a quiet deal if you don't want it widely known in your industry that your business is up for sale.

As always, it's best if you can get a personal introduction from a mutual friend/colleague—so milk your lawyers, accountants, board of directors and anyone else you can think of in your network for contacts. If you don't get an introduction you'll have to make a cold call—these days, this normally means a coordinated two pronged attack on the buyers' voice-mail and e-mail systems.

Present to Buyers

Potential buyers are obviously interested in learning about your product and technology; however, this is the best opportunity you're going to get to deliver all the benefits of a potential merger or acquisition. Remember to switch into sales mode—all communication with the buyer is part of the negotiation process (see *Switch into Sales Mode*, page 314).

Here are some points to bear in mind:

- *Demonstrate momentum*—show marked progress and a positive buzz around the company. As always, photographs and video clips of expert endorsements and customer testimonials can very effective.
- *Be sensitive to questions*—potential buyers often have specific questions that need to be answered before the discussions can proceed. Listening carefully can help you gauge their level of interest and identify any potential obstacles (see *Connect with the Individual*, page 315).
- *Practice your presentation until your message is clear and concise*—lock yourself in a hotel room with a video camera for several hours beforehand. In preparing for any presentation, a stopwatch is also an essential piece of equipment (see *Present to Investors*, page 338).
- *Showcase your most impressive team members*—and be prepared to answer questions on the market, competition, technology, and virtually any other topic.

In addition to a slideshow, you may want to take the buyer on a tour of the facilities and introduce him/her to key members of staff. A live product demonstration is always more interesting than a canned pre-recorded demo—but it's usually more risky.

My personal style is to deliver all the selling points and allow the buyer to reach his/her own conclusions. People are often resistant to someone else's ideas but they're inclined to approve of their own—or ideas they believe to be their own.

It's not difficult to add a voice narration to your slideshow and make it all available on the web (see *Cloned Presenter*, page 175). I'm convinced that the Internet is going to be used much more extensively in future to deliver presentations, documents, product demonstrations and virtually everything the buyer needs to know, however, there's no replacement for a live meeting or presentation.

Negotiate Terms

Negotiating terms is obviously a crucial part of selling the company. This obviously involves finding a mutually agreeable price but it also involves agreeing on the currency and the structure of the deal (see *Getting what you Want—The Negotiation Process*, page 313).

Negotiate the Price

When it comes to selling the company, you can make your estimates of valuation, but the real price is what a buyer is actually prepared to pay—and this is driven to a great extent by the strength of your negotiator, the number of potential buyers and the degree of competition between them (see *What's it Worth? Valuing the Company*, page 301). In a *Cash Flow Sale*, where you're selling the company as a viable stand-alone business, valuation techniques such as *Discounted Cash Flow, Comparable Deals, Earnings Multiple* and *Revenue Multiple* can be used. In an *Asset Sale,* where you're selling the technology or product as an asset, the only reasonable techniques to consider are *Build Cost Plus, Rule of Thumb* and *Comparable Deals.*

Negotiate the Structure & Currency

In many cases, the way the deal is structured is more important than the price. There's no cookie-cutter technique for structuring the merger or acquisition of a technology company. In fact, to increase their billable hours, lawyers, accountants and M&A advisors have composed a myriad of complicated alternatives. Every buyer and seller is unique and each company's size, cash position, debt, tax situation and ownership can have an impact on how a deal is structured. Cross-border deals can create additional complexities and problems that have to be resolved. Of course, it makes sense for you to have the most experienced, inventive and expensive bloodsucking advisors, lawyers and accountants guide you through this process. Knowing the proper structure for you and your business requires substantial experience and knowledge of what is happening in the industry on a real-time daily basis. As the seller, it's really in your interests to manage the structuring of the deal.

The buyer is often prepared to pay a higher price if the seller is prepared to bear some of the risk and offer some flexibility in the structure:

✓ *Integration*—the deal structure is often affected by the buyers' plans for integration (see *Meet the Parents*, page 368)—whether the company lives on as an independent subsidiary or is absorbed into the parent without trace. It's important that the chosen structure takes into consideration the needs and incentives of the team—specifically the employees that are going to be hired into the parent. Members of the dependent team, the group without which the technology would be worthless, need an incentive to stay and like to feel they're getting a fair deal.

✓ *Tax*—as a shareholder of the selling company, the way the deal is structured could have a huge impact on the amount of tax you end up paying to Uncle Sam. You could find yourself paying long term capital gains tax of 20% or, you could end up paying 30% tax as a corporation and an additional 30% as an individual. The difference between 20% and 60% tax can be huge, so, again, make sure you pay for good advice. You also need to be prepared to negotiate hard on this point as what's generally a good tax structure for the buyer is a poor one for the seller—and vice versa.

✓ *Currency*—large public companies usually pay for their acquisitions with cash and/or stock. Smaller pre-public private companies use private stock and warrants. Earn-outs are common for the acquisition of small owner/operator companies. The form of payment can have an effect on the price. The valuation techniques (see *What's it Worth? Valuing the Company*, page 301) assume that the full consideration is paid in cash—if the buyer wants to pay in stock, kind, buttons or IOU's, then you should increase the valuation and price of the deal to compensate for the loss of liquidity. High technology M&A transactions range from all cash to all earn-out, with myriad combinations of taxable and tax-deferred structures in between. The introduction of currency alternatives to cash can often break a deadlock situation when negotiations on price grind to a halt (see *Introduce Alternative Currencies*, page 323).

Deal Currency—Getting Paid in Stock instead of Cash

The buyer often prefers to pay in stock to preserve its cash. The seller often prefers stock to defer tax. Many buyers are reluctant to make an all-cash offer and stock is a popular form of currency in technology transactions.

In the good old days (way back in the 1990's) there was a huge tax incentive for buyers if they could acquire the company for stock and position the transaction as a 'pooling of interests'. To qualify, the companies had to agree to certain restrictions and jump through various hoops. This tax loophole has now been closed and pooling no longer offers an incentive to structure an all-stock transaction.

If you're acquired by a public company and paid in stock, you might be forgiven for thinking that you can sell the stock and convert it to cash whenever you feel the urge. That's the beauty of publicly traded stock, right? Wrong. When I was negotiating selling my company to a public corporation for stock, along with the other shareholders, I was restricted from selling any of my new stock for over 12 months. Then there were blackout periods and other restrictions aimed at preventing us from dumping our stock on the public market. Believe it or not, Wall Street is somewhat unpredictable and, over a 12 month period, the buyers' stock price can fluctuate dramatically. If the stock plummeted during the 12 month lockout I would have walked away with nothing—except a huge tax bill. For some unfathomable reason, in this scenario I was liable to pay tax on revenues that I never actually received. So in selling for stock, you are exposed to a downturn in the stock price, however, your losses can be limited by the use of a sort of insurance policy called a 'collar'.

Deal Currency—Selling the Assets Instead of Your Company Stock

By buying all your company stock, the acquirer inherits your company's debts and liabilities. This can be something of a turn-off to a buyer, especially if the company has impending law suits or there are any other dangers lurking. By simply buying the assets from the company, the acquirer can avoid taking on these liabilities. After the acquisition, your company stays in existence as a separate company from the buyer. Obviously this structure can be very appealing to a buyer; however, it can be complicated and lead to a double tax whammy for the seller.

Deal Currency—Earn-Outs

A business that's driven by a powerful leader, or management team, could collapse after an acquisition that results in these individuals leaving the company or losing motivation. This is a common situation for smaller owner-operator businesses that are heavily dependent on their founders. If you sold your company in an earn-out situation, you'd have an employment contract to stay with the company and, instead of being bought out in one lump sum, you'd likely be paid out over a number of years. You can also expect a non-compete clause to restrict you from setting up in competition after the earn-out is finalized. The amount you're paid is dependent on how you and the company perform after the acquisition—normally a formula is agreed that ties your pay-out to future sales and profits. So you have an incentive to stick around and make the company perform—and the acquirer buys some time to find your replacement.

This all sounds great in theory, but in practice it can be very problematic. One business that I was involved with was in an earn-out situation. The founder had received a small up-front lump sum on selling his company and his earn-out was calculated at $2 for every $1 in net profit that the company delivered to the parent corporation over a 3 year period. If he delivered $3m in profit over the 3 year period, he would receive $6m in earn-out. If he delivered no profit, then he would have nothing in the way of earn-out. As you can imagine, this was a man that was totally focused on making profit. Of course he was working hard to increase sales, but he was also obsessed with keeping costs to a bare minimum. The way he saw it, every dollar the company spent was two dollars out of his own pocket—so if the company paid $100 for a hotel room, it would cost him $200 from his earn-out. As a result, I've never known a company that was so tight with its money. When the staff traveled on business, which they did a great deal, they would be forced to choose the cheapest hotels in town and sleep 3 or 4 to a room. Of course this meant that the acquirer inherited a lot of disgruntled employees. Then the new parent decided to make changes and start to dictate how the company was to be run. The seller was none too pleased—he was not going to agree to anything that involved spending any money and he was determined to keep total control of the business until his earn-out was over. As you can imagine, there was a good deal of tension between the buyer and seller in this situation—and the earn-out structure didn't work for either of them.

If you find yourself in an earn-out, you should be aware that things can get even worse than this. Imagine that you deliver your profit figures only to find that the parent company imposes an overhead cost that dramatically slashes the profit calculation and your subsequent earn-out payment. This happens all the time and many entrepreneurs have been devastated to find that, after the buyer cooks the books, earn-out payments don't come close to meeting their expectations.

An earn-out has more chance of working out if, after the acquisition, the company continues to operate as a totally independent entity. This can be a real problem for the buyer—especially if there's some disagreement over strategy or management, as there often is. The financial arrangements have to be very clearly defined and every possible eventuality has to be anticipated.

Earn-outs can be very complicated for small owner/operator businesses, but they're even more problematic for larger companies where external investors are involved. If they're left out of the earn-out, they're obviously going to get very upset, but how can external investors, that are not employees of the company, contribute towards its future performance after the acquisition is complete? Sharing the pie between the employees and the external shareholders can be very difficult.

If you sell your company in an earn-out, don't be surprised to find yourself in a legal dispute with the buyer, or even your own external shareholders. Of course, you need to pay for the best advice if you're thinking of entering into an earn-out situation. You're likely to find some very willing professional advisors—a complicated earn-out with a high probability of litigation is a dream scenario for accountants and lawyers. I wonder who came up with this idea in the first place?

Agree Terms

When you finally agree terms, get them onto paper as quickly as possible in the form of a letter of intent. The letter of intent is not positioned as a binding agreement; however, many of the terms are actually binding and have to be taken seriously. In some countries, and under certain conditions, the buyer and seller, by their actions, can give rise to an implied contract which is, in fact, enforceable. However, if you bring a lawyer into the process before the letter of intent has been finalized, you're likely to expand its scope to the point that it looks like the definitive agreement. The decision-makers on both sides of the negotiating table usually like to work with short, friendly letters of intent but their lawyers like to make things as complicated as possible. Try to keep the letter of intent focused on the business terms and save the legal wrangling for the definitive agreement. If either side brings in hard line lawyers, you'll find yourselves spending time discussing legal minutia—in this case you may as well skip the letter of intent all together and go straight to the definitive agreement.

Board & Other Approvals

Selling the company is a serious undertaking that normally requires official approval from the board of directors and some, or all, of the shareholders. Some deals also have to win approval from state and federal regulators and various regulatory bodies. Depending how the company is structured, the investors, as preference shareholders, may have the rights to veto a proposed sale. Hopefully, you won't have reached this point without some understanding and indication as to what they're prepared to accept and the deal will go through without a hitch. However, some selling and arm-twisting may be required at this point to win the approval you need and the ultimate decision may come down to a vote. If there is disagreement in the ranks, you're well advised to keep this under your hat as a savvy negotiator on the other side may use this information to his/her advantage.

A letter of intent that's agreed by both parties and approved by their respective boards and shareholders is a significant milestone in the process of selling the company. But don't celebrate just yet—there's still serious work to do before the deal is closed.

Prepare Agreements

The definitive agreement is actually a set of many different contracts, attachments and schedules that define the terms and structure of the transaction, establish the legal obligations of both parties and disclose tons of information about the buyer as well as the seller.

You're likely to get into a great deal of negotiation at this point regarding risks, liabilities, representations, warranties and indemnification. But don't be confused by the legal jargon. Basically, the buyer says: "I'm buying your company on the basis that the information you've provided me with and, as a result, I'm taking on all your company's liabilities. You're telling me that there are no hidden skeletons in the closet and I believe you—but if I find one after the deal closes, I want you to pay all the costs associated with removing it." This sounds like a reasonable request from the buyers' perspective but it could put you in a very difficult position. If you only receive $1m from the proceeds of the deal, would you want to be personally liable to pay for the removal of the skeleton if it costs $1m or even more? You're going to want to limit your liability here to a reasonable figure—certainly a figure that's smaller than your proceeds from the sale. The buyer doesn't want to pay for the removal of undisclosed skeletons inherited from the seller, so you have a potential stalemate that, if not handled carefully, could hold up the whole transaction.

In all likelihood, a portion of the sale price will end up being held back to pay for unforeseen liabilities (skeleton removal). As possession is nine tenths of the law, it's much better for you to have the cash that's held back sitting in your bank account rather than the buyers account—of course it will be subject to escrow and it won't be officially yours until the escrow period is over. Unless you set clear boundaries, the buyer can nickel and dime you at this point demanding compensation to correct minor defects it discovers after the deal closes. Unless you say that the escrow funds can only be touched if the total costs exceed a minimum figure, of several thousand dollars, you could find the funds being repeatedly tapped for the cost of broken pencils and other petty items.

Complete Due Diligence

The buyer, especially if it's a public company, has a duty to its shareholders to carry out extensive checks on your business to find all the skeletons in the closets before rather than after the deal is closed (see *Carry out Financial Audit and Due Diligence*, page 208). A sophisticated buyer will provide you with a boilerplate check-list of documents that it needs to make a fair assessment of the benefits and liabilities of the acquisition. If you've prepared properly, the ground rules and scope of the due diligence process will have been agreed in the letter of intent—together with an estimated timeline and you'll have most of the documents sitting in binders ready to respond.

You could be held personally liable if any of the information you provide is found to be untrue or inaccurate. Let's say that again: You could be held personally liable if any of the information that you provide is found to be untrue or inaccurate. Your exposure here could be enormous. Keep records of all the buyers' requests and your responses. As the seller, you must be responsive, accurate and truthful in your answers. In fact you need to disclose specific problems or liabilities that could be of interest to the buyer and attach them to the definitive agreement. Or course, you might come up against a deal-breaker of a problem that derails the whole transaction. Alternatively, the buyer may well want to hold back some money to pay for any unforeseen costs related to skeletons or closets uncovered in the due diligence process.

Remember that until the deal is closed and the money's in the bank, it could fall apart at any stage and you need to continue selling throughout the process. Lawyers working on the definitive agreements and managers working on the due diligence documents can easily kill the deal if they allow themselves to get into a squabble with individuals on the opposing side—believe me, this can happen. Make sure that everyone on your team understands how important it is to stay in sales mode until the deal is closed.

Close the Sale

Phew. After dodging several bullets and going through a few near-death experiences, you've actually made it to the closing. You probably missed the first closing date, but don't let that upset you—just make sure you find a date that you can actually close. If your deal is not overly large or complex, you'll probably be able to sign the papers and close on the same day. It's likely to be a nail-biting experience as you wait for those final documents to pop out of the Fedex system and arrive through your door.

When it's all over, your hands are aching from all the signatures and the funds have been successfully transferred to your account, it's time to celebrate. Congratulations.

Meet the Parents

As soon as the ink on the contract is dry, it's time to announce the deal, to the employees and the outside world, and start the process of integration with the new parent company. The integration process can be something of a challenge. In fact, a surprisingly large number of acquisitions are seen as failures. This is partly due to the culture shock experienced by employees, partly due to skeletons being discovered in closets, and partly due to a lack of management support for the deal. Your chances of success are improved if the integration process is well structured and carefully managed.

When you announce the deal to your employees, even if you handle it perfectly, be prepared for an explosion of emotions. However, good the deal may be, don't expect to be able to please all the people all the time! There's sure to be some suspicion and resentment. After I'd announced the pending sale of my company, I returned to my office to find a line of red faced employees standing outside. After meeting with a couple of them I was shocked at what was going on. They were all scrambling to negotiate themselves a bigger share of the pie. They wanted to know what their colleagues were getting out of the deal and they had various creative justifications for demanding last minute stock option grants. It was like a feeding frenzy. This was normally a very calm and friendly team. One 'stockless' contractor tearfully demanded I give him half of my stock and actually brought in his lawyer to help convince me that this was a reasonable request. Employees also want to know precisely what this means for each of their jobs. Will they be laid off? Get a new boss? Get a raise? Promotion? More responsibility? What about their sales commissions? The list of concerns goes on and on. It can be overwhelming if you're not prepared for it. It's also a tremendous time drain—productivity can fall to non-existent levels as people tie up hour after hour on these issues.

As a result, you need to be careful about when and how news of the deal reaches employees—one of my colleagues was upset to hear that her company had been acquired by reading it in the newspaper. When you announce the deal, make sure you have answers to all the most likely questions. Sophisticated buyers prepare welcome packs for the employees and make Frequently Asked Questions and other information available on an intranet site. It's important that you tell employees what to expect and you don't make promises that you're not in a position to keep—some people don't like change, but you just can't guarantee that they're not going to be affected by significant changes. Employees look to key managers for guidance and inspiration—so you need buy-in from key staff to ensure that they contribute to the development of the integration plan, cooperate publicly and help sell the deal to the employees. Announcing the deal in conjunction with a staff retention plan can make it very palatable to most employees, even the miserable ones. Welcome bonuses, stock option grants, profit sharing bonus plans and benefits packages can put a smile on the face of most employees.

There are countless ways of integrating the two companies together. At one end of the spectrum each department could be immediately (or quickly) absorbed into the parent and your company would virtually disappear without trace. At the other end, you could continue to operate as an autonomous business with little to show that the ownership had changed hands.

Company is Integrated as a Self-Contained Subsidiary

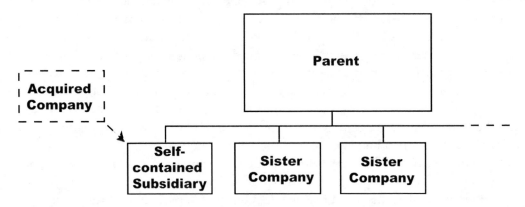

In a *Cash Flow Sale*, where the company is already operating as a self-sustaining entity in its own right, the buyer may decide to keep the operation intact. In this case, many of the employees may be or unaffected by the sale—it's just business as usual as far as they're concerned. The bulk of the interaction with the new owners will be through the CEO and accountant—as the focus will be on delivering financial results to the parent.

Company is Absorbed into Parent

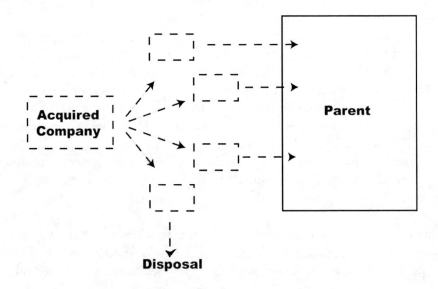

In an *Asset Sale*, the buyer is typically taking your product and technology (as an asset) and delivering it to customers through its own route to market—its established sales, marketing and distribution channels. The asset, and the technology team on which it depends, are often absorbed into divisions of the parent and the old company disappears with little trace. Some, or all, of the management, sales and marketing teams may be disposed of—as they're excess to requirement in the parent company (see *Short Sprint to Destination Asset Sale*, page 227).

The integration may be a long-term process that starts with the company operating as an autonomous business and ends with a complete assimilation after several years of step-by-step integration.

Integration Plan

Most deals fail when it comes to the amalgamation of the new subsidiary with the parent. This is hardly surprising considering that they have to create a single corporate culture and meld together disparate product lines, sales and marketing activities, human resources, accounting and IT systems. Melding different cultures and corporate philosophies into a single company can be a real challenge. Employees coming from acquired companies are often brainwashed with the parents' values in an attempt to meld a single corporate culture and management style.

As the seller, this is when you find out what's really been going on behind the scenes in the buying company—you get to know which individuals supported the deal and want it to succeed and which ones opposed the deal and want to see it fail. After buying my Windows-based technology, one bright spark in the new parent company, who was not exactly supportive of the deal, decided that the whole software platform had to be converted to Unix. It didn't make sense. The porting process would take 18 months, cost several million dollars—and achieve very little. An integration plan should have been worked out and these issues should have been discussed in the due diligence stage—before the deal was actually closed. Corporations that are accustomed to making acquisitions recognize the importance of integration. They have well thought-out strategies and teams dedicated to making their acquisitions a success.

Streamlining the M&A Process

Believe it or not, unless your company is worth $50m or more, some of the bulge bracket investment banks can hardly afford to take on the assignment and sell it. As the IPO market has dried up, even the elite firms are hurting for business, and they're now stooping to compete for smaller deals, however, many still don't have the cost structure to sell companies worth $10m or less.

In an interesting dichotomy, many vendors on eBay can now sell products for a couple of dollars and still make a profit. Surely, new technology can be harnessed to streamline the traditional M&A process? In the last 25 years, I've seen computers invade virtually all aspects of business and our daily lives. I suspect that the traditional M&A business is about to be transformed by technology—and the initial match-making part of the process will soon resemble eBay.

Of course, important negotiations will still be conducted face-to-face, however, buyers will not have to look much further than their computer screens to find valuable companies and assets to buy. Of course, business plans, financial statements, technology white papers and all forms of documents can be delivered to the buyers' PC—but many people still don't realize that slideshow presentations, with software demonstrations and voice narrations can be piped directly through this channel as well (see *Cloned Presenter*, page 175). There's no need to put the CEO on a plane and send him/her to the buyers office with a laptop, PowerPoint presentation and projector—the whole presentation can be delivered over the Internet.

Finding a company or technology to buy is becoming more convenient and efficient at online sites where the buyer can search through listings at a rapid pace. There are no faxes, e-mails and printed documents to collate or meetings to attend—all the information the buyer needs can be available in one convenient site.

Of course, selling a company is not quite the same as selling your old record collection on eBay. For one thing, you might want to keep the sale confidential and avoid broadcasting it to your staff, competitors and the rest of the world. Guess what? Restricting access to qualified buyers and keeping the information anonymous is not impossible online. In fact, these issues have already been successfully addressed by sites like the TechnologyTradingExchange. You can spread the net and find genuine buyers online without giving away your trade secrets.

Internet technology can streamline and improve the matchmaking process linking buyers with sellers, it can also help to smooth the two way communications. On the other hand, it will always make sense to have real-life human experts take care of the negotiation process. Technology can't entirely replace the M&A process, but it will surely streamline it in the coming years—especially for smaller companies and asset-sale deals.

Selling the Company in a Hurry

In reality, many technology startups don't have the luxury of a 6-12 month window when they decide to sell up. In many cases, the 'For Sale' sign goes up when the wolves can be heard scratching at the door, or at least howling in the distance. When you're selling your company in a hurry, you're in a race against time. If you lose the race and run out of cash, your company is probably worth nothing, or something bearing a painful resemblance to nothing. If you're perceived as a distressed company in a fire-sale situation with only one potential buyer, you're sure to get beaten up on valuation (see *What's it Worth? Valuing the Company*, page 301). Well aware that you're running out of cash, a sensible buyer will allow the clock to tick in the knowledge that the valuation will likely continue to drop with every passing day. You have a fighting chance of maintaining a fair price if you have the time to generate an auction environment with a number of competing buyers. It's important to keep one eye on the clock when you're forced to sell the company in a hurry.

No Short Cuts when it comes to Preparation

Just because the wolves are at the door, it doesn't mean that you can skip some of the steps of the sales process. Fortunately, with a little work some of the steps, such as selecting an intermediary, identifying and approaching potential buyers, negotiating and structuring the deal can be compressed. Other steps, like preparing tons of financial, marketing and due diligence documents still have to be completed—whether you have weeks, months or years to sell up.

The Sales Team

Depending on whether you're looking at a sale in the range of $5m or $500m, hiring an investment bank may or may not be an option. Making cold calls to potential buyers is tough and it can be difficult to get through the voice-mail system and speak to a live person, unless you're calling from Morgan Stanley or Goldman Sachs. However, a top-tier agent or investment bank may be reluctant to take on any company in a fire sale situation.

When selling the company is priority number one, a good CEO may want to personally lead the charge. It can work quite well if this individual is not calling cold and has some form of introduction to the potential buyers. Selling a company is a complicated and specialist activity and even the most talented and experienced CEO could benefit from the support of an M&A advisor. You may want to consider hiring a specialist M&A consultant or lawyer on an hourly rate (plus success bonus) rather than an investment bank on a retainer and commission. A good advisor will have plenty of ideas to overcome negotiation and deal-structuring stalemate situations, and naturally tag team with the CEO in the good guy/bad guy game.

New Internet-based services can accelerate the process of dressing the company up for sale, identifying, approaching and presenting to buyers. Cyberspace offers a fast and efficient platform for buyers and sellers to meet up.

Valuation

It's in your interests to complete a thorough valuation analysis and arm your negotiator with a credible valuation report (see *What's it Worth?—Valuing the Company*, page 301). The valuation will eventually depend on the experience of your negotiating team, the credibility of your valuation comparisons, the number of potential buyers you're talking to and the amount of time you have before your cash burns out. When time is not an issue, it's in your interests to delay any discussion about valuation as long as you possibly can. When the wolves are at the door, you don't really have time to delay anything, so when asked, you might as well go ahead and give the buyer your opening valuation estimate.

Before you go into negotiation with the buyer, poll your major investors and board members to get some idea as to how much flexibility there's likely to be on the issue of valuation. If it's a choice between having the company acquired or shutting down, it's important that everyone is aware of this—your negotiator is going to need some price flexibility in this situation. If there are a number of interested buyers and you're choosing between several realistic options, it's important that your negotiator knows what everyone is looking for and where the bottom line is. You don't want to enter the negotiation phase without a clear understanding of the valuation objectives and boundaries.

Approaching Potential Buyers

Your CEO could make the initial approach to a potential buyer with a call and follow-up e-mail. If there's not much time to beat about the bush, the message has to be direct and to the point:

> *"I've always felt that there's a great deal of synergy between our companies. We're currently involved in some M&A activity. Before we go much further, I'd like to present you with our story and look into a potential fit with your organization. Do you have any time slots available to meet on Wednesday afternoon?"*

By carefully choosing your words, you may be able to create the impression that there are a number of interested potential buyers. You may get away with a vague statement like—*'we're talking to other buyers'*—even if you only have one serious contender. Hey, you're saying that you're talking to them, you're not saying that they're talking back, or that they've expressed any form of interest whatsoever! Take care here—creating an auction atmosphere doesn't mean misrepresenting the status of the company. Remember that any interested buyer is going to go through a pretty thorough due diligence process that will identify all the skeletons in the closets sooner or later. In fact, to give you more time to deal with them, you really want the buyer to find the skeletons sooner rather than later—nasty surprises are the last thing you want as you drive to close the deal.

Accelerated Negotiation

You're going to need a creative and experienced team to negotiate and structure a deal when you're in a hurry. Ideally your negotiating team will have lots of experience, creative ideas and know-how to deal with everything that's thrown at it during the negotiation process. Fancy footwork can be useful when it comes to quickly overcoming obstacles, maintaining momentum and keeping discussions on track.

You can buy yourself time and the buyer can demonstrate commitment and goodwill if you negotiate a bridge loan or deposit to carry the company through the potentially lengthy M&A process.

If you don't manage to secure a bridge loan from the buyer, and find that you're losing the race against time, as well as seeing the valuation heading south, don't be surprised to see the structure of the deal go through some form of shocking transmutation. Instead of acquiring the stock and taking on the company as a going concern, the buyer may offer to simply buy some or all of the assets, leaving the company shell with any debts and liabilities behind. In extreme cases, instead of buying with cash, debt or public stock, the buyer may offer employment agreements or earn-outs to the key staff. In these situations it's important that your negotiating team keeps the discussions flowing—an experienced M&A advisor without an emotional bond to the company can make all the difference here.

Bypass the Letter of Intent

Drawing up an official letter of intent is not a necessary part of the sales process and it can take up valuable time, but it would be a mistake to avoid this step completely. You might not want the lawyers to spend time drawing up an 'official' document, but it's always nice to have your agreement written down, even if it's a simple list of bullet points on an e-mail message or the back of an envelope. Your next challenge is to keep the momentum going through the due diligence process, so as well as stating clearly what the deal points are, make sure your letter of intent sets some guidelines for the due diligence, a closing date and some milestone dates for people to aim at along the way.

Due Diligence Process and Preparation of the Definitive Agreement

So you're in a race against time and your deal is now in the hands of lawyers—not exactly the fastest people on earth. It's not good news that the lawyers drawing up the definitive agreements are probably working for the buyer, and they're not under your control, but the real bad news is that it may be in the buyers interests to pass papers back and forth and drag the due diligence process out as long as possible.

The best thing you can do is take control of the process by appointing yourself, or someone on your team, as project manager, unofficially of course. Have both sides agree on the process, identify the individual steps and commit to a timeline broken down into individual milestones. Like any good project manager, make sure everyone in the team knows exactly what he or she is expected to do by when. On your side, you obviously need to make sure that your team is highly responsive to due diligence requests. On the buyers' side, you need to build some sort of relationship that gives each individual an incentive to stay on track—challenge them, make them look good in front of their bosses, do whatever it takes to encourage them to keep this project at the top of their 'to do' lists.

It's not easy to sell the company in a hurry, and normally involves one or more near-death experiences, but it can be done and is normally well worth all the effort.

Appendix 5—Every Journey Tells a Story

Journeys don't always go as smoothly as we'd like. We don't always stay on course and we don't always reach our target destinations. Let's looks at some of the alternative routes your startup could take. Remember, the longer the journey, the more cash the company is likely to burn—so short, direct routes are much more rewarding than long, meandering ones.

Investors Founders Creditors
&
Employees

IPO

Zero

Zero-to-IPO Direct

You set out targeting IPO, progress smoothly through each of the stages hitting all the milestones along the route and reach IPO without meandering or hanging around. You probably go through various rounds of funding, but this direct journey is relatively quick and not excessively expensive. The IPO should generate a healthy company valuation—investors get a good return on investment and even employee stock options start to carry some significant value. Yippee!

It doesn't get much better than this! (Unless you can follow the *Zero-to-IPO Diversion* route—page 391).

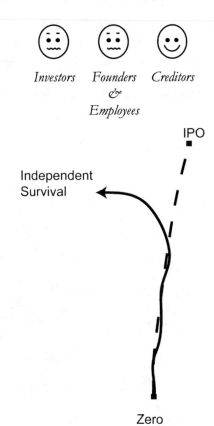

Zero-to-Independent Survival

You set out on the route to IPO, hit your early milestones and successfully managed to build a viable stand-alone business. With positive cash flow, the business is able to survive indefinitely—congratulations. However, it will take years, probably decades, to provide a return for the investors through the distribution of profits in the form of share dividends—how long are the investors prepared to wait for an exit route? Unless the company reached this position without raising investment funds, it's just a matter of time before investors push for an acquisition or IPO.

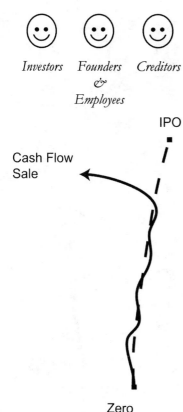

Investors   Founders   Creditors
&
Employees

Zero-to-Cash Flow Sale Diversion

You set out heading for IPO, hit your milestones and start to attract attention in the market. When the business turns a profit and starts to generate positive cash flow, you receive an acquisition offer. You choose to sell the company rather than continue to pursue IPO. The company could be absorbed and disappear without a trace, or it could be operated as a stand-alone subsidiary that continues to deliver profits and positive cash flow to the parent.

Congratulations—with positive cash flow, the company valuation should be quite reasonable. Investors, founders, employees and all the shareholders should be able to cash out with a smile.

Zero-to-Cash Flow Sale Backtrack

After hitting all your milestones and building a profitable stand-alone business, you fail to make it all the way up the final ascent to IPO. Perhaps you failed to hit IPO-qualifying numbers or the route is temporarily closed due to inclement conditions on Wall Street. Whatever the reason, you don't make it all the way to IPO and decide to backtrack and sell the company instead.

As the company is generating positive cash flow, you should find a number of potential buyers and sell out for a healthy price. The valuation may not be as high as you'd achieve through IPO (often 15-30% lower) but the chances are that you get paid out in cash, or shares that you can sell at any time—you don't have to wait a year or so for the lock up to expire as you would with IPO. Assuming the sale price is reasonable, this should be seen as a good result for the investors, founders, employees and everyone involved.

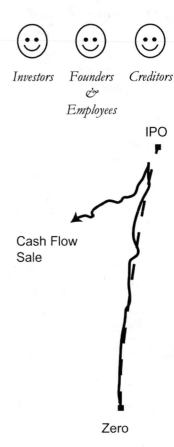

Investors   Founders & Employees   Creditors

IPO

Cash Flow Sale

Zero

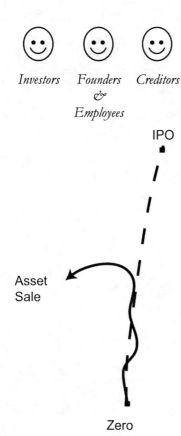

Zero-to-Asset Sale Diversion (Intentional)

You start out aiming for IPO, manage to build a valuable product but realize that creating your own route to market is a pretty tall order—without decades of investment, you figure you have little chance of building a viable stand-alone business. Instead of building your own route to market, you decide to sell out to someone that has one in place already.

After raising a modest level of funding—perhaps $2-5m in your seed and early rounds—you decide not to pump gazillions of dollars into building a sales and marketing operation. Instead, you focus on building a valuable product that you sell, with the development team and the company, before your cash burns out. As you didn't struggle on blindly investing in sales and marketing, you avoided burning up too much cash and there's a good chance that the investors, founders and employees will be pleased with the proceeds of the sale.

Zero-to-Asset Sale Diversion (Unsolicited Offer)

Heading out toward IPO, you start by building a valuable product that attracts the attention of existing players in the market. Before you manage to build your sales channels and start to generate positive cash flow, you receive an unsolicited offer to buy the company and decide to sell out. As the company is not yet generating positive cash flow, the buyer sees the company as a wrapper for the intellectual property and the supporting team. When the sale is complete, the product is integrated with others in the buyers' line-up and the corporate entity is disposed of—the company is simply a disposable wrapper for the product and other assets.

As the acquisition takes place before you established an expensive sales and marketing operation, your investor list should be relatively short and the proceeds of the *Asset Sale* should be sufficient to provide a healthy return for the investors—and provide a nice lump sum for each of the founders and employees.

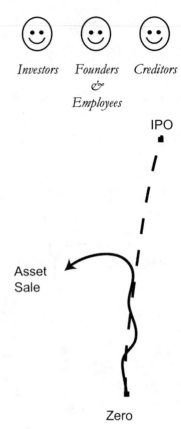

Investors   Founders & Employees   Creditors

IPO

Asset Sale

Zero

Zero-to-Asset Sale Backtrack

You build a valuable product, raise funding and hit many of your milestones. However, you fail to generate sufficient sales to turn a profit. As the company continues to burn up cash and report a loss, it's not possible to *IPO* or achieve a healthy price through *Cash Flow Sale*. Sooner or later, the company is sure to hit a cash crisis and head for *Shutdown* or *Bankruptcy*. *Asset Sale* is the only viable alternative.

Investors *Founders* *Creditors*
&
Employees

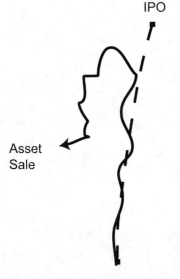

The board, investors and management team agree to make a radical 'U'-turn and switch target destinations to *Asset Sale*. In a major shift in thinking, the board of directors decides to give up the attempt to generate sales or build a viable stand-alone business. Instead, you strip the company down to a bite-size unit that's structured and dressed up to appeal to a corporate buyer. You cut the burn rate by slashing costs—this involves offloading the sales and marketing teams and other staff not directly required to develop and support the product. You shed all the components of the business that are unlikely to appeal to an established buyer—typically a corporate buyer with its own management resources and established routes to market. With a hot product and a low burn rate, you find a buyer and sell out. The product is integrated alongside the existing line-up of the corporate buyer, the product team is assimilated, the management team and company are disposed of.

This has not been a direct journey—you raised money to fund the development of your sales and marketing channels but failed to generate sufficient sales to turn a profit, so the amount of money raised from external investors likely runs well into eight figures. After the investors have taken their share of the sale proceeds, they'll be unlikely to cover their costs. There's little chance of having anything left over for the founders and employees.

Zero-to-Shutdown Direct

You plot out your route to *IPO*, but for one reason or another, you fail to raise sufficient funds—perhaps you raise seed funds but fail to bring in a venture investor for your first round. After paying off any outstanding creditors, you shut the company down.

It may look like the company was driven directly toward oblivion and, on first glance, it doesn't appear that management made a very serious attempt to build a valuable business. However, you implemented an *Orderly Shutdown* without bearing the expense of a long journey and managed to avoid a messy bankruptcy— compared to some of the stories below, this is a relatively happy ending!

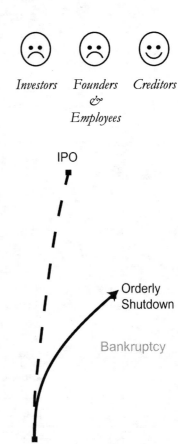

Investors   *Founders*   *Creditors*
&
Employees

Zero-to-Bankruptcy—Direct

This journey follows the same route as
the Zero-to-Shutdown route above,
however, you fail to act quickly enough,
you find yourself with insufficient cash in
the bank to pay off the creditors and the
company is forced into *Bankruptcy*. The
creditors are never very happy when this
happens—in some circles, the board of
directors and management team are sure
to be somewhat unpopular.

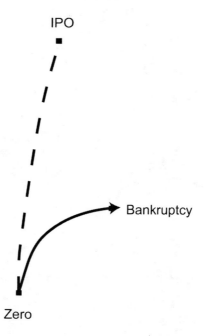

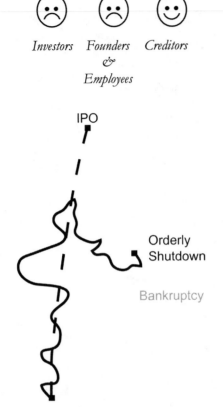

Investors   Founders   Creditors
             &
             Employees

IPO

Orderly
Shutdown

Bankruptcy

Zero

Zero-to-Shutdown Popular Route

After heading out hoping to reach IPO, you manage to hit some milestones, perhaps build an interesting product and come close to reaching *Asset Sale*. However, for one reason or another, you fail to close the deal and the acquisition doesn't go through.

You struggle on, trying to create your own routes to market and build a viable stand-alone business, but cash continues to burn. You realize that the only way to avoid a messy bankruptcy is to act quickly and shut down while you still have sufficient funds to pay off the outstanding creditors. The company is shutdown in an orderly fashion, but the shares and stock options end up being worthless—investors end up losing their stakes and there's no upside for the founders and employees.

Zero-to-Bankruptcy Popular Route

Unfortunately, this is the journey taken by many technology startups. The company heads out targeting *IPO*, hits some milestones, raises some funds but fails to generate sufficient sales to turn a profit and build a viable stand-alone business. Management fails to cut or slash cost sufficiently to slow the rate at which the company is burning cash, fails to target and drive toward *Asset Sale*—and without an obvious exit route, it fail to raise new funds. The company passes the point at which it has sufficient funds to carry out an *Orderly Shutdown* and then ends up in *Bankruptcy*.

Everyone seems to lose out here—the investors lose their stake, the creditors bills are left unpaid, the founders and employees have stock options that are worthless and the management team members come away with black marks on their resumes. Ouch!

Investors   *Founders & Employees*   *Creditors*

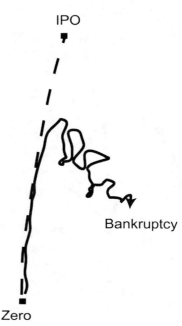

IPO

Bankruptcy

Zero

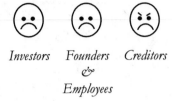

Investors   Founders   Creditors
&
Employees

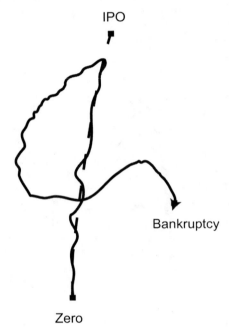

IPO

Bankruptcy

Zero

The Costly Routes to Bankruptcy and Shutdown

This is a long, expensive journey. You hit your milestones, raise your seed, venture, strategic and mezzanine rounds of funding, build your route to market, generate profitable sales and build a viable stand-alone business. However, you then fail to achieve IPO—perhaps the company struggles to hit its numbers or Wall Street develops an allergy to new stock issues. Whatever the reason, IPO is not attainable so you decide to look at selling the company in a *Cash Flow Sale*. You do the dance with a number of potential buyers but the M&A process doesn't reach a conclusion—you fail to sell the company as a profitable going-concern.

Then you lose momentum, perhaps the M&A discussions distract the team and the company stumbles. Sales fail to cover costs and the company once again starts to burn up cash. You investigate the possibility of

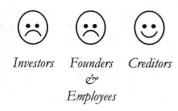

Investors Founders Creditors
&&
Employees

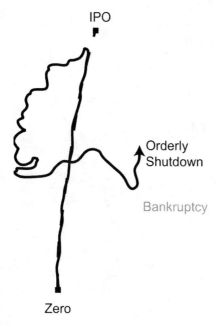

selling the company for its product in an *Asset Sale*—but these efforts also fail and the company continues burning through its cash. Management struggles on, fails to raise new funds and the company goes into a freefall. One day, someone realizes that there's insufficient cash to pay off the creditors and the company goes into bankruptcy.

A long, expensive journey with bankruptcy at the end is a disaster for virtually everyone involved. The management team hardly walks away with an impressive track record, the founders lose many years of their working lives, all the seed, venture, strategic and mezzanine investors lose their shirts and the creditors are left high and dry. It doesn't get much worse than this!

Management can salvage some of its reputation if it acts quickly and decides to pay off the creditors when there's sufficient cash in the bank to avoid *Bankruptcy*—and stage an *Orderly Shutdown*.

Zero-to-Asset Sale Direct

You set out targeting Asset Sale, raise relatively small amount of funding, build an insanely great product, establish pilots to prove the market exists, identify potential acquirers with their own routes to market and sell the company. The acquirer gets a great new product to add to its line-up, a capable development team and most likely disposes of the corporate shell.

As the journey relatively short and inexpensive, the investors achieve a healthy return from the proceeds of the sale. The founders and employees should come away with some hard cash, stock options in the parent company and other incentives to stay on-board. This journey can take less than two years.

Investors   *Founders*   *Creditors*
&
Employees

Asset Sale

Zero

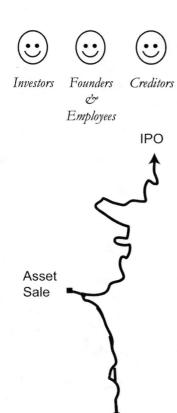

Investors   Founders   Creditors
&
Employees

Zero-to-IPO Diversion

The company heads out for *Asset Sale* and soon starts to generate good momentum—quickly hitting its milestones and stepping stones along the way. It builds a valuable product and starts to think about preparing to sell the company to a buyer that has its own routes to market. No serious investment is made in sales and marketing but orders start flowing in. The company likely receives acquisition offers from interested buyers, but the decision is made to switch destinations, raise more funding, invest in sales and marketing and build a viable stand-alone business. Distribution channels are established and the route to market becomes productive—the company soon starts to generate impressive sales and turn a profit. The company successfully reaches its new destination—*IPO*.

By setting out on the route to *Asset Sale*, the company developed a culture whereby costs were kept under tight control. As a result, the journey to IPO was relatively inexpensive—the investors, employees and founders hit pay dirt. The ultimate result!

Appendix 6—Resource Guide

Note: Any printed directory of resources in Silicon Valley and the technology sector is sure to be outdated as new companies emerge, old ones disappear, others change their names, change their web sites, merge together and do whatever they can to scupper all publishers attempts to track them. The only way to keep the directory up-to-date is to publish it online. As part of the entrepreneurship knowledgebase available through Astecs, the Association of Technology Entrepreneurs, this resource guide is now updated, reorganized and more comprehensive. Check it out online at www.astecs.org.

Executive Resources

Business Planning Resources

Google Directory
http://directory.google.com/Top/Business/Small_Business/Finance/Business_Plans/

Yahoo Directory
http://dir.yahoo.com/Business_and_Economy/Business_to_Business/Corporate_Services/Business_Development/Business_Plans/

Bond & Pecaro
www.bondpecaro.com

Bplans.com - the planning people
www.bplans.com

Business Plans International Inc (BOI)
www.businessplansintl.com

Forward Action Inc
www.forwardaction.com

FundingEdge.com
www.FundingEdge.com

IRA Networks
www.businessplanfunding.com

Mount Vernon Strategies
www.mvstrat.com

Planware
www.planware.org

Professional Planning Associates, Inc.
www.proplana.com

vFinance.com - Business Plan Development
www.vfinance.com/home.asp?bps=1&ToolPage=bps_main.asp

WizBizWeb, LLC
www.wizbizweb.com

WSJ.com StartUp Journal
http://wsj.miniplan.com

Organizations for Technology Entrepreneurs

Asian-Silicon Valley Connection
www.asvc.org

Churchill Club
www.churchillclub.org

Forum for Women Entrepreneurs
www.fwe.org

SD Forum
www.sdforum.org

SVASE
www.svase.org

The IndUS Entrepreneur
www.tie.org

Women in Technology (WITI)
www.witi.org

Young Entrepreneurs Organization
www.yeo.org

Young Presidents Organization
www.ypo.org

Entrepreneur & Startup Resources

Google Directory
http://directory.google.com/Top/Business/Venture_Capital/Resources_for_Entrepreneurs/

All Business
www.allbusiness.com/index.jsp

Alternative Technologies
www.alternativetech.com

Browne, Berlin and Gallo
www.mconsultants.com
Business Week Online
www.businessweek.com
Business.com
www.business.com
BuyerZone.com
www.buyerzone.com
Complete Toolkit for Boards
www.mapnp.org/library/boards/boards.htm
Doculabs
www.doculabs.com
**Dunn & Bradstreet: Small Business
Solutions**
http://sbs.dnb.com
Entrepreneur.com
www.entrepreneur.com
Entrepreneurial Edge
http://edge.lowe.org
EntreWorld.org
www.entreworld.org
**Forum for Women Entrepreneurs
(FWE)**
www.fwe.org
inc.com
www.inc.com
MoreBusiness.com
www.morebusiness.com
Recurrent Technologies, Inc.
www.recurrent.com
Red Herring
www.herring.com
**Silicon Valley Small Business
Development Center**
www.siliconvalley-sbdc.org
The Goodwin Group
http://goodwin-group.com
TheCFO.com LLC
www.thecfo.com
**United States Small Business
Administration**
www.sbaonline.sba.gov
Upside
www.upside.com
USA Diligence
www.usadiligence.com

vFinance inc.
www.vfinance.com
WSJ.com Startup Journal
http://startupjournal.com
Yahoo Directory
http://dir.yahoo.com/Business_and_Econo
my/Finance_and_Investment/Financing/Cor
porate_Financing/Venture_Capital/
Yahoo Directory! Small Business
http://smallbusiness.yahoo.com
YoungEntrepreneur.com
http://youngentrepreneur.com

Finance

Accountant Lists & Directories

CPA Directory
http://cpadirectory.com
EZ Directory
www.cpafinder.com
Google Directory
http://directory.google.com/Top/Business/
Accounting/Firms/Directories/
Yahoo Directory
http://dir.yahoo.com/Business_and_Econo
my/Business_to_Business/Financial_Services
/Accounting/Directories/

Large Accounting & Auditing Firms

BDO
www.bdo.com
Deloitte and Touche LLP
www.deloitte.com
Ernst and Young
www.ey.com
Grant Thornton, LLP
www.grantthornton.com
KPMG
www.us.kpmg.com
PricewaterhouseCoopers
www.pricewaterhouse.com

Bookkeeping & Accounting Software

Google Directory
http://directory.google.com/Top/Computers/Software/Accounting/

Yahoo Directory
http://dir.yahoo.com/Business_and_Economy/Business_to_Business/Financial_Services/Accounting/Software/

CPA Online
www.findaccountingsoftware.com

Accubooks 2000
www.accubooks2000.com

Cognos
www.cognos.com

Cougar Mountain Software
www.cougarmtn.com

Icode
www.icode.com

Intuit
www.Intuit.com

MYOB
www.myob.com

Oracle - Small Business Suite
http://oracle.com

Peachtree
www.peachtree.com

Incubators

Google Directory
http://directory.google.com/Top/Business/Venture_Capital/Incubators/

Yahoo Directory
http://dir.yahoo.com/Business_and_Economy/Business_to_Business/Corporate_Services/Business_Development/Incubators/

Austin Technology Incubator
www.ic2-ati.org

Communications Technology Cluster (CTC)
www.ctcluster.com

Idealab!
www.idealab.com

International Business Incubator (IBI)
www.ibi-sv.org

Mobius Venture Capital
www.sbvc.com

National Business Incubation Association
www.nbia.org

Panasonic Incubator
www.vcpanasonic.com

San Jose Software Business Cluster
www.sjsbc.org

socalTECH.com - Incubators
www.socaltech.com/incubate.html

TEN-The Enterprise Network
www.ten-net.org

The Technology Innovation Center
www.theincubator.com

Venture Frogs
www.vfrogs.com

Women's Technology Cluster
www.womenstechcluster.org

Investment Bank Lists

Google Directory
http://directory.google.com/Top/Business/Financial_Services/Investment_Banks/

Yahoo Directory
http://dir.yahoo.com/Business_and_Economy/Business_to_Business/Financial_Services/Finance_and_Receivables/Financing/Corporate_Finance/Consulting/Investment_Banks/

Business Finance
www.businessfinance.com/investment-banks.asp

Investment Banking Resources
www.investment-banking-resources.com/investment_banks/index.html

Investment Banks—*Largest Based on Nasdaq IPO's 2000*

Bear Stearns
www.bear.com

Chase H&Q
www.jpmhq.com

Credit Suisse First Boston
www.csfb.com

Deutsche Bank Alex Brown
www.db.com/corporatefinance/

Donaldson, Lufkin & Jenrette
www.dlj.com
Goldman Sachs
www.gs.com
Lehman Brothers
www.lehman.com
Merrill Lynch
www.ml.com
Morgan Stanley Dean Witter
www.morganstanley.com
Solomon Smith Barney
www.salomonsmithbarney.com

Investment Banks—*Selection*

A G Edwards
www.agedwards.com
ABN AMRO Rothchild
www.abnamro.com
Adams, Harkness & Hill
www.ahh.com
Banc of America Securities
www.bofasecurities.com
BNP Paribas
www.bnpparibas.com
CIBC World Markets
www.cibcwm.com
Credit Lyonnais Securities
www.creditlyonnais.com
Dain Rauscher Wessels
www.rbcdain.com
Deutsche Banc Alex Brown
https://www.alexbrown.db.com
First Union - Wachovia Securities
http://wachovia.firstunion.com
Friedman, Billings, Ramsay
www.fbr.com
George K. Baum & Company
www.gkbaum.com
Harris Direct
www.harrisdirect.com
ING Barings
www.ingbarings.com
JP Morgan Chase
www.jpmorgan.com
KBC Securities
www.kbcsecurities.com

Lehman Brothers
www.lehman.com
Needham
www.needhamco.com
Nesbitt Burns Securities
www.bmonesbittburns.com
Paribas Corporation
www.bnpparibas.com
Paulson Investment Company
www.paulsoninvestment.com
Piper Jaffray
www.piperjaffray.com
Prudential Securities
www.cm1.prusec.com
RBC Capital Markets
www.rbccmresearch.com
RBC Dominion Securities
www.rbcds.com
Robert W. Baird & Co
www.rwbaird.com
Roth Capital Partners
www.rothcp.com
SC Investment Banking
www.cowen.com
SG Cowen Securities
www.cowen.com
Stephens
www.stephens.com
TD Securities
www.tdsecurities.com
Thomas Weisel Partners
www.tweisel.com
U.S. Bancorp Piper Jaffray
www.piperjaffray.com
UBS Warburg
www.ubswarburg.com
William Blair & Company
www.wmblair.com
Wit Soundview
www.soundview.com
WR Hambrecht + Co
www.wrhambrecht.com

Investor Conferences & Events

Google Directory
http://directory.google.com/Top/Business/
Venture_Capital/Resources_for_Entrepreneu
rs/Conferences/

Yahoo Directory
http://dir.yahoo.com/Business_and_Econo
my/Business_to_Business/Financial_Services
/Finance_and_Receivables/Financing/Corpo
rate_Finance/Venture_Capital/Conventions_
and_Conferences/

Demo
www.idgexecforums.com/demo/

J P Morgan H & Q
http://conference.hamquist.com/

Red Herring
www.redherring.com/mediakit/conferences.h
tml

Showcase

Upside
www.upside.com

IPO Resources and Information

Google Directory
http://directory.google.com/Top/Business/I
nvesting/Stocks_and_Bonds/Investment_Res
earch/Specialties/IPO/

Yahoo Directory
http://dir.yahoo.com/Business_and_Econo
my/Finance_and_Investment/Initial_Public_
Offerings/Hoovers Online:

IPO Central
www.hoovers.com/ipo/0,1334,23,00.html

IPO Home
www.ipohome.com

IPO Resource
www.iporesources.org

IPO.com
www.ipo.com

Nasdaq
www.nasdaq.com

National Association of Securites Dealers
www.nasd.com

Securities Exchange Commission
www.sec.gov

vFinance.com
www.vfinance.com

Merger & Acquisition Intermediaries

See investment banks.

Google Directory
http://directory.google.com/Top/Business/
Consulting/Mergers_and_Acquisitions/

Yahoo Directory
http://dir.yahoo.com/Business_and_Economy/
Business_to_Business/Financial_Services/Finan
ce_and_Receivables/Financing/Corporate_Fina
nce/Consulting/Mergers_and_Acquisitions/

Advance Ventures
www.advanceventures.com

BDO Seidman LLC
www.bdo.com

Black Mountain Capital
www.blackmountaincapital.com

Broadview
www.broadview.com

Corum Group
www.corumgroup.com

Directory of M&A Intermediaries (Book)
www.sdponline.com

Google Directory
http://directory.google.com/Top/Business/
Consulting/Mergers_and_Acquisitions/

Investment Banking Resources
www.investment-banking-
resources.com/mergers_acquisitions/index.html

MergerCentral.com
www.mergercentral.com

Parallax Capital Partners LLC
www.parallaxcap.com

TECHaquisitions
www.techacquisitions.com

The Mergers & Acquisitions Advisor Online
www.maadvisor.com

Business Brokers

Google
http://directory.google.com/Top/Business/
Real_Estate/Commercial/Business_Brokers/
Business Broker Directory
www.businessbrokerdirectory.com
Business Brokerage Group
www.businessbrokeragegroup.com
California Association of Business Brokers
www.cabb.org
IBBA - International Business Brokers Association
www.ibba.org

Investor Lists & Match-Making Services

Google Directory 1
http://directory.google.com/Top/Business/
Venture_Capital/
Google Directory 2
http://directory.google.com/Top/Business/
Venture_Capital/Resources_for_Entrepreneu
rs/Capital_Access_-_Financing/
Yahoo Directory
http://dir.yahoo.com/Business_and_Econo
my/Business_to_Business/Financial_Services
/Finance_and_Receivables/Financing/Corpo
rate_Finance/Venture_Capital/Industry_Spec
ific/Technology/
Access Capital
https://www.accesscapital.com
American Venture
www.avce.com
Business Finance
www.businessfinance.com/venture-capital.asp
BusinessPartners.com
www.businesspartners.com
Capogee
www.capogee.com
Forbes Midas List
www.forbes.com/midas/
Galante
www.assetnews.com/products/dir/galante.htm
National Venture Capital Association
www.nvca.com/members.html

National Venture Capital Association
www.nvca.org
Pratts Guide to Venture Capital Sources (book)
www.amazon.com/exec/obidos/ASIN/0914
470094/venlogic-20/103-1262749-4799866
RaisingMoney.com
www.raisingmoney.com
The Directory of Venture Capital Firms (book)
www.greyhouse.com/venture.htm
The Venture Capital Resource Library 2002 CD
www.vfinance.com
VCAOnline.com
www.vcaonline.com
VentureExchange
www.ventureexchangenetwork.com
vFinance
www.vfinance.com

Angel Investor Lists

Angel Capital Network
www.bayangels.com
Angel Investor Magazine
www.angelinvestormagazine.com
Band Of Angels
www.bandangels.com
Business Finance Angel List
www.businessfinance.com/angel-search.asp
BusinessPartners.com
www.businesspartners.net
Capital Match
www.capmatch.com
International AngelInvestors.Org
http://angelinvestors.org
Investorguide.com - Angel Investors
www.investorguide.com/angelsmore.html
Next Wave Stocks - Angel Directory
www.nextwavestocks.com/angeldirectory.html
The Angels' Forum
www.angelsforum.com
vFinance - AngelSearch
www.vfinance.com/home.asp?ToolPage=ang
elsearch.asp

Prominent VC Investors—*Selection*

3i
www.3i.com

Accel Partners
www.accel.com

Alexander Hutton Venture Partners
www.ahvp.com

Arch Venture Partners
www.archventure.com

Baker Capital
www.bakercapital.com

Battery Ventures
www.battery.com

Benchmark Capital
www.benchmark.com

Bessemer Venture Partners
www.bvp.com

Charles River Ventures
www.crv.com

CMGI
www.cmgi.com

Crosspoint Ventures
www.crosspointvc.com

Draper Fisher Jurvetson
www.dfj.com

Flatiron Partners
www.flatironpartners.com

Greylock
www.greylock.com

Hummer Winblad Venture Partners
www.hummerwinblad.com

Idealab
www.idealab.com

Integral Partners
www.integralcapital.com

InterWest Partners
www.interwest.com

IVP
www.ivp.com

JAFCO Ventures
www.jafco.com

Kleiner Perkins Caufield & Byers
www.kpcb.com

Lightspeed (Weiss, Peck & Greer)
www.lightspeedvp.com

Madrona Venture Group
www.madrona.com

Matrix Partners
www.matrixpartners.com

Mayfield
www.mayfield.com

Menlo Ventures
www.menloventures.com

Mobius Venture Capital (Softbank)
www.sbvc.com

Mohr, Davidow Ventures
www.mdv.com

NEA - New Enterprise Associates
www.nea.com

Norwest Venture Partners
www.norwestvc.com

Oak Investment Partners
www.oakinv.com

OVP Venture Partners
www.ovp.com

Polaris Venture Partners
www.polarisventures.com

Redpoint Ventures
www.redpoint.com

Sequoia Capital
www.sequoiacap.com

Sevin Rosen Funds
www.srfunds.com

Sigma Partners
www.sigmapartners.com

Spectrum Equity Investors
www.spectrumequity.com

Summit Partners
www.summitpartners.com

Sutter Hill Ventures
www.shv.com

TA Associates
www.ta.com

Technology Crossover Ventures
www.tcv.com

Trinity Ventures
www.trinityventures.com

US Venture Partners
www.usvp.com

Vanguard Venture Partners
www.vanguardventures.com

Venrock Associates
www.venrock.com

Walden
www.waldenvc.com

VC Information & Resources

Google Directory
http://directory.google.com/Top/Business/
Venture_Capital/
Yahoo Directory
http://dir.yahoo.com/Business_and_Econo
my/Business_to_Business/Financial_Services
/Finance_and_Receivables/Financing/Corpo
rate_Finance/Venture_Capital/
European Venture Capital Journal
www.evcj.co
National Venture Capital Association
www.nvca.org
NVST
www.nvst.com
Red Herring
www.redherring.com
Upside
www.upside.com
Venture Capital Journal
www.venturecapitaljournal.net
Venture Wire
www.venturewire.com

Valuation Information Sources

Assetnews
www.assetnews.com
Bond & Pecaro
www.bondpecaro.com
Bond & Pecaro - CyberValuation
www.cybervaluation.com
Deloitte & Touche - Growth Company Services
www.deloitte.com/us/growth
Google Directory
http://directory.google.com/Top/Business/
Opportunities/Valuation_Services/
IPO.com
www.ipo.com
Securities Data Publishing (Thomson Financial)
www.sdponline.com/index.html
Venlogic
www.venlogic.com

Venture Economics
www.venturEConomics.com
VentureOne
www.ventureone.com
vFinance - Deal Monitor
www.vfinance.com/home.asp?ToolPage=vci
m_search.asp
vFinance inc.
www.vfinance.com
Venture Leasing
DiBari Group
www.dibarigroup.net
Dominion Ventures
www.dominion.com
Forum Financial Services Inc.
www.forumleasing.com
IFC Credit Corporation
www.ifccredit.com
VCapital
www.vcapital.com
Venture-Leasing.com
www.venture-leasing.com

Legal

Corporation Formation Services

Google Directory
http://directory.google.com/Top/Business/
Consulting/Business_Formation/
Yahoo Directory
http://dir.yahoo.com/Business_and_Econo
my/Business_to_Business/Corporate_Service
s/Incorporation_Services/
Business Filings Incorporated
www.bizfilings.com/index.asp
Delaware Corporations LLC
www.delawarecorp.com
Delaware Intercorp
www.delawareintercorp.com
Incorporate U.S.A
www.inc123.com

Immigration Lawyers & Resources

Google Directory
http://directory.google.com/Top/Regional/North_America/United_States/Business_and_Economy/Immigration/

Yahoo Directory
http://dir.yahoo.com/Government/U_S__Government/Law/Immigration_and_Naturalization/

American Immigration Network
www.usavisanow.com/immigrationvisakits.htm

OnlineVisas.com
www.onlinevisas.com

The INS Online
www.ins.usdoj.gov/graphics/index.htm

U.S. Immigration Services
www.immigrationlawusa.com

Visa Services
www.immigrationvisas.com

WorkPermit.com
www.workpermit.com

Lawyer Lists

Google Directory
http://directory.google.com/Top/Society/Law/Services/Lawyers_and_Law_Firms/Directories/

Yahoo Directory
http://dir.yahoo.com/Business_and_Economy/Shopping_and_Services/Law/Directories/

Findlaw
http://directory.findlaw.com/

Lawyer.com
www.lawyers.com

IPO Lawyers—*Largest based on 2000 Nasdaq IPOs*

Brobeck, Phleger & Harrison
www.brobeck.com

Cooley Godward
www.cgc.com

Fenwick & West
www.fenwick.com

Hale and Dorr LLP
www.haledorr.com

Hogan & Harston
www.hhlaw.com

Morgan, Lewis & Brockius
www.morganlewis.com

Pillsbury Madison & Sutro LLP
www.pillsburywinthrop.com

Ropes & Gray
www.ropesgray.com

Skadden Arps Slate Meagher & Flom
www.skadden.com

Testa, Hurwitz & Thibeault
www.tht.com

Wilson Sonsini Goodrich & Rosati
www.wsgr.com

Boutique Law Firms

White & Lee LLP
www.whiteandlee.com

IPO Lawyers

Brobeck Hale and Dorr International
www.bhd.com

Brobeck Phleger & Harrison
www.brobeck.com

Buchanan Ingersoll
www.bipc.com

Cahill Gordon & Reindel
www.cahill.com

Chadbourne & Parke
www.chadbourne.com

Chamberlain, Hrdlicka, White, Williams & Martin
www.chamberlainlaw.com

Clifford Chance
www.cliffordchance.com

Friend Frank Harris Shriver & Jacobson
www.internationallawoffice.com

Goodwin, Procter & Hoar
www.goodwinprocter.com

Greenberg Traurig LLP
www.gtlaw.com

Heller Ehrman White & McAuliffe
www.hewm.com

Helms Mulliss & Wicker, PLLC
www.hmw.com

Holland & Knight LLP
www.hklaw.com

Holme Roberts & Owen LLP
www.hro.com
Hutchins, Wheeler & Dittmar
www.hutch.com
Kirkland & Ellis
www.kirkland.com
Latham & Watkins
www.lw.com
Manatt Phelps & Phillips, LLP
www.manatt.com
Mintz Levin Cohn Ferris Glovsky and Popeo, P.C
www.mintz.com
Morgan, Lewis & Bockius
www.morganlewis.com
Morrison & Foerster LLP
www.mofo.com
Morrison & Foerster LLP
www.mofo.com
Nixon Peabody LLP
www.nixonpeabody.com
Palmer & Dodge
www.palmerdodge.com
Perkins Coie
www.perkinscoie.com
Piper Marbury Rudnick & Wolfe LLP
www.piperrudnick.com
Schmeltzer, Aptaker & Shepard, P.C
www.saspc.com
Shaw Pittman Potts & Trowbridge
www.shawpittman.com
Shearman & Sterling
www.shearman.com
Smith Gambrell & Russell
www.sgrlaw.com
Stibbe Simont Monahan Duhot
www.stibbe.com
Stradling, Yocca, Carlson & Rauth
www.sycr.com
Sullivan & Cromwell
www.sullcrom.com
Wachtell, Lipton, Rosen & Katz
www.wlrk.com

Legal Resources

Findlaw
www.findlaw.com

Google Directory
http://directory.google.com/Top/Society/Law/Legal_Information/Resources/Directories/
Nolo.com
www.nolo.com
White & Lee - white papers
www.whiteandlee.com/papers.html
Yahoo Directory
http://dir.yahoo.com/Government/Law/Web_Directories/

Trademark, Patent & IP Lawyer Lists

Database of patent attorneys on U.S.PTO site:
www.uspto.gov/web/offices/dcom/olia/oed/roster/index.html#attorney_agent_search
InventNet
www.inventnet.com/patattn.html
Trademark Patent Lawyers
www.trademark-patent-lawyers.com
United States Patent and Trademark Office
www.uspto.gov

Human Resources

Benefit Brokers & Resources

A G Sieben & Associates
www.agsieben.com
Benefit News
www.benefitnews.com
BuyerZone - Benefits
www.buyerzone.com/benefits/
Clark/Bardes Consulting
www.crgworld.com
Coty & Bruce Benefits, Inc.
www.cb-benefits.com

Large Executive Search Firms

Google Directory
http://directory.google.com/Top/Business/Human_Resources/Compensation_and_Benefits/

Yahoo Directory
http://dir.yahoo.com/Society_and_Culture/Issues_and_Causes/Employment_and_Workplace_Issues/Employee_Benefits/

A. T. Kearney
www.atkearney.com

Accord Group
www.accordgroup.net

Amrop
www.amrop.com

Boyden
www.boyden.com

Egon Zehnder International
www.zehnder.com

Heidrick & Struggles
www.heidrick.com

Horton International
www.horton-intl.com

IIC Partners
www.iicpartners.com

InterSearch
www.intersearch.org

Korn/Ferry International
www.kornferry.com

Norman Broadbent International
www.normanbroadbent.com

Ray & Berndtson
www.rayberndtson.com

Russell Reynolds Associates
www.russreyn.com

Spencer Stuart
www.spencerstuart.com

Ward Howell International
www.whru.com

Health Insurance & Resources

Google Directory
http://directory.google.com/Top/Business/Human_Resources/Compensation_and_Benefits/Health_and_Welfare_Plans/

Yahoo Directory
http://dir.yahoo.com/Business_and_Economy/Business_to_Business/Financial_Services/Insurance/Health/Corporate_Benefits_Plans/

1st Health Insurance Quotes
www.1sthealthinsurancequotes.com

1st Insurance
www.1st-insurance-health-insurance-quotes.com

1st U.S. Health Quotes
www.ushealthquotes.com

About Health Insurance
http://about-health-insurance.com

Aetna
www.aetna.com

Blue Cross, etc.
www.bluecross.com

Cigna
www.cigna.come

HealthInsurance.com
www.ehealthinsurance.com

find Health Insurance
http://find-health-insurance.com

Health Insurance Finder
www.healthinsurancefinders.com

HealthNet
www.healthnet.com

HealthPlanDirectory.com
www.healthplandirectory.com

Kaiser Permanente
www.kaiserpermanente.org

Lifeguard
www.lifeguard.com

QuoteMonster
www.quotemonster.com

HR & Payroll Resources

Google Directory
http://directory.google.com/Top/Business/Financial_Services/Payroll_Services/

Yahoo Directory
http://dir.yahoo.com/Business_and_Economy/Business_to_Business/Financial_Services/Accounting/Payroll/

ADP
www.adp.com

California Chamber of Commerce
www.calchamber.com

Execustaff
www.execustaff.net

HR California
www.hrcalifornia.com

Salary Source
www.salarysource.com
Salary.com
www.salary.com
Survey Research Associates LLC
www.salaries.com

Outsourcing

Google Directory
http://directory.google.com/Top/Business/
Consulting/Outsourcing/
Yahoo Directory
http://dir.yahoo.com/Business_and_Econo
my/Business_to_Business/Corporate_Service
s/Human_Resources/Outsourcing/
Accountants Inc.
www.accountantsinc.com
Administaff
www.administaff.com
Ajilon Consulting
www.ajilonconsulting.com
BCB Consulting
www.geocities.com/bfbradstreet/
CFO Connection
www.cfo-connection.com
CTO4Rent
www.cto4rent.com
eDiligence
www.ediligence.com
eWork
www.ework.com
ExecuStaff
www.execustaff.net
Growth Process Group
www.growthprocess.com
Latte Services Corp.
www.latteservices.com
Murdock and Associates
http://hornmurdockcolesv.com
The Controller's Office
www.tco-inc.com
Travis Consulting
www.travis-consulting.com

Recruitment

Google
http://dir.yahoo.com/Business_and_Economy
/Business_to_Business/Corporate_Services/H
uman_Resources/Recruiting_and_Placement/
Yahoo Directory
http://dir.yahoo.com/Business_and_Econo
my/Business_to_Business/Corporate_Service
s/Human_Resources/Recruiting_and_Placem
ent/Directories/
Adecco, Inc.
www.adecco.com
Ajilon Consulting
www.ajilonconsulting.com
**ALG Systems - Maker of
VisualRecruiter**
www.visualrecruiter.com
**Allen Associates - Executive Search
Advisors**
www.allensearch.com
ArkProfessional
www.arkprofessional.com
Bliss & Associates Inc.
www.blissassociates.com
Brainbuzz
www.brainbuzz.com
BrassRing
www.brassring.com
BridgeGate
www.bridgegate.com
Calamia and Associates
www.calamiaandassociates.com
CareerMosaic
www.CareerMosaic.com
CareerPath
www.CareerPath.com
CeleraSearch LLC
www.celerasearch.com
Clark/Bardes Consulting
www.crgworld.com
ComputerJobs
www.ComputerJobs.com
Dice
www.dice.com
FreeAgent
www.FreeAgent.com

Guru
www.Guru.com
Headhunter.net
www.Headhunter.net
HotJobs.com
www.hotjobs.com
HR Advisors, Inc.
www.hradvisors.comcontrol.html
JobOptions
www.JobOptions.com
Jobs
www.Jobs.com
JobsOnline
www.JobsOnline.com
Kelly Services
www.kellyservices.com
Kforce
www.Kforce.com
Lee Stephens & Associates
www.leestephens.com
Lyons Pruitt International, Inc.
www.lyonspruitt.com
Manpower International
www.manpower.com
Monster.com
www.monster.com
myrecruiter.com
www.myrecruiter.com
NationJob
www.NationJob.com
Net-Temps
www.Net-Temps.com
Russell Reynolds Associates, Inc.
www.russellreynolds.com
Skillsvillage
www.Skillsvillage.com
Snelling
www.snelling.com
Techies
www.Techies.com
TMP Worldwide Inc. - eResourcing
http://na.eresourcing.tmp.com

Yahoo
http://careers.yahoo.com

Operations

Internet Domain, Search & Registraton
Yahoo
http://dir.yahoo.com/Computers_and_Internet/Internet/Domain_Name_Registration/
Google
http://directory.google.com/Top/Computers/Internet/Domain_Names/

Web Hosting Services
Google Directory
http://directory.google.com/Top/Computers/Internet/Web_Design_and_Development/Hosting/
Yahoo Directory
http://dir.yahoo.com/Business_and_Economy/Business_to_Business/Communications_and_Networking/Internet_and_World_Wide_Web/Network_Service_Providers/Hosting/Web_Site_Hosting/
Yahoo! Website Services
http://website.yahoo.com/
Yahoo! GeoCities
http://geocities.yahoo.com/home/
CNET Internet Services
www.cnet.com/internet/0-3761.html
Doteasy.com
www.doteasy.com
HostIndex.com
www.hostindex.com
HostSave.com
www.hostsave.com
Microsoft bCentral
www.bcentral.com/services/bws/default.asp
TopHosts.com
www.tophosts.com

Marketing

Advertising & Marketing Agency Lists

Google Directory
http://directory.google.com/Top/Business/
Advertising/Directories/

Google Directory
http://directory.google.com/Top/Business/
Advertising/Agencies/

Yahoo Directory
http://dir.yahoo.com/Business_and_Econo
my/Business_to_Business/Marketing_and_A
dvertising/Advertising/

AdForum.com
http://ww0.adforum.com/index.asp

Agency ComPile
www.agencycompile.com

agencyfinder.com
www.agencyfinder.com

AmericanAdAgencies.com
www.americanadagencies.com

Horah Direct
www.horah.com

King-TeleServices
www.King-TeleServices.com

MarketIt Right
www.marketitright.com

MediaPost
www.mediapost.com

Sharrow & Assoc.
www.dnai.com/~sharrow/agencies.html

UT Austin - Dept of Advertising
http://advertising.utexas.edu/world/Agencies_
Menu.html

PR Agency Lists

Public Relations Society of America
www.prsa.org

Google Directory
http://directory.google.com/Top/Business/
Marketing/Public_Relations/Agencies/

Yahoo Directory
http://dir.yahoo.com/Business_and_Economy
/Business_to_Business/Corporate_Services/Pu
blic_Relations/

Selected PR Agencies

Access Communications
www.accesspr.com

Alexander Ogilvy
www.alexanderogilvy.com

Applied Communications
www.appliedcom.com

Atomic
www.atomicpr.com

Blanc & Otus
www.bando.com

Brodeur Worldwide
www.brodeur.com

Burson Marsteller
www.bksh.com

Citigate Cunningham
www.cunningham.com

Cohn & Wolfe
www.cohnwolfe.com

Edelman Public Relations Worldwide
www.edelman.com

Fitzgerald Communications
www.fitzgerald.com

Fleishman Hillard
www.fleishman.com

FutureWorks
www.future-works.com

GCI Group/APCO Associates
www.gcigroup.com

Gibbs & Soell
www.gibbs-soell.com

Golin Harris
www.golinharris.com

Hill & Knowlton
www.hillandknowlton.com

Horn Group
www.horngroup.com

Ketchum
www.ketchum.com

Lippert/Heilshorn & Associates
www.lhai.com

Magnet Communications
www.magnetcom.com

Manning, Selvage & Lee
www.mslpr.com

Morgen Walke
www.fdmw.com

Neale-May & Partners
www.nealemay.com
Pacifico
www.pacifico.com
Peppercom
www.peppercom.com
Porter Novelli
www.porternovelli.com
Porter Novelli International
www.porternovelli.com
PR21
www.pr21.com
Publicis Dialogue
www.publicis-usa.com
Ruder Finn
www.ruderfinn.com
S & S Public Relations Inc.
www.sspr.com
Schwartz Communications
www.schwartz-pr.com
Springbok Technologies
www.springbok.com
Sterling Hager
www.sterlinghager.com
Text 100
www.text100.com
The Hoffman Agency
www.hoffman.com
The Hoffman Agency
www.hoffman.com
The MWW Group
www.mwwpr.com
Radiate
www.radiatepr.com
Waggener Edstrom
www.wagged.com
Weber Group
www.webergroup.com
Weber Shandwick Worldwide
www.webershandwick.com

PR Resources

Council of Public Relations Firms
www.prfirms.org
PR Week
www.prweek.com

Public Relations Society of America
www.prsa.org

Press Release Distribution Services

Advanced PR
www.advanced-pr.com
eReleases
www.ereleases.come
Worldwire
www.eworldwire.com
PR Web
www.prweb.com
Press Release Network
www.pressreleasenetwork.com
Pressi.com
www.pressi.com
U-Wire
www.uwire.com/services/release.html
Xpress Press
www.xpresspress.com

Web Developer Lists

Google Directory
http://directory.google.com/Top/Computers/Internet/Web_Design_and_Development/Designers/
WebDeveloperDirectory.com
www.webdeveloperdirectory.com
Yahoo Directory
http://dir.yahoo.com/Business_and_Economy/Business_to_Business/Communications_and_Networking/Internet_and_World_Wide_Web/Web_Site_Designers/
a2z Web Design Source Directory
www.a2zwebdesignsource.com
About
http://webdesign.about.com/library/designers/bldirectory.htm
Elance
www.elance.com

Web Site Promotion Services

Google Directory
http://directory.google.com/Top/Computers/Internet/Web_Design_and_Development/P

romotion/Search_Engine_Submitting_and_P
ositioning/Submitting_Services/

Yahoo Directory
http://dir.yahoo.com/Computers_and_Inter
net/Internet/World_Wide_Web/Searching_t
he_Web/Search_Engines_and_Directories/S
ubmit_a_Site/

Company Information & Research

D & B
www.dnb.com

Hoover's Online
http://hoovers.com

**US Securitites & Exchange
Commission - EDGAR**
www.sec.gov/edgar.shtml

**US Securitities & Exchange
Commission**
www.sec.gov

Market Surveys & Research

Google Directory
http://dir.yahoo.com/Computers_and_Intern
et/Internet/World_Wide_Web/Searching_the
_Web/Search_Engines_and_Directories/Sub
mit_a_Site/

Yahoo Directory
http://dir.yahoo.com/Business_and_Econo
my/Business_to_Business/Marketing_and_A
dvertising/Market_Research/

**Commercial Business Intelligence,
Inc**
www.cbintel.com

Current Analysis
www.currentanalysis.com

e-FocusGroups
www.e-focusgroups.com

ElectroniCast
www.electronicast.com

Forrester
www.forrester.com/ER/Home/0,1361,0,FF.
html

Gartner Group
http://gartner11.gartnerweb.com/public/stati
c/home/home.html

iResearch
www.iresearch.com

Jupiter Communications
www.jup.com/home.jsp

Market Facts
www.marketfacts.com

**Marketing & Management Resources,
Inc**
www.mmrconsulting.com

Marketing Research Association
www.mra-net.org

OnlineSurveys
www.onlinesurveys.com

Predictive Research Group
www.prg3.com

Primary Intelligence
http://primary-intel.com

Research Info
www.researchinfo.com

SurveySite
www.surveysite.com

The Olinger Group
www.olingergroup.com

Virtual Research Room
www.vrroom.com

WebSurveyor.com
www.websurveyor.com

Wirthlin Worldwide
www.wirthlin.com

Index

Dear Reader,

Writing this book has taken the best part of two years, over 2,000 hours and 1,200 cappuccinos. Like most entrepreneurial journeys, writing this book was much longer and more arduous than I first envisaged—by a factor of at least ten! Now that this edition is printed, I can concentrate on other activities aimed at helping entrepreneurs survive startup and cash out:

✓ Capturing the essence of entrepreneurship in Silicon Valley on video by interviewing successful entrepreneurs, investors, lawyers, bankers and other experts.
✓ Compiling the video clips, audio podcasts and other materials captured in the interviews into a comprehensive entrepreneurship knowledgebase that's made available online to entrepreneurs, students and educators online (www.astecs.org).
✓ Directing my latest and most exciting startup to date—Tynax, the Technology Trading Exchange (www.tynax.com).
✓ Teaching entrepreneurship and helping business schools and law schools better prepare their graduates for life in the real world.
✓ Speaking at seminars, conferences and events.

I hope this book helps you and other entrepreneurs to navigate the difficult terrain you're sure to encounter and reach your target destinations in one piece.

I hope you enjoy the book and find it useful. I welcome your comments and suggestions by email:

DavidSmith@Zero-To-IPO.com

Best of luck!

David Smith

PS—you will find a roadmap, startup simulation game and other related materials on the www.Zero-To-IPO.com web site.